STUDIES IN EARLY MODERN CULTURAL,
POLITICAL AND SOCIAL HISTORY

Volume 14

REMAKING ENGLISH SOCIETY
SOCIAL RELATIONS AND SOCIAL CHANGE IN EARLY MODERN ENGLAND

Studies in Early Modern Cultural, Political and Social History

ISSN: 1476–9107

Series editors
Tim Harris – Brown University
Stephen Taylor – Durham University
Andy Wood – Durham University

Previously published titles in the series
are listed at the back of this volume

Keith Wrightson on Hampstead Heath, 2012
(Photo: Eva Wrightson)

REMAKING ENGLISH SOCIETY

SOCIAL RELATIONS AND SOCIAL CHANGE IN EARLY MODERN ENGLAND

Edited by

Steve Hindle, Alexandra Shepard and John Walter

THE BOYDELL PRESS

First published 2013
The Boydell Press, Woodbridge
Reprinted in paperback 2015

ISBN 978–1–84383–796–1 hardback
ISBN 978–1–78327–017–0 paperback

The Boydell Press is an imprint of Boydell & Brewer Ltd
PO Box 9, Woodbridge, Suffolk IP12 3DF, UK
and of Boydell & Brewer Inc.
668 Mt Hope Avenue, Rochester, NY 14620–2731, USA
website: www.boydellandbrewer.com

A CIP record for this book is available
from the British Library

The publisher has no responsibility for the continued existence or
accuracy of URLs for external or third-party internet websites referred
to in this book, and does not guarantee that any content on
such websites is, or will remain, accurate or appropriate.

This publication is printed on acid-free paper

For Keith
with gratitude and affection

Contents

Illustrations, Figures, Maps and Tables

Acknowledgements

The editors gratefully acknowledge the industriousness and patience of all the contributors; and the enthusiasm and attention to detail of the editorial and production staff at Boydell. Thanks are due also to Sally Phillips for compiling the index and to the Fletcher-Jones Endowment at the Huntington Library for financing her contribution. We would also like to thank Eva Wrightson for supplying the photograph of Keith and engaging in subterfuge with the editors over this volume, and for the support and encouragement she has offered to the contributors over a number of years. Most of all, however, we are grateful to Keith Wrightson himself, to whose contribution the dedication of this volume hardly begins to do justice.

Contributors

HELEN BERRY is Professor of Early Modern History at Newcastle University. Her publications include *Gender Society and Print Culture in Late-Stuart England* (2003), *Creating and Consuming Culture in North-East England* (co-edited with Jeremy Gregory, 2004), *The Family in Early Modern England* (co-edited with Elizabeth Foyster, 2007), *Northern Landscapes: Representations and Realities of North-East England* (co-edited with Thomas Faulkner and Jeremy Gregory, 2010) and, most recently, *The Castrato and His Wife* (2011).

ADAM FOX is Reader in Economic and Social History at the University of Edinburgh. He is the author of *Oral and Literate Culture in England 1500–1700* (2000), and co-editor of *The Experience of Authority in Early Modern England* (1996) and *The Spoken Word: Oral Culture in Britain, 1500–1850* (2002). He is currently working on the development of popular print in Edinburgh, 1680–1760.

HENRY FRENCH is Professor of Social History at the University of Exeter. He has published works on masculinity and landed society with Dr Mark Rothery, and the social identity of the middle sort of people in provincial England, 1600–1750, and a jointly authored monograph on the decline of the small landowner in Earls Colne, Essex, with Professor Richard Hoyle, as well as a number of articles on social identity, agrarian development, common lands and early modern electoral politics.

MALCOLM GASKILL is Professor of Early Modern History at the University of East Anglia. He is the author of *Crime and Mentalities in Early Modern England* (2000), *Hellish Nell: Last of Britain's Witches* (2001), *Witchfinders: a Seventeenth-Century English Tragedy* (2005) and *Witchcraft: a Very Short Introduction* (2010). His latest project is a history of English culture and identity in seventeenth-century America.

PAUL GRIFFITHS is Professor of Early Modern British Cultural and Social History at Iowa State University. He is the author of *Lost Londons: Change, Crime, and Control in the Capital City, 1550–1660* (2008) and *Youth and Authority: Formative Experiences in England, 1560–1640* (1996); co-editor of *The Experience of Authority in Early Modern England* (1996); and joint-editor of *Londinopolis: Essays in the Cultural and Social History of Early Modern London* (2000) and *Penal Practice and Culture: Punishing the English 1550–1850* (2004).

STEVE HINDLE is Director of Research at the Huntington Library in San Marino, California. He is the author of *The State and Social Change in Early Modern England, 1550–1640* (2000) and *On the Parish? The Micro-Politics of Poor Relief in Rural England, c.1550–1750* (2004), and has published a series of articles on social relations in English rural communities. He is currently working on a study of the Warwickshire parish of Chilvers Coton, provisionally entitled *The Social Topography of a Rural Community*.

CRAIG MULDREW is Reader in Early Modern Economic and Social History and Fellow of Queens' College, Cambridge. He is the author of *The Economy of Obligation: The Culture of Credit and Social Relations in Early Modern England* (1998) and *Food, Energy and the Industrious Revolution: Work and Material Culture in Agrarian England, 1550–1780* (2011), and he has also written articles in the field of legal history concerning debt litigation and its relationship to the nature of community, and articles on the cultural nature of money and wages in the early modern period.

LINDSAY O'NEILL is Lecturer in the History Department at the University of Southern California and is currently working on a project about the intersection of letter writing, social networks and the wider British world, provisionally entitled 'Speaking Letters: Communication Networks in the Early Modern British World', based on her 2008 Yale University PhD thesis, researched under the supervision of Keith Wrightson.

ALEXANDRA SHEPARD is Reader in Early Modern History at the University of Glasgow. She is the author of *Meanings of Manhood in Early Modern England* (2003) and several essays on gender and social relations in early modern England. She is co-editor of *Communities in Early Modern England* (2000) and *Gender and Change: Agency, Chronology and Periodisation* (2009), and is currently finishing a book on worth, status and the language of self-description in England between 1550 and 1730.

TIM STRETTON is Professor of History at Saint Mary's University in Nova Scotia. His publications include *Women Waging Law in Elizabethan England* (1998), a Camden Society Volume entitled *Marital Litigation in the Court of Requests 1541–1641* and articles on women, law and litigation, the use of legal records, the Elizabethan author George Puttenham and Shakespeare's *The Merchant of Venice*.

NAOMI TADMOR is Professor of History at Lancaster University. She is the author of *Family and Friends: Household, Kinship, and Patronage in Eighteenth-Century England* (2001) and *The Social Universe of the English Bible: Scripture, Society and Culture in Early Modern England* (2010); co-editor of *The Practice and Representation of Reading in England* (1996); and joint guest editor of *Kinship in England and beyond, 500–2000, a special issue of Continuity and Change* (2010). She has published articles on the history of the family, the history of reading and the culture of the Bible in early modern England.

JOHN WALTER is Professor of History at the University of Essex. He is the author of *Understanding Popular Violence in the English Revolution: The Colchester Plunderers* (1999) and *Crowds and Popular Politics in Early Modern England* (2006), and co-editor of *Famine, Disease and the Social Order in Early Modern Society* (1989) and *Negotiating Power in Early Modern Society: Order, Hierarchy & Subordination in Britain & Ireland* (2001). He is currently preparing a book on State oaths and political culture in the English Revolution.

PHIL WITHINGTON is Professor of Early Modern History at the University of Sheffield. He is the author of *The Politics of Commonwealth: Citizens and Freemen in Early Modern England* (2005) and *Society in Early Modern England: The Vernacular Origins of Some Powerful Ideas* (2010). He has edited *Citizens and Soldiers in Britain, Ireland and the Wider World* (2011), and co-edited *Communities in Early Modern England* (2000). He is currently working on a book about intoxicants and early modernity.

ANDY WOOD is Professor of Social History at the Durham University. His publications include *The Politics of Social Conflict: The Peak Country, 1520–1770* (1999), *Riot, Rebellion and Popular Politics in Early Modern England* (2002) and *The 1549 Rebellions and the Making of Early Modern England* (2007). He is currently completing a book for Cambridge University Press entitled *The Memory of the People: Custom and Popular Senses of the Past in Early Modern England.*

Abbreviations

Place of publication is London unless otherwise stated.

AHR	American Historical Review
C&C	Continuity and Change
EcHR	Economic History Review
HJ	Historical Journal
HWJ	History Workshop Journal
JBS	Journal of British Studies
JSH	Journal of Social History
Levine & Wrightson, Whickham	David Levine and Keith Wrightson, The Making of an Industrial Society: Whickham 1560–1765 (Oxford, 1991)
P&P	Past & Present
SH	Social History
TLS	Times Literary Supplement
TRHS	Transactions of the Royal Historical Society
Wrightson, EN	Keith Wrightson, Earthly Necessities: Economic Lives in Early Modern Britain (New Haven, 2000)
Wrightson, ES	Keith Wrightson, English Society 1580–1680 (1982)
Wrightson & Levine, Terling	Keith Wrightson and David Levine, Poverty and Piety in an English Village: Terling 1525–1700 ([1979]; 2nd edn, Oxford, 1995)

1

The Making and Remaking of Early Modern English Social History

STEVE HINDLE, ALEXANDRA SHEPARD AND JOHN WALTER

Understanding ourselves in time

There cannot be a 'new history' in quite the sense that Einstein founded a 'new physics'. ... Nevertheless the shift of interest towards inquiries of the sort which are reported with such brevity and sketchiness in this book, ought perhaps to be called a new branch of history.

The phrase 'sociological history' has been occasionally used here ... as its title.... This is mainly to register a distinction in subject matter, for confessedly historical writing has not previously concerned itself with births, marriages and deaths as such, nor has it dwelt so exclusively on the shape and development of social structure. But the outlook is novel as well as the material, at least in its emphasis. Perhaps the distinctive feature of the attitude is the frank acceptance of the truth that all historical knowledge, from one point of view, and that an important and legitimate one, is knowledge about ourselves, and the insistence on understanding by contrast.   Peter Laslett (1965)[1]

When I read Peter Laslett's *The World we have Lost* (1965) I literally sat up all night to finish it, and it made me want to sign up for the 'new social history' under his supervision. His phrase 'understanding ourselves in time' encapsulates for me what this enterprise is all about.   Keith Wrightson (2011)[2]

This volume offers a tribute to Keith Wrightson. It brings together essays by many of the doctoral students whose research Keith stimulated and supervised and who have subsequently contributed to our knowledge of the social, economic and cultural history of early modern England.[3] Through both his own body of work, and the publications of those he has taught

---

[1]   Peter Laslett, *The World We Have Lost* (1965) (written 1960–65), 230–1.
[2]   Keith Wrightson, interview, *The British Scholar Society*, August 2011: britishscholar. org/publications/2011/08/15/august-2011-keith-wrightson.
[3]   Those invited to contribute to this volume – and not all were able to accept – had

and inspired, Keith has played a leading role in establishing the distinctive nature and historical development of early modern English society.[4] In acknowledgement of Peter Laslett's maxim that the project of social history is that of 'understanding ourselves in time',[5] this introductory essay offers a double analysis of the making of what has come to be called 'the new social history' and, within that context, of the making of Keith Wrightson as a historian of early modern England.

Fifty years after the 1963 *Past & Present* conference on 'History, Sociology and Social Anthropology', itself but one of the quickly multiplying markers of a profound historiographical shift, this is an appropriate moment to reflect on the origins and development of 'the new social history', a genre now sufficiently old to have attracted its own history.[6] But since no historiographical discussion has yet adequately captured the particular inflections of this developing field in the context of the study of sixteenth- and seventeenth-century England, and because Wrightson (like all historians) necessarily forged his own path through the methodological landscape, we pay particular attention here to the making of *early modern* social history. In this introduction, we review briefly the converging trends that created 'the new social history', before going on first to analyse the distinctive ways in which early modern social history in particular drew on these influences and then to discuss the making of Wrightson himself as a social historian. We consider the significance of his contribution to our understanding both of continuity and of change in the history of early modern England, which are themselves the two abiding themes in his work. In a final section, we explain how Wrightson has influenced our recovery and writing of that history; and we survey developments since the publication in 1982 of his path-breaking *English Society*.

The making of 'the new social history'

> No historian writes a book alone and this is no exception to that rule. It would not have been conceived had it not been for the wave of new thinking about English social history which swept through the universities of the English-speaking world in the 1960s and 1970s. Keith Wrightson (1982)[7]

completed a Ph.D. under Keith Wrightson's supervision, had subsequently published a monograph and now hold a permanent university post.

[4]   For a comprehensive bibliography of Wrightson's own publications, see appendix.

[5]   The title of the concluding chapter of Laslett, *World We Have Lost* .

[6]   See 'History, Sociology and Social Anthropology: Conference Report', *P&P* 27 (1964), 102–9. Although we believe that the phrase 'the new social history' is problematic, we nonetheless retain this shorthand in the text to refer to the historical moment of the 1950s and early 1960s when earlier developments converged to shape the subsequent development of social history as a genre.

[7]   Wrightson, *ES*, 9.

Given the variety of the strands which contributed to the development of 'the new social history', the dating of its emergence and the identification of the precise complex of disciplinary traditions which informed its development are necessarily difficult. This was, after all, an international movement with common origins and inspirations, but local inflection.[8] There is, nonetheless, broad agreement that the late 1950s through to the mid 1970s represented a critical period in the development of the field.[9] This is true in terms of individual historians, of academic institutions and of intellectual influences. The flagship journal *Past & Present* was established in 1952 (in its first incarnation as 'A Journal of Scientific History'). 1958 saw the emergence of the Society for the Study of Labour History, whose *Bulletin*, first appearing in 1960, was to be particularly significant for early modern social history. The Cambridge Group for the Study of Population and Social Structure was founded in 1964; both the *Journal of Social History* and the History Workshops began in 1967; and the Centre for the Study of Social History was created at the University of Warwick in 1968. In 1963, in an interesting pointer to the otherwise little-remarked precociousness of medievalists in writing about social history, Rodney Hilton was appointed Professor of Medieval Social History at Birmingham University, while the more familiar professorial appointment of Harold Perkin to the first British Chair in Social History occurred at Lancaster University in 1967.[10] The establishment in 1976 of both the Social History Society and the journals *Social History* and *History Workshop Journal* signalled the coming-of-age of the field.

A further marker of this historiographical development was the renaming of (often only recently formed) 'economic history' departments in British universities as departments of 'economic and social history'. Both this rebranding and the subsequent wave of academic appointments naturally reflected the important contribution made to the emergence of social history *within* the discipline of economic history. From this perspective, the precocious work of R. H. Tawney and others, mobilised by political concerns over early twentieth-century social problems and policy, long anticipated the traditionally accepted birth-date for 'the new social history' and addressed

[8] See, e.g., the subtle differences in the definitions of the subject in the inaugural issue of the *JSH* 1 (1967), 3–16. For early British discussions, see Harold Perkin, 'Social History', in *Approaches to History: A Symposium*, ed. H. R. P. Finberg (1953, rev. 1962), 51–82; Jeffrey N. Wasserstrom, 'New Ways in History', *HWJ* 64 (2007), 271–94.
[9] E. J. Hobsbawm, 'From Social History to the History of Society', *Daedalus* 100 (1971), 20–45.
[10] Jim Obelkevich, 'New Developments in History in the 1950s and 1960s', *Contemporary British History* 14 (2000), 140–1.

many of its defining topics.[11] To this extent, although 'the new social history' was in part a reaction against the cliometrics of 'the new economic history', it continued its engagement with an earlier tradition of economic history, especially in those regional studies of the history of specific places that appeared in the 1950s and 1960s.[12] This was particularly true of the pioneering work of what subsequently came to be known as the Leicester School of English Local History, whose focus on the historic landscape and on interactions between environment and local society paralleled developments in the increasingly influential *Annales* 'school' in France.[13] But over and above this, the ongoing dialogue with economic history profoundly influenced the dominant theoretical premise of 'the new social history': that is, the determination of the economic base within the sovereignty of 'the social'.

A full-scale analysis of the emergence of 'the new social history' would necessarily demand consideration of a wide range of factors. Appropriately, both its defining ambitions and its objects of study reflected far broader societal trends. The expansion in higher education and the changing social profile of undergraduates which this facilitated, together with the dissolution of disciplinary boundaries within the schools of the new universities of the 1960s, contributed to what might be called a 'democratisation' in the subject matter of the historical discipline.[14] For good or ill, this development both shifted the focus from elites to the people; and encouraged the writing of a history of society that offered more than a simple reflection of the thoughts and writings of the literate classes about subordinate groups. The expansion in higher education also stimulated the significant increase in doctoral research where much of the pioneering work in social history

[11] See, e.g., E. M. Leonard, *The Early History of English Poor Relief* (Cambridge, 1900); Alice Clark, *The Working Life of Women in the Seventeenth Century* (1919) and, of course, R. H. Tawney, *Religion and the Rise of Capitalism: A Historical Study* (1926).
[12] J. D. Chambers, 'The Vale of Trent, 1670–1800: A Regional Study of Economic Change', *EcHR* Supplement 3 (1957).
[13] On the Leicester School, see Mike Thompson, Pam Fisher, Alan Fox and Christopher Dyer, *English Local History at Leicester: A Bibliography and History, 1999–2008* (Leicester, 2009): www.le.ac.uk/el/documents/Bibliography_1999_2008.pdf. On the influence of *Annales*, see Maurice Aymard, 'The *Annales* and French Historiography (1929–72)', *Journal of European Economic History* 1 (1972), 491–511; 'The Impact of the *Annales* School on the Social Sciences', *Review* 1 (1978); Stuart Clark, 'The *Annales* Historians', in *The Return of Grand Theory in the Human Sciences*, ed. Quentin Skinner (Cambridge, 1985), 177–98; Lynn Hunt, 'French History in the Last Twenty Years: the Rise and Fall of the *Annales* Paradigm', *Journal of Contemporary History* 21 (1986), 209–24; Peter Burke, *The French Historical Revolution: The Annales School, 1929–89* (Cambridge, 1990).
[14] Peter Burke, *History and Social Theory* (Cambridge, 2005) discusses his own experience of interdisciplinarity when, as a historian at the University of Sussex in the early 1960s, he taught a course on 'Social Structure and Social Change'. See also his autobiographical 'Invitation to Historians: An intellectual Self-Portrait, or the History of an Historian', *Rethinking History* 13 (2009), 269–81.

was first undertaken. And it was paralleled by the establishment of Research Councils, which from the founding of the Social Science Research Council (SSRC) in 1965, later the Economic and Social Research Council (ESRC), began to fund (often large-scale) research projects in social and economic history. In turn, this democratisation reflected a political engagement with broader post-1945 social and political trends. Keith Wrightson was both the product and beneficiary of these trends.

The intellectual influences behind these societal, educational and institutional developments were manifold. But central to the emergence of 'the new social history' within the universities was a recognition of the benefits of interdisciplinarity. This was heralded in a series of historiographical pronouncements (perhaps better described as manifestos) which reflected contemporaneous developments across various disciplines. In a famous set of lectures delivered in 1961, E. H. Carr argued that 'the more sociological history becomes and the more historical sociology becomes, the better for both'.[15] The 1963 *Past & Present* Conference was convened specifically 'to examine the relationship between the disciplines of history, sociology and social anthropology in the context of the widely held view that there is today a marked convergence of interests and methods'. In the same year, the journal published Keith Thomas's pioneering article on 'History and Anthropology'.[16] By 1966, the *Times Literary Supplement* could publish a series of articles advocating 'new ways in history'. Famously, Thomas's contribution to that issue – 'The Tools and the Job' – argued that if the job of social history was the reconstruction of past social and cultural systems, then the conceptual tools developed by anthropologists and sociologists would be not only helpful but *necessary*.[17]

Central to these interdisciplinary exchanges was the recognition that sociology and history shared a common set of problems in analysing the processes involved in the production, reproduction and transformation of societies. History, it was argued, could provide sociologists (many of whom carried out their research at a conspicuously shallow historical depth) with a longer chronological perspective on the history of social change, thereby ensuring that sociological research was (or should be) engaged in the study of what Philip Abrams described as the '(historical) process of structuring'.[18] Sociology, conversely, could not only offer historians the concepts necessary to analyse past societies, but also extend the range of the very subjects that historians might study. Within this broad agreement, however, there were significant differences, with some critics arguing that interdisciplinarity should induce historians both to critique much of sociology's often histori-

15 E. H. Carr, *What Is History?* (Harmondsworth, 1961), 84.
16 'History, Sociology and Social Anthropology', 102; Keith Thomas, 'History and Anthropology', *P&P* 24 (1963), 3–24.
17 Keith Thomas, 'The Tools and the Job', *TLS* (7 April, 1966).
18 Philip Abrams, *Historical Sociology* (Shepton Mallet, 1982), 304.

cally shallow theorising of social change and to develop historically rich theory.[19] But for the most part the growing ambitions of this 'new social history' were represented by the fruitful borrowing of what might be called 'intermediate theory'. This was especially true in an emerging British social history, which was arguably more comfortable (and certainly more successful) in assimilating what Geoff Eley describes as social-scientific 'techniques' rather than in adopting social theory per se, and in which eclecticism was seen (by historians at least) as a virtue.[20] This engagement with sociological concepts and methods nurtured what Adrian Wilson has christened 'the social-history paradigm'.[21]

Similar arguments were made about the beneficial returns which might follow from an exchange between history and anthropology.[22] It was suggested that anthropologists (for whom the otherness of their subject was constructed by space and by distance) offered historians (whose otherness was constructed by the notion of the past as 'a foreign country' where time itself was distance) the conceptual tools which might facilitate the analysis of 'pre-industrial' societies.[23] If many of the societies that historians studied were dominated by peasantries, then anthropology could offer the findings of field-work with 'real' peasants, providing what Thomas characterised as 'direct experience of matters about which historians have only read in books'.[24] (This was of course a pre-lapsarian age before anthropologists began to critique the poetics and politics of their own practice.)[25] Anthropology also encouraged those who wanted to study the lived *experience* of subordinate groups in past societies. As Thomas himself noted of his encounter with E. E. Evans-Pritchard's *History and Anthropology*, 'the concentration

---

[19] Gareth Stedman Jones, 'The Poverty of Empiricism', in *Ideology in Social Science*, ed. R. Blackburn (1972), 96–115, a challenge carried into the manifesto of the *HWJ*, reprinted in *History Workshop Collecteana 1967–1991*, ed. Raphael Samuel (Oxford, 1991).

[20] Geoff Eley, *A Crooked Line: From Cultural History to the History of Society* (Ann Arbor, 2005), 40.

[21] Adrian Wilson, 'A Critical Portrait of Social History', in *Rethinking Social History: English Society 1570–1920 and its Interpretation*, ed. Adrian Wilson (Manchester, 1993), 15–20.

[22] See the discussions of 'Anthropology and History in the 1980s', in *The New History: The 1980s and Beyond*, ed. Theodore K. Rabb and Robert I. Rotberg (Princeton, 1982), 227–78; Thomas, 'History and Anthropology'. For a more critical, but still sympathetic, response see E. P. Thompson, 'Anthropology and the Discipline of Historical Context', *Midland History* 1 (1972), 41–55; idem, *Folklore, Anthropology, and Social History* (Studies in Labour History Pamphlet, 1979).

[23] Bernard S. Cohn, 'Anthropology and History in the 1980s', in *The New History*, ed. Rabb and Rotberg, 227–52; idem, 'History and Anthropology: the State of Play', in his *An Anthropologist among the Historians: A Field Study* (Delhi, 1990).

[24] Thomas, 'History and Anthropology', 8.

[25] *Writing Culture: The Poetics and Politics of Ethnography*, ed. James Clifford and George E. Marcus (Berkeley, 1986).

on everyday life was perfectly normal, and even central, rather than inci-
dental and peripheral'.[26] Anthropology, especially the British social anthropology that first attracted historians, provided not only detailed studies of an
extended range of social forms in which family, kin and gender were central
categories of analysis, but also a holistic argument about the inter-relationships between these forms that was held to explain (perhaps too successfully
in its 'functionalist' formulation) how societies were structured and reproduced themselves. At its best, moreover, the anthropological emphasis on
cultural relativism (most evident in analysis of the relationships between
belief and behaviour) could help social historians protect the past from the
'condescension' of historians. This was to be immediately realised in those
studies of witchcraft and of 'popular religion' which rescued the investigation of past mental worlds from the inherited prejudices of protestant and
catholic reformers.

Most fundamentally of all, of course, both historians and social scientists wanted to develop causal explanations for social change. This shared
focus encouraged the widespread advocacy within a comparative historical
method of sociological models and 'ideal types' as part of the attempt to
isolate and highlight the causes of change.[27] Over this shared problematic
of 'big structures and large processes' loomed the challenges of explaining
and charting the consequences of the major transformation represented by
the Industrial Revolution.[28] This agenda, entangled as it was with theories
of modernisation, had profound implications for the emergence of social
history in general and for early modern social history in particular. At its
worst, modernisation theory produced a 'looking-glass' history, in which
change was described as a series of radical discontinuities and where *pre-
industrial* societies were perceived in terms of negative inversions. 'Pre-
industrial' social forms and experiences were, accordingly, characterised
in opposition to what was thought to be 'modern'.[29] The example of the
nuclear family, itself supposedly a product of industrialisation, provides one
notorious case study of this tendency, the construction of the characteristics
defining a (in fact, an ahistorical) peasantry perhaps another.[30]

[26] Interview with Keith Thomas in Maria Lúcia G. Pallares-Burke, *The New History:
Confessions and Conversations* (Cambridge, 2002), 90–1.
[27] See Theda Skocpol, 'Sociology's Historical Imagination', in *Vision and Method in
Historical Sociology*, ed. Theda Skocpol (Cambridge, 1984), 1–21.
[28] The phrase originates with Charles Tilly, *Big Structures, Large Processes, Huge
Questions* (New York, 1984).
[29] Burke, *History and Social Theory*, 145.
[30] See, for example, the comments in Peter Laslett, 'Introduction: The History of the
Family', in *Household and Family in Past Time: Comparative Studies in the Size and Structure
of the Domestic Group over the Last Three Centuries*, ed. Peter Laslett and Richard Wall
(Cambridge, 1972), 1–90; or the debate over Alan Macfarlane, *The Origins of English
Individualism: The Family, Property and Social Transition* (Oxford, 1978), reviewed in
Macfarlane, *The Culture of Capitalism* (Oxford, 1987), 191–222.

One particular variant of modernisation theory, the Marxism which dictated much of the agenda of social science, proved particularly attractive to British social historians. Even those who anxiously distanced themselves from politically engaged Marxism nonetheless employed a 'vulgar Marxism', which implied a materialist analysis ascribing a larger causative role in historical change to the economic and the social and explaining human agency (or its absence) primarily in terms of the process of class formation. Central, therefore, even to this 'soft' variety of historical materialism was a preoccupation with the universalising category of *class*, which emerged as the defining idiom of a 'realist' social history, and which was itself regarded as having been generated largely by the social relations of production.

The centrality to the 'new social history' of a materialist, causative analysis of past societies, as practised by historians who identified themselves as Marxists, was directly related to the emergence of what became known as 'history from below'. This term was apparently first deployed in Thompson's contribution to the *Times Literary Supplement* issue on 'new ways in history'.[31] But 'history from below' had deeper roots in the activities of the British Communist Party historians group (whose ranks included George Rudé, Eric Hobsbawm and Rodney Hilton, all of whom subsequently became influential historians of popular movements);[32] in the contributions made by those writing and teaching history *outside* the academy, notably in the extra-mural work of the Workers' Educational Association (of whom R. H. Tawney was an early apostle, and E. P. Thompson and Raymond Williams perhaps the most famous members);[33] and in the older tradition of a people's history.[34] Whatever its origins, the emergence of 'history from below' provided a keystone for much of 'the new social history'. Its influence was emphasised in Raphael Samuel's later insistence that social history was fundamentally 'oppositional': it dealt with 'real life' as opposed to abstractions; with 'ordinary' rather than privileged people; and with the everyday.[35] It encouraged in the precocious development of 'Labour History', for example, a switch from the history of institutions and of ideology to the study of crowds and of the culture of labouring people. Thompson himself argued that social change could best be understood through the historical reconstruction not only of the *experience* but also of the *agency* of subordinate groups. This

---

[31] E. P. Thompson, 'History from Below', *TLS* (7 April 1966).

[32] Harvey J. Kaye, *The British Marxist Historians: An Introductory Analysis* (Cambridge, 1984).

[33] See R. H. Tawney, *The Agrarian Problem in the Sixteenth Century* (1912), dedication; [J. R. Williams, R. M. Titmuss, F. J. Fisher], *R. H. Tawney: A Portrait by Several Hands* (1960).

[34] Raphael Samuel, 'British Marxist Historians, 1880–1980: Part One', *New Left Review* 120 (1980), 21–96.

[35] Raphael Samuel, 'What is Social History?', *History Today* (March 1985), 34. On the development of the History Workshops, see his *History Workshop Collecteana*.

inspirational (and rhetorically powerful) approach amounted to a manifesto for the reconstruction of the 'popular mentalities of subordination', and its influence – embodied for early modernists in particular in the essays later collected in Thompson's *Customs in Common* – resonates still in the work of all practitioners of the genre, Wrightson included.[36]

Under these influences, 'the new social history' significantly expanded the range of issues which fell within the historian's domain. Following Marc Bloch's famous dictum that 'the good historian is like the giant of the fairy tale ... he knows that wherever he catches the scent of human flesh, there his quarry lies', social historians began to address an ever-widening range of topics, including the histories of the family, of work and community, of crime and deviancy, of social movements and protest, of popular culture, of the sociology of religion and, slightly later (first under the impact of feminism in the guise of 'women's history') of gender.[37] The subsequent and ongoing extension of the list of topics whose history can be recovered reflects the multiplying ambitions of social history to recover what Wrightson himself characterised as the 'ancestry of our every act'.[38] The 'new social history' of the 1960s therefore enjoyed what Geoff Eley characterises as a doubled genealogy: 'identifying with the people and learning from social science'.[39]

The influence of these innovations was very quickly felt across the historical discipline. By 1971, Eric Hobsbawm could declare that 'It is a good moment to be a social historian.'[40] It was clear by then that social historians did not conceive of themselves merely as practitioners of yet another 'adjectival history'. Under 'the sovereignty of the social', the ambition now was to write *societal* history, which itself would provide the backbone to other areas of historical analysis.[41] In place of an earlier 'residual' social history (with the politics left out) and avoiding the charge that the genre was just another sub-discipline, 'the new social history' was to be *vertebraic* to the study of the past. This amounted to the emergence of a social history that Adrian Wilson has characterised as 'a totalising historiography'.[42] Nearly ten years after Hobsbawm's claim, Peter Burke's definition signalled the maturity of a field: for Burke, social history was nothing less than the history of social relations, of social structure, of social solidarities and social conflicts, of social classes and groups, and of everyday and private life.[43]

---

[36] E. P. Thompson, *Customs in Common* (1991).

[37] Marc Bloch, *The Historian's Craft: Reflections on The Nature and Uses of History and the Techniques and Methods of Those Who Write It* (Manchester, 1992 edn), 22.

[38] Keith Wrightson, 'The Enclosure of English Social History', in *Rethinking Social History*, ed. Wilson, 60.

[39] Eley, *Crooked Line*, 47.

[40] Hobsbawm, 'From Social History', 43.

[41] Eley, *Crooked Line*, 26.

[42] Wilson, 'Critical Portrait', 20–4.

[43] Peter Burke, *Sociology and History* (1980), 31.

By the early 1980s, the emergence of a sociologically informed social history and of a fully conceptualised historical sociology promised the realisation of E. H. Carr's hopes.[44] The shared concern of historians and sociologists in addressing 'the problematic of structuring' in analysing the transformation of societies was elegantly captured by Philip Abrams:

> Both [historians and sociologists] seek to understand the puzzle of human agency and both seek to do so in terms of the process of social structuring. Both are impelled to conceive of that process chronologically; at the end of the debate the diachrony-synchrony distinction is absurd. Sociology must be concerned with eventuation, because that is how structuring happens. History must be theoretical, because that is how structuring is apprehended.[45]

Abrams' manifesto for historical sociology proved particularly influential for Keith Wrightson who, in offering his own definition of social history, wrote of 'the attempt to produce, from a variety of perspectives, properly contextualised explanatory accounts of the manner in which social, cultural, economic and institutional structures have been created, maintained and transformed over time'.[46]

'Cold rooms and warm beer':[47] the making of early modern English social history

> In preparing and writing this book I have incurred many debts. The greatest and longest-standing is to the many research students and scholars of diverse nationality who contributed, however briefly, to the discussion of English social history in and around the Cambridge research seminars of the early 1970s. No-one who participated in that activity, much of it informal, is ever likely to forget it or to escape its influence.   Keith Wrightson (1982)[48]

In the late 1980s, attendees at an International Postgraduate Summer School at the University of Essex were startled to hear one participant, now a distinguished early modernist in her own right, confess that she took Keith Wrightson to bed with her every night. It transpired that she had meant to say that her frequent bedtime reading was Wrightson's *English Society*. Both episode and elision point to the enduring influence of that work. *English*

---

[44] For a critical review, see Craig Calhoun, 'The Rise and Domestication of Historical Sociology', in *The Historic Turn in the Human Sciences*, ed. Terrence J. MacDonald (Ann Arbor, 1996), 305–37.
[45] Abrams, *Historical Sociology*, ix–x. Cf. Christopher Lloyd, *Explanation in Social History* (Oxford, 1986).
[46] Wrightson, 'Enclosure', 73.
[47] The phrase is David Levine's in the preface to Wrightson & Levine, *Terling*, xi.
[48] Wrightson, *ES*, 9.

Society (together with its co-authored monographic companion, *Poverty and Piety in an English Village*) epitomises both the development of 'the new social history' of early modern England in general and the making of Keith Wrightson as a social historian in particular. Wrightson's own practice not only reflects the shared influences discussed above, but also demonstrates their particular significance for the study of the early modern period, and for the distinctive ways in which that study was carried out in Cambridge University in the early 1970s when he undertook his doctoral research.

Keith Wrightson was sired by Peter Laslett out of Christopher Hill. As shorthand, this thoroughbred metaphor captures the immediate genealogy of Wrightson's making as a historian of early modern England. In different ways the work of Laslett and of Hill connected Wrightson with the key intellectual influences in the making of 'the new social history', and more significantly they gave it a particular early modern inflection. Given the disagreements that separated these two historians during their lives, it is ironic that their two most influential works – Hill's collection of essays, *Society and Puritanism in Pre-Revolutionary England*, and Laslett's *The World We Have Lost* – might, taken together, be regarded as the founding texts of early modern social history.

Hill's work (the product of teaching he undertook for the Workers' Educational Association) was an exercise in the sociology of religion, designed to explore 'the roots of Puritanism in English society'.[49] *Society and Puritanism* took Puritanism out of the church and into society. It sought to identify 'the non-theological reasons for supporting the Puritans, or for being a Puritan'. As this suggests, Hill's work drew upon R. H. Tawney's *Religion and the Rise of Capitalism*, a text that Hill's former student Keith Thomas also acknowledged as 'a deep influence' on his own thinking as a historian.[50] And behind Tawney, Hill's essays engage with the work of the theorist who might be regarded as one of the first historical sociologists, Max Weber. Although neither Weber nor Tawney feature much in the footnotes of *Society and Puritanism*, their thinking structures what was effectively an early essay in the historical sociology of English local society. Exploring the appeal of Puritanism to 'the industrious sort of people' (the group that Wrightson would subsequently describe as the 'middling sort'), Hill's essays explored issues that became fundamental to 'the new social history' of early modern England: the social contours of popular religion; the role of the church courts; the relationship between religious discourse and the structure of social relations in household and community; the place of the poor in the parish. The centrality of many of these themes to what came to be known as the 'Wrightson thesis' should be immediately apparent. Hill's influence,

[49] Christopher Hill, *Society and Puritanism in Pre-Revolutionary England* (1964), 9.
[50] Keith Thomas, interviewed by Alan Macfarlane in 2009: www.sms.cam.ac.uk/media/1132829.

however, extended still further, for his *From Reformation to Industrial Revolution* (1967) discusses social differentiation between the beneficiaries of developing agrarian and commercial capitalism (yeoman farmers and merchants) and its victims (artisans and the labouring poor), an argument that, more carefully worked out, became fundamental to the reading of social change in Wrightson's *English Society*.[51] Hill was, therefore, not only practising the kind of history from below which appealed to Wrightson, but he was specifically engaged in the historical analysis of Puritanism as a social phenomenon which profoundly influenced Wrightson's work, from his doctoral thesis – on the Puritan reformation of manners – on.[52]

The influence on Wrightson of Peter Laslett is more easily identified. In 1998, the Institute of Historical Research staged a conference on 'New Developments in History in the 1950s and 1960s'.[53] Many of the participants in the 'Witness Seminar', themselves key players in that interdisciplinary historical moment, emphasised the significance of anthropology, rather than sociology, in the formation of 'the new social history'. This is striking testimony to the role that anthropology has subsequently played in social- and cultural-historical analysis (and undoubtedly reflects the personal intellectual trajectories of those commentators). Although it is true that, for reasons we discuss below, the anthropological turn shaped the subsequent development of early modern history, the emphasis on anthropology arguably misrepresents the sequencing and hierarchy of influences within the gestation of 'the new social history'. Strikingly, one of the few dissenters from the anthropological orthodoxy at the 1998 seminar was Wrightson's doctoral supervisor Peter Laslett, who explicitly framed his testimony on the development of demographic history within the context of historical sociology and whose own work developed the concept of 'social structural time'.[54] Disciplinary boundaries are, of course, never neatly drawn. It will nevertheless be argued in what follows that for Wrightson sociology rather than anthropology provided initial and ongoing conceptual inspiration; and that, even within his sociological reading, Wrightson had distinct preferences: he consistently engaged more with middle-range theories and methodology rather than with classical theory, and even where he did discuss the founding fathers he followed Laslett in drawing less from Marx than from

---

[51] Christopher Hill, *Reformation to Industrial Revolution* (1967), 119–20.
[52] 'I loved the way Christopher Hill revealed an alternative history that gave a place and a voice to the common people. When I read him for the first time there was a sense of discovering a history that I had suspected was there, but had never before had the chance to read about': britishscholar.org/publications/2011/08/15/august-2011-keith-wrightson.
[53] Jim Obelkevich, 'Witness Seminar: New Developments in History in the 1950s and 1960s', *Contemporary History* 14 (2000), 143–67.
[54] See, e.g., the essays collected in Peter Laslett, *Family Life and Illicit Love in Earlier Generations: Essays in Historical Sociology* (Cambridge, 1977).

Weber, whose writings seemed more attuned to analysing the particularities and peculiarities of early modern society.

A Cambridge-based doctoral student pursuing a research agenda in sixteenth- and seventeenth-century English social history at the dawn of the 1970s almost inevitably drew inspiration from all three of the nascent traditions discussed above – of what were beginning to be known then as historical sociology, as historical anthropology and as history from below. This was a methodological inheritance shared by the cohort of Cambridge doctoral students – among them David Cressy, John Walter, David Levine, Vivienne Brodsky-Elliott and Ann Kussmaul – of which Wrightson was part. All of them subsequently produced studies of specific aspects of early modern English society that betray these different influences in various ways.[55] But even more significant in local (and ultimately also in more general) terms was the influence of historical demography as practised by the Cambridge Group for the Study of Population and Social Structure.

If in Cambridge, the interdisciplinary agenda of the late 1960s derived – at least initially – rather more from sociology than anthropology (and from *inter alia* economic history, historical geography and development studies), the significance of the Cambridge Group cannot be overestimated. The Group was distinctive as the sort of collaborative research unit that early proponents of 'the new social history' had envisaged, and it offered a practical example of interdisciplinary work, a meeting-place for cross-disciplinary and cross-cultural exchanges and not least, via its international networks, a rich library of largely unpublished papers. Wrightson himself was never formally associated with the Group. But indirectly through collaborations with the doctoral students working with E. A. ('Tony') Wrigley and Roger Schofield, under the tutelage of his own doctoral supervisor Peter Laslett (the principal populariser of the unit's findings), and with the Group's subsequent Director Richard Smith, the Group exercised an enduring influence on Wrightson's thinking about social-structural and demographic trends in the English past. Both the Group's informal 'seminar' – what Peter Laslett called 'a loose-ish association around a coffee party which meets each day' – and its regular research seminar brought together visiting scholars from different disciplines and cultures.[56] For regular attendees, Wrightson among

---

[55] See, *inter alia*, John Walter and Keith Wrightson, 'Dearth and the Social Order in Early Modern England', *P&P* 71 (1976), 22–42; David Levine, *Family Formation in an Age of Nascent Capitalism* (New York, 1977); David Cressy, *Literacy and the Social Order: Reading and Writing in Tudor and Stuart England* (Cambridge, 1980); Ann Kussmaul, *Servants in Husbandry in Early Modern England* (Cambridge, 1985); John Walter, *Understanding Popular Violence in the English Revolution: The Colchester Plunderers* (Cambridge, 1999); and the essays collected in John Walter, *Crowds and Popular Politics in Early Modern England* (Manchester, 2006), all of which emerged (sooner or later) from doctoral research undertaken in Cambridge in the early and mid 1970s.
[56] '"The Family Way": Interview with Peter Laslett', *CAM* 59 (2000), 20.

them, the Group was the forum for a first encounter with the approaches, concepts and individuals associated with the *Annales* school.

The work of the *Annales*, most obviously the regional studies which formed part of what has been called the second wave of *Annaliste* historiography (and especially those of Pierre Goubert), proved particularly important for Wrightson's own methodological thinking.[57] The hierarchy of determinations – from ecology through economy to society and then to culture – adopted by second-wave *Annalistes* itself reflected a distinctive response to the interdisciplinary moment, in their case offering a causative analysis that was by definition social-scientific but at the same time fundamentally structuralist. The writing of regional studies according to these determinations is clearly reflected in the methodological approach of both *Poverty and Piety* and *English Society*. But Wrightson's exercises in reconstructing historical communities (like those of Alan Macfarlane whose influence is discussed below) also drew upon more indigenous traditions. Wrightson's frequent citation of W. G. Hoskins' pioneering study, *The Midland Peasant* (written during the Second World War but not published until 1957), points to the considerable influence of the Leicester School of Local History. Its ecologically driven analysis of regional patterns of rural social structure, paralleled in its most ambitious work by the attempt to relate the enduring structures of climate, landscape and settlement to the conjunctures of mentalities and belief-systems, echoed the concerns of the *Annalistes*.[58]

Wrightson's conceptual and methodological horizons were therefore widening at a time and in a place where the findings of the Cambridge Group were (at least partly under the influence of the *Annales* school, and fully cognisant of developments in English local history) cumulatively demythologising the social history of early modern England. English men and women in the sixteenth and seventeenth century, Wrigley and Schofield demonstrated, married much later; tended to live in smaller households; and migrated for the purposes of apprenticeship, employment, courtship and marriage much more frequently than had once been thought.[59] The painstaking reconstruction – on the basis of parish registers and 'census type-listings' – of these structural characteristics was, Laslett argued, fundamental to the project of 'understanding ourselves in time' and would accordingly

---

[57] Pierre Goubert, *Beauvais et le Beauvaisis de 1600 à 1730* (Paris, 1960); *idem*, *The French Peasantry in the Seventeenth Century* (Cambridge, 1986).
[58] W. G. Hoskins, *Provincial England* (1963); Joan Thirsk, *English Peasant Farming: The Agrarian History of Lincolnshire from Tudor to Recent Times* (1957); *The Agrarian History of England and Wales, IV: 1500–1640*, ed. Joan Thirsk (Cambridge, 1967); Alan Everitt, *Landscape and Community in England* (1985); Margaret Spufford, *Contrasting Communities: English Villagers in the Sixteenth and Seventeenth Centuries* (Cambridge, 1974); David G. Hey, *An English Rural Community: Myddle under the Tudors and Stuarts* (Leicester, 1974).
[59] Laslett, *World We Have Lost*; *Household and Family*, ed. Laslett and Wall.

inform Wrightson's analysis of the complex interactions between enduring structures and processes of social change.

A second major influence within (but arguably more significantly beyond) the Cambridge History faculty of the early 1970s was represented by the King's College Social History Seminar. This very influential group of scholars met from 1973 to 1975, with Wrightson himself speaking in the seminar's first season.[60] Its themes during those three years – social control, historical community studies and social bonds – reflect the impact on social history of the exchange with the social sciences. Run by Oxford émigrés Alan Macfarlane and Martin Ingram, both doctoral students of Keith Thomas, this network promoted an early engagement with anthropology. Macfarlane convened two important SSRC-supported conferences in 1975 and 1977 on history and anthropology, at which Wrightson was an attendee and paper-giver. Macfarlane himself had been the direct beneficiary of Thomas's hugely influential 1971 study *Religion and the Decline of Magic*, and his own post-doctoral 1970 monograph *Witchcraft in Tudor and Stuart England* not only explicitly signalled the arrival of historical anthropology in the historiography of early modern England, but also started him down a path that was to see him train and subsequently teach as an anthropologist.[61] Two years later, Macfarlane sub-titled his study of the family life of a seventeenth-century clergyman *An Essay in Historical Anthropology*.[62]

In 1972, Macfarlane began another collaborative and pioneering SSRC-funded project, originally conceived as a comparative historical reconstruction of two rural parishes: Kirkby Lonsdale in Cumberland and Earls Colne in Essex. This extraordinarily ambitious project sought systematically to reconstitute the two historical communities from the archives of church, state and manor over the *longue durée*. It sponsored important theoretical discussions about the nature of 'the community' as a bounded social entity and about the methodologies for undertaking historical community studies.[63] In its ultimate form, recovering and transcribing the entire public archive

---

[60] We are grateful to Martin Ingram for providing copies of the seminar's programme for these years.

[61] Keith Thomas, *Religion and the Decline of Magic: Studies in Popular Beliefs in Sixteenth- and Seventeenth-Century England* (1971); Alan Macfarlane, *Witchcraft in Tudor and Stuart England: A Regional and Comparative Study* (1970); idem, 'Historical Anthropology', *Cambridge Anthropology* 3 (1977), 1–21. There is an informative 2008 filmed interview with Macfarlane about his career: www.youtube.com/watch?v=hIbv5BybJCo. Macfarlane's website is a treasure trove for those interested in his role in the development of historical anthropology: www.alanmacfarlane.com/contents_web.html.

[62] Alan Macfarlane, *The Family Life of Ralph Josselin: A Seventeenth-Century Clergyman. An Essay in Historical Anthropology* (Cambridge, 1970).

[63] Alan Macfarlane, 'History, Anthropology and the Study of Communities', *SH* 2 (1977), 631–52; Craig J. Calhoun, 'History, Anthropology and the Study of Communities: Some Problems in Macfarlane's Proposals', *SH* 3 (1978), 363–73; idem, 'Community: Towards a Variable Conceptualization for Comparative Research', *SH* 5 (1980), 105–29.

of the single village of Earls Colne, the project introduced social historians to the possibilities of systematic *serial* research and record linkage across multiple archival sources.[64] (Macfarlane's work also demonstrated how 'the new social history', especially in its impulse to quantify in fields like the history of crime,[65] was facilitated both by the otherwise little-discussed and generally post-Second World War revolution in archives collection and management, and by the technological changes associated with computing in which his group also played a pioneering role.)[66] In sketching out the archival parameters and methodological possibilities for the reconstruction of historical communities, Macfarlane's thinking helped Wrightson, in conjunction with David Levine, think about how local social systems might best be studied. More specifically, Macfarlane's painstaking reconstruction of the social, cultural and economic factors which might explain the highly localised pattern of witchcraft accusations in Elizabethan and early Stuart Essex helped Wrightson and Levine identify an appropriate focus for their own archival research. The result was the justly famous co-authored study of the Essex parish of Terling: *Poverty and Piety in an English Village*.[67]

This central focus on the nature and significance of 'community' in late medieval and early modern social history inevitably drew on theoretical work in the social sciences then dominated by the mobilisation of models and ideal types for the construction of a continuum along which specific social formations might be placed and social change evaluated.[68] Perceived parallels between early modern English rural society and other peasant societies saw important exchanges in fora like the Peasant Studies seminar at the School of Oriental and Asian Studies, in the *Peasant Studies Newsletter* and later in the *Journal of Peasant Studies*, to which Wrightson was an early contributor.[69] The engagement with case studies and empirical sociology led Wrightson in turn to the rediscovery of an earlier generation of 'community

---

[64] Alan Macfarlane, in collaboration with Sarah Harrison and Charles Jardine, *Reconstructing Historical Communities* (Cambridge, 1977); *Earls Colne. Records of an English Village, 1375–1854*: www.dspace.ca.ac.uk/handle/1810/195838. For Kirby Lonsdale, see Alan Macfarlane, 'The Myth of the Peasantry: Family and Economy in a Northern Parish', in *Land, Kinship and Life-Cycle*, ed. R. M. Smith (Cambridge, 1984), 333–49.

[65] See, for example, J. A. Sharpe, *Crime in Seventeenth-Century England: A County Study* (Cambridge, 1983).

[66] For a discussion of this silent revolution in the archive, see Alan Macfarlane, *A Guide to English Historical Records* (Cambridge, 1983).

[67] Wrightson & Levine, *Terling*.

[68] Robert Redfield, *The Little Community: Viewpoints for the Study of the Human Whole* (Chicago, 1955); *idem*, *Peasant Society and Culture: An Anthropological Approach to Civilization* (Chicago, 1956).

[69] For a helpful review of the development of peasant studies, see Henry Bernstein and Terence J. Byers, 'From Peasant Studies to Agrarian Change', *Journal of Agrarian Change* 1 (2001), 1–56.

studies', whose genealogy could be traced back to the pioneering influence of the Chicago school of urban sociology; and to a close reading of contemporaneous studies of particular communities.[70] Underpinning both these fields was an earlier interdisciplinary exchange in which the pioneering work of the social scientists Arensberg and Kimball had informed George Homans' classic 1942 study of *English Villagers of the Thirteenth Century*.[71] It was in this interdisciplinary context that the later work of W. M. Williams on Ashworthy and on Gosforth, or of Margaret Stacy on Banbury, was to loom large in Wrightson's thinking in the 1970s.[72] At the same time, he familiarised himself with the methodologies developed by sociologists as they encountered difficulties in defining communities as bounded social entities. Of particular importance in this respect was social network theory, first adapted in the English historical context by the Cambridge-based historical geographer Richard Smith in his study of medieval peasant communities.[73]

None of this is, of course, to deny that 'the new social history' was flowering elsewhere, especially in Oxford, at Warwick and at Lancaster. Much of the pioneering research on the social history of crime, for instance, took place under the supervision of historians (E. P. Thompson included) who lay beyond the orbit of the historical demography and historical anthropology which preoccupied Wrightson and his contemporaries in Cambridge. But when given the chance to bring these various strands together and to crystallise what was then known about English society in the late sixteenth and seventeenth centuries Wrightson grasped the opportunity with both hands. The result was *English Society 1580–1680*, which rapidly became recognised as a considerable achievement in and of itself. By the time of its publication in 1982, Wrightson had already (by virtue of the collaborative work both with John Walter and with David Levine) earned a reputation as a new and significant voice in a rapidly developing historiography. *English Society* not only confirmed but elaborated that status. Given the intellectual, methodological and psychological matrix from which it emerged, it is hardly surprising that it was a highly complex book both in idiom and argument. Even its genre is somewhat misleading. Commissioned as part of the

---

70 For an overview, see Ronald Frankenberg, *Communities in Britain: Social Life in Town and Country* (Harmondsworth, 1969).

71 Conrad M. Arensberg and Solon T. Kimball, *Family and Community in Ireland* (Cambridge MA, 1940); George C. Homans, *English Villagers of the Thirteenth Century* (Cambridge MA, 1942).

72 W. M. Williams, *A West Country Village: Ashworthy* (1963); idem, *The Sociology of an English Village: Gosforth* (1964). Margaret Stacy, *Tradition and Change: A Study of Banbury* (Oxford, 1960).

73 J. A. Barnes, 'Class and Committees in a Norwegian Island Parish', *Human Relations* 7 (1954), 39–58; J. Boissevain and J. Clyde Mitchell, *Network Analysis: Studies in Human Interaction* (The Hague, 1973). R. M. Smith, 'English Peasant Life-Cycles and Socio-Economic Networks: A Quantitative Geographical Case Study' (unpublished University of Cambridge Ph.D., 1975).

Hutchinson Social History of England series in which the preceding volume was to have been written by Charles Phythian-Adams and the succeeding volumes (by Pamela Horn and Bob Malcolmson) had already appeared, it is on the face of it an undergraduate text, and at the time it appeared it was competing with volumes by Holderness and by Coleman (and was to compete subsequently with volumes by both Clay and Sharpe).[74] What Wrightson in fact produced has come to be regarded as *the* creative synthesis of the 'new social history' of early modern England. In fact, much of the influence of *English Society* derived from its conception less as a textbook than as an interpretative essay on the relationship between enduring structures and social change in the century after 1580. Wrightson's timing was also, however, undoubtedly advantageous, for he crested a breaking wave of archival research in what was still in the late 1970s and early 1980s a relatively novel field of historical enquiry. He was able to benefit, for instance, from the recent publication of David Cressy's painstaking analysis of literacy rates; from discussions with John Walter about his rigorous exploration of the highly ambiguous evidence for the nature and scale of popular protest; and from the still unpublished Cambridge Group working papers which would shortly see the light of day as Wrigley and Schofield's *Population History of England*.[75] Add into this mix his own analysis of the reformation of manners as it was fought out (in Terling and elsewhere) over the punishment of extra-marital sexuality and the regulation of alehouses, and spice it up with the interpretative polarisation of the debate over history and continuity in the nature of affective relations between husbands and wives and parents and children in the wake of the publication of Lawrence Stone's *Family, Sex and Marriage*, and it is possible to see just how and why *English Society* became so much more (and in some ways less) than a textbook.[76]

---

[74] Pamela Horn, *The Rural World, 1780–1850: Social Change in the English Countryside* (1980); Robert W. Malcolmson, *Life and Labour in England 1700–1780* (1981); B. A. Holderness, *Pre-Industrial England: Economy and Society, 1500–1750* (1976); D. C. Coleman, *The Economy of England, 1450–1750* (Oxford, 1977); C. G. A. Clay, *Economic Expansion and Social Change: England, 1500–1700*, 2 vols (Cambridge, 1984); J. A. Sharpe, *Early Modern England: A Social History 1550–1760* (1987).

[75] Cressy, *Literacy*; Walter and Wrightson, 'Dearth and the Social Order'. E. A. Wrigley and R. S. Schofield, *The Population History of England, 1541–1871: A Reconstruction* (1981) was in press as Wrightson's volume went into production.

[76] Keith Wrightson and David Levine, 'The Social Context of Illegitimacy in Early Modern England' and Keith Wrightson, 'The Nadir of English Illegitimacy in the Seventeenth-Century', both in *Bastardy and its Comparative History*, ed. Peter Laslett, Karla Oosterveen and Richard M. Smith (1980), 158–75, 176–91; Keith Wrightson, 'Two Concepts of Order: Justices, Constables and Jurymen in Seventeenth-Century England', in *An Ungovernable People: The English and their Law in the Seventeenth and Eighteenth Centuries*, ed. John Brewer and John Styles (London, 1980), 21–46; *idem*, 'Alehouses, Order and Reformation in Rural England, 1590–1660', in *Popular Culture and Class Conflict 1590–1914: Explorations in the History of Labour and Leisure*, ed. Eileen

English Society established definitively what we knew then about the history of marriage and the family, about the changing balance of population and resources, and about the ways in which a polity obsessed with notions of hierarchy coped with the threat of significant social disorder.

English Society and the contribution of Keith Wrightson

> My manuscript was completed in the early autumn of 1980, but in an important sense work of this kind is never finished. In a rapidly developing subject any attempt at interpretive synthesis must of necessity remain provisional. Challenging new work continues to appear. It will be enough, however, if I have succeeded even partially in my two most important objectives. One is that of conveying something of the texture of the social experience of this period to those as yet unfamiliar with its history. The other is that of putting forward arguments about the nature and development of English society in the past which will stimulate as much as persuade. Keith Wrightson (1982)[77]

If the interdisciplinary environment of Cambridge University was influential for the emergence of early modern English social history in the 1970s, Keith Wrightson had a highly personal and distinctive take on that intellectual inheritance. He came to share the assumption, implicit in Thomas's manifesto for a closer relationship between history and anthropology, that although social scientists might offer concepts and models which informed the fundamental questions about the nature of historical change, the answers to those questions could be found only in empirical historical research, much of it closely focused.[78] From its very first flowerings in his (unpublished) Cambridge doctoral thesis and the articles associated with it, through his collaborations with David Levine on the historical reconstructions of Terling, and into his first great work of synthesis in 1982 and beyond, his approach has consistently proved to be conceptually sophisticated, archivally informed and politically engaged.[79]

The conceptual sophistication of Wrightson's work has almost always been implicit rather than explicit. It is abundantly clear that Wrightson has read his sociology, both in the classics produced by the 'founding fathers' (by Marx, by Tönnies and especially by Weber) but also in the more recent agendas set first by the practitioners of empirical sociology in the British

Yeo and Stephen Yeo (Brighton, 1981), 1–27; Lawrence Stone, *The Family, Sex and Marriage in England 1500–1800* (1977); Alan Macfarlane, 'Review of *The Family, Sex and Marriage in England 1500–1800*, by Lawrence Stone', *History and Theory* 18 (1979), 103–26.

[77] Wrightson, *ES*, 'Preface'.

[78] Thomas, 'History and Anthropology'. Cf. Thompson, 'Historical Anthropology'.

[79] Keith Wrightson, 'The Puritan Reformation of Manners with Special Reference to the Counties of Lancashire and Essex 1640–1660' (unpublished University of Cambridge Ph.D., 1974).

tradition as that field developed in the 1950s and 1960s; and subsequently by Laslett and by Abrams in their manifestos for a genuinely *historical* sociology.[80] By the late 1980s, he was rehearsing Abrams' notion that 'historical time is a medium of continuity as well as of change'.[81] From this methodological perspective, *English Society* is itself probably best characterised as a work of historical sociology in the empirical tradition. Just occasionally the urge to conceptualise became explicit: both in his rejoinder to Miranda Chaytor's work on kinship in sixteenth-century Ryton in 1979 and in his 1997 manifesto for the rejuvenation of the historiography of the family, Wrightson insisted that the 'credibility problem' of social history as a genre could be overcome not simply by more stringent and empirical procedures of *verification* (more source criticism, more systematic quantification, more rigorous comparison) but by more sophisticated *conceptualisation* of processes of social change.[82]

But even when he did not wear his sociology on his sleeve, Wrightson's history was invariably informed by a profoundly sociological imagination, a peculiarly insightful grasp (by no means instinctive to all practitioners of social history) of how social systems might function and of the social relations to which those systems gave shape. There are some splendid expressions of this sociological thinking in the pages of *English Society* in particular: the argument that marriage was understood in early modern England 'as a privilege rather than a right'; the idea that the sanctions implied by the poor law constituted 'a powerful reinforcement of habits of deference and subordination'; or the notion that the gradual incorporation of local communities into processes of government added a 'a new depth and complexity to their local patterns of social stratification'.[83] These elegant formulations are all the more striking, and have been all the more influential, precisely because at the time of their publication they were essentially intuitive, since the empirical research which might verify them was only then underway. It almost goes without saying that intensive archival work both by Wrightson himself and by others has subsequently vindicated these insights.

Conceptualisation might have been necessary to Wrightson's approach but it was by no means sufficient. From the very earliest stages Wrightson took archives very seriously. Working both on his own and with Levine, Wrightson got his hands dirty in the archival evidence which survived in

[80] For the founding fathers, see Wrightson, *EN*, ch. 1. For Stacy and Williams, see Keith Wrightson, 'Kinship in an English Village: Terling, Essex 1500–1700', in *Land, Kinship and Life-Cycle*, ed. Smith, 313 n. 1, 317 n. 7.

[81] Abrams, *Historical Sociology*, 178, cited in Levine & Wrightson, *Whickham*, 430 n.1.

[82] Wrightson, 'Household and Kinship', *HWJ* 12 (1981), 151–8; *idem*, 'The Family in Early Modern England: Continuity and Change', in *Hanoverian Britain and Empire: Essays in Memory of Philip Lawson*, ed. Stephen Taylor, Richard Connors and Clyve Jones (Woodbridge, 1998), 12–15.

[83] Wrightson, *ES*, 70, 181, 224.

both local and central repositories. Rather than sampling or serendipitously selecting examples as previous historians had often done, he undertook systematic and serial research across bodies of evidence. It is hard now to recapture the exploratory nature of this research, for which there was then little knowledge or training. But the vignettes of Wrightson abruptly terminating his first day's research on the Lancashire records on discovering that, when he had eventually tamed the unflattened quarter session rolls and deciphered the clerk's hand, they were written in Latin (he went back and mastered both the next day), or at the Essex Record Office having to introduce his own supervisor, Peter Laslett, to bastardy examinations, suggest the pioneering nature of the research undertaken in the second wave of 'the new social history'. In line with the nascent emphasis on quantification, Wrightson was perfectly prepared to count and did so rigorously. But for him quantification was also matched by sensitivity to the social and juridical processes that had generated the sources and which gave meaning to the statistical patterns uncovered. This allowed him to offer closely focused local studies of the rural communities of Terling and of Whickham, and, most recently, of the urban networks of seventeenth-century Newcastle.[84] In particular, his archival mastery of the procedures of the ecclesiastical courts – especially in respect of their jurisdiction over marriage and over probate – enabled Wrightson to offer highly original and richly textured studies of kinship and of moral regulation and to locate those studies in painstaking reconstruction of the local demographic and economic context (of birth and death rates, of wage levels and tenurial patterns) in which these social dramas played out.[85] As Wrightson himself has recently noted, regarding 'small scale, intense focus, and painstaking record linkage':

> I get a lot of satisfaction out of that kind of craftsmanship, and the way that it can reveal things previously unsuspected and answer large questions that are otherwise inaccessible. I was trying to do that sort of thing, under the influence of the best English local history, and of sociological and social anthropological case studies, before the term 'microhistory' was coined. But now that the label exists, I am happy to wear it. I've done plenty of large scale, big sweep history, but the microhistory is what I really most enjoy.[86]

The locales on which Wrightson chose (initially at least) to undertake archival research were emphatically *rural*. Narrowing the scale of observation to relatively small communities facilitated the systematic exploitation of the available sources and, acknowledging the influence of social

---

[84] Wrightson & Levine, *Terling*; Levine & Wrightson, *Whickham*; Keith Wrightson, *Ralph Tailor's Summer: A Scrivener, His City and the Plague* (New Haven, 2011).
[85] For kinship, see Wrightson 'Kinship'; Levine & Wrightson, *Whickham*; for moral regulation, see Wrightson & Levine, *Terling*.
[86] britishscholar.org/publications/2011/08/15/august-2011-keith-wrightson.

anthropology, the detailed exploration of the inter-relationships between the stories that they could be encouraged to tell. The unpublished experiment in the reconstruction of the parish of Burnham-on-Crouch and the fully realised study of Terling were planned, researched and executed under the influence of Laslett's view that the analysis of small-scale communities would permit the reconstruction of face-to-face relations in a way that would be entirely impossible on the much larger canvas implied by urban history.[87] This consistent interest in rural social relations found expression in his very first publications, especially in the early review essay on 'Villages, Villagers and Village Studies' and in the study of 'Aspects of Social Differentiation'.[88] Even when the analysis of social relations in the parish of Whickham submerged the Elizabethan community chapter-by-chapter into the increasingly urbanised Durham coalfield, Wrightson consistently recognised the distinctiveness of the local and of the particular.[89] As we have suggested, this profound sense of the significance of space and place was indebted in part to the Leicester School of Local History, but at the same time it retained a recognition (not generally characteristic of the Leicester School) of the significance of demographic context and a striking sensitivity to both the structure and the content of local social relationships.

If Wrightson and Levine were unusually rigorous in their approach to the demographic context in which local social systems could be reconstructed, they were also extremely ambitious in exploiting the demographic evidence to pose questions about the nature and quality of social relations. It is no accident that the first collaboration with Levine was to reconstruct the intimate social arenas in which illegitimate births might arise, the one aspect of demographic history where the laconic record of parish registers could be linked to the richer qualitative evidence surviving in the archives of ecclesiastical and secular (that is, quarter sessions) jurisdictions.[90] This was a significant step forward from the statistical analysis of illegitimacy offered by Laslett and his collaborators and it allowed Wrightson and Levine to investigate in detail the nature and causes of the notorious 'boomlet' in bastardy ratios which occurred at the end of the sixteenth century, and to argue for the significance of interrupted courtship rather than rampant promiscuity as a proximate cause of this remarkable inflation in the rate of illegitimate conceptions.[91] A similar approach informed his fundamentally important

---

[87] For Burnham-on-Crouch see Wrightson, 'Two Concepts of Order', 40–4; *idem*, 'Alehouses', 14–15, 19, 22. For Terling, see Wrightson & Levine, *Terling*.

[88] Keith Wrightson, 'Villages, Villagers and Village Studies', *HJ* 18 (1975), 632–9; *idem*, 'Aspects of Social Differentiation in Rural England, c.1580–1660', *Journal of Peasant Studies* 5 (1977), 33–47.

[89] Levine & Wrightson, *Whickham*, 274–427.

[90] Wrightson and Levine, 'The Social Context of Illegitimacy'.

[91] For the 'boomlet' see Edward Shorter, *The Making of the Modern Family* (Ann Arbor, 1977). Cf. Levine, *Family Formation*.

studies of kinship in the reconstruction of social relations in Terling and in Whickham. Building upon the demographic record as it was captured on family reconstitution forms, and linking this data to other evidence (especially the concentric circles of scribes, executors, appraisers, witnesses and beneficiaries referred to in wills and other probate material), Wrightson was able to assess the relative importance of neighbourliness, a concept whose centrality to past social relationships he has done most to establish, over and above kinship, in the social horizons of early modern men and women.[92]

These various themes were ultimately synthesised in *English Society*, but the book's *leitmotiv* is its consistent emphasis on the sixteenth and seventeenth centuries in general (and on the period 1580–1640 in particular) as a site of *social change*. The Wrightson of *English Society* was certainly at pains to characterise the 'enduring structures' which shaped patterns of social relations, but he was insistent in arguing that those very patterns were themselves subject to extraordinary (and, in many respects, unprecedented) pressures in this period. He was certainly not the first historian to associate this period with profound social transformation: this was, after all, 'Tawney's century', and as we have seen Hill, Thomas and Macfarlane had each in different ways sketched out the rise and fall of specific social, economic and cultural phenomena during this period. The novelty of Wrightson's analysis lay, rather, both in its fully integrated discussion of the relationship between various historical trends and in its sensitivity to the impact of those trends on specific social groups. In discussing the course of social change in *English Society*, Wrightson singled out the distribution of resources, the nature of social order, and processes of learning and godliness as three distinctive arenas of social transformation. And although it was hidden under the anodyne title of the volume's conclusion, there was (in 'Nation and Locality') an even stronger emphasis on the developing processes of governance themselves as a fourth index of change. Although the periodisation of the 'textbook' series in which *English Society* had been commissioned led Wrightson to focus on the peculiar experience of the generations that lived at the turn of the sixteenth and seventeenth century, his more expansive formulations (encouraged by the broader canvas of *Earthly Necessities* in particular and of his more synthetic later essays in general) have developed increasingly sophisticated readings not only of the overall course of social change but also of the class-related experience of those developments in which different social groups had varying economic opportunities according

---

[92] The trajectory of this line of interpretation can be traced from Wrightson 'Kinship', through Levine & Wrightson, *Whickham*, and into the later essays on neighbourliness: Keith Wrightson, 'Mutualities and Obligations: Changing Social Relationships in Early Modern England', *Proceedings of the British Academy* 139 (2006), 157–94; *idem*, 'The "Decline of Neighbourliness" Revisited', in *Local Identities in Late Medieval and Early Modern England*, ed. Norman L. Jones and Daniel Woolf (Basignstoke, 2007), 19–49.

to their estate or degree.[93] By the time *Earthly Necessities* was published in 2000, Wrightson had elaborated the concept of 'life-chances' as a model to explain the differentiation in the experience of economic opportunity among different social groups across the entire period from 1450 to 1760.[94]

Wrightson's reading of the class-specific experience of social change reflects the strong sense of political engagement that underpins his work. This is arguably a function of his own personal experience of the general social developments occurring in Britain in the 1950s and 1960s. It is also a reflection of his enormous capacity for empathy, born of an eye for the telling detail or vivid anecdote which brings his historical subjects to life. This sympathetic instinct allowed him to offer a very close but nonetheless highly intuitive reading of the diaries, autobiographies and correspondence of the period, an engagement which littered the pages of *English Society* in particular with glistening fragments of the personal lives of Ralph and Mary Josselin of Earls Colne (Essex), of Adam and Susannah Eyre of Penistone (Yorkshire) or of Roger Lowe and Emm Potter of Ashton-in-Makerfield (Lancashire). These anecdotes are no less characteristic of the writing in *Earthly Necessities*, but by 2000 the degree of imaginative sympathy had grown even more acute, with Wrightson envisaging the patriarch dipping first into the dish to prove who was the master of the household, or the farm worker holding his hat in his hand yet still daring to remind his employer that he might earn more elsewhere.[95]

It is, moreover, no accident that the most striking examples of Wrightson's empathy are those in which the experience of subordinate groups is validated and arguably even valorised. Perhaps the most explicit examples are the suggestion that the wearing of the parish badge causes a shudder of pain to vibrate down the centuries; or the argument that although Whickham might not have been depopulated, its fields and territories had nonetheless been turned inside-out.[96] But there are others, including most recently the indictment of Robert Jenison's elaborate justification for leaving the plague-ridden city of Newcastle in the summer of 1635 as 'a masterpiece of self-serving cant'.[97] This politically engaged tone has sometimes led explicitly to present-centeredness: after all, *The Making of an Industrial Society* is dedicated 'to the people of the Durham coalfield past and present', and even

[93] Keith Wrightson, 'Estate, Degrees, and Sorts: Changing Perspectives of Society in Tudor and Stuart England', in *Language, History and Class*, ed. Penelope J. Corfield (Oxford, 1991), 30–52; *idem*, '"Sorts of People" in Tudor and Stuart England', in *The Middling Sort of People: Culture, Society and Politics in England, 1550–1800*, ed. Jonathan Barry and Christopher Brooks (New York, 1994), 28–51; *idem*, 'Decline of Neighbourliness'; *idem*, 'Mutualities and Obligations'.
[94] Wrightson, *EN*, 221.
[95] *Ibid.*, 64, 327.
[96] Wrightson & Levine, *Terling*, 185; Levine & Wrightson, *Whickham*, 134.
[97] Wrightson, *Ralph Tailor's Summer*, 59.

without that direct reference (all the more poignant given that the heart had been ripped out of Durham coalmining communities during the very years in which Levine and Wrightson were reconstructing their histories), it does not require too close a reading of the book to recognise in its analysis of the social relations which held Elizabethan Whickham together an argument for the re-creation of those very bonds of neighbourhood and kinship which would enable the pit villages to survive in a post-industrial environment.

All these elements – conceptual sophistication, archival mastery and political engagement – have remained consistent features of Wrightson's work since the publication of *English Society*. Taken together these characteristics have informed a research agenda which has always taken very seriously the material inequalities of sixteenth- and seventeenth-century life yet has never been less than fully sensitive to the idiom in which those inequalities were described and to the rituals that gave them meaning. The group of essays on contemporary understandings of the social order in early modern England, for instance, might in some ways be seen as extended footnotes to *English Society*, each of them gradually refining the analysis of social differentiation that had shaped that book, but all of them based on very close readings of the languages of social description employed not only by those at the apex of the social hierarchy but also by those in its middling strata.[98] Cumulatively these essays offered a view of social order not from above but from within, and they demonstrated that however finely graded English society might have been, it nonetheless contained recognisable social clusters. In emphasising the significance of the informal language of sorts, moreover, they inspired a wave of subsequent research on self-perceptions among middling and subordinate social groups. At a time when the first systematic attacks were being made on class as a viable category of historical analysis, Wrightson's reconstruction of the cultural dissociation between various 'sorts of people' demonstrated that studies of material inequality and of linguistic representation need not be incompatible. If this first trio of essays might be read in the context of the ongoing debate over the significance of class, then a subsequent trio were equally engaged in a defence of the capacity of the social history project to conceptualise, verify and explain patterns of social change.[99] This is most obvious in his subtle

---

[98] Keith Wrightson, 'The Social Order of Early Modern England: Three Approaches', in *The World We Have Gained: Histories of Population and Social Structure*, ed. Lloyd Bonfield, Richard M. Smith and Keith Wrightson (Oxford, 1986), 177–202; *idem*, 'Estates, Degrees, and Sorts; *idem*, 'Sorts of People'.

[99] Keith Wrightson, 'The Politics of the Parish in Early Modern England', in *The Experience of Authority in Early Modern England*, ed. Paul Griffiths, Adam Fox and Steve Hindle (Basingstoke, 1996), 10–46; *idem*, 'Mutualities and Obligations'; *idem*, 'Decline of Neighbourliness'.

and nuanced attempt to rehabilitate the notion of 'a decline of neighbourliness' in the historiography of seventeenth-century England, and to a lesser extent in his discussion of changing patterns of mutuality and obligation in early modern society. But it is also a significant concluding theme in his conceptualisation of 'the politics of the parish', which (besides responding to Patrick Collinson's manifesto for a new political history) urges social historians to retain their focus on questions of societal development even if they agree with post-modern critics that the old master narratives no longer suffice.[100]

Taken together, these essays suggest that Wrightson might have produced persuasive monographs on class and the languages of social identity, or on neighbourliness and social change in early modern England. Instead, however, he accepted the commission to produce another synthesis, this time in the Penguin Economic History of England series. *Earthly Necessities*, which appeared to significant acclaim in 2000, was structured around the notion that patterns of economic development were conditioned by the changing attitudes of different groups within the social order to the possibilities and pitfalls created by a changing commercial context. In some respects the book might be read as a cultural history of economic attitudes *towards* the market rather than merely an economic history of the material culture produced *by* the market. If so, it too succeeded in fusing the traditional concerns of materialist social history with the emerging preoccupation of cultural historians with language and representation. Although change remained a central theme, the chronology sketched in *Earthly Necessities* was only partially familiar. The patterns of economic differentiation in the two or three generations after 1580 which underpinned the notion of cultural polarisation that had been so central to *English Society* could by 2000 be more fully documented than was possible in 1982. There were, nonetheless, some striking new emphases, especially in the analysis of late seventeenth-century developments, associated now less with the *consolidation* than with the *acceleration* of existing trends, a phenomenon made possible by the relative weakness of the demographic and cultural restraints which had choked off expansion in the mid seventeenth century. The chronology of the volume was also significant, for it offered highly original analyses of social and economic conditions in the half-centuries both before and after the conventional periodisation of early modern history. By seriously engaging with early sixteenth- and early eighteenth-century social change, to say nothing of its valiant attempt to reconstruct the *British* context in which economic attitudes and practices evolved, the book reshaped the mould of early modern social history which Wrightson had himself helped to create.

---

[100] Wrightson, 'Politics of the Parish'; Patrick Collinson, *De Republica Anglorum: Or, History with the Politics Put Back* (Cambridge, 1990).

The running theme of Wrightson's own work in the twenty or so years after *English Society* had made his reputation has, therefore, been the interconnectedness of social, economic and cultural processes of change. This agenda was crystallised in the opening chapter of *Earthly Necessities*, which traced the discipline of economic history back to its origins. Wrightson persuasively argued that the earliest (eighteenth- and nineteenth-century) practitioners of economic history (Hume, Steuart, Millar and Marx) and, before them, contemporary commentators on sixteenth- and seventeenth-century economic behaviour (Dudley, More, Smith, Harrison, Harrington and King) believed economic history to be properly concerned not only with material existence and the distribution of resources but also with social organisation and cultural values. One part of Wrightson's narrative is, therefore, the experience of the 'shock of disruption' brought by demographic growth, price inflation and commercialisation.[101] But it has a logical corollary in the contemporary 'urge to understand' that shock in terms of the shifting practices, values and assumptions of those who were regarded (and often regarded themselves) as the protagonists or victims of change. *Earthly Necessities* is a big book, but its manifesto for the writing of a social and cultural history of demographic and economic change contains the seeds of his subsequent monograph. If the historiographical imperative was to reconstruct the 'shock of disruption' and to analyse the contemporary 'urge to understand', a tightly focused study of a devastating plague epidemic gave Wrightson a glorious opportunity to narrow the scale of observation to reveal (warts and all) a face-to-face to society and to vindicate through archival heroism and narrative skill Camus's famous observation that 'what we learn in time of pestilence is that there are more things in men to admire than to despise'.[102] And it is no accident that those to be admired in *Ralph Tailor's Summer* are the people of Wrightson's own city of Newcastle. The result is a moving portrait of a civic community pulling both together and apart as it faced the threat of radical social and demographic dislocation. In this self-declared experiment in microhistory, Wrightson's idiosyncrasies and preferences as a historian of early modern England finally come together: a reading of social relations underpinned by a sophisticated grasp of historical demography; an evocation of a sense of place through archival mastery and emotional sympathy; a sensitivity to the harsh realities of unequal life chances through the exercise of a profoundly sociological imagination; and a deft juxtaposition of the micro and macro.

[101] Wrightson, *EN*, 12.
[102] Quoted in Wrightson, *Ralph Tailor's Summer*, 161.

Early modern English social history after *English Society*

> Can the new generation of cultural historians ... find ways to give greater preci-
> sion to the depiction of change, to strengthen accounts of causation which are
> sometimes allusive and underspecified, even to reformulate the inherited 'general
> outline'?   Keith Wrightson (2010).[103]

The enduring value of Wrightson's distinctive agenda is evident in the
continued importance of *English Society* as the starting point for students,
and as the bedrock for subsequent and related research (not only amongst
historians, but literary scholars too).[104] It is testimony to the quality of analysis and vision in *English Society* that there has been no further undertaking,
since J. A. Sharpe's in 1987, to produce a successor.[105] Indeed, the narrative framework and conceptual structure of *English Society* set the agenda for
a wealth of ensuing research developing the book's central themes, much
(although by no means all) of which originated in doctoral work supervised by Wrightson himself, some of it represented in the essays that follow.
In relation to the 'enduring structures' which shaped early modern English
society, we now know considerably more about the 'degrees of people' it
comprised, and about the subtleties of social differentiation below the level
of the gentry – in particular about the critical importance of the 'middling
sort' whose significance was first identified by Wrightson.[106] The character
of social relations – in both rural and urban settings – has been reassessed
in terms ranging from reconciliation, custom and corporate culture to

---

[103] Review of Keith Thomas, *The Ends of Life*, in *English Historical Review* 125 [no.512]
(2010), 178.

[104] See, e.g., Richard Wilson, *Will Power: Essays on Shakesperean Authority* (Hemel
Hempstead, 1993), esp. 82, 212; Louise Montrose, *The Purpose of Playing: Shakespeare
and the Cultural Politics of the Elizabethan Theatre* (Chicago, 1996), esp. 78, 115, 181.

[105] Sharpe, *Early Modern England*. This is in sharp contrast to the number of textbook
accounts of the period's political events.

[106] See *The Middling Sort of People*, ed. Barry and Brooks; Margaret Hunt, *The Middling
Sort: Commerce, Gender and the Family, 1680–1780* (Berkeley, 1996); Joan Kent, 'The
Rural "Middling Sort" in Early Modern England, circa 1640–1740: Some Economic,
Political and Socio-Cultural Characteristics', *Rural History* 10 (1999), 19–54; H. R.
French, *The Middle Sort of People in Provincial England 1600–1750* (Oxford, 2007). On
labouring folk, see A. Hassell Smith, 'Labourers in Late Sixteenth-Century England: A
Case Study from North Norfolk', *C&C* 4 (1989), 11–52, 367–94; Alexandra Shepard,
'Poverty, Labour and the Language of Social Description in Early Modern England', *P&P*
201 (2008), 51–95; Craig Muldrew, *Food, Energy and the Creation of Industriousness: Work
and Material Culture in Agrarian England, 1550–1780* (Cambridge, 2011). See also the
essays by Fox and Muldrew below. The focus on non-elites has not been exclusive. For
work on the gentry that originated under Wrightson's supervision, see Mark S. Dawson,
Gentility and the Comic Theatre of Late Stuart London (Cambridge, 2005).

simulated deference and class conflict.[107] The patriarchal dynamics of early modern social relations have been further explored with reference to gender, age and household structure and to marriage, the family and kinship.[108] Refining the course of social change charted in *English Society*, analysis on the one hand of the experience of poverty and on the other of emergent cultures of consumption has sharpened our understanding of the shifting balance of population and resources and of consequent social polarisation.[109] The principles and practices associated with (re-)ordering society have been extensively studied with reference to civil and criminal litigation; to forms of social exclusion; to waves of local regulation; and to modes of protest and resistance.[110] Re-evaluation of oral and literate culture, popular beliefs and early modern associational culture has elucidated the cultural fissures

[107] See, for example, Craig Muldrew, 'The Culture of Reconciliation: Community and the Settlement of Economic Disputes in Early Modern England', *HJ* 39 (1996), 915–42; Andy Wood, 'The Place of Custom in Plebeian Political Culture: England 1550–1800', *SH* 22 (1997), 46–60; Phil Withington, *The Politics of Commonwealth: Citizens and Freemen in Early Modern England* (Cambridge, 2005); Andy Wood, 'Fear, Hatred, and the Hidden Injuries of Class in Early Modern England', *JSH* 39 (2006), 803–26. See also the essays below by Hindle, Gaskill, Shepard, Withington and Wood.

[108] For work on gender see the discussion on pp. 32–35 below and the essays in this volume by Berry, Shepard and Tadmor. Examples on the other themes mentioned here include Paul Griffiths, *Youth and Authority: Formative Experiences in England 1560–1640* (Oxford, 1996); L. A. Botelho, *Old Age and the English Poor Law, 1500–1700* (Woodbridge, 2004); Naomi Tadmor, 'The Concept of the Household Family in Eighteenth-Century England', *P&P* 151 (1996), 111–40; *The Family in Early Modern England*, ed. Helen Berry and Elizabeth Foyster (Cambridge, 2007); Diana O'Hara, *Courtship and Constraint: Rethinking the Making of Marriage in Tudor England* (Manchester, 2000); Amy M. Froide, *Never Married: Singlewomen in Early Modern England* (Oxford, 2005); Naomi Tadmor, 'Early Modern English Kinship in the Long Run: Reflections on Continuity and Change', *C&C* 25 (2010), 15–48.

[109] Select examples include Steve Hindle, *On the Parish? The Micro-Politics of Poor Relief in Rural England, c.1550–1750* (Oxford, 2004); Lorna Weatherill, *Consumer Behaviour and Material Culture in Britain 1660–1760* (1988); Mark Overton, Jane Whittle, Darron Dean and Andrew Hann, *Production and Consumption in English Households, 1600–1750* (2004). See also the essays below by Berry, Fox, French, Hindle and Withington.

[110] See, for example, Cynthia B. Herrup, *The Common Peace: Participation and the Criminal Law in Seventeenth-Century England* (Cambridge, 1989); Tim Stretton, *Women Waging Law in Elizabethan England* (Cambridge, 1998); Craig Muldrew, *The Economy of Obligation: The Culture of Credit and Social Relations in Early Modern England* (Basingstoke, 1998); Malcolm Gaskill, *Crime and Mentalities in Early Modern England* (Cambridge, 2000); Garthine Walker, *Crime, Gender and Social Order in Early Modern England* (Cambridge, 2003); C. W. Brooks, *Law, Politics and Society in Early Modern England* (Cambridge, 2008); Steve Hindle, *The State and Social Change in Early Modern England, c.1550–1640* (Basingstoke, 2000); *The Politics of the Excluded c.1500–1850*, ed. Tim Harris (Basingstoke, 2001); Andy Wood, *Riot, Rebellion and Popular Politics in Early Modern England* (Basingstoke, 2002); Andy Wood, *The 1549 Rebellions and the Making of Early Modern England* (Cambridge, 2007); Walter, *Understanding Popular Violence*; idem, *Crowds and Popular Politics*. See also the essays by Griffiths and Stretton below.

associated with social change, generating in turn serious historiographical fissures over the place of religion and in particular over the contribution of godliness to the tenor of social differentiation.[111]

Much of this work was undertaken in defiance (even in ignorance) of, but in some ways also contributed to, the chorus of criticism which was increasingly directed against the conceptual and methodological foundations of 'the new social history' throughout the 1980s and 1990s. The post-structural privileging of the analysis of representation above the reconstruction of experience, and the challenge posed by 'the new cultural history' to the explanatory primacy of agency over structure, amounted to an onslaught against the totalising claims and master narratives implicit in models of social structural change. Rejecting the 'base–superstructure' binary, according to which culture is reflective rather than constitutive of social reality, the 'central task of cultural history' was defined as '[t]he deciphering of meaning … rather than the inference of causal laws of explanation'.[112] As such, cultural history was, in an abrogation of the dialogue with 'hard-edged' social science, heavily indebted both to cultural anthropology and to linguistic theory. Besides adding layers to the overview provided by *English Society* – through critical engagement as well as endorsement – subsequent scholarship has therefore contributed a range of methodological innovations and conceptual challenges, some departing significantly from the founding concerns of 'the new social history' and others extending and reworking them.

One of the richest, and least contested, areas of development has emerged from explorations of the linked terrain of society and politics. While older totalising claims that social history provides *explanations* for political change have been relinquished, the interconnectedness of politics and society has been secured as the lynch-pin for understanding the formation of the early modern state, building on Wrightson's observation that social differentia-

---

[111] Adam Fox, *Oral and Literate Culture in England 1500–1700* (Oxford, 2000); Tessa Watt, *Cheap Print and Popular Piety, 1550–1640* (Cambridge, 1991); Peter Clark, *British Clubs and Societies 1580–1800: The Origins of an Associational World* (Oxford, 2002); Mark Hailwood, 'Sociability, Work and Labouring Identity in Seventeenth-Century England', *Cultural and Social History* 8 (2011), 9–29; Phil Withington, 'Intoxicants and Society in Early Modern England', *HJ* 54 (2011), 631–57; Martin Ingram, 'Religion, Communities and Moral Discipline', in *Religion and Society in Early Modern Europe, 1500–1800*, ed. K. Von Greyerz (1984), 177–93; Marjorie K. McIntosh, *Controlling Misbehavior in England, 1370–1600* (Cambridge, 1998); Christopher Marsh, 'Sacred Space in England, 1560–1640: The View from the Pew', *Journal of Ecclesiastical History* 53 (2002), 286–311. For the extremes of historiographical difference, see Margaret Spufford, 'Puritanism and Social Control', in *Order and Disorder in Early Modern England*, ed. A. Fletcher and J. Stevenson (Cambridge, 1985), 41–57 and the postscript to the second edition of Wrightson & Levine, *Terling*, 197–220.

[112] Lynn Hunt, 'Introduction: History, Culture, and Text', in *The New Cultural History*, ed. Lynn Hunt (Berkeley, 1989), 1–22, p. 12.

tion was both cause and effect of the increasing presence of the state in the local community.[113] Particularly associated with the work of Steve Hindle and Michael J. Braddick, recent accounts of state formation are premised on an expanded definition of 'politics' that both acknowledges forms of political participation amongst those who were theoretically 'excluded' and maps 'the extent to which the governed played a role in their own governance'.[114] The resulting convergence of the 'new political history [that explores] the social depth of politics' advocated by Patrick Collinson with social history's traditional focus on 'the social distribution and use of power', while not without differences of emphasis, has fused the concerns of both.[115] This was in no small part due to what John Morrill has described as the 'Wrightson revolution' which 'had a huge impact on those ... who were more interested in high politics'.[116] This novel emphasis on the social dynamics of state formation is a powerful example of the way in which social history might, as Wrightson had hoped, 'transform understanding of the whole'.[117]

In a related development, social conflict and popular politics have been reassessed in terms of the *negotiation* of power relations, reflecting a continued commitment to recovering the agency of subordinated groups. The most influential theoretical tributary swelling the tide of recent research flows from the conceptualisation by the social anthropologist James C. Scott of a negotiated 'public transcript', which establishes the terms of deference and authority but exists alongside a 'hidden transcript' of veiled resistance.[118] In its most sophisticated reworking, Scott's template has influenced the construction of a 'more elaborate model of the multivalency of power relations' in the form of 'an early modern power grid' constituted by the intersection of multiple hierarchies, thereby challenging the blunt dichotomies between elite and popular or between governors and governed

---

[113] More recent work has also demonstrated that this process had deeper chronological roots than acknowledged by Wrightson: John Watts, 'Public or Plebs: The Changing Meaning of "the Commons", 1381–1549', in *Power and Identity in the Middle Ages: Essays in Memory of Rees Davies*, ed. Huw Pryce, J. Watts and R. R. Davies (Oxford, 2007), 242–60; David Rollison, *A Commonwealth of the People: Popular Politics and England's Long Social Revolution, 1066–1649* (Cambridge, 2010).

[114] Ethan H. Shagan, *Popular Politics and the English Reformation* (Cambridge, 2003), 19. For Wrightson's pioneering engagement with these issues, see 'Two Concepts of Order'. See also Hindle, *The State and Social Change*; M. J. Braddick, *State Formation in Early Modern England c.1550–1700* (Cambridge, 2000); *Politics of the Excluded*, ed. Harris.

[115] Collinson, *De Republica Anglorum*, 15; Wrightson, 'Politics of the Parish'.

[116] Interview with John Morrill, 2008, part of the IHR 'Making History' series, www.history.ac.uk/makinghistory/resources/interviews/Morrill_John.html, accessed 13 December 2011.

[117] Wrightson, 'Enclosure', 60.

[118] James C. Scott, *Weapons of the Weak: Everyday Forms of Peasant Resistance* (New Haven, 1985); *idem*, *Domination and the Arts of Resistance: Hidden Transcripts* (New Haven, 1990).

that structured much of the early 'new social history'.[119] An additional and related binary opposition, between deference and social conflict, is rejected by Andy Wood whose critical reading of Scott and re-engagement with the Gramscian concept of hegemony has informed his attempt to rehabilitate the relevance of class for our understanding of early modern society – not in order to trace 'antecedents of modern class identities', but, as he argues in his contribution below, as a *necessary* corollary to the deeply engrained paternalism of the period.[120]

The most profound and controversial shifts affecting the subsequent development of the field have arguably been those associated with the emergence of gender as a category of analysis, itself one of the priorities of 'the new cultural history'. The resurgence of women's history in conjunction with the tide of second-wave feminism in the 1970s not only established the inadequacies of analysing class in isolation from patriarchy but also vastly expanded the remit of definitions of the 'political' to include interpersonal relations between the sexes.[121] Building on the pioneering work of Alice Clark, this led to the re-evaluation of women's work, initially in terms of narratives of the progress or decline of women's economic standing relative to men, a project resulting in conflicting conclusions about the impact of capitalism on the changing position of women.[122] More recently, and partly in response to the shortcomings of measuring change in whiggish terms of the improvement or regression of the status of 'women' conceived as a monolithic group, women's work has been approached in relation to the balance of production and consumption associated with the 'industrious revolution' – to which the character and extent of women's varied contributions, it is clear, were critical.[123] Although gender has never taken centre-

---

[119] Michael J. Braddick and John Walter, 'Introduction. Grids of Power: Order, Hierarchy and Subordination in Early Modern Society', in *Negotiating Power in Early Modern Society: Order, Hierarchy and Subordination in Britain and Ireland*, ed. Michael J. Braddick and John Walter (Cambridge, 2001), 1–42, pp. 10, 39.

[120] Wood, 'Hidden Injuries', 804.

[121] For the theoretical underpinnings of these developments, see Sylvia Walby, *Theorizing Patriarchy* (Oxford, 1990). For an editorial reflecting the turning point associated with feminist analysis in the 1970s, see Sally Alexander and Anna Davin, 'Feminist History', *HWJ* 1 (1976), 4–6.

[122] For a summary, see Amy Erickson's introduction to Alice Clark, *Working Life of Women in the Seventeenth Century* (1992 edn), vii–lv.

[123] Jan de Vries, *The Industrious Revolution: Consumer Behaviour and the Household Economy, 1650 to the Present* (Cambridge, 2008); Jane Whittle, 'Housewives and Servants in Rural England, 1440–1650: Evidence of Women's Work from Probate Documents', *TRHS* 15 (2005), 51–74; Amanda Flather, *Gender and Space in Early Modern England* (Woodbridge, 2007); Craig Muldrew, '"Th'ancient Distaff" and "Whirling Spindle": Measuring the Contribution of Spinning to Household Earnings and the National Economy of England, 1550–1770', *EcHR* (Online early, 2011); Jane Whittle, 'The House as a Place of Work in Early Modern Rural England', *Home Cultures* 8 (2011), 134–50. Cf. the dissertation (supervised by Keith Wrightson) by J. D. Melville, 'The

stage in Keith Wrightson's work, his characterisation of non-elite marriages as economic partnerships has been confirmed by ongoing research into early modern women's economic activities that has not only reiterated the importance of the *household* economy (as opposed to an anachronistic focus on the work performed by adult males) but which is also opening up questions about definitions of 'work' itself and the relatively fluid character of occupational identities. Research in this vein alerts us to the multi-faceted character of socio-economic status as inflected by gender and the life-cycle and it has questioned the extent to which *coverture* restricted the working activities and identities of early modern women.[124] Additionally, women's importance as providers of capital to the lending networks that sustained early modern economic expansion is increasingly being recognised in ways that establish gender roles less as a casualty than as a *driver* of capitalist development. In its most radical formulation, this analysis attributes the precocious emergence of a capitalist market economy in England to its distinct forms of marital property law.[125] Much of this work has been influenced by broader concerns with women's agency in the context of patriarchal oppression that have extended more general analyses of processes of domination and resistance to provide a richer picture of the tenor of social conflict and the social distribution of power.[126]

These inroads have been made alongside the growing predominance of gender itself as a category of analysis, with two important consequences. First, while objections have been voiced that the shift from women's history to gender history forfeited the political impetus behind the former, in many

Use and Organisation of Domestic Space in Late Seventeenth-Century London' (unpublished University of Cambridge Ph.D., 1999).

[124] Amy L. Erickson, 'Married Women's Occupations in Eighteenth-Century London', *C&C* 23 (2008), 267–307. See also Amy L. Erickson, 'Possession – and the Other One-Tenth of the Law: Assessing Women's Ownership and Economic Roles in Early Modern England', *Women's History Review* 16 (2007), 369–85; Joanne Bailey, 'Favoured or Oppressed? Married Women, Property and "Coverture" in England, 1660–1800', *C&C* 17 (2002), 351–72; Alexandra Shepard, 'The Worth of Married Women in the English Church Courts, c.1550–c.1730', in *Married Women and the Law in Northern Europe, c.1200–c.1700*, ed. Cordelia Beattie and Matthew Stevens (Woodbridge, forthcoming).

[125] Amy L. Erickson, 'Coverture and Capitalism', *HWJ* 59 (2005), 1–16. See also Craig Muldrew, '"A Mutual Assent of her Mind"? Women, Debt Litigation and Contract in Early Modern England', *HWJ* 55 (2003), 47–71; Marjorie K. McIntosh, 'Women, Credit, and Family Relationships in England, 1300–1620', *Journal of Family History* 30 (2005), 143–63; Judith Spicksley, 'Usury Legislation, Cash and Credit: The Development of the Female Investor in the Late Tudor and Stuart Periods', *EcHR* 2nd ser. 61 (2008), 277–301.

[126] Select examples include Susan D. Amussen, *An Ordered Society: Gender and Class in Early Modern England* (New York, 1988); Laura Gowing, *Common Bodies: Women, Touch and Power in Seventeenth-Century England* (New Haven, 2003); Bernard Capp, *When Gossips Meet: Women, Family, and Neighbourhood in Early Modern England* (Oxford, 2003). See also the essays by Shepard and Tadmor below.

ways gender history shares the feminist objective to transform, rather than merely supplement, understandings of the whole. Women did not live their lives in a separate chapter; and men did not operate in gender-free terrain as the norm against which women derived their (gendered) 'otherness'. In the mid 1970s, Natalie Zemon Davis astutely observed 'that we should be interested in the history of both women and men' and 'that we should not be working only on the subjected sex any more than an historian of class can focus entirely on peasants'.[127] Around two decades later the history of masculinity finally began to gather a momentum that (while not without its pitfalls) has the potential to refine explorations of the practice of patriarchy, envisaged not in terms of a monolithic form of oppression, but of a multi-lateral matrix of power, built on the (gendered) differences *within* each sex as well as the differences between them.[128] Work in this vein clearly also chimes with social history's preoccupation with the processes of differentiation and identification that propelled and accompanied social change, and offers new opportunities for analysis of the dual operation of gender and class.[129]

The second, and arguably more contentious, consequence of the development of gender analysis has been its poststructuralist emphasis on the discursive production of gender identities and the ways in which discourses of gender in turn signified power.[130] While this has proved indispensible for analysing sexuality in the past, and has also usefully dissolved some of the conceptual boundaries between the 'public' and the 'private', between politics and culture, and between family and state – in the early modern case specifically through exploration of the metaphorical and metonymical elision of body, household and state – it has also generated misgivings both about divorcing discursive processes from social experience, and about

[127] Natalie Zemon Davis, 'Women's History in Transition: The European Case', *Feminist Studies* 3 (1975–76), 83–103, p. 90.
[128] For a summary of these developments, see Alexandra Shepard, 'Manhood, Patriarchy, and Gender in Early Modern History', in *Masculinities, Childhood, Violence: Attending to Early Modern Women – and Men*, ed. Amy E. Leonard and Karen L. Nelson (Newark NJ, 2011), 77–95.
[129] See also, for example, Susan Amussen, '"The Part of a Christian Man": The Cultural Politics of Manhood in Early Modern England', in *Political Culture and Cultural Politics in Early Modern England*, ed. Susan Amussen and Mark Kishlansky (Manchester, 1995); Alexandra Shepard, *Meanings of Manhood in Early Modern England* (Oxford, 2003); and the essays by Berry and Shepard in this volume.
[130] For the classic statement, see Joan Scott, 'Gender: A Useful Category of Analysis', *AHR* 91 (1986), 1053–75. In response, see, e.g., Joan Hoff, 'Gender as a Postmodern Category of Paralysis', *Women's History Review* 3 (1994), 149–68. For more measured critical engagement, with reference to the early modern period, see Jeanne Boydston, 'Gender as a Question of Historical Analysis', *Gender and History* 20 (2008), 558–83.

denying gender any ontological status.[131] One response has been to re-engage with the psychic and somatic dimensions of subjectivity;[132] another recommends that historians 'should refuse the disconnect between cultural and social forms of analysis and focus instead on understanding how social and cultural forms are mutually constitutive of one another'.[133] No longer simply a discursive construct, gender in the former case serves narratives of continuity over change, while in the latter case, gender becomes implicated in *explanations*, rather than descriptions, of change over time. Gender history thereby re-engages with larger questions of periodisation (epitomised by the gauntlet long since thrown down by Joan Kelly's question, 'Did women have a Renaissance?') that underpinned the transformational promise of feminist history.[134]

Many of these debates have not been exclusive to gender history but are both indicative of wider historiographical fault-lines and reflective of the position of gender history at the leading edge of the linguistic turn. There has been much recent reflection on the fate of social history in the wake of the cultural turn, but this retrospective impulse has largely overlooked the pathways taken by early modernists.[135] There remains general disagreement over whether the cultural turn was 'something different from social history, even a danger to it, or rather an innovation within it'.[136] One might argue that it was all three, not least because it has encompassed such a variety of approaches that have played out differently across diverse fields and academic settings, although the level of 'danger' threatened by the cultural turn appears to have been wildly exaggerated. The relationship of cultural history with early modern social history has in many ways been extremely productive, although unresolved differences and competing

---

[131] Joan Scott, *Gender and the Politics of History* (New York, 1988); Amussen, *An Ordered Society*, 34–66; Moira Gatens, *Imaginary Bodies: Ethics, Power and Corporeality* (1996).

[132] The pioneering manifesto for 'incorporat[ing] ... the corporeal' is Lyndal Roper, *Oedipus and the Devil: Witchcraft, Sexuality and Religion in Early Modern Europe* (1994), 18.

[133] Laura Lee Downs, *Writing Gender History* (2004), 101.

[134] Joan Kelly-Gadol, 'Did Women Have a Renaissance?', in *Becoming Visible: Women in European History*, ed. Renate Blumenthal and Claudia Koonz (Boston, 1977), 175–201. On the implications of the history of masculinity for periodisation, see the special feature of the *JBS* 44 (2005), ed. Karen Harvey and Alexandra Shepard. See also *Gender and Change: Agency, Chronology and Periodisation*, ed. Garthine Walker and Alexandra Shepard (Oxford, 2009).

[135] See, e.g., *Beyond the Cultural Turn: New Directions in the Study of Society and Culture*, ed. Victoria E. Bonnell and Lynn Hunt (Berkeley, 1999); the special issue of *JSH* 37 (2003) devoted to an assessment of the field; Peter Mandler, 'The Problem with Cultural History', *Cultural and Social History* 1 (2004), 94–117; Eley, *Crooked Line*; and the forum on Eley's *A Crooked Line*, AHR 113 (2008), 391–437; Patrick Joyce, 'What is the Social in Social History?', *P&P* 206 (2010), 212–48. For a recent survey of early modern historiography, see *Writing Early Modern History*, ed. Garthine Walker (2005).

[136] Peter N. Stearns, 'Social History Present and Future', *JSH* 37 (2003), 9.

priorities continue to raise questions about future historiographical trajectories. In very general terms, the best of the cultural turn has fostered new forms of interdisciplinary and theoretical dialogue; greater sophistication of textual analysis; and a renewed concern with broadly based power relations (albeit discursively constructed). Positive developments have arisen from assertions of the constitutive possibilities of 'the cultural' *as well as* 'the social' that concede a dynamic relationship between them rather than simply jettisoning the latter in preference for the former.

Keith Wrightson's own work – particularly on the 'language of sorts' and on the parochial 'politics of subordination and meaning' (whereby social relations were 'rearticulated' through 'processes of redescription' that lent cultural authority to economic and political change) – reflects the ways in which the cultural turn can both build upon yet retain roots within social history.[137] Much of the doctoral work supervised by Wrightson has exploited the opportunities presented by the *dialectic* (rather than any intrinsic competition) between social and cultural history, which has implications for our understandings of 'early modern' society, especially in respect of continuity and change in the character of social relations. One example is provided by the ways in which individualism has been reassessed in terms of the relationship between self and society (not to mention with reference to understandings of neighbourhood, parish and 'community'). In perhaps the most radical departure from purely 'social' historical roots, Michael Mascuch's work on self-identity recasts the concept of individualism and its links to modernity by approaching autobiography as a historically specific cultural practice.[138] Theoretically and conceptually polymathic, Mascuch's study challenges both social historical accounts that have emphasised the material basis of individualism and literary approaches to autobiography as a genre in a formalist sense, specifically by arguing that 'the first English individualist' autobiographer did not emerge until 1791, albeit with extensive and complex precursors. The implications of this chronology for social history have a direct bearing on materialist accounts of 'early modernity' by both asserting the *cultural* basis of subjective identity rooted in discursive production, while also reiterating the later eighteenth century as a decisive turning point. While questionably 'an innovation within' social history, this manifestation of the cultural turn hardly constitutes a 'danger to it', offering instead a novel perspective on subjective identity that engages with, remains relevant to and indeed re-inscribes larger narratives of change.[139]

[137] Wrightson, 'Politics of the Parish', 31–5.
[138] Michael Mascuch, *Origins of the Individualist Self: Autobiography and Self-Identity in England, 1591–1791* (Oxford, 1997). See also *idem*, 'Continuity and Change in a Patronage Society: the Social Mobility of British Autobiographers, 1600–1750', *Journal of Historical Sociology* 7 (1994), 177–97; *idem*, 'Social Mobility and Middling Identity: the Ethos of British Autobiographers, 1600–1750', *SH* 20 (1995), 45–61.
[139] A 'cultural revolution' in understandings of selfhood has also been attributed to

Similarly sophisticated textual analysis underpins Naomi Tadmor's histor-icisation of the concepts of 'family' and 'friend' which censures historians' uncritical borrowing of terms such as 'nuclear' and 'extended' from social anthropology, and pioneers analysis of the categories used by historical actors themselves to make sense of familial relations – thereby exposing the anachronistic terms of the debate over the origins, timing and historical specificity of the 'affective individualism' heralded by Lawrence Stone in his modernisation narrative charting the emergence of the 'closed domesticated nuclear family'.[140] Tracing the *meanings* of 'family' in the past, rather than attempting to judge its emotional complexion, Tadmor rejects not only the terms of the 'individualism' trumpeted by Stone, but also (unlike Mascuch) *any* narrative of change that revolves around the emergence of individualist tendencies however defined, both arguing that individualism and familism went hand in hand in the enterprising families of the eighteenth century and doubting 'whether there was a single chronology that could embrace so many relationships'.[141] If anything, Tadmor's is a story of persistence rather than change.

The relationship between self and society, and its links to concepts and practices of individualism, has also been radically redrawn by Craig Muldrew's exercise in 'deconstructing capitalism' which, in his elucida-tion of the ways in which the 'culture of credit' elided wealth and reputa-tion, has 'collapse[d] the notion of the "economic" and the "social" into one'. The rise in debt litigation associated with an expanding economy provides not only further evidence of the co-option of the institutional authority of the state to resolve disputes, but also another counterpoint to prevailing notions of paternalism, deference and patriarchy in the form of 'the equality expounded in contemporary social theories of bargaining and market exchange'.[142] Exposing the limits of neoclassical economic theory by *combining* qualitative and quantitative analysis, Muldrew emphasises the emotive rather than rational basis of economic trust that underpinned early modern commercial expansion, and reinterprets social relations in terms of the judgement of creditworthiness, the unit of assessment being – signifi-cantly – that of the household rather than the individual. Finally, Muldrew also invokes a longer-term shift towards conceptions of social interaction in terms of the happiness of the 'self', individualistic conceptions of authority

the late eighteenth century: Dror Wahrman, *The Making of the Modern Self: Identity and Culture in Eighteenth-Century England* (New Haven, 2004), 48.
[140] Naomi Tadmor, *Family and Friends in Eighteenth-Century England: Household, Kinship, and Patronage* (Cambridge, 2001); Lawrence Stone, *The Family, Sex and Marriage in England 1500–1800* (1977). For his critique of the 'affect' debate, see Wrightson, 'The Family'.
[141] Tadmor, *Family and Friends*, 17; Tadmor, 'Early Modern English Kinship'.
[142] Muldrew, *Economy of Obligation*, 156, 271.

and the institutional brokering of credit, that speaks in interesting ways to the findings of both Mascuch and Tadmor.

These three examples, all drawn from those whose doctoral work Keith Wrightson supervised, extend the traditional concerns of 'the new social history' with social relations and social identities, and yet retain a commitment to the diachronic and synchronic exploration of experience alongside meaning. They demonstrate the value of historicising concepts – such as 'self', 'household', 'credit' and (in the recent work of Phil Withington) even 'modern' and 'society' – as articulations of social practice that might produce continuity and/or change and which was at the very least related to, if not determined by, economic context.[143] Research in this vein is in this respect evidence of the extent to which 'the new cultural history' has depended on rather than supplanted the 'new social history' that preceded it, and of the potential fruits of 'a proper cultural history' – identified by Malcolm Gaskill as 'a history of social meanings' or 'the way ordinary folk thought about their everyday lives' – designed to *complement* rather than to replace history from either above or below.[144] Such work, as well as the best of gender history, does not warrant many of the generic criticisms of cultural history that have surfaced in recent reflections, such as its lack of a longer-term perspective and engagement with periodisation, its neglect of material parameters, its disproportional focus on the margins, or its privileging the microhistorical at the expense of the macrosocietal.[145]

This is not, however, to argue that there are no remaining differences or concerns, particularly regarding (non-)explanations of change and the loss of 'the bigger picture of society as a whole', which makes Keith Wrightson's continued commitment to the social historical project all the more important.[146] Research indebted to the cultural turn has done much to establish the eighteenth century as the gateway to 'modernity', albeit on very different terms than once conceived, with reference no longer to industrialisation or class formation but to 'revolutions' in identity and sexuality, yet retaining a profoundly teleological emphasis.[147] By contrast, the 'late medieval/early modern' boundary has received a more sustained challenge on a wider range of fronts.[148] The contours within the sixteenth and seventeenth centuries,

[143] Phil Withington, *Society in Early Modern England: The Vernacular Origins of Some Powerful Ideas* (Cambridge, 2010).
[144] Malcolm Gaskill, *Crime and Mentalities in Early Modern England* (Cambridge, 2000), 4.
[145] Jürgen Kocka, 'Losses, Gains and Opportunities: Social History Today', *JSH* 37 (2003), 21–9; Paula S. Fass, 'Cultural History/Social History: Some Reflections on a Continuing Dialogue', *JSH* 37 (2003), 39–46.
[146] Eley, *Crooked Line*, 11.
[147] Wahrman, *Making of the Modern Self*; Faramerz Dabhoiwala, *The Origins of Sex: A History of the First Sexual Revolution* (Oxford, 2012).
[148] See, for example, Richard M. Smith, '"Modernisation" and the Corporate Medieval Village Community in England: Some Sceptical Reflections', in *Explorations in Historical*

on the other hand, remain largely in place, not least due to the continued tendency for historians to confine themselves to the periods either before or after the arguably artificial and unhelpful divide of the mid seventeenth century, with the crisis of the 1640s either entirely absent or treated as a separate entity – thus perpetuating a historiography that is 'at best uneven and at worst broken-backed'.[149] As for explaining change, trading 'lost causes' for 'lost causality' is clearly an unsatisfactory bargain,[150] the risk of which has inspired renewed calls both for diachronic analysis and for explorations of what Wrightson himself has termed 'the interconnectedness of the historical process'.[151] As William Sewell has argued, moving beyond mere nostalgia for the founding ambitions of 'the new social history' is likely to require both a renewed interdisciplinary dialogue with the social sciences and a re-engagement with Marxist concepts of capital accumulation as well as class.[152] It should also embody Wrightson's commitment to rendering our accounts (and explanations) of continuity and change in the past accessible rather than obfuscated by jargon. As he has repeatedly reminded his students (courtesy of Duke Ellington), 'it don't mean a thing if it ain't got that swing'.

Amidst all this, Keith Wrightson has maintained the demanding and ambitious brief that historians should be concerned 'with the nature of social organisation and cultural values in past societies – with changes in the manner in which human relationships have been ordered and invested with meaning'.[153] Contributors to this volume were duly asked to focus on the relationship between enduring structures and the impact of social and cultural change in early modern England, and encouraged to address issues which lie at the heart of their current research agenda but which also speak to the development of the field as a whole. Their essays attest to the healthy state of the discipline of 'social history' as it is currently practised, as well as some of the differences of emphasis and (at times) opinion within it. Some of the methodological variety and chronological dissonance sketched above is clear in the essays below. Conflicting judgements about the character of early modern social relations have opened up shades of interpretative difference along an axis of optimism versus pessimism. Tim Stretton's

Geography, ed. Alan R. H. Baker and Derek Gregory (Cambridge, 1984), 140–79; *Culture and History 1350–1600: Essays on English Communities, Identities and Writing*, ed. D. Aers (Chichester, 1992).

[149] Wrightson, 'Enclosure', 62.

[150] Patrick Collinson, *The History of a History Man: Or, the Twentieth Century Viewed from a Safe Distance* (Woodbridge, 2011), 51.

[151] Wrightson, 'Enclosure', 60.

[152] William H. Sewell Jr, 'Crooked Lines', AHR 113 (2008), 393–405. See also Mandler, 'The Problem with Cultural History'.

[153] Wrightson, *EN*, 1.

essay, for example, remains sceptical of the extent to which litigation in seventeenth-century England was reconciliatory as opposed to hostile, while (on the other hand) Malcolm Gaskill's analysis rehabilitates a more positive vision of neighbourliness even amidst the contention of witchcraft accusations. The extremes of social polarisation – a foundational theme of *English Society* and of all Wrightson's subsequent work – are questioned in Phil Withington's discussion of the urban evidence for alehouse sociability, while a more familiar picture of social differentiation is presented by Adam Fox (with reference to novel evidence relating to the consumption of food and drink) and by Alexandra Shepard (in relation to parochial responses to illegitimacy). Some of the negative consequences of the growth of the parish state are further elaborated in the contributions by Paul Griffiths and Naomi Tadmor. In turn, Steve Hindle and Craig Muldrew's relatively optimistic appraisals of the material prospects (both real and imagined) of labouring people in the later seventeenth and eighteenth centuries similarly contrast with Helen Berry's novel (and negative) take on the impact of market forces on the commodification of individuals and with Henry French's examination of poor relief payments in eighteenth-century Terling. French's essay additionally alerts us to the complexities of measuring the relative fortunes of individuals and groups in either 'optimistic' or 'pessimistic' terms, and, along with Andy Wood's contribution, cautions against assumptions that differing models of social relations were either sequential or mutually exclusive.

In bringing these essays together and suggesting how they reflect and amplify the themes that have preoccupied Keith Wrightson over almost forty years of scholarship, we hope to have demonstrated that the new social history had particular significance for the historiography of sixteenth- and seventeenth-century England. To be sure, the influences that shaped *Ralph Tailor's Summer* differ in many respects from those that shaped 'The Puritan Reformation of Manners'. That in itself is an index of the way in which 'the new social history' has responded to the challenges presented by the new cultural history and more radically by postmodernism. But the project of 'understanding ourselves in time' remains as central to the Wrightson of 2011 as it did to the Wrightson of 1974, however much the mode in which that understanding is articulated has changed. There is, of course, no consensus over what social history is and should be in 2013 any more than there was over what 'the new social history' was or should have been in 1963. But the very fact that the achievements and failures, perhaps even the missed opportunities, of the social history project are so readily revealed by a reconstruction of Wrightson's own intellectual and methodological journey (replicated, refined and sometimes even rejected in the essays that follow) suggests his centrality to its making.

2

Brokering Fatherhood:
Illegitimacy and Paternal Rights and
Responsibilities in Early Modern England

ALEXANDRA SHEPARD

The 'family' has been consistently central to Keith Wrightson's ongoing interrogation of the interconnectedness of daily life with broader social trends in early modern England. *English Society* contains one of the most nuanced accounts of the practice of patriarchy in seventeenth-century English households, explaining how the complex bonds of authority, dependence and reciprocity between spouses and between parents and children contributed to the 'enduring structures' of the seventeenth century.[1] Wrightson does not portray early modern family life as unchanging, however. While he rejects a unilinear model of change associated with narratives of modernisation, he remains sceptical of arguments that solely stress continuity. He has instead called for historians of early modern England to attend to the socially differentiated experience of familial relations as the material and cultural contexts in which they were conducted shifted to produce a 'growing diversity of family experience'.[2] This essay responds to that call with reference to a comparatively neglected aspect of early modern family life and male gendered identity: fatherhood. In particular, it probes the links between paternity and the social roles associated with fatherhood to argue that the former did not guarantee the latter, especially in cases of illegitimate birth. This was in part owing to demographic uncertainties but also to the uneven distribution of patriarchal dividends that accompanied the processes of social polarisation through which English society was remade in the early modern period.

---

[1] Wrightson, *ES*, part I. See also Wrightson, *EN*, chs 1–2.
[2] Keith Wrightson, 'Mutualities and Obligations: Changing Social Relationships in Early Modern England', *Proceedings of the British Academy* 139 (2006), 157–94, p. 190. See also Keith Wrightson, 'The Family in Early Modern England: Continuity and Change', in *Hanoverian Britain and Empire: Essays in Memory of Philip Lawson*, ed. Steven Taylor, Richard Connors and Clyve Jones (Woodbridge, 1998), 1–22.

Despite being labelled over a decade ago as 'something of a cross-cultural growth industry', the history of fatherhood amongst early modernists has until very recently resembled a minor cottage activity largely subsisting through piecework for the history of the family.[3] Our impressions of fathering in early modern England have not benefited from its analysis being subsumed within debates over the extent of pre-modern parents' devotion to their children, characterised by 'unseemly rows' among a generation of scholars pursuing the 'sentiments approach' to the history of the family.[4] Besides the methodological problems of conceptualisation, verification and credibility detailed by Wrightson,[5] two significant blind spots have limited work in this vein: the assumption of a biological bond between parents and children; and the absence of gender analysis, particularly regarding the parental roles performed by men.

In the context of the 'affect' debate triggered by Lawrence Stone's *The Family, Sex and Marriage*, parenthood has been understood as an emotional relationship premised upon a biological bond, rather than a range of roles which might be performed by a variety of surrogates.[6] As Naomi Tadmor's work has shown, this approach stems from an anachronistic interpretation of the meaning of 'family', which to early modern people denoted the members of a household.[7] More particularly this approach not only collapses the distinction between 'social' and 'genetic' fatherhood but also ignores what the anthropologist E. N. Goody has termed 'pro-parenthood', whereby some or even all of a series of parental obligations are performed by proxy, often distributed between an assortment of adults rather than concentrated in the nuclear family. Beyond reproduction, many of the social and cultural roles comprising parenting – such as the provision of status identity, nursing, tutoring (moral and technical) and sponsoring the assumption of adult status – are transferable. Particularly when it is not restricted to crisis situations, 'pro-parenthood' can function as an important form of social cement forging links between a range of adults and children in particular and between the

---

[3] Robert L. Griswold, 'Introduction to the Special Issue on Fatherhood', *Journal of Family History* 24 (1999), 251–4, p. 251.

[4] Wrightson, 'The Family', 1. For the 'sentiments approach', see Michael Anderson, *Approaches to the History of the Western Family 1500–1914* (Basingstoke, 1980), ch. 3.

[5] Wrightson, 'The Family', 12–15.

[6] Lawrence Stone, *The Family, Sex and Marriage in England, 1500–1800* (1977). For responses see Linda A. Pollock, *Forgotten Children: Parent–Child Relations from 1500 to 1900* (Cambridge, 1983); Ralph A. Houlbrooke, *The English Family 1450–1700* (Harlow, 1984); Alan Macfarlane, *Marriage and Love in England: Modes of Reproduction 1300–1840* (Oxford, 1985).

[7] Naomi Tadmor, 'The Concept of the Household-Family in Eighteenth-Century England', *P&P* 151 (1996), 111–40; Naomi Tadmor, 'Early Modern English Kinship in the Long Run: Reflections on Continuity and Change', *C&C* 25 (2010), 15–48.

generations more generally.[8] Such a situation clearly existed in early modern England, since a great deal of parenting was performed by a variety of surrogates as a result of choice as well as necessity. Paternity guaranteed neither the authority associated with fatherhood nor the performance of parental duties by men.

The second blindspot characterising debates over levels of parental affection relates to the workings of gender. Despite an uneasy relationship between women's history and the history of the family, motherhood as a gendered identity has at least been subject to some sustained analysis by early modernists.[9] By contrast, it is only now in the context of a burgeoning history of masculinity that fatherhood is beginning to receive the gender-sensitive analysis required to differentiate it from parenthood.[10] Approaching fatherhood as a gendered category, with complex links both to concepts of manhood and to the practice of patriarchy, provides a more nuanced perspective not only on male parenting but also on the gendered distribution of authority between and within the sexes, reflecting the shifting interstices of gender and class in early modern England.

This essay focuses specifically on the complex links that existed in early modern England between paternity (here used to denote a biological identity) and fatherhood (more broadly understood as a cultural construct central to the formulation of normative manhood and a series of social roles that could be transferred or shared between men). What follows will, first, briefly review the ways in which fatherhood was idealised as a source of authority and positive male identity. The essay will then focus on circumstances in which the link between paternity and fatherhood could be severed, forcing

[8]   E. N. Goody, 'Forms of Pro-Parenthood: The Sharing and Substitution of Parental Roles', in *Kinship: Selected Readings*, ed. Jack Goody (1971), 331–45.

[9]   Megan Doolittle, 'Close Relations? Bringing Together Gender and Family in English History', *Gender & History* 11 (1999), 542–54. Patricia Crawford, 'The Sucking Child: Adult Attitudes to Child Care in the First Year of Life in Seventeenth-Century England', *C&C* 1 (1986), 23–52; *Women as Mothers in Pre-Industrial England*, ed. Valerie Fildes (1990); Linda Pollock, 'Childbearing and Female Bonding in Early Modern England', *SH* 22 (1997), 286–306; David Cressy, *Birth, Marriage and Death: Ritual, Religion and the Life-Cycle in Tudor and Stuart England* (Oxford, 1997); Laura Gowing, *Common Bodies: Women, Touch and Power in Seventeenth-Century England* (New Haven, 2003), chs 4–6.

[10]   See especially Patricia Crawford, *Blood, Bodies and Families in Early Modern England* (Harlow, 2004), 113–39; *idem, Parents of Poor Children in England, 1580–1800* (Oxford, 2010). Fatherhood receives passing mention in Elizabeth A. Foyster, *Manhood in Early Modern England: Honour, Sex and Marriage* (Harlow, 1999) and Alexandra Shepard, *Meanings of Manhood in Early Modern England* (Oxford, 2003). See also Helen Berry and Elizabeth Foyster, 'Childless Men in Early Modern England', in *The Family in Early Modern England*, ed. Helen Berry and Elizabeth Foyster (Cambridge, 2007); Joanne Bailey, '"A Very Sensible Man": Imagining Fatherhood in England c.1750–1830', *History*, 95 (2010), 267–92; Joanne Bailey, 'Masculinity and Fatherhood in England c.1760–1830', in *What is Masculinity? Historical Dynamics from Antiquity to the Contemporary Worlds*, ed. John Arnold and Sean Brady (Basingstoke, 2011), 167–88.

parental roles to be transferred or overridden. In particular, it will examine the implications of illegitimate parenthood for men from the late sixteenth-century peak in illegitimacy ratios through to the mid-seventeenth-century nadir that provided one of the starting points for Wrightson's analysis of early modern familial and social relations.[11] An exploration of arrangements made for illegitimate children suggests that fatherhood as a positive male identity was not always premised on paternity and paternity did not always carry the endorsement associated with fatherhood. This disjunction was partly due to the disruption caused by high mortality rates in early modern England, but it was also a product of severe social and economic disloca-tion. Fatherhood as a transferable identity helped to shore up the authority of male household heads deemed central to the maintenance of an ordered society. As a result, the ways in which fatherhood was claimed, conferred and denied in early modern England played a role in mediating relations of authority between men as well as between men and women in ways which served not only to uphold the patriarchal order but also increasingly to restrict access to its dividends.

I

Although it will be argued below that paternity in early modern England did not always secure the positive associations of fatherhood, the act of genera-tion was nonetheless a celebrated aspect of manhood. John Tosh has argued that, cross-culturally, paternity is linked to concepts of virility and to the endowment of future generations.[12] Such themes were certainly common in early modern discourse. 'Virility', in an early seventeenth-century dictionary, was equated with manhood in its definition as 'man's estate'.[13] This echoed medical discussions of reproduction which also treated conception in terms of manliness.[14] Aristotelian theories of conception accorded men the power to determine the sex and disposition of the child, and these ideas were more

[11] Keith Wrightson and David Levine, 'The Social Context of Illegitimacy in Early Modern England' and Keith Wrightson, 'The Nadir of English Illegitimacy in the Seventeenth-Century', in *Bastardy and its Comparative History*, ed. Peter Laslett, Karla Oosterveen and Richard M. Smith (1980). See also Peter Laslett and Karen Oosterveen, 'Long-Term Trends in Bastardy in England: A Study of the Illegitimacy Figures in the Parish Registers and in the Reports of the Registrar General, 1561–1960', *Population Studies* 27 (1973), 255–86; Richard Adair, *Courtship, Illegitimacy and Marriage in Early Modern England* (Manchester, 1996).
[12] John Tosh, *A Man's Place: Masculinity and the Middle Class Home in Victorian England* (New Haven, 1999), 80.
[13] John Bullokar, *An English Expositor: Teaching the Interpretation of the Hardest Words Used in Our Language* (1616), sig. P2.
[14] Mary Fissell, 'Gender and Generation: Representing Reproduction in Early Modern England', *Gender & History* 7 (1995), 433–56.

broadly reflected in the popular belief that children inherited the appearance and characteristics of their fathers. So in 1629 Mary Bryan declared to the daughter of Anne Hudspeth in Newcastle, 'Thou ... is John Hedley's bastard ... see thou art as like John Hedley as if he had spit thee out of his mouth.'[15] Humoural theory likewise linked the hot-bloodedness associated with men to the attribute of virility. Sir Thomas Elyot's *Castel of Health*, for example, declared that a man of a hot temperament displayed '[g]reat appetite to the act of generacyon. Ingendryng men children', while inferior men with cold 'genitoryes' (testicles) suffered diminished 'puissance', evident in their lack of pubic hair, limited sexual appetite and (if conception were possible) the spawning of female children, and as a result such men were characterised as effeminate.[16] Virility was more explicitly linked to lineage and posterity in advice literature extolling the benefits of marriage for men. An argument against bachelorhood claimed that it forced a man to 'leave the world without memorie of his name', and a childless marriage was represented as a source of discredit for a man, 'whereby he shameth to accompany men, as seeming himself to be lesse than a man'.[17] *The Office of Christian Parents* inversely declared it 'a very honourable dignitie ... to be head of the family, the fountain of the ofspring, and the true cause of the childrens beeing'.[18]

However, despite their frequent rehearsal, concepts of virility and lineage were by no means the principal elements in the celebration of fatherhood as a category of male identity. Just as the physical rites of passage such as menarche, pregnancy and menopause were not used as markers of female life-cycle phases in early modern England, so the numerous accounts of the various ages of man singled out neither paternity nor even fatherhood more generally as a specific developmental stage for men.[19] Manhood, 'man's age' or 'man's estate' (as opposed to childhood, youth or old age) was defined in terms of physical and behavioural characteristics that made little or no direct mention of fatherhood. Physically, manhood (beginning between the ages of twenty-five and thirty-five and lasting until fifty) was not linked with puberty, but was the age during which the male body ideally

---

[15] Elizabeth Foyster, 'Silent Witnesses? Children and the Breakdown of Domestic and Social Order in Early Modern England', in *Childhood in Question: Children, Parents and the State*, ed. Anthony Fletcher and Stephen Hussey (Manchester, 1999), 57–73, p. 58.

[16] Sir Thomas Elyot, *The Castel of Health* (1561), fol. 7. See also Levine Lemnius, *The Touchstone of Complexions* (1633), 130, and Thomas A. Foster, 'Deficient Husbands: Manhood, Sexual Incapacity, and Male Marital Sexuality in Seventeenth-Century New England', *William and Mary Quarterly* 56 (1999), 723–44.

[17] Nicholas Breton, *A Poste with a Madde Packet of Letters* (1609), sig. E4; *A Discourse of the Married and Single Life* (1621). See also Berry and Foyster, 'Childless Men'.

[18] *The Office of Christian Parents: Shewing How Children Are to be Governed Throughout All Ages and Times of Their Life* (1616), 7.

[19] Sara Mendelson and Patricia Crawford, *Women in Early Modern England* (Oxford, 1998), 77.

achieved humoural balance and temperamental moderation. Behaviourally, it was characterised primarily in terms of self-government and control, and was related to marriage and house-holding status rather than explicitly to fatherhood. Within this framework, fatherhood was represented as a single – although no less important – strand in a web of hierarchical relationships from which male household heads derived their authority, and upon which the patriarchal order was founded: husbands over wives; parents over children; and masters over servants. Fatherhood was constructed as a social role, involving the management of one of a range of subordinates, rather than as a biological feat of generation.

It was through this entanglement with other aspects of male authority that fatherhood derived its significance as a cornerstone of patriarchal privilege. Male household heads were characterised as 'governors', and in certain contexts 'pastors', over their families, just as the command of kings and, to a lesser degree, clergy and teachers was justified in terms of fatherly rule.[20] As a 'little commonwealth', the household was represented both as a microcosm of the polity and as the primary unit of society, so that 'a conscionable performance of household duties' by its male head 'may be accounted a publicke worke'.[21] Although the oft-rehearsed fifth commandment exhorted listeners to honour father *and* mother, contemporary commentators were in no doubt that the father was the pre-eminent parent, since as a result of the gender hierarchy that placed husbands over wives men were better positioned than women to benefit from the association between householding and civic responsibility. According to William Gouge, 'father' was 'a title of great dignitie', and since he was 'the chief and principal Governour, and hath the greatest charge', so he should have 'the greatest care' even in matters that were common to both parents. Should disagreements arise between spouses over a child's care or instruction, it was the father who must be obeyed.[22] This hierarchy of parental authority is also reflected in the gendered division of labour expected by conduct writers such as Gouge, who privileged the roles performed by fathers above those of mothers: '[t]he mothers paines and care in bringing forth the childe is indeed the greater, and it may be also the greater in bringing up the childe, especially while it is young ... yet afterwards the fathers exceedeth in providing fit calling, sufficient meanes of maintenance, yea and portion or inheritance for it, and that

[20] Gordon J. Schochet, *Patriarchalism in Political Thought: The Authoritarian Family and Political Speculation and Attitudes Especially in Seventeenth-Century England* (Oxford, 1975); Susan Dwyer Amussen, *An Ordered Society: Gender and Class in Early Modern England* (Oxford, 1988); Crawford, *Parents of Poor Children*, 22–3.
[21] William Gouge, *Of Domesticall Duties*, 18.
[22] *Ibid.*, 136, 485. See also Hugh Cunningham, *Children and Childhood in Western Society since 1500* (Harlow, 1995), ch. 3.

after he himself is dead.'[23] Another tract declared that fathers who neglected this last aspect of their duties – posthumous provision – were 'unworthie to have children'.[24] In return, filial obedience overrode other status distinctions that could arise between fathers and their sons (the assumption being that this concern did not apply to daughters), with Gouge declaring that 'no honour is comparable to the dignity of fatherhood: it giveth a greater eminency to the parent over his childe, then any other honour can to the childe over his parent'.[25] In such situations, fathers were also in a position to claim their son's achievements as a lasting memorial to their good name.[26] A stake in their sons' good conduct was the driving force behind the genre of father–son advice that proliferated in print during the early modern period.[27]

Fatherhood was therefore broadly conceived as one of the pillars of order in early modern England and a central component of adult male authority. Crucially, fatherhood carried expectations not merely of a man's provision for his children but also of his direct and sustained involvement in, and responsibility for, their socialisation and nurturing, and these were roles from which fathers could derive emotional rewards as well as patriarchal authority.[28] The pleasure of parenting for men can occasionally be glimpsed, as in Whickham (County Durham) when an estate worker's fondness for his newborn son was reported in 1712: 'he got it in his armes the morning it was born … and said "Honny thou's my Darlin and shalt want for nothing as long as I am able to worke for thee".'[29] Although we still know far too little about the character of father–child relations in early modern England, the affect debate between historians has featured several similar examples of the very deep sentiments fathers developed for their children and the agonies they suffered when a child went astray or suffered misfortune, even in adulthood.[30] It is also clear that the present and future provision for

---

[23] Gouge, *Domesticall Duties*, 546. See also John Dod and Robert Cleaver, *A Godly Form of Householde Government: For the Ordering of Private Families* (1612), 60.

[24] Dod and Cleaver, *A Godly Form of Householde Government*, 253.

[25] Gouge, *Domesticall Duties*, 437. See also Dod and Cleaver, *A Godly Form of Householde Gorvernment*, 345.

[26] Keith Thomas, *The Ends of Life: Roads to Fulfilment in Early Modern England* (Oxford, 2009), 257.

[27] One of the most frequently printed examples was William Cecil, *The Counsell of a Father to his Sonne, in Ten Severall Precepts* (1617). For a fuller discussion of this genre, see Shepard, *Meanings of Manhood*, 30–8.

[28] John R. Gillis, 'Bringing up Father: British Paternal Identities, 1700 to Present', *Masculinities* 3 (1995), 1–27.

[29] Levine & Wrightson, *Whickham*, 321.

[30] For a summary, see Wrightson, ES, 108–18. See also Elizabeth Foyster, 'Parenting was for Life, not Just for Childhood: The Role of Parents in the Married Lives of their Children in Early Modern England', *History* 86 (2001), 313–27.

dependants was the principal goal of the majority of household economies.[31] Normatively, then, the duties of fatherhood comprised a delicate balance of authority, nurture, instruction and maintenance.

It was additionally acknowledged that parental duties were extensive and frequently distributed far beyond the family of origin – not least in concerns that not all surrogates performed their roles as conscientiously as natural parents. The transferable character of parenting was necessitated by a youth-heavy age structure and a high-pressure mortality regime which left many children parentless. In the Sussex port of Rye between 1553 and 1604 only 26.7 per cent of fathers survived to see any of their children reach adulthood, and 59.3 per cent of fathers died before any of their children had reached the age of fourteen. In seventeenth-century Clayworth (Nottinghamshire) as many as 40 per cent of unmarried persons had suffered the loss of one parent (more likely a father than a mother). Rough estimates suggest that between a third and a fifth of English youths experienced parental deprivation in the early modern period.[32] Service, apprenticeship and guardianship were the main means by which the fatherless were provided for, and following the death of a parent these arrangements were ideally mediated by bonds of neighbourliness and mutual obligation that could cross social boundaries to serve as a form of patronage for the orphaned and of charitable display for the guardian.[33] The significant limits to such bonds are, however, evident in the animus often associated with step-parenthood; in anxieties over the proper protection of orphans' goods as well as their persons; and also in the many disputes that arose over pauper apprenticeship, whereby children from indigent families were removed to other households through the intervention of parish officials in measures that smacked more of punishment than patronage.[34]

The arrangements put in place in response to the death of one or both parents and/or to diffuse charges on parish rates and to inculcate labour discipline provide an important context for understanding situations in which fatherhood was transferred even when the biological father remained alive. Such arrangements served to channel some of the privileges of fatherhood, if not all its responsibilities, on the basis of social and economic

[31] Wrightson, EN, ch. 2; Crawford, Parents of Poor Children, ch. 3.

[32] Graham Mayhew, 'Life-Cycle Service and the Family Unit in Early Modern Rye', C&C 6 (1991), 201–26, p. 205; Peter Laslett, Family Life and Illicit Love in Earlier Generations (Cambridge, 1977), 161–73. See also Houlbrooke, English Family, 215–21.

[33] Will Coster, 'To Bring Them Up in the Fear of God': Guardianship in the Diocese of York, 1500–1668', C&C 10 (1995), 9–32.

[34] Houlbrooke, English Family, 215–21; Pamela Sharpe, 'Poor Children as Apprentices in Colyton, 1598–1830', C&C 6 (1991), 253–70; Steve Hindle, 'Waste Children? Pauper Apprenticeship under the Elizabethan Poor Laws, c.1598–1697', in Women, Work and Wages in England, 1600–1850, ed. Penelope Lane, Neil Raven and K. D. M. Snell (Woodbridge, 2004), 15–46.

distinctions. The remainder of this essay will focus particularly on the sever-ance of links between paternity and fatherhood in cases of illegitimacy in ways which regulated relations not only between the generations but also between different groups of adult men. Parenthood of an illegitimate child has been represented by historians as something men all too readily wished to escape, either literally through flight or through negotiations (sometimes covert) whereby a mother or her parish were paid off thereby minimising the paternal role to one of indirect maintenance at most.[35] It will be argued here that while the differential treatment of mothers and fathers of children born out of wedlock can indeed be viewed as an extension of the sexual double standard, arrangements made for the care of illegitimate children sometimes convey expectations about the involvement of putative fathers. Furthermore, severance of the link between paternity and fatherhood, by enforcing the pecuniary responsibility of the former without the rewards of the latter, sometimes functioned as much to restrict men's access to patriar-chal authority as to enable them to benefit from patriarchal privilege over women.

II

Whether the relative fluidity of potential arrangements for the care of the young was an advantage or disadvantage to putative fathers of illegitimate children is debatable. On the one hand, it is clear that many sought to dodge both the shame and responsibility attached to parenting a bastard using a variety of strategies (some of which rested on the patronage and active collusion of other men). On the other hand, there is evidence that the active involvement of putative fathers in their children's upbringing, beyond the payment of maintenance, could be demanded by magistrates and was sometimes even desired by the men concerned. With this in mind, it is possible that some situations in which genetic fathers lost responsibility for their offspring were the consequence of similar judgements about fitness for parenting that informed the arrangement of pauper apprenticeship. Puta-tive fathers' impulses to flee and the punitive attitude adopted by parish authorities were mutually reinforcing, yet while this resulted in high levels of parental loss for the children involved the consequences for their fathers were not straightforwardly beneficial and might equally be viewed in terms of deprivation. This is not to argue simplistically that the genetic fathers were 'victims' of their circumstances (and certainly not when compared with the fates of the women concerned), but to suggest that the decision-making consequent on an illegitimate birth was governed as much by the

---

[35] Gowing, *Common Bodies*, ch. 6; Crawford, *Parents of Poor Children*, ch. 2.

unequal division of patriarchal dividends between men as by the differential treatment of women and men.[36]

Church court cases disputing the identity of putative fathers and quarter sessions orders for the maintenance of illegitimate offspring are the chief sources in which negotiations concerning paternal responsibilities towards children conceived and born out of wedlock come to light. This is a problematic body of evidence since it is a highly impressionistic record of deviancy and dispute. The majority of affiliation arrangements did not involve the courts, and even the formal negotiations between justices of the peace [JPs], parish officials and putative fathers may have masked informal aspects of a child's care that left no record. However, despite their bias towards the more contentious end of the spectrum of possible consequences of illegitimacy, even these sources suggest that paternity of an illegitimate child had varied outcomes for the men concerned.[37] While the cases that came to court were dominated by concerns regarding reputation and provision, they also reveal other considerations that determined the nature of putative fathers' involvement with their offspring that were linked in turn to their access to normative masculinity and its associated patriarchal authority.

Although the negative consequences of an illegitimate birth were rarely as devastating for the father as they were for the mother, paternity in the wrong circumstances – that is, not legitimised by wedlock – could nonetheless be a source of disgrace and material damage for the men concerned.[38] Parents of illegitimate children could be ordered to perform penance by the church courts, and were liable to public shaming, especially if there were ideological axes to be ground as in the case of the couple who were ordered to be whipped until they bled in Glastonbury high street with two fiddles playing before them in order 'to make known their lewdness in begetting [a] base child upon the Sabbath day coming from dancing'.[39] Such rituals for those charged with fornication were more commonly suffered by women than by men and also appear to have declined over time. In cases where the child's maintenance was likely to become chargeable to the parish, the mother was to be whipped and committed to the house of correction for

[36] For caution about casting men as victims of patriarchal relations see Toby L. Ditz, 'The New Men's History and the Peculiar Absence of Gendered Power: Some Remedies from Early American Gender History', *Gender & History* 16 (2004), 1–35; Alexandra Shepard, 'Manhood, Patriarchy, and Gender in Early Modern History', in *Masculinities, Childhood, Violence: Attending to Early Modern Women – and Men*, ed. Amy Leonard and Karen Nelson (Newark NJ, 2011), 77–95.

[37] Alan Macfarlane, 'Illegitimacy and Illegitimates in English History', in *Bastardy*, ed. Laslett, Oosterveen and Smith, 71–85.

[38] Bernard Capp, 'The Double Standard Revisited: Plebeian Women and Male Sexual Reputation in Early Modern England', *P&P* 162 (1999), 70–100; Shepard, *Meanings of Manhood*, 157–73.

[39] E. H. Bates, ed., *Quarter Sessions Records for the County of Somerset, I: James I 1607–1625*, Somerset Record Society 23 (1907), 211.

one year and, when possible, the 'reputed' father was to be bound to save the parish harmless from all costs associated with the child's upbringing and could be gaoled until he provided sufficient security to do so.[40] However, it was the wider social opprobrium rather than the weight of the law or even the financial responsibility of maintenance that many putative fathers apparently feared.

Accusations of paternity out of wedlock formed the basis of many slander cases brought by men before the church courts. Such cases were likely to have been initiated as strategic bids to deflect claims for maintenance, but the litigation turned as much on the wider social stigma as on the pecuniary consequences of the affiliation of a bastard child. One witness in a defamation suit from Devon in 1594 claimed that, by stating that Ambrose Pooke had 'a bastard in the town' whose maintenance he had paid for almost a year and that 'after a while it will be brought home to him', the defendant had done Pooke 'so muche wronge' that the witness could not 'tell howe he should be hable to recompence him'.[41] Various implications of fathering a bastard were spelled out in other cases. In attesting to the damage suffered by John Skurrell following Joanne Campe's declaration that he was the father of her child, one witness described how Skurrell had been 'flowted at, and mocked and taunted with the wordes of scandal … amongest honest and grave persons'.[42] Besides esteem, it is clear that offices, livelihoods and inheritances could be at stake. As the suspected father of his maid's illegitimate child, it was reported in 1600 that the Cambridge brewer 'goodman Hardinge … ys lyke to loose one of his offices, because he … loved yonge fleshe' and that he 'was hardlye thought on for the same matter'.[43] In different circumstances, putative fathers could be more concerned about their own father's wrath than with their responsibilities to an unborn or newborn child. When in 1629 Jane Russell accused a young fellow of Pembroke College, Cambridge, of fathering the child she was carrying, he (according to her account) 'did upon his knees intreate [her] not to laye the beggettinge of the child … unto him because yf his father did knowe of it he should be undone'.[44] Anxieties about fathering illegitimate children did not only appear in the predictable context of defamation litigation and paternity suits. In a debt case of 1584, for example, doubts were raised about the honesty of Robert Archer, a tailor, who had been called as a witness. It emerged that an illegitimate child had been laid on Archer's stall, which

---

[40] For a contemporary summary of the legal position of parents of 'base-born' children, see Michael Dalton, *The Countrey Justice, Conteyning the Practise of the Justices of the Peace out of Their Sessions* (1618), 31–2.

[41] Devon Record Office, Chanter 864, fol. 49.

[42] Norfolk Record Office [NRO], DN/DEP30/32, fol. 45v.

[43] Cambridge University Library [CUL], Cambridge University Archive [CUA], Comm. Ct.II.9, fol. 3r–v.

[44] CUL, CUA, V.C.Ct.II.25, fol. 20v.

child had been 'begotten unlawefullie' on his former maidservant, and it was 'reported by some that he was father of yt, & by other some that a shoemaker was the father thereof'. Even though – as Archer claimed – he had cleared himself of the charge, the symbolic gesture of placing the child on his shop-front had proved enough to cast doubt on his reliability as a witness in a totally unrelated matter several months subsequently.[45]

That such allegations of paternity could have so damaging an impact on men's reputations is also suggested by their attempts to offload the shame associated with illegitimacy onto other men. Disputes over the paternity of illegitimate children are indicative both of the mistrust with which women's words were treated in early modern England, and of the complex negotiations between men, women, neighbours and kin that could be part of the process of naming a father (which in turn compounded the mistrust of mothers).[46] Women of illegitimate children were put under harrowing pressure while in childbirth, threatened with refusals of help by midwives and gossips demanding confirmation of the identity of the father.[47] These rituals often occurred after protracted bargaining in which the material interests of the mother and child were set against the social stigma of paternity. In 1620, widow Corby of Offpuddle in Dorset informed her neighbour that the father of Thomasina Valence's child was of 'to[o] to[o] great a calling to be named or questioned … and that there would be another father for the child found in Whitechurch'. Subsequently Thomasina duly confessed that she had named Thomas Squib as the father, because 'the trew father therof was to[o] great of bloud to mary her or to be approached for the father'.[48]

It is not clear in this case whether the 'true father' was involved in negotiating Thomas Squib's fate, but there are examples of allegations of paternity being foisted upon the defenceless, such as the deaf and dumb or the recently deceased.[49] The most unlikely of such scenarios is a case from Norfolk in which Edmund Man, the curate of Sheringham and the suspected father of an illegitimate child, according to one witness 'did suffer

[45] CUL, CUA, Comm.Ct.II.2, fols 71, 74.
[46] Laura Gowing, 'Ordering the Body: Illegitimacy and Female Authority in Seventeenth-Century England', in *Negotiating Power in Early Modern Society: Order, Hierarchy and Subordination in Britain and Ireland*, ed. Michael J. Braddick and John Walter (Cambridge, 2001), 43–84; Gowing, *Common Bodies*, ch. 6.
[47] Laura Gowing, 'Secret Births and Infanticide in Seventeenth-Century England', *P&P* 156 (1997), 87–115; Linda A. Pollock, 'Childbearing and Female Bonding in Early Modern England', *SH* 22 (1997), 286–306. See also Steve Hindle, 'The Shaming of Margaret Knowsley: Gossip, Gender and the Experience of Authority in Early Modern England', *C&C* 9 (1994), 391–419.
[48] *The Case Book of Sir Francis Ashley, J.P., Recorder of Dorchester 1614–1635*, ed. J. H. Bettey, Dorset Record Society 7 (Dorchester, 1971), 68.
[49] E.g. S. A. H. Burne, ed., *The Staffordshire Quarter Sessions Rolls*, IV: 1598–1602 (Kendal, 1936), 388; S. C. Ratcliff and H. C. Johnson, eds, *Warwick County Records*, II: *Quarter Sessions Order Book Michaelmas, 1637, to Epiphany, 1650* (Warwick, 1936), 226.

John Walker ... of the age of seven or viij yeares to answere for the child'.[50] It is also clear that some fathers bribed expectant mothers to name another man, or bought off proxy progenitors, demonstrating that although they might be willing to accept the financial burden of paternity, they sought to avoid both the shame associated with it and the social responsibility of fatherhood. William Foster, for example, the fellow of Pembroke College who was concerned to avoid the shame of paternity (mentioned above), appears to have bribed his college servant to shoulder the blame for Jane Russell's pregnancy by offering him £10, and was ultimately cleared of the charge when Russell named this servant in Foster's place.[51] Worcestershire JPs were informed of a similar situation in 1619 after a servant confessed that 'his late master caused him to absent himself from his service' and offered him £15 to take on his master's illegitimate child and to 'make the world think the child was his'.[52]

Putative fathers could be assisted in their attempts to shift or dodge responsibility by family and friends, despite the costs this might incur for those abetting flight.[53] The support networks offered to men in the wake of a paternity charge that come to light in the records of quarter sessions were more patriarchal than fraternal in character, suggesting that younger men could be protected by their seniors from bearing responsibility towards the women and children concerned. Just as some masters attempted to shift the blame from themselves onto a servant, others helped their servants escape charges, such as the constable of Nuneaton (Warwickshire) who in 1628 was ordered to appear before JPs to answer for his negligence, having either allowed his servant to escape (following an accusation of paternity) or colluded in his being 'secretly conveyed away'.[54] Sureties for absent fathers could find themselves liable for a child's maintenance until the reputed father was bound to undertake his duty of provision, and there is occasional evidence of men's attempts to escape being aided by their peers. But it was fathers of men charged with paternity who were most often in the frame for shielding their sons from the burdens associated with answering for an illegitimate child. For example, a widow petitioned the Worcestershire sessions in 1619 on behalf of her daughter, requesting that the father of one William Coles (a tailor) who was 'the father of her daughter's child, & who has been sent away by his father' be ordered to contribute towards the child's

---

[50] NRO, DN/DEP30/32, fols 54v–55v.

[51] CUL, CUA, V.C.Ct.III.30, nos 114–15.

[52] *Worcestershire County Records. Division I. Documents Relating to Quarter Sessions*, I: 1591–1643, part I, comp. J. W. Willis Bund (Worcester, 1900), 307.

[53] For examples of help extended to mothers of illegitimate children, see Dave Postles, 'Surviving Lone Motherhood in Early-Modern England', *The Seventeenth Century* 21 (2006), 160–83.

[54] S. C. Ratcliff and H. C. Johnson, eds, *Warwick County Records*, I: *Quarter Sessions Order Book Easter, 1625, to Trinity, 1637* (Warwick, 1935), 53.

maintenance, which he was duly required to do at the weekly rate of 6*d* until he produced his son before JPs.[55] Occasionally, fathers of defaulting fathers who became complicit in their sons' negligence might find themselves directly charged with a child's care. In 1606, two Staffordshire JPs ordered that the yeoman Roger Bromley, having failed to bring his son John Bromley to 'receive order touching a bastard son which he has confessed to have begotten', was to keep the child himself, which child was to be handed over by his mother and the parish constable into Roger Bromley's care.[56]

Familial loyalties between fathers and sons that jeopardised the material well-being of the mother and her illegitimate child could create considerable conflict within a parish. A protracted dispute arose between the parishioners of Bilton (Warwickshire) and their parson, John Enewes, after he advised his son (who had impregnated one of his father's servants while also working as a servant in his father's household) to 'run away and to leave the charge upon the said inhabitants of Bilton'. According to a petition from the parishioners, Richard Enewes had been willing to marry the child's mother before being dissuaded by his own father John. In 1642, some nine years after the child's birth, the quarter sessions ordered that John should 'take the said bastard child ... to be his apprentice for nine years next ensuing' and repay the overseers of the poor all reasonable charges and damages so far associated with providing for the child. This order was made on account of the 'good temporal means' possessed by John Enewes, none of which had been forthcoming to support the child despite John's promise to save the parish from any charge and several attempts by the parish to extract maintenance.[57] Fathers who failed to take order regarding their son's indiscretions might also find themselves charged with incontinent living besides becoming financially liable for the consequences. In 1628, the churchwardens of Wisborough Green (Sussex) not only presented John Nightingall and Mary Lewer (his father's servant) for incontinency following Lewer's confessions that she was pregnant by John, but also Robert Nightingall, John's father, 'for a very bawd'. This was because he had for several months 'bin told, both [by] our vicar and also by divers others, what great familiarity was spoken of to be betwixt his said sonne John and Mary Lewer' but had failed 'either to cause them for to be marryed or els to put them asunder ... which maketh many people uppon great presumptions for to suggest that the said Mary is an harlot common both with the father and also with his sonne'. As a consequence all three were 'kept backe from the Lord's table, for the great suspicion of their incontinency'.[58]

[55] *Worcestershire County Records*, 308.
[56] S. A. H. Burne, ed., *The Staffordshire Quarter Sessions Rolls*, V: 1603–1606 (Kendal, 1940), 305.
[57] *Warwick County Records*, II, 110.
[58] Hilda Johnstone, ed., *Churchwardens' Presentments (17th Century)*, Part I: Archdeaconry of Chichester, Sussex Record Society 49 (Lewes, 1948), 127.

Measures whereby grandparents were ordered to take responsibility for their children's children reflected a wider framework of familial protection that could be extended to parents of 'base-born' children. While this some-times incurred punitive consequences at the instigation of churchwardens and overseers seeking to limit charges to parish funds, grandparental involve-ment – and expenditure – was often voluntary and did not necessarily entail competing loyalties towards children and grandchildren. While it was more often maternal grandparents of illegitimate children that featured in quarter session orders both being compelled and volunteering to take on the respon-sibility for their grandchildren's maintenance, fathers of putative fathers can also be glimpsed substituting their own means on behalf of their sons. JPs in Somerset in 1616 discharged Gyles Capell from paying 8d weekly towards the support of 'the base-born child of Mary Browne, whereof his son Thomas is the reputed father ... in respect that he doth henceforth keep the child himself, and give sufficient security unto the parishioners of Tintinhull ... for the discharge of the said parish', adding further that George Browne (possibly Mary's father) 'shall not detain the said child any longer but deliver him to the said Gyles Capell'.[59] A similar arrangement appears to have been brokered between the grandparents of the child Alice Martin was carrying in 1640, of which the labourer Thomas Spencer was the reputed father. William Martin, Alice's father, 'did voluntarily undertake to keep her ... until she could be delivered', after which John Spencer, Thomas's father, undertook to 'keep the said child' on account of his withholding consent from his son to marry Alice 'unless he should be compelled by law'.[60] As in this last case, fathers of putative fathers often stepped in to let their sons off the hook and such actions mirrored the kind of arrangements that could be put in place for the care of legitimate children who had been pre-deceased or deserted by their fathers. These measures could therefore function as a form of licensed desertion or figurative death, and may well have deprived both the illegitimate children and their 'reputed' fathers of the opportunity to form lasting bonds. However, it is also possible that such arrangements (many of which would have been brokered out of court) actually served to facilitate paternal contact and prioritise it above maternal claims on either the putative father or their child.

Similar interpretative ambiguities regarding attitudes to putative fathers arise from measures put in place by JPs to secure the maintenance of ille-gitimate children. On the one hand, magisterial orders were principally motivated by the need to limit pressure on the charges borne by ratepayers, and they were therefore focused on extracting a financial commitment from putative fathers. This had a punitive as well as pragmatic dimension, divorcing maintenance from those concepts of honesty and respectability

[59] *Quarter Sessions Records for the County of Somerset*, I, 183.
[60] *Warwick County Records*, II, 71.

that were normatively associated with a man's provision for his dependants. Orders sometimes stipulated that payments should be made after divine service at the communion table or in the church porch, in rituals of reparation which were public and which may have therefore carried associations of shame.[61] On the other hand, the preoccupation with maintenance was not always severed from expectations that fathers would play an active role in the upbringing of their offspring, although – significantly – such expectations appear to have diminished over the course of the seventeenth century.[62] While this might be judged to have been beneficial to the men concerned, freeing them from the direct responsibilities of parenthood in ways that were increasingly unthinkable for the mothers of illegitimate children (particularly during infancy), it also more decisively severed the links between paternity and parenthood in cases when fathers were deemed incapable of maintenance, thereby channelling patriarchal dividends out of the hands of the poor.

Many putative fathers were not shielded by their families of origin from either the charges or even the practicalities of caring for illegitimate children. Securing a child's maintenance without charge to ratepayers was the main preoccupation of JPs concerned with giving orders to 'reputed' fathers. However, it was not unheard of, particularly in the earlier part of the period, for JPs to expect more paternal involvement than the basic provision of regular maintenance payments and sufficient security to protect parish rates. A few maintenance orders issued by JPs stipulated a division of labour between mothers and fathers of illegitimate children that entailed fathers taking over direct responsibility, usually after infancy or early childhood, at the very least for decision-making concerning the child's future if not for its day-to-day care. JPs in Staffordshire in 1601 ordered that John Sabin should pay 10d weekly towards the maintenance of the child he fathered on Alice Godwin until its second birthday, after which he was to 'take charge of the child', receiving 1d weekly from Alice until the child was able to get its own living.[63] At the Wiltshire Sessions in 1615 it was similarly ordered that an illegitimate child should be nursed and brought up by his mother until he 'shall accomplishe the full age of three years', during which time the father was to pay 10d weekly towards his maintenance. After this point the father was to 'keep and maintaine the childe untill he be fitt yeares to be bound as an apprentice in some Trade or mistrie' during which time the mother was to contribute 4d weekly to the father's costs.[64]

In determining a period of payment, it was not unusual for maintenance

[61] *Quarter Sessions Records for the County of Somerset*, I, 277, 278.
[62] Walter J. King, 'Punishment for Bastardy in Early Seventeenth-Century England', *Albion* 10 (1978), 130–51.
[63] *Staffordshire Quarter Sessions Rolls*, IV, 393.
[64] B. Howard Cunningham, ed., *Records of the County of Wilts, being Extracts from the Quarter Sessions Great Rolls of the Seventeenth Century* (Devizes, 1932), 50.

orders to oblige putative fathers to undertake weekly contributions until they took over the child's care or arranged a place in service or apprenticeship, and it is possible that fathers were expected to take direct responsibility for such placements in a division of labour that would have mirrored the duties of fathers towards their legitimate offspring.[65] In the early 1560s the Durham church courts presided over a settlement between the parents of a 'bais begotton' girl to the effect that her father William Brandling was to 'have the rewll, order and government' of the child while her mother agreed from henceforth to have 'no medlynge with the said wench, to enties hir frome any servic order or apointment lawfullye by the said William the wench shall be assigned unto'. William, in the meantime, was to compensate the mother for her former charges associated with bringing up their child with a bundle of lint or flax annually for the following four years.[66] A quarter sessions order from Warwickshire in 1639 confirmed that the inhabitants of Priors Marston were no longer obliged to pay maintenance to William Carter for the care of an illegitimate child born to his daughter Agnes Carter, since the child's father had 'taken away the said child ... and bound him apprentice in London'.[67]

Very occasionally fathers could be expected to take on the care of an illegitimate child from birth or during early infancy. Petitions lodged with JPs sometimes included expectations that putative fathers should take on direct and immediate responsibility for a child's care, such as that lodged by Eleanor Raynolds in 1619 requesting that the father of her child, a butcher, be ordered 'to breed up the said child or give her money wherewith to maintain it'.[68] The fellmonger Augustine King was similarly issued with the choice between taking on 'the whole keeping and nourishing' of his bastard child or paying a weekly sum of 12d to the overseers of the poor 'for its upkeep and education until it can be placed in service'.[69] That a request for a father to take on his illegitimate child was not merely an empty threat designed to extract maintenance payments is suggested by orders that presumed paternal responsibility, such as that issued by Warwickshire JPs in 1662 subsequent to Elizabeth Morrell's affiliation of her child to William Search during her delivery. On the basis of the testimony of midwives present at the birth it was ordered that Search 'shall from henceforth receive, provide for and maintain the said bastard male child', free the parish of Milverton from any

---

[65] Alexandra Shepard, 'Family and Household', in *The Elizabethan World*, ed. Susan Doran and Norman Jones (2010).

[66] *Depositions and other Ecclesiastical Proceedings from the Courts of Durham extending from 1311 to the Reign of Elizabeth*, Publications of the Surtees Society 22 (1845), 72.

[67] *Warwick County Records*, II, 41.

[68] *Worcestershire County Records*, 308.

[69] *Kent at Law 1602: The County Jurisdiction: Assizes and Sessions of the Peace*, ed. Louis A. Knafla (1994), 168. See also 178.

charge relating to his maintenance and pay James Morrell, in whose house the child had been born, his 'reasonable charges' for Elizabeth's lying in.[70]

In a few instances, sessions records provide fleeting references to puta-tive fathers voluntarily taking on direct responsibility for their children's welfare. In 1665 the Warwickshire bench ordered that the child of Anne Wilcox be removed from her care in the county gaol on the petition of its father who was 'contented to maintain and provide for the said child' and who was exhorted to 'take care that the said child be carefully provided for'.[71] This may have been a temporary measure, as in the case of Richard Jones who had been entrusted with the care of the child he had fathered on Elizabeth Smyth while she remained in the house of correction, which arrangement ceased when she was freed as a consequence of inheriting 'some reasonable estate whereby she … is of ability to maintain herself in good sort'.[72] However, it is important that we do not discount the possibility in at least some cases of genuine affection on the part of fathers towards their illegitimate children. Such emotions are unlikely to have surfaced in the routine orders issued for maintenance – not least since most cases came to the attention of the quarter sessions as a consequence of some kind of default – but they can very occasionally be discerned elsewhere. The senti-ments of Richard Smyth, for example, servant to Elizabeth Watson, were recorded in 1617 after she was suspected of drinking a substance concocted to destroy the child she was carrying, fathered illegitimately by Richard. He confessed to a number of witnesses that, having often lain with him, 'my dame nede not a gone awaye frome me thus for I dide never deserve it at her hand', declaring that 'she is a beaste' and that 'she nede not agone aboute to a destryed it for I am as licke a man as enye of hir husbones ware for I woulde never a stored from hir for I would neaver a bene a shamed of it'.[73]

The ability of fathers to assume direct responsibility for their illegitimate offspring's care depended on a range of factors besides willingness – which, it should not be denied, was often clearly lacking. It is not perhaps coin-cidental that many of the orders discussed above involving direct paternal involvement of some kind related to men with specific occupational titles that suggest they may have been householders of sufficient substance rather than youths more dependent on the patronage and goodwill of parents or employers – although the distress of Richard Smyth at his mistress's attempt to destroy their child suggests that not all men in this position automati-cally looked to flight, denial or protection as the most attractive options.

[70] S. C. Ratcliff and H. C. Johnson, eds, *Warwick County Records*, IV: *Quarter Sessions Order Book Easter, 1657, to Epiphany, 1665* (Warwick, 1938), 173.
[71] S. C. Ratcliff and H. C. Johnson, eds, *Warwick County Records*, V: *Orders Made at Quarter Sessions Easter, 1665, to Epiphany, 1674* (Warwick, 1939), 2.
[72] *Warwick County Records*, II, 39.
[73] CUL, Ely Diocesan Records, E7/2/14. See also E7/2/13.

In the case of married men charged with paternity the action taken would most likely have involved spousal negotiation, with some wives colluding in attempts to have another man named as the putative father of any children born of their husband's adulterous liaisons and others willing to accommodate them within their own households. A petition by Anne, the wife of John Aldridge, submitted to the Warwickshire sessions in 1657 illustrates the circumstances in which it might have been in a wife's interest to house another woman's child, reputedly fathered by her husband. Protesting against John's long imprisonment for being the 'supposed' father of a child begotten on Bridget Darbey, Anne offered to take the child and 'breed it up with her own children rather than her husband should lie in prison, she being confident of her husband's honesty notwithstanding the harlot's affirmation in the time of her travail'.[74] It was clearly less damaging to the household's material well-being to take on the burden of an additional child than to suffer the costs of John's absence, even if this did not vindicate his reputation in the way Anne might have desired. It should also be remembered that it was not unusual for households to absorb children from former relationships, however unharmoniously, and that fostering arrangements were also commonplace, providing a context in which the boundary between legitimate and illegitimate children could be blurred.

Over the course of the seventeenth century there was, however, a subtle shift in the dynamics governing the negotiation of paternal responsibilities towards and involvement with illegitimate offspring as the intervention of parish authorities became more routine regarding arrangements for the care, education and (most pressingly) the maintenance of the poor children who were deemed a threat to parish rates. This has already been charted with reference to the practice of placing pauper children as apprentices, which became increasingly commonplace from the early seventeenth century and which reflected the growing scepticism of parish authorities about the ability of poorer parents to socialise as much as provide for their children.[75] Conversely, the power of parish officers to place children in foster care (on account of their poverty or parental deprivation) could also constitute a form of patronage to the receiving households through the provision of a welcome source of labour, income and claims to civic entitlement. In Southampton, for example, widow Grundie promised to take in an orphaned child until he was old enough to be bound apprentice to her son, '[i]n Considerac'on whereof she was p[ro]missed that she should contynewe Alehowse keeping' in addition to receiving the sum of 20s, while a porter, Thomas Pitties, took in a child 'at his owne charges' on condition that he, his wife and the boy

---

74 *Warwick County Records*, IV, 26.
75 Hindle, 'Waste Children'; *idem, On the Parish? The Micro-Politics of Poor Relief in Rural England, c.1550–1750* (Oxford, 2004), ch. 3.

had 'a spare Roome in the lower Almeshowse'.[76] The transfer of parental roles in such cases could be informed by distinctions between the 'deserving' and 'undeserving' poor and often involved the subtle redistribution of scant resources between them. Just as 'marriage and family formation … was a privilege rather than a right' in early modern England, with some parish officers actively preventing nuptials between couples of limited means, fitness for fatherhood was also judged in socio-economic terms, and this was of particular relevance in cases of illegitimacy in which parish overseers became involved.[77]

During the first half of the seventeenth century, the numbers of orders requiring fathers' direct paternal involvement in or responsibility for their illegitimate offspring's care diminished markedly.[78] Instead, it became routine to demand weekly maintenance payments from putative fathers in cases when officials were not satisfied that an illegitimate child would be provided for either by a one-off payment of a lump sum and/or a bond supported by sureties saving the parish harmless. Increasingly, as the mechanisms for administering poor relief became established at the level of the parish, these payments were channelled through the overseers of the poor. In Warwickshire, for example, maintenance payments from fathers were less often paid directly to their children's carers but were increasingly administered and redistributed by parish officials over the course of the seventeenth century. This occurred not only when the parish authorities took on responsibility for arranging a child's care (perhaps after the return to work, death or desertion of its mother), but also even when the child remained in the mother's hands. Besides a cluster of cases during the Interregnum in which the bench ordered maintenance to be paid directly to the child's mother or foster carer, and two cases involving men of substantial means (one a gentleman and the other settling with a lump sum), overseers of the poor were increasingly specified as the recipients and distributors of payments. So in 1684, JPs ordered that Thomas Rawbone should pay 12d weekly to the overseers of Radford towards the maintenance of his illegitimate son, which sum would be paid to the child's mother providing she continued to 'keep and nourish him … according to her ability' until he reached the age of eight at which point Rawbone was to pay a further £5 towards apprenticing the boy.[79] While it might have benefited some mothers to have parish officials policing maintenance payments on their behalf, orders such as this

---

[76] J. W. Horrocks, ed., *The Assembly Books of Southampton*, IV: 1615–1616 (Southampton, 1925), 41; idem, ed., *The Assembly Books of Southampton*, I: 1602–1608 (Southampton, 1917), 52.

[77] Wrightson, *ES*, 70; Steve Hindle, 'The Problem of Pauper Marriage in Seventeenth-Century England', *TRHS* 6th ser. 8 (1998), 71–89.

[78] King, 'Punishment for Bastardy'.

[79] H. C. Johnson, ed., *Warwick County Records*, VIII: *Quarter Sessions Records Trinity, 1682, to Epiphany, 1690* (Warwick, 1953), 89.

may also have served to limit fathers' direct contact with their children and responsibility for decision-making about their future, reducing their investment to a financial commitment alone. Diminished paternal involvement in such cases should not therefore be ascribed to the elevation of maternal above paternal bonds, since it was most likely the cost-effectiveness of maternal breast-feeding (compared with the expense of a wet nurse) that lay behind parochial pressure on mothers of chargeable illegitimates to keep their children. Divesting putative fathers of paternal responsibilities beyond maintenance stemmed from the assumptions of 'civic fathers' (so described and documented by Patricia Crawford) that poor men 'lack[ed] the masculine virtues of independence and autonomy' and were to be treated themselves 'as children who required paternal supervision'.[80]

III

While on the one hand it is possible to discern the collusion of men to shield putative fathers from the responsibilities of fatherhood in ways which may have been beneficial to the men involved, this was far from the whole story behind the varied arrangements made for the care of illegitimate children. There was a degree of consensus that young men were unfit for the demands of fatherhood, lacking both the means and authority to maintain their offspring, and in many cases their own fathers stepped in either to take on the duty of care (sometimes following parochial or magisterial pressure) or to aid a youth's flight from the situation. Men of substance could attempt to pay off others to take on responsibility for their illegitimate children – some avoiding the shame of affiliation altogether – while others were in a position to absorb an additional child into their own households. Poorer men lacking either means or patronage, however, were more likely to cede both their authority and agency as fathers to parish authorities, not wholly escaping responsibility but having their paternal role reduced to a pecuniary obligation to the *parish* rather than to their child, and stripped bare of any of the patriarchal privileges associated with fatherhood. This was made explicit in the case of Richard White who was ordered in 1645 to enter into a bond to pay 16d weekly towards his illegitimate child's maintenance until it reached the age of twelve while undertaking not to 'take the said child from the place where now it is or otherwise dispose of it without the order of this court or the consent of the churchwardens and overseers of the said parish'.[81] Sessions orders, it should be reiterated, may well have masked informal contact and the forging of bonds between fathers and their illegitimate offspring. Indeed, in this case, the order appears to

---

80 Crawford, *Parents of Poor Children*, 208.
81 *Warwick County Records*, II, 127.

have been an active attempt to limit such bonds by depriving White of autonomy regarding the decision-making affecting his child's future. Maintenance orders that placed parish officials at the centre of arrangements for illegitimate children certainly did not preclude paternal involvement when all parties were willing. It is also important to remember that the majority of illegitimate births (especially those that were not brought to the attention of the sessions of the peace) were most likely the consequence of disrupted marriage plans between those most vulnerable to economic dislocation in times of crisis, and it seems appropriate to assume paternal goodwill in many instances.[82]

However, it is also significant that the increase in the proportion of sessions orders specifying parish officers' involvement occurred alongside two other trends: first, with the decline in illegitimacy ratios towards the mid seventeenth century, 'bastardy was becoming more exclusively the province of the poor and the obscure', and secondly, during the same period, 'bastardy was felt increasingly to be the sole responsibility of the mother of the child'.[83] While it is impossible to generalise about the extent to which the social incidence of illegitimacy shifted downwards over the course of the period, it is clear that the regulation and punishment of putative fathers in particular became focused on those unable to make financial recompense.[84] If these trends were not merely coincidental, it might be argued that fathers – and specifically poorer fathers – were being pushed out. Although it is clear that many putative fathers did not wish to translate paternity into fatherhood, we must not assume this was the only factor governing the denial of parental roles in cases of illegitimacy. Just as the redistribution of children associated with pauper apprenticeship was often against their parents' will, so some of the broken links between paternity and fatherhood constituted a loss for putative fathers as well as their children as a consequence of the growing intervention by local officials in the family life of the poor. Even the most unpromising sources provide glimpses of affection felt by some fathers for their illegitimate children, confirming historiographical scepticism towards a longer-term, linear shift from authority to

---

[82] David Levine, *Family Formation in an Age of Nascent Capitalism* (New York, 1977), ch. 9; *Bastardy*, ed. Laslett, Oosterveen and Smith.

[83] Levine and Wrightson, 'Social Context of Illegitimacy', 165; Adair, *Courtship*, 79. For the diminishing social status of bastard bearers see also Wrightson & Levine, *Terling*, 126–32; Martin Ingram, 'The Reform of Popular Culture? Sex and Marriage in Early Modern England', in *Popular Culture in Seventeenth-Century England*, ed. Barry Reay (1985), 129–65, pp. 150–6; David Underdown, *Fire from Heaven: Life in an English Town in the Seventeenth Century* (New Haven, 1992), 106–8. Cf. Peter Kitson, 'Occupationally Specific Prenuptial Pregnancy in Early Modern England: the Case of Gainsborough, 1564–1812' (unpublished paper, www.ehs.org.uk/othercontent/kitson.htm, accessed 27 October 2011).

[84] King, 'Punishment for Bastardy'.

nurture in parenting modes.[85] However, just as maternal bonds were neither always assumed nor respected, so paternal claims both to responsibility and affection for their children could be overridden. Far from cementing ties between the generations and between different social groups, the practices of 'pro-parenting' in circumstances such as these served to shore up hierarchies of masculinity by excluding certain men from parts of the patriarchal portion – namely the honesty and authority associated with providing for and governing dependants.

Paternal experiences and identities in early modern England were not simply the consequence of varying levels of 'affect' but were negotiable, not least because of the degree to which demographic and economic realities conspired against the formation and maintenance of stable households that were deemed the basis of social order. These negotiations, involving judgements about who was fit to parent, were shaped by the interplay of class and gender during a period of transition that witnessed the concentration of patriarchal dividends alongside material resources into fewer hands. As the honesty and status associated with house-holding became unobtainable for an increasing proportion of men (reflected more broadly in the dramatic rise in the proportions never marrying over the course of the seventeenth century), so familial relations became more socially differentiated not just in terms of household size and structure but, more importantly, in terms of shaping access to the culturally endorsed roles and identities associated with normative masculinity. That fatherhood should be transferable was in the interests of householders, and of stakeholders in the social order, not only because it enabled the care of needy children and the patching up of broken households, but also because it endorsed normative concepts of manhood and concentrated patriarchal privilege within the hands of the minority of men designated fit as governors of both the next generation and the 'meaner' sorts. The extent to which this was in the interests of some of the fathers involved – not to mention their children – remains doubtful.

---

[85] Joanne Bailey, 'Paternal Power: the Pleasures and Perils of "Indulgent" Fathering in Britain in the Long Eighteenth Century', in *History of the Family* (forthcoming). I am grateful to the author for sharing a draft of this article prior to its publication.

3

Gender, Sexuality and the Consumption of Musical Culture in Eighteenth-Century London

HELEN BERRY

The craze for Italian opera started in England in the early 1700s and it continued to be popular with many adaptations and local appropriations throughout the century. It presented the English with a dazzling new form of foreign entertainment. In the long term, opera in its various forms was to make a substantial contribution to the development of diverse social, cultural and economic activities within the burgeoning leisure sector in the metropolis and leading provincial towns throughout the British Isles. The stars of eighteenth-century opera were Italian *castrati* – male singers who had been castrated as boys to preserve their unbroken voices. Their arrival provoked the English into writing and sometimes publishing explicit commentaries on themes which were often otherwise unrecorded, particularly in relation to gender and sexuality. The English debated, for example, whether castrati were 'real' men. Though they had been associated with homosexuality in seventeenth-century Europe, and there were notorious examples of castrati who were the lovers of powerful men, in eighteenth-century England contemporary authors commented upon the appeal of castrati among female opera-goers. This was thought to derive as much from the promise of sexual pleasure without reproductive consequences that castrati appeared to offer as from their astonishing vocal skill.[1] The castrato

---

[1]   For example, the relationship between Grand Prince Ferdinando de Medici and the castrato Domenico Cecchi ('Cecchino'). J. R. Hale, *Florence and the Medici: the Pattern of Control* (Plymouth, 1977), 187–192. Although the specialist literature on castrati is extensive, the social history of castrati in the British Isles is less well known beyond musicology. For authoritative works on the subject, see John Rosselli, 'The Castrati as a Professional Group and a Social Phenomenon, 1550–1850', *Acta Musicologica* 60 (1988), 143–79; Roger Freitas, 'The Eroticism of Emasculation: Confronting the Baroque Body of the Castrato', *Journal of Musicology* 20:2 (2003), 196–249; and a special edition dedicated to Farinelli (Carlo Broschi) of the *British Journal for Eighteenth-Century Studies* 28:3 (2005).

was also an extreme example of what the continental and 'Popish' fashion for Baroque art could produce, and shocked metropolitan consumers into reflecting upon whether the marketplace for entertainment (and, by extension, English society at large) had any moral limits in a rapidly changing world.

This chapter focuses upon the social milieu of opera singers and their wealthy patrons through a case study of one particular castrato, Giusto Ferdinando Tenducci. It proposes that as fashions in musical taste changed during the second half of the eighteenth century, the vogue for castrato voices was no longer confined to the upper end of the social and cultural spectrum. Tenducci was instrumental in the popularisation of opera sung in English for a wide middling-sort fan-base. As such, the commercialisation of the castrato's voice was of a piece with the wider socio-economic and cultural transformation of Britain in this period which has been delineated so insightfully in the work of Keith Wrightson. As Wrightson demonstrates, by the mid eighteenth century, an 'upward spiral of economic growth' was under way, witnessed in the expansion of new metropolitan markets and the swelling ranks of middling consumers, made up of families of independent means with prospects.[2] Armed with 'social capital' in the form of access to credit and networks of 'association, obligation and support', their status as respectable and prosperous citizens was enhanced by the new kinds of 'cultural capital' that London offered, and which fashionable urban centres throughout the British Isles were eager to emulate.[3] The middling sorts, as Wrightson reminds us, not only sought to 'ape' their social betters, however, but to establish a distinctive identity via their domestic consumption, leisure and sociability. They thus not only distanced themselves from their social inferiors, but forged 'the social capital of group membership and the cultural capital of public reputation'.[4]

In this context, one more new 'commodity' available to the middling sorts was the castrato. An exclusive Italian 'import', his commodification among bourgeois consumers would not have been possible without the exponential growth in the print trade – the production and widespread circulation of newspapers, periodicals, sheet music, even pin-up portraits – in the course of the eighteenth century. Through their command of enormous fees, mass-markets for their concerts and print controversies surrounding their talent and ambiguous sexual appeal, castrati became iconic symbols of the new demand for luxury, primarily in London, but increasingly in other urban centres across the British Isles. They provoked widespread discussions of the implications of socio-economic and cultural change, especially concerning

[2] Wrightson, *EN*, esp. ch. 13, quoting p. 6.
[3] *Ibid.*, 290–1, 298–300.
[4] *Ibid.*, 300.

the effects of market-driven profit motives upon human rights, consumer preferences and the economy of sex.

I

The London career of the castrato Giusto Ferdinando Tenducci provides a detailed insight into the transformation of castrato voices for mass consumption, the controversies that castrati provoked by their presence in England and the changing social attitudes towards foreign fashions in music and other forms of visual and performing arts in the second half of the eighteenth century. Born in Siena around 1735 to a family of humble origins, and schooled in one of the great Neapolitan musical conservatories, Tenducci first appears in the classified advertisements section of the London newspapers towards the end of 1758.[5] The *Public Advertiser* announced on 16 December that Signor Tenducci would appear in 'an Opera call'd Demetrio' at the King's Theatre in the Haymarket. The performance was also given the additional puff of social cachet in the advertisement with the suggestion that it was being staged 'by particular Desire of several Persons of Quality'.[6] By the end of his first season in June 1759 Tenducci had a growing fanbase among the English opera-going public. He had given fifty-five performances of five operatic works at the King's Theatre. During the summer of that same year, the *Whitehall Evening Post*, *London Evening Post* and *Public Advertiser* issued serial advertisements about the installation of the earl of Westmoreland as the new chancellor of Oxford University. For this prestigious social occasion, held at St Mary's, the University church, the vice-chancellor arranged for the entire 'Opera Band, Vocal and Instrumental' from the King's Theatre to be moved 'at prodigious expense' out of London so that they could perform their most recent London production with the original cast of singers and musicians in Oxford. The *London Chronicle* listed 101 persons of note in attendance, including dukes and duchesses, the lord mayor of London, courtiers and members of parliament, and 'a very splendid appearance of other gentry, too numerous to be here inserted'.[7]

In March 1760, a benefit concert was held for Tenducci at the King's Theatre, a mark of the esteem with which he was regarded by the company. Tenducci himself sold tickets from his own lodgings, which provided

---

5 Though he has an entry in *Grove's Dictionary of Music* and the *Oxford Dictionary of National Biography*, there is no extant biography of Tenducci besides a pen-portrait as one of the three Sienese opera stars profiled in Antonio Mazzeo, *I Tre 'Senesini' Musici ed Altri Cantanti Evirati Senesi* (Siena, 1996). For Tenducci's early life, see Helen Berry, *The Castrato and His Wife* (Oxford, 2011).
6 *Public Advertiser*, no. 7530 (16 December 1758).
7 *London Chronicle, or Universal Evening Post*, no. 398 (14 July 1759).

an important opportunity for the singer to meet useful patrons.[8] Tickets were also sold at the King's Theatre box office and were saved as souvenirs by Tenducci's growing number of fans. The newspaper advertisements for Tenducci's benefit concert promised in advance that the singer would perform three new songs, in appreciation of his supporters. This was an early example of the way in which rising stars of the London stage built their rapport with the English public by placing advertisements in the press, a practice which was relatively new, but at which Tenducci proved adept.

By the early 1760s, Tenducci had already built up a powerful patronage network and a degree of celebrity that was made possible via the flourishing print culture of eighteenth-century London.[9] His swift rise to fame was marked by his early successes at the King's Theatre and his immediate access to powerful patrons who saw him perform. Within the first decade after his arrival in London, Tenducci had sung at the four leading theatres in the capital: the King's Theatre, Haymarket; the Theatre Royal, Covent Garden; Drury Lane Theatre; and the Theatre Royal, Haymarket. Many of the other venues where he appeared in concert were within a one-mile radius of the Piazza in Covent Garden, where there was a cluster of theatres, concert halls and assembly rooms. Newspaper reports from the period contain over 300 advertisements for operas, concerts and other public entertainments featuring Tenducci by name, although the actual number of his performances was far greater, allowing for under-recording of repeat public performances and the unadvertised private engagements which he undertook in the course of his career as a singer and as a composer in his own right. Tenducci carried out a large number of charitable engagements in the form of benefit concerts for other singers and musicians, at venues such as the Hanover Square Concert Rooms, Hickford's Great Room in Brewer Street, the Great Room in Dean Street, Soho, and Pasquali's Rooms in the newly built Tottenham Court Road. He also performed sacred music in churches for commemorations, such as a special service held at the Lock Hospital Chapel and an event for the freemen of the City of London at Haberdashers' Hall, one of London's oldest and most prestigious guildhalls.[10]

During the 1760s and 1770s, Tenducci came to be associated with Ranelagh, a venue which proved critical to the commercialisation of his talent as a vocalist and composer. Located in Chelsea, Ranelagh was the

[8] *Public Advertiser*, no. 7870 (12 February 1760). On the history of benefit concerts, a customary means of raising money for singers of note, see Simon McVeigh, 'Introduction', in *Concert Life in Eighteenth-Century Britain*, ed. Susan Wollenberg and Simon McVeigh (Aldershot, 2004), 1–15, pp. 8–10

[9] Felicity Nussbaum, *Rival Queens: Actresses, Performance, and the Eighteenth-Century British Theatre* (Philadelphia, 2010), 13 and *passim*.

[10] See for example *Public Advertiser*, no. 8875 (13 April 1763), no. 9440 (2 February 1765) and no. 9448 (12 February 1765); *Morning Post*, no. 1728 (2 May 1778); *Gazetteer and London Daily Advertiser*, no. 15623 (10 March 1779).

more prestigious of London's two leading pleasure gardens (the other was south of the River Thames at Vauxhall). In 1742, Ranelagh had opened its famous Rotunda and Gardens with a celebratory public breakfast. The Rotunda was an extraordinary structure made entirely of wood and resembled a covered amphitheatre some 150 feet in diameter. Inside its cathedral-like interior, finely dressed men and women paraded, took tea and ate bread and butter and fancy cakes in one of fifty specially constructed booths. The whole edifice was illuminated with chandeliers, so that 'painting, carving, and gilding, enlightened with a thousand golden lamps that emulate the noonday sun' dazzled the assembled company.[11] It was in the magnificent Rotunda at Ranelagh that Tenducci sang popular songs in English, many of his own composition. These were expressive, sentimental ballads, competently set to music in a style suited to the taste of the day, telling stories of love lost and found. Songs written by Tenducci were composed and marketed via pleasure-garden performances and publication in popular songbooks available widely through the print shops in London and the provinces, aimed at a socially diverse audience of middling and elite pleasure-garden patrons. The lyrics were in English (rather than Italian), had a strong melodic line (they were 'catchy tunes'), adapted for domestic performance on keyboard and wind instruments that could be found in even middle-class homes and expressed universal sentiments of love and loss. 'Fair's my Lucy as the Day/ Brighter than the Glooming May' found its counterpart in another of his compositions, 'O Cruel Maid they scorn forbear/ Nor thus my tender bosom tear …'. John Johnson's shop opposite Bow Church in Cheapside stocked copies of the sheet music at 3s a time, a price well within the range of the polite middling sort of concert-goer, as well as the gentry. Once purchased and taken home, these songs could then be sung again at social gatherings in the privacy of polite drawing-rooms, accompanied by the harpsichord and bassoon or other instruments suitable for amateur domestic performance.[12] The *Public Advertiser* began serialising the words of Tenducci's songs 'to oblige our Readers and frequenters of Ranelagh'.[13] Meanwhile, the socially ambitious customer paying in cash for his silk waistcoats at Mr Lorrain's, a tailor's shop in the Strand, could finesse his fashionable gentility by picking up a copy of 'The favourite songs now sung at Ranelagh by Mr. Tenducci'.[14] The singer even made an appearance in Tobias Smollett's novel *Humphrey Clinker*, when the heroine Lydia Melford writes to a friend that she has fallen in love with the singer after hearing him 'warbling so divinely'

[11] The account of Ranelagh is taken from N. Wroth, *London Pleasure Gardens of the Eighteenth Century* (1896), 199–205.
[12] Bodleian Library, Oxford, Harding MUS. E474, 'Six New English Songs Composed by Ferdinando Tenducci and to be Sung by him at Ranelagh' (c.1763).
[13] *Public Advertiser*, no. 8910 (26 May 1763).
[14] *Ibid.*, no. 9198 (23 April 1764).

at Ranelagh.[15] Having an opinion about Italian music, if not actually attempting to perform it, came to be a mark of social aspiration. 'I think, we are a reasonable, but by no means a pleasurable People', mused the poet Thomas Gray on the subject of the English national character, '& to mend us we must have a Dash of the French, & Italian'.[16]

II

Tenducci proved adept at building socially diverse and numerous audiences for his musical talent, in socio-economic circumstances that were favourable to the commercial entertainment of which he was a pioneering example. From the late seventeenth century, acceleration in trade, imperial expansion and social migration, both within the British Isles and between Britain, Europe and the wider world, brought a cross-pollination of cultural influences, witnessed in the development of the African slave trade, the opening up of new markets through mercantilist colonial ambitions and London's emergent role as the world's leading entrepôt for luxury commodities.[17] The 'luxury debates' which attended the creation of a bourgeois consumer society were divided broadly between those who championed new capitalism and (to paraphrase Bernard Mandeville) the profits of greed, and the traditional interests of Christian moralists whose voices were raised against excessive material comfort and sensory pleasure.[18]

Commodification of the male body through the castration of barely pubescent boys was designed to produce an aural commodity that was at first only available to a highly restricted luxury market, a private pleasure reserved for the social elite. But in England, thanks to the efforts of theatre impresarios, concert organisers and some castrati themselves, performances by 'Italian singers' (as castrati were known euphemistically) had come within the reach of wider middle-class consumption. The German music connois-

---

[15] Tobias Smollett, *The Expedition of Humphrey Clinker* [1771], ed. Lewis M. Knapp (Oxford, 1966), 92.

[16] Thomas Gray to John Chute and Sir Horace Mann (?July 1742), *Correspondence of Thomas Gray*, ed. Paget Toynbee and Leonard Whibley, 3 vols (Oxford, 1935), I, 214. On the popularity of the Grand Tour and Italian culture in London, see Jason M. Kelly, *The Society of Dilettanti: Archaeology and Identity in the British Enlightenment* (New Haven, 2009); Jeremy Black, *The British Abroad: the Grand Tour in the Eighteenth Century* (1999).

[17] Wrightson, *EN*, 238–40 and *passim*.

[18] See *Luxury in the Eighteenth Century: Debates, Desires and Delectable Goods*, ed. Maxine Berg and Elizabeth Eger (Basingstoke, 2003), 7–27; John Sekora, *Luxury: The Concept in Western European Thought from Eden to Smollett* (Baltimore, 1977); Christopher Berry, *The Idea of Luxury: A Conceptual and Historical Investigation* (Cambridge, 1994); John Brewer, '"The Most Polite Age and the Most Vicious": Attitudes Towards Culture as a Commodity, 1660–1800', in *The Consumption of Culture 1600–1800: Image, Object, Text*, ed. Ann Bermingham and John Brewer (1995), 341–61.

seur Johann Mattheson noted in the early 1700s that 'he who in the present time want to make a profit out of music betakes himself to England. The Italians exalt music: the French enliven it; the Germans strive after it, the English pay for it well.'[19] London's rapid demographic expansion featured market processes of specialisation and diversification in the retail and leisure sectors of the capital. The chronological limit of Mattheson's survey was 1750, but the continuing effects of metropolitan development were plain for visitors to England to see from mid-century onwards. In 1758, the same year that Tenducci had his first English season, tax officials counted that there were 21,603 shops, warehouses and other retail outlets in the capital, selling foodstuffs and merchandise from all corners of the globe.[20] Since the Restoration, 200 different venues had opened in London for entertainment, ranging from theatres, fairground booths and music rooms to taverns and pleasure gardens.[21] Depending upon personal taste (that watch-word of the discerning Georgian consumer), it was possible to visit Don Saltero's coffee house in Chelsea or to inspect the collections of artefacts and curiosities at the British Museum, to see the galleries of the Royal Academy of Arts or to pay an admission fee to Bedlam Hospital to view the inmates.[22] Disposable income was necessary in order to participate in these various entertainments, and although many forms of paid entertainment were still beyond the reach of the majority of England's population,[23] the scale of the metropolitan consumer market for musical concerts was demonstrated in 1749 at the first performance of Handel's *Music for the Royal Fireworks*. Commissioned by George II to commemorate the Peace of Aix-la-Chapelle, the rehearsal alone attracted 12,000 ticket-buying spectators to Green Park, paying 2s 6d each.[24] In a wider European perspective, the phenomenon of mass ticket-paying audiences witnessed in Georgian London was unusual, since deliberate measures were taken elsewhere to preserve certain cultural

[19] Frederick C. Petty, *Italian Opera in London, 1760–1800*, Studies in Musicology 16 (Ann Arbor, 1972), 4.

[20] John Brewer, *The Pleasures of the Imagination: English Culture in the Eighteenth Century* (1997), xxvii and ch. 1, on the cultural diminution of the English court.

[21] Edward A. Langhans, 'The Theatres', in *The London Theatre World, 1660–1800*, ed. Robert D. Hume (Amsterdam, 1980), 35–65, p. 56

[22] Jeremy Black, *A Subject for Taste: Culture in Eighteenth-Century England* (2005), especially chs 1, 6 and 9.

[23] See for example, Ben Fine and Ellen Leopold, 'Consumerism and the Industrial Revolution', *SH* 15 (1990), 151–79; E. A. Wrigley, 'Urban Growth and Agricultural Change: England and the Continent in the Early Modern Period', in Wrigley, *People, Cities and Wealth: The Transformation of Traditional Society* (Oxford, 1987), 157–8 and *passim*. The complex debate over disposable incomes in this period is summarised in Hans-Joachim Voth, 'Living Standards and the Urban Environment', in *The Cambridge Economic History of Britain*, I: *Industrialisation, 1700–1860*, ed. Roderick Floud and Paul Johnson (Cambridge, 2004), 268–94.

[24] Brewer, *Pleasures of the Imagination*, 27.

activities such as opera-going as elite pleasures. In Dresden, for example, opera was funded under the patronage of the electors of Saxony, and there was an actual ban on payment for tickets.[25]

Curiosity, fear and prurient interest underpinned many of the fictional and anecdotal stories which circulated in private correspondence and in print about Italian castrati in London. While some English commentators greeted Italian singers with scorn and ridicule, others raved about their spectacular voices and their personal attributes. Samuel Pepys implied he was not like other people when he noted in his diary that he did not 'dote of the Eunuchs', although he later succumbed and engaged a castrato for a private concert.[26] John Evelyn went especially to a Catholic chapel in London to hear the castrato Siface sing, observing that there was 'much crowding, little devotion' in church that day.[27] The Whig informant Roger Morrice remarked in his 'entring book' for February 1687 that an unnamed 'Italian eunuch' (most probably Siface) had sung at Whitehall several times before the king, and that 'he is reported to sing better than any man that this century has produced'.[28]

In Hanoverian England, there was an enduring suspicion that Italian opera was a means for Romish priests to infiltrate the nation. The anonymous author of A Protestant Alarm (1733) urged the 'Nobility, Gentry and others whom it may concern' to take care that Handel and one of his leading stars, the castrato Senesino, were true Protestants, 'well affected to the present Government'. Since English audiences could not by and large understand the words of Italian operas, it was suspected that opera singers were hiding 'Jesuitical Quibbles, or other Papistical Legerdemain' among the words of the *libretti* sung in Italian. One solution, suggested the *Protestant Alarm*, could be for parliament to insist that people should not be allowed to sing 'in an unknown Tongue'. Since many of the leading castrati had risen to fame by singing in the pope's private chapel, it was even suggested that opera was an alternative way of celebrating the Catholic mass.[29] Though satirical in character, the fact that the popular literature of this period chose to focus upon Italian opera as a flashpoint for religious, political and social commentary is indicative of the wider awareness of this imported fashion

[25] Angus Heriot, *The Castrati in Opera* (1956), 58–61.

[26] John Evelyn recorded that 'Mr. Pepys' invited Siface to his house to perform to 'a select number of persons'. *Diary and Correspondence of John Evelyn* (19 April 1687), ed. William Bray (1827), 460.

[27] *Ibid.*, 457.

[28] *The Entring Book of Roger Morrice, 1677–1691*, I: *Roger Morrice and the Puritan Whigs*, ed. Mark Goldie (Woodbridge, 2007), 421.

[29] Anon., *Do You Know What You are About? Or, a Protestant Alarm to Great Britain: Proving Our Late Theatric Squabble, a Type of the Present Contest for the Crown of Poland; and that the Division between Handel and Senesino, has more in it than we imagine. Also, That the Latter is No Eunuch, but a Jesuit in Disguise; with Other Particulars of the Greatest Importance* (1733), 1–18.

beyond the social elite and the curiosity of the English towards this Baroque art form.

Remarkably similar anxieties were expressed about the public enthusiasm for other foreign fashions and imported luxuries at the time. As Adam Fox demonstrates in chapter 7 of this volume, consumption of exotic foodstuffs was one means by which the city elites distinguished themselves from the 'common people', especially those living outside of the metropolis. London consumers were eager to sample new exotic beverages in the first Restoration coffee houses, for example, but were mocked for being 'English apes', copying the manners of other countries and willingly adopting their dress, habits and (it seemed to some) morals for the sake of novelty. 'Like Apes, the English imitate all other people in their ridiculous Fashions', observed the author of A Character of Coffee and Coffee-Houses in 1661. Just as coffee was becoming the preferred social lubricant of city merchants and news-readers, some self-styled virtuosi wanted to associate themselves with the Italian idea of expertise and connoisseurship. Other English commentators, however, criticised the fact that their fellow-countrymen seemed perilously receptive to all manner of foreign influences. If the fashion in Paris were for pantaloons, it was said, 'the English-man will be à la mode de France. With the Barbarous Indian he smoaks Tobacco. With the Turk he drinks coffee.'[30] This opinion would have found sympathy from the author who railed against the 'amazing depravity of taste' among his countrymen for elevating castrati to the status of 'Grand Seignors', like the rulers of the Ottoman Empire, for 'it is not possible to conceive a more nauseous and odious creature than a Castrato'.[31]

With music, as in other forms of consumption, English audiences seemed to be able to hold the contradictions in tension, both despising all things foreign, especially 'Popish', while simultaneously enjoying the exoticism of imported style.[32] Henry Purcell composed Baroque musical odes which were performed at the court of William and Mary, which celebrated the saints (such as Cecilia, the patron saint of music) beloved of the nation's Catholic enemies. Sir Christopher Wren's construction of the new St Paul's Cathedral as England's most stunningly Baroque building raised concerns among some Anglican clergy. The purchase of paintings to add to the interior was later rejected (perhaps rather belatedly, given the surroundings) as overly 'Popish'.[33] While many English authors despised the Baroque style for

---

[30] 'M. P.', A Character of Coffee and Coffee-Houses (1661), 1.

[31] Anon., Queen of Quavers, 8.

[32] This ambivalence towards, for example, French Catholicism, whilst revelling in French taste, is explored in Robin Eagles, Francophilia in English Society, 1748–1815 (Basingstoke, 2000), which nuances the analysis of xenophobia and anti-French sentiment presented in Linda Colley, Britons: Forging the Nation, 1707–1837 (New Haven, 1992).

[33] Clare Haynes, Pictures and Popery: Art and Religion in England, 1660–1760 (Aldershot, 2006), 13.

embodying all that was idolatrous and absolutist, there was also the sense that historically, when it came to art and music, Catholicism was the 'parent of taste'.[34] Part of the pleasure evoked by Italian castrati, the stars of the London opera houses, was therefore not only their vocal ability and the macabre novelty factor of their predicament as castrated men, but also their dangerous connotations of Popish decadence and crypto-Catholicism.

It was the composer Handel who, as a German Protestant loyal to the Hanoverian regime, made Italian opera acceptable to elite English audiences.[35] London's Royal Academy of Music had been founded in 1719 under the patronage of George I, who gave £1,000 towards the cost of setting up the academy specifically to promote opera under the directorship of the lord chamberlain.[36] The opera produced by the Royal Academy, with Handel as its musical director, included successful productions which became the height of fashion among the *beau monde*, although the expense of staging them meant that they seldom made a profit.[37] By mid-century, Thomas Gray reflected that opera had been supported in England 'at a great expence for so many years ... by the admiration besto'd on a few particular voices, or the borrow'd taste of a few Men of condition'. The gentry and aristocracy who had the opportunity to go on the Grand Tour 'learn'd in Italy how to admire', but he believed that their patronage of opera was inspired more by the cachet of being associated with all things Italian rather than 'any genuine love we bear to the best Italian musick'. [38] Gray attributed the lack of development of English opera 'in great measure to the language', since although 'I by no means wish to have been born any thing but an Englishman; yet I should rejoice to exchange tongues with Italy'.[39] He recorded how he had observed first-hand the hostility of the English public beyond the rarefied world of the 'better sort' towards foreign performers and imported music, such that he had witnessed riots in the common theatres during Italian *Buffo* comic performances ('I have known candles lighted, broken bottles and penknives thrown on the stage, the benches torn up, the scenes hurried into the street & set on fire, the curtain drew [drawn] up ...').[40]

But it was Tenducci, in collaboration with the English composer Thomas

[34] Colin Haydon, *Anti-Catholicism in Eighteenth-Century England, c.1714–1780* (Manchester, 1998), 102.
[35] Patrick Barbier, *The World of the Castrato: the History of an Extraordinary Operatic Phenomenon*, trans. Margaret Crosland (1997), 182; *Handel: A Celebration of His Life and Times, 1685–1759*, ed. Joseph Simon (1985), 14–16.
[36] Brewer, *Pleasures of the Imagination*, 364.
[37] Lowell Lindgren, 'The Staging of Handel's Operas in London', in *Handel Tercentenary Collection*, ed. Stanley Sadie and Anthony Hicks, Royal Musical Association (Basingstoke, 1987), 93–117.
[38] Thomas Gray to Conte Francesco Algarotti (9 September 1763), in *Correspondence of Thomas Gray*, ed. Toynbee and Whibley, II, 809.
[39] *Ibid.*
[40] *Ibid.*

Arne, who succeeded in making opera accessible to the middling sorts. Handel's death in 1759 ushered in new opportunities for the next genera-tion of composers and vocalists. In 1762, Tenducci appeared as the hero Arbaces in Arne's opera *Artaxerxes*. The production was highly experi-mental, since it was the first all-sung opera in English. The plot, like so many eighteenth-century operas, was extremely convoluted and explored questions of honour, duty and sacrifice, played out by royalty and with reso-nances for contemporary politics among the dynastic struggles that were then taking place between and within the great European royal houses.[41] Tenducci, as Arbaces, played the part of a young man fighting to clear his name when faced with a murder accusation and to win the hand of his sweetheart Mandane. *Artaxerxes* proved an instant success, with which Tenducci became forever associated. His rendition of the aria 'Water Parted from the Sea' was a lament which found universal appeal in its expression of sentimental longing for home.

Successful arias such as these found a market beyond those who could afford expensive tickets and subscriptions to opera performances, since the music and lyrics were quickly printed in bulk and sold in shops, simpli-fied for performances in domestic salons and tavern singing-clubs.[42] In John Johnson's shop in Cheapside, for example, a popular songbook of arias from *Artaxerxes* was advertised alongside works by Haydn and Purcell, transposed for amateur performance.[43] The degree of popular celebrity which Tenducci came to enjoy as a result of the widespread popularisation of his aria in *Artaxerxes* is reflected by one contemporary's recollection that in Dublin every barrow-boy at this time was said to be humming 'Water parted from the *Say*'.[44] Well into the nineteenth century, Arne's aria popularised by Tenducci became a favourite drawing-room piece for domestic performance; Jane Austen confessed she had grown tired of *Artaxerxes* because she had heard it so many times.[45] Via the pleasure gardens and print shops, Tenduc-ci's music reached wider audiences than would have been possible in the opera house alone, so that like other popular musicians and artists of the day he eventually became a celebrity pin-up, his portrait engraved and sold as a single sheet for his fans to display in their homes (see illustration 3.1).

[41] On the history of *opera seria* (opera with a serious or tragic rather than comic theme) see *The Cambridge Companion to Eighteenth-Century Opera*, ed. Anthony R. DelDonna and Pierpaolo Polzonetti (Cambridge, 2009).

[42] For recent studies of music and English culture before 1800, see Brian Robins, *Catch and Glee Culture in Eighteenth-Century England* (Woodbridge, 2006); Peter Borsay, 'Sounding the Town', *Urban History* 29 (2002), 92–102; Christopher Marsh, *Music and Society in Early Modern England* (Cambridge, 2010); T. C. W. Blanning, *The Triumph of Music: Composers, Musicians and their Audiences from 1700 to the Present* (2008).

[43] Preface to *Six New English Songs Composed by Ferdinando Tenducci* (1763) [n. p.]

[44] John Kay, *A Series of Original Portraits and Character Etchings*, II (Edinburgh, 2007).

[45] Todd Gilman, 'Arne, Handel, the Beautiful and the Sublime', *Eighteenth-Century Studies* 42 (2009), 529–55, p. 530.

3.1. A broadsheet pin-up of Tenducci holding a copy of the musical score to 'Water Parted from the Sea', the famous aria by Thomas Arne from the opera *Artaxerxes* (1762). Painting by J. Bruscetti (c.1770)

The old suspicions that Italian opera was a mask for crypto-Catholicism were confounded when people could understand and be moved by the simple, pastoral sentiments of Tenducci's most famous arias and his own compositions in English. Tenducci was therefore one of the leading agents in the transformation of the form of Italian opera in a process of Anglicisation that took it beyond being only an elite leisure activity to make it also a popular money-making entertainment accessible to the middling sorts. Tenducci and Arne engaged in the commercialisation of the castrato by appealing to a wide social range of people in London and across the British Isles via the mass circulation of newsprint and sheet music. They were also skilled in capitalising upon one of the most distinctive features of the castrato's marketability in the new cultural marketplace of eighteenth-century Britain: his appeal to female consumers.

III

Castrati were insultingly and routinely described as 'neuter', or 'things', unsexed and essentially unappealing, a living testimony to the horrors inflicted upon man by his fellow man in the name of luxury and art. For all her admiration of his singing, Lydia Melford, Smollett's fictional heroine in *Humphrey Clinker*, described Tenducci as 'a thing from Italy – It looks for all the world like a man, though they say it is not.'[46] But there is much evidence that, as well as the aesthetic pleasure bestowed by hearing them sing, these neutered men had, for many people, a powerful erotic appeal. There seems to have been no sense in which English audiences found the casting of castrati as male romantic leads to have been problematic, even though they were often mocked for their physical status as 'capons', 'geldings' or other kinds of castrated animals.[47] Castrati, with their boyishly smooth faces, statuesque height and exquisite voices, were thought by many at the time to be highly desirable and convincing love-objects. The ambivalence which their voices aroused – desire, without the promise of consummation – was expressed by Lydia Melford, for whom Tenducci's voice 'to be sure, is neither man's nor woman's: but it is more melodious than either ... while I listened, I really thought myself in paradise'.[48]

Though their castration was thought to have rendered castrati 'colder' and more effeminate than other men (an idea which in modern times became stereotypically associated with homosexuality), according to early modern ideas effeminacy in a man was actually a sign of being deeply attracted to

---

46 Smollett, *Humphrey Clinker*, 92.
47 See Martha Feldman, 'Strange Births and Surprising Kin: the Castrato's Tale', in *Italy's Eighteenth Century: Gender and Culture in the Age of the Grand Tour*, ed. Paula Findlen, Wendy Wassyng Roworth and Catherine M. Sama (Paolo Alto, 2009), 176–85.
48 Smollett, *Humphrey Clinker*, 92.

women. The caricature of the fop, as Philip Carter has argued, was of a man of fashion in thrall to Italian luxuries who became effeminate rather because he loved women too much than because he eschewed them altogether.[49] In many respects castrati matched the aesthetics of an idealised form of male beauty beloved by eighteenth-century Europeans, and they were convincingly staged, to contemporary audiences, as romantic, lustily hetero-sexual heroes. Women were thought to be more responsive and attracted to men who displayed signs of effeminacy, although their actual views on the subject usually went undocumented for reasons of propriety. Women's responses to castrati must have been as variable as they were numerous. One rare appreciation of the fashionable ideals of male beauty written by a woman is among the *Letters from Italy* (1776) by Lady Anna Miller. Lady Anna recorded her damning verdict upon the famously muscular statue of the Farnese Hercules: 'if all mankind were so proportioned, I should think them very disagreeable and odious'. By contrast, she was drawn to the lithe and youthful statue of the Apollo Belvidere, which epitomised the contem-porary ideal of male beauty, exuding 'angelic sweetness'.[50] In this era, being tall was associated with male authority, a remnant of the time when martial valour was a test of aristocratic male virtue and virility.[51] The castrato's body was therefore something of a paradox. In some respects, men like Tenducci conformed to idealised notions of male beauty and bearing at the time, but other aspects of their physiology inevitably meant that they became cruel targets for comments inspired by the spectre of castration.

Critics did not have to look far for further evidence that castrati were highly effeminate, almost-women, since their roles on stage were often interchangeable with female sopranos who took 'breeches parts'. In certain circumstances, gender roles could be reversed, with female sopranos playing male leads or castrati playing female parts, but this tended to be only [?] if there were no other options available. As manager of the King's Theatre, Giardini's instructions to Leone, his agent in Italy during the 1760s, were to hire either 'a Woman of a good figure' who could 'occasionally perform in Mens Cloaths' or 'a young Castrato with a good voice' who could sing both male and female parts.[52] Another illustration of this was the shared arias in the repertoires of Tenducci and a leading female soprano, Charlotte Brent, mistress and muse to the composer Thomas Arne. In 1762, the words set to a 'Scotch air' in the overture to *Thomas and Sally*, a successful pastoral

---

[49] Philip Carter, *Manhood and the Emergence of Polite Society, Britain 1660–1800* (2001).
[50] See Roger Frietas, 'Sex without Sex: an Erotic Image of the Castrato Singer', in *Italy's Eighteenth Century*, ed. Findlen *et al.*, 203–15, p. 209.
[51] Keith Thomas, *The Ends of Life: Roads to Fulfilment in Early Modern England* (Oxford, 2008), 44–77.
[52] Curtis Price, Judith Milhouse and Robert D. Hume, *The Impresario's Ten Commandments. Continental Recruitment for Italian Opera in London, 1763–64*, Royal Musical Association Monographs 6 (1992), 10.

opera composed by Arne, were sung in Italian by Tenducci at Ranelagh and in the same season at Vauxhall Gardens in English by 'Miss Brent'.[53] Each, however, sang different lyrics to the same melody. Tenducci's was a general paean of praise to love, sung in Italian, in terms that would have been appropriate for any male singer (though few in the audience would have been able to translate his high-minded sentiments). Charlotte Brent meanwhile sang the same air in the part of an innocent country girl, Sally, fending off an over-lusty suitor. Given that Charlotte Brent's lyrics were in keeping with the plot of *Thomas and Sally*, it suggests that the libretto was reworked specifically to make it more suitable for Tenducci to sing as a male vocalist. Tenducci did once sing a 'female' role: that of Mary, Queen of Scots, although in the course of his entire thirty-year career, this was exceptional.[54] Another leading female soprano, Mrs Mattocks, sang the 'breeches' part in Tenducci's most famous role, Arbaces in *Artaxerxes*, inviting critical comparison between her interpretation and Tenducci's.[55] This could work both ways: Tenducci sang a male part in Bath, that of Alphonso in Samuel Arnold's *Castle of Andalusia*, which the press referred to as 'Mrs Kennedy's Part'.[56] At the centre of fashionable eighteenth-century culture there was therefore a close professional connection between castrati like Tenducci and the leading female vocalists of the day. Though some castrati were known for performing women's roles on stage, Tenducci's preference in the vast majority of his career was for playing romantically doomed classical heroes, such as Orpheus, and legendary men, including Montezuma, King of the Aztecs.[57]

The vogue for castrati among female consumers was of a piece with the new leisure culture that began to flourish in London and provincial towns throughout the British Isles. In provincial England, as Naomi Tadmor has observed in her contribution to this volume, women often had limited access to the 'circuits of male sociability' which were conduits of local power and authority. In the metropolis, social networking, and the gendering of political affiliations, was more complicated. As a detailed study of actresses and the 'economy of celebrity' in the London theatre world by Felicity Nussbaum has recently shown, women were a visible – and vocal – presence on stage and among theatre and concert audiences throughout the

[53] *The Winter's Amusement, Consisting of Favourite Songs and Cantatas … The Whole Composed by Thomas Arne* (n.d. [1762?]). A rare copy of this collection of songs is in the Beinecke Library, Yale University.

[54] Anon., *Queen Mary's Lamentation, As Sung by Mr. Tenducci at the Pantheon, London* (Dublin, n.d. [1773?]).

[55] *Morning Chronicle*, no. 1505 (21 March 1774).

[56] *Public Advertiser*, no. 15453 (6 December 1783).

[57] *Gazetta Toscana*, no. 6 (February 1772), reported Tenducci's recent triumph playing the role of 'Motezuma [sic], Emperor of the Aztecs' at the Teatro di Roma.

Georgian period.[58] Leading actresses like George Anne Bellamy, the mistress of Charles James Fox, effectively orchestrated seating arrangements so that men seeking patronage received privileged access to the king's minister, and she pocketed the resulting profits.[59]

The importance of opera performances as an opportunity for elite women to meet one another and exchange news and the overlap between musical events and other types of female cultural production are evident in a letter from Susanna Phillips, née Burney, to her sister Fanny. Susanna reported how Fanny's new novel, Cecilia, had been received: 'though your praises were not sung at the opera on Sat[urda]y night, I heard nothing [else] talked of'. She heard this first from a visit to 'the Eldest Miss Bull, who has a delightful Box on the ground floor just over the Orchestra', then from Lady Mary Duncan, who said 'she was sure you'd never have acquired so much knowledge of the world', and then finally 'After this I made a Visit to the other Miss Brett who was in Lady Clarges' Box.'[60] Though they were somewhat atypical, coming from an exceptionally musical and literary family, the Burney women were keen documenters of the wider social and sexual mores of London society and showed how connoisseurship of opera could be a mark of good taste for others of their own rank and sex, albeit with bluestocking inclinations. The castrato Pacchierotti, the darling of aristocratic women, was 'immensely wealthy' by the 1780s and retired on the proceeds of their donations.[61]

Contemporary evidence suggests that the popularity of castrati owed much to their appeal among women, to which there was a romantic, if not explicitly erotic, dimension. Earlier in the century, an Englishwoman had notoriously shouted from the audience during an operatic production by the greatest castrato of them all 'One God, one Farinelli!', at a stroke breaking the taboo of a woman raising her voice in public, blaspheming and making a spectacle of her desire, in a manner which would have been inconceivable were the object of her devotion a 'normal' man (that is, unless she was a courtesan or actress with no respectable reputation to lose).[62] In this respect, the 'unnatural' castrato was thought to provoke 'unnatural' behaviour in women. There are distinct lesbian overtones in John Dryden's verdict upon women who found castrati erotic: 'There are those in soft eunuchs place their bliss/ And shun the scrubbing of a bearded kiss.' Women who found 'softness' appealing in castrati were perversely giving up their devotion to men and the special form of bristling masculinity that they should have

---

[58] Nussbaum, Rival Queens, ch. 1 and passim.

[59] Ibid., 54.

[60] British Library, Egerton MS 3690, fol. 18r (Susanna Burney to Fanny Burney, 6 November 1782).

[61] Michael Kelly, Reminiscences of Michael Kelly of the King's Theatre and Theatre Royal Drury Lane, 2nd edn, 2 vols (1826), I, 105

[62] Barbier, World of the Castrato, 183

prized as the most virile and desirable. Simultaneously, of course, Dryden also playfully acknowledged the appealing sensuality of castrati compared to the brutishness of other members of his own sex.[63]

Though such poetic musings evidently provided the cultural commentary which framed people's reactions to castrati, this was more than just a literary conceit. When it came to castrati, respectable women could 'play the field', displaying their affections publicly and going from one castrato to another at their pleasure. Unlike common prostitutes, however, their virtue remained intact owing to the apparently undisputed sexual incapacity of their chosen love-objects. In heterosexual terms, castrati were as appealing, and as dangerous, as life-size dolls, colourfully presented and flamboyant, safe for women to dress up, buy presents for and play with, but pass over according to their whim. Like the giant Brobdingnag 'Maids of Honour' in *Gulliver's Travels*, who held the doll-like tiny Gulliver to their oversized bosoms, castrati were the ultimate in a rich woman's toy box, little better than a lap-dog to be cosseted and lavished with gifts without fear of jeopardising their reputations.[64] This dynamic produced sentimental love-relationships akin to romantic friendships between women, of a kind which were especially fashionable in eighteenth-century literary circles. 'I dare say we remember one another daily (I'm sure I do *you*)', wrote the blue-stocking Catherine Talbot to Elizabeth Carter. Likewise, the 'Queen of the Blues', Elizabeth Montagu, pined at separation from her friend: 'how can my grief be childish when it is all that is not childish in me that weeps for the absence of Miss Carter!'[65]

Some castrati, like Pacchierotti, evidently reciprocated the adoration of their female admirers, and became embroiled in love affairs expressed through correspondence which was framed in similarly heightened and passionate language, which owed much to the conventions of the newly invented epistolary novel. Susanna Burney recorded her great joy at hearing Pacchierotti's carriage arrive outside of her father's house: 'Lord – I was so glad!' she enthused in her private letter-book.[66] On another occasion, she told the singer, 'You spoil me when you sing, Signor Pacchierotti, for everything else – before you begin I am occupied by thoughts of the pleasure I have to come, and after you sing everything is flat and insipid.' Pacchierotti replied in similar vein, telling Susanna with tear-filled eyes that 'I ought not to come too often because it makes it harder for me to leave you – Indeed I know it.'[67] However, society expected that friendship between a virgin girl and a castrato, like that between romantic friends of the same sex, would

---

[63] John Dryden, *Poems of John Dryden*, ed. J. Kinsley (Oxford, 1958), II, 708.

[64] Jonathan Swift, *Gulliver's Travels* (1726), ed. Paul Turner (Oxford, 1986), 106–7.

[65] Quoted in Susan B. Lanser, 'Bluestocking Sapphism and the Economies of Desire', *Huntington Library Quarterly* 65 (2002), 257–75, pp. 267, 271.

[66] Kelly, *Susanna, the Captain and the Castrato*, 103–10 and *passim*.

[67] Ibid., 71, 77, 102.

be no more than a testing ground for harmless expressions of heterosexual attraction that would be superseded when a suitable marriage partner came along.[68]

IV

Tenducci's rumoured relationships with women provoked reflections on the shifting dynamics of relations between 'normal' men and women under pressure from changing market conditions.[69] In real life, Tenducci's actual elopement in the summer of 1766 with Dorothea Maunsell, the daughter of an Irish barrister, was widely regarded as folly, although (unlike in his native Italy) it was not actually illegal for a castrato to marry under English law.[70] The test case that resulted from Dorothea's subsequent petition for the marriage to be annulled in the London Consistory Court provided the only explicit ruling on the castrato's presumed inability to consummate a marriage, which by legal definition had to entail insemination – the potential for the act to lead to pregnancy – as well as sexual intercourse.[71] Though some castrati may have been capable of penetrative sex, they were by definition incapable of fathering children. The Tenducci marriage was eventually annulled. Dorothea's second marriage was formally legitimised, as was at least one child to whom she had already given birth whose father was William Kingsman, the man she subsequently married.[72]

Dorothea Maunsell went further than her peers in actually eloping with a castrato, but she was not alone in finding them attractive. In the generation after Tenducci, Rauzzini, 'a beautiful, animated, young man, with a sweet, clear, and flexible voice', was beloved of Louisa Harris, a well-born young woman, who wrote him love-letters until she transferred her loyalty

---

[68] See Ruth Perry, *Novel Relations: the Transformation of Kinship in English Literature and Culture, 1748–1818* (Cambridge, 2004), chs 1 and 6.

[69] For a full account of Tenducci's elopement with Dorothea Maunsell see Berry, *Castrato and his Wife*. On the pressures of commercialisation and competition upon the family, see Keith Wrightson, 'Mutualities and Obligations: Changing Social Relationships in Early Modern England', *Proceedings of the British Academy* 139 (2006), 157–94, pp. 180–1.

[70] For Dorothea's supposed version of events, see *A True and Genuine Narrative of Mr and Mrs Tenducci in a Letter to a Friend at Bath, Giving a Full Account, from their Marriage in Ireland to the Present Time* (1768).

[71] Helen Berry and Elizabeth Foyster, 'Childless Men in Early Modern England', in *The Family in Early Modern England*, ed. Helen Berry and Elizabeth Foyster (Cambridge, 2007), 158–74.

[72] The original court records for the London Consistory Court in the case of 'Kingsman, falsely called Tenducci v. Tenducci' are in the L[ondon] M[etropolitan] A[rchives], DL/C/557/102/Exhibits, depositions and interrogations, 1775–76; DL/C/558/20–21 Sayings and depositions, 1775–76; DL/C/639/Deposition book, 1772–77; and DL/C/177/ Allegations, Libels and Sentence Book, 1772–77.

to another castrato. Miss Harris, observed Lady Clarges over tea with Lady Hales, 'is now quite *Notorious* with Pacchierotti ... first with Rauzzini – then Pacchierotti – it's really being what I call quite common'.[73] Some eighteenth-century women, like Louisa Harris and Dorothea Maunsell (who was able to remarry another man of her choice who could father children), took the opportunity to express desire and affection for a male love-object in a castrato, finding a 'loophole' that could provide an escape from the sexual double standard.[74]

Castrati like Tenducci inevitably inspired debates about sex and gender in public commentaries and in their private lives. Unlike previous generations, where some castrati were associated with homosexual relationships among the European social elite of cardinals and royalty, the stereotyping of the castrato in England during the eighteenth century centred upon his heterosexual appeal to a wider audience of female fans, as well as to men who may or may not have found castrati erotically appealing. Many women admired castrati on stage but never met them in person; their admiration was based upon their appreciation of these singers' talent. Many eighteenth-century Englishmen were nonetheless vexed that Italian castrati inspired droves of women, if not to fall in love with them, then at least to express more than cerebral pleasure at hearing them sing. When the subject of castrati came up in conversation, a certain Mr Blakeney, an acquaintance of Fanny Burney, recalled, 'Why now, there was one of these fellows at Bath last season, a Mr. Rozzini [Rauzzini] – I vow I longed to cane him every day! Such a work made with him! All the *fair females* sighing for him! Enough to make a man sick!'[75] The vitriol that some male authors heaped upon castrati was a mocking check upon the spectacle of such public expressions of female devotion. One satirist lampooned Frances Brooke, the female manager of one of the prime London venues for Italian opera, the King's Theatre, Haymarket, as the 'Queen of Quavers' for promoting uncontrolled 'quavering' – that is, an intoxicating and unaccountable love of Italian opera.[76] The nub of these anonymous male authors' complaint was that castrato singers 'can command our most enchanting females, especially those that are not yet initiated into the mysteries of the *naked truth*'.[77] In *The Ladies Lamentation for the Loss*

73 Kelly, *Susanna, the Captain and the Castrato*, 78.
74 Keith Thomas, 'The Double Standard', *Journal of the History of Ideas* 20 (1959), 195–216; see also Bernard Capp, 'The Double Standard Revisited: Plebeian Women and Male Sexual Reputation in Early Modern England', *P&P* 162 (1999), 70–100.
75 *The Early Diary of Frances Burney, 1768–1778*, ed. Annie Raine Ellis (1907), II, 122–3.
76 Ian Woodfield, *Opera and Drama in Eighteenth-Century London: The King's Theatre, Garrick, and the Business of Performance* (Cambridge, 2001), 171–2.
77 'J. Democritus' and 'W. Diogenes' [Anon.], *The Remarkable Trial of the Queen of Quavers and Her Associates for Sorcery, Witchcraft and Enchantment at the Assizes held in the Moon, for the County of Gelding before the Rt. Hon. Sir Francis Lash, Lord Chief Baron of the Lunar Exchequer* (1777/78?), 7.

of Senesino (1735) an anonymous male author lampooned the grief of the castrato's female fans at the singer's departure from England for the Continent, nobles bowing before him, ladies weeping and trying to make him stay, with servants following and carrying hand-barrows loaded with 'Ready Money', the profits of his talent. As one female fan, a 'beautiful Creature', laments his loss, she admits her love is hopeless: 'Tis neither for Man, nor for Woman' that she is crying; her 'sweet Darling of fame', Senesino, 'Is a Shadow of something, a Sex without Name'.[78]

In relation to the potential for disruption to the gendered ordering of society, it was just a short step in the chain of responses from rendering a castrato from a monster into a commodity, a less-than-human *thing*; being 'neither man nor woman', he was something 'betwixt the human species and the brute creation, like a monkey, and may be properly termed an outlaw of nature'.[79] Castrati were likened by some commentators to 'exotick animals', which for eighteenth-century Londoners would have recalled the imported wild beasts caged in the menageries at St James's Park and the Tower of London, which visitors paid to gawp at as part of the regular tourist trail for foreigners and provincial visitors to the capital.[80] But, unlike other imported luxury commodities – from exotic beasts to porcelain cups – the castrato was human and had emotional, perhaps even sexual, needs of his own. As the second half of the eighteenth century progressed, there arose a new enthusiasm for moral campaigns against the human suffering and the effective commodification of human cargo. Castrati, like African slaves on sugar plantations, suffered bodily harm to satisfy the luxurious tastes of the affluent. It is no coincidence that increasingly public expressions of disgust at the fashion for castrato voices coincided with the rise of abolitionism as a serious political movement.[81]

Fashions changed rapidly in the political climate of the 1770s. Britain made significant gains as an imperial power as a result of the Seven Years War (1756–63), but already faced rebellion in the American colonies.[82] Foreign influences and luxury imports were indicted with increasing regularity in the press for threatening British morals. The *Morning Post* opined

---

[78] Anon., *The Ladies Lamentation for the Loss of Senesino* (1735) [quoting the printed verse at the foot of the cartoon].

[79] Anon., *Trial of the Queen of Quavers*, 9.

[80] Woodfield, *Opera and Drama*, 172.

[81] For an introduction to the extensive literature on this subject, see *Gender and Slave Emancipation in the Atlantic World*, ed. Pamela Scully and Diana Paton (Durham NC, 2005).

[82] On related themes, see Kathleen Wilson, *The Island Race: Englishness, Empire and Gender in the Eighteenth Century* (2003); Michèle Cohen, 'Manliness, Effeminacy and the French: Gender and the Construction of National Character in Eighteenth-Century England', in *English Masculinities, 1660–1800*, ed. Tim Hitchcock and Michèle Cohen (Basingstoke, 1999), 44–61.

that English singers were superior to Italian ones since they had 'derived their musical education from the principles of nature, and reason', a sentiment which chimed with emerging Enlightenment principles.[83] In February 1777, Tenducci was criticised for incurring 'ruinous expence' upon the Drury Lane Theatre owing to the fact that he was 'suddenly seized with a hoarseness, which injuring the *emasculate* delicacy of his voice, an apology was obliged to be made to the audience'. The editorial concluded that the episode was 'proof [of] how little this very expensive train of foreigners are considered by an English audience, as an *essential* part of their entertainment'.[84] Another critic, writing under the influence of the leading Enlightenment philosopher Jean-Jacques Rousseau, dismissed Tenducci's talent, since it was tainted by being contrary to nature:

> Rousseau affirms, that singing does not appear natural to man; for though the savages of America sing, because they talk, yet the true savage never sings; *ergo* castration was invented, and Tenducci is ... a fresh wonder ... Heavens preserve any man from such natural notes! He neither sings in tune, nor with any new cantabile.[85]

For some critics, castrati continued to represent the kind of absolutist political system and high Baroque fashion that was becoming increasingly outdated in an era when radical ideas circulated among intellectual circles. Among society at large, the appeal in the press to the wider public of middling concert-goers and amateur musicians in promoting home-grown British talent was an equally forceful rationale for eschewing the castrato and his outmoded glamour. During the last quarter of the eighteenth century, Enlightenment critics defended nature against the deforming influences of human excesses, including the production of 'chirruping' castrati.[86]

Tenducci himself had shown his ability to adapt with the times, changing his repertoire in the 1770s and 1780s to include Scottish ballads that suited the supposedly simpler tastes of the age. He was a victim more of his own profligacy than of public rejection, however: the circle of his creditors closed in upon him during the spring of 1788.[87] Though his talent had regularly brought riches, as with many celebrated performers of the day, it appears he

---

[83] *Morning Post*, no. 1353 (20 February 1777).

[84] *Gazetteer and London Daily Advertiser*, no. 14985 (5 March 1777).

[85] *Ibid.* See also Jean-Jacques Rousseau, *Appendix to Grassineaus's Musical Dictionary, Selected from the* Dictionnaire de Musique *of J. J. Rousseau* (1769), which quotes in English the origins of Rousseau's idea that 'Singing does not appear to be natural to man, for tho' the savages of America sing, because they talk, the true savage never sings', 41.

[86] Martha Feldman, 'Denaturing the Castrato', *Opera Quarterly* 24 (19??), 178–99.

[87] An advertisement for the auction of his personal effects appeared in the *Morning Post*, no. 4706 (17 April, 1788).

never fully escaped the threat of bankruptcy. He fled to Italy, where he died having taken refuge in the household of a Genoese nobleman, in January 1790.[88]

V

The social and cultural history of castrati in eighteenth-century London provides the opportunity for new insights into the intersections between the history of consumption and consumer behaviour that have come to the fore in studies of this period since the mid 1990s and into the history of gender and sexuality, which has also received much attention from historians during the past two decades.[89] Masculinity has come to be problematised and scrutinised as part of the wider remit to consider the dynamics of gender history, rather than conflating 'gender' and 'women' as categories of historical analysis.[90] The history of body modification, like the history of disability, offers new insights into diverse subjectivities and the wider social and cultural responses against which normative standards of gender were measured.[91]

The presence of Italian castrati in eighteenth-century London forced the British to confront a range of disturbing possibilities. One was to consider the implications of a rising number of female consumers who endorsed a new marketplace for sexual pleasure without reproductive consequences. The commercialisation of castrati as love-objects offered at least a theoretical alternative to the obligations of patriarchal marriage and childbearing, contemplation of which alone was sufficient to provoke widespread critical comment. As with African slaves, when it came to castrati Christian moralists and Enlightenment thinkers raised voices of concern over the brutal

---

[88] Previously unknown details of his final years are in Berry, *Castrato and his Wife*, ch. 9.

[89] For a summary of the extensive literature and key debates on eighteenth-century consumption, see Sara Pennell, 'Consumption and Consumerism in Early Modern England', *HJ* 42 (1999), 549–64; more recently, Jan de Vries, *The Industrious Revolution: Consumer Behaviour and the Household Economy, 1650 to the Present* (Cambridge, 2008). Further examples of studies at the nexus between consumption and gender are Karen Harvey, 'Men Making Home: Masculinity and Domesticity in Eighteenth-Century England', *Gender & History* 21 (2009), 520–40; Margot Finn, 'Men's Things: Masculine Possession in the Consumer Revolution', *SH* 26 (2000), 133–56; Amanda Vickery, *Behind Closed Door: At Home in Georgian England* (New Haven, 2010).

[90] See Karen Harvey and Alexandra Shepard, 'What Have Historians Done with Masculinity? Reflections on Five Centuries of British History, circa 1500–1950', *JBS* 44 (2005), 274–80.

[91] For other examples of this approach, see Naomi Baker, *Plain Ugly: The Unattractive Body in Early Modern Culture* (Manchester, 2010); Helen Deutsch and Felicity Nussbaum, *'Defects': Engendering the Modern Body* (Ann Arbor, 2000). My thanks to Caroline Neilsen and Luc Racaut for stimulating discussions on this subject.

commodification of humanity. The reality in the long term, however, was that increasingly powerful market forces ensured that consumer demands for novel commodities, the agenda of a nascent idea of human rights and the traditional moral framework imposed by the church would be in constant tension. In this, the traces of some of the most fundamental dilemmas of modern society are all too evident.

4

Where was Mrs Turner? Governance and Gender in an Eighteenth-Century Village

Naomi Tadmor

On Wednesday 5 May 1756, several members of the parish vestry of East Hoathly, Sussex, met together at the public house to discuss important affairs. The main item on the agenda concerned the 'putting out' of pauper children, one of the chief duties of parochial care, initially stipulated some 211 years earlier.[1] The public meeting of 5 May was duly announced at the local church on a preceding Sunday.[2] The authority of the parishioners involved (who included the local shopkeeper, the butcher, a victualler, and two farmers) was strongly reflected in their words. They agreed to put out one pauper girl to a neighbour at a cost of 18d per week for 'so long as the parish shall think proper'. Her younger sister was to be dispatched elsewhere and maintained for the same sum, with the reiterated provision 'to take either of them away at any time whensoever the parish shall think proper'. The drinks consumed by the parishioners present amounted to a total cost of 2s 6d (just under a fortnight's maintenance for each of the girls concerned), to be charged to the parish account, but the bill remained unpaid. This was, after all, one of many similar meetings, held at the same place and attended by more or less the same men. Payment could be deferred to be balanced quarterly, as usual, alongside other bills, with reciprocal reckoning of credit and debt. Later that evening, the men returned to their homes. The young girls' family, in contrast, was at that night dismantled. The head of the family lost his guardianship of his daughters. The two sisters – Ann Braiser aged nine and Lucy aged eleven – were separated, probably never to live again under the same roof.

---

[1] I Edw. VI c. 3 (1547). See Paul Slack, *The English Poor Law, 1531–1782* (Cambridge, 1990), 51; 'The Bill for bringing up of poor Mens Children', *Journal of the House of Commons, I: 1547–1629* (1802), 1 [www.british-history.ac.uk/report.aspx?compid=8413, accessed 26 September 2010].
[2] Yale University Library, Thomas Turner's Papers, Manuscripts and Archives: Diary of Thomas Turner, 1754–65 [hereafter Diary], 2 May 1756.

In the following days, parish affairs continued smoothly. The removal of pauper children from their parents' home and their placement elsewhere was a familiar procedure in East Hoathly. Parents were given notice 'to bring their children to the Vestry', following which the meeting of the 'public vestry' was held and the children were put out.[3] Between May 1784 and December 1790, no fewer than sixty-seven such arrangements were recorded in the parish's vestry minutes.[4] Luckily for the paupers of East Hoathly, their parish generally kept the removed children relatively close to home with a range of service, apprenticeship, and boarding arrangements (unlike the burgeoning nearby parish of Brighthelmstone, or Brighton, for example, where around the same time the removal of poor children to Lancashire was explored).[5] The two sisters, Ann and Lucy Braiser, thus probably still had many opportunities to see each other: at church, in the village shop, down country lanes, and so on, and they could probably also visit their parents on occasion.

As time went by, however, increasing difficulties arose. At first, Ann's mistress, Dame Trill, herself a pauper in receipt of relief, typically employed by the parish to foster others, started complaining that the money allotted for the keeping of Ann 'was not enough'. When the overseer suggested adding an occasional shilling, she asserted 'she would not except of it' and 'have more or none'.[6] One can only imagine how her dissatisfaction might have affected her treatment of Ann. The fact that Dame Trill also had a daughter of her own, who continued to live at home and evidently enjoyed preferential care, may have also been a source of unease.[7] Before long, reports reached the overseer that young Ann was being 'very saucy and impertinent'. Worse still, by the spring Lucy clearly also had difficulties in adjusting to her new place. Her behaviour deteriorated to the point that the public vestry had to be called to authorise her master to punish her. The master, to judge from his low level of taxation, must have valued the stipend

---

[3]   East Sussex Record Office [hereafter ESRO], PAR 378/31/1 (overseers' account book, 1761–1779), fols 52, 254–5, 262 (including notices concerning parish children); e.g. PAR 378/12/2 (vestry minutes); AMS 5841/22, 58, 61 (bills for keeping paupers).
[4]   ESRO, PAR 378/12/2 (in Thomas Turner's hand); K. Young, 'The Workings of the Parish Office and the Parish Vestry: A Case Study Based on the Diary of Thomas Turner of East Hoathly and Sussex Records (unpublished University of Sussex MA thesis, 2009), 34.
[5]   See broader discussion, Steve Hindle, *On the Parish? The Micro-politics of Poor Relief in Rural England c.1550–1750* (Oxford, 2004), esp. 203–23. See also the stipulations preventing parishes from intentionally shifting the care of paupers to other parishes: Richard Burn, *The Justice of the Peace and the Parish Officer*, 2 vols (1756), e.g. II, 244.
[6]   Diary, 26 July 1756; see also, e.g., 5 October 1756, 7 March 1757.
[7]   See Dame Trill and her daughter visiting Turner and drinking tea: Diary, 26 February 1757.

allotted to him for keeping the girl.[8] But once he 'corrected' her by order of the vestry, the girls' father, Master Braiser, intervened. At this point he declared that his daughter Lucy was 'abused', and that she would live with her master no longer.

Three months passed, and Master Braiser was feeling the pinch: trade was depressed in Sussex, and prices were high.[9] With another mouth to feed, he had no choice but to appeal to the parish; and when the parish refused, he went as far as addressing the local magistrate to force the parish to give him and his daughter relief. But now the authorities clenched their fist. The magistrate sided entirely with the parish. The local overseer, a God-fearing man with an impeccable reputation, took care to 'lay the story' before the magistrate 'impartially'. But he was convinced that the father was 'pretending', and he had no doubt that the parish was right in supporting the master and correcting the saucy girl. The justice ruled, to the overseer's satisfaction, that Lucy must return to service; indeed he advised the father to 'beg of the parish Officers' that she should be returned to the same place, and be put once more under the authority of the same master.[10]

Later that day, the men of East Hoathly assembled again: the shopkeeper, the butcher, the local chandler (who happened to be the butcher's brother), the local brick maker, several farmers, as well as the rector, and the steward of the local estate. This time they enjoyed a lavish meal: a roasted sirloin of beef, buttock of beef, boiled brisket of beef, seasonal vegetables, and a fine raisin bread suet pudding. When dinner was over, they stayed and smoked a pipe. The wife of the parish officer who recorded the events – the shop-keeper Thomas Turner – stayed at home and awaited her husband's return. For her, too, this was a busy day. With a house and shop to run, two boys to foster, and a husband away on parish affairs, there was a great deal to do. And so she, the maidservant, and the boys stayed at home and dined on the remains of yesterday's dinner.

I

Two historical fields can be brought together to reflect on the significance of these localised episodes in 'the politics of the parish', importantly defined by Keith Wrightson.[11] The first pertains to the history of the poor law and the early modern 'parish state';[12] the second to the history of women and gender

---

[8]   Diary, 7 April 1757 (17s 6d collected for the poor tax). The rate for 1757 was 3s 6d in the pound, Diary, 5 March 1757.

[9]   'Never, never was money so scarce as now', Diary, 22 July 1757.

[10] Diary, 5 November 1757.

[11] Keith Wrightson, 'The Politics of the Parish in Early Modern England', in *The Experience of Authority in Early Modern England*, ed. Paul Griffiths, Adam Fox and Steve Hindle (Basingstoke, 1996), 10–46.

[12] John Clare, *The Parish, A Satire* [c.1823–27], ed. E. Robinson (Harmondsworth, 1985),

relations. Both concern the history of the 'middling sort', whose social and cultural consolidation is likewise examined by Wrightson.[13] The more power was wielded by the butcher, the shopkeeper, and the farmer in the manage-ment of their local affairs, and the more the exercise of that power fed into the streams of male sociability and conviviality, the more we may ask the question: where was Mrs Turner? And what was the relationship between the operation of the 'parish state' and the changing disposition of gender relations? A snapshot from eighteenth-century East Hoathly cannot possibly aim to reveal the full view of women's roles in the historical 'parish state', but it can highlight several features and provide food for thought. The oper-ation of the parochial system of governance, this chapter suggests, had an impact on the social roles of women and on gender roles and relations in a parish such as East Hoathly. The personal diary of the middling shopkeeper and parish officer, Thomas Turner, offers a rare source for consideration, alongside contemporary legal and local documents.

The following discussion, then, aims to bring together two historiograph-ical fields. While the administration of the parish has been widely discussed, and the history of women and gender relations in early modern England have also been extensively studied, central arguments in these historiographies proceed along parallel tracks with insufficient interconnections. Pioneering works on women's history portrayed the seventeenth and eighteenth centu-ries as a period of change, in which women were increasingly relegated to the 'private sphere' of the home owing mainly to economic transformation. The scene of local rule did not occupy centre stage in such debates, and historians tended to focus on women of the middling and upper ranks. More recently revisionist critiques have questioned both the old chronology of economic change employed by pioneering historians and the definitions of the 'private' and 'public' spheres; yet discussions have hardly reached the structure of parish rule.[14] At the same time, historians have tended to move

63, line 1289; David Eastwood, *Government and Community, 1700–1870* (Basingstoke, 1997), 47, 56; Peter King, 'Edward Thompson's Contribution to Eighteenth-Century Studies: The Patrician-Plebeian Model Re-examined', *SH* 21 (1996), 215–28, esp. 227; Steve Hindle, 'Power, Poor Relief and Social Relations in Holland Fen, *c.*1600–1800', *HJ* 41 (1998), 67–96, pp. 94–6.

[13] See especially Keith Wrightson, 'The Social Order of Early Modern England: Three Approaches', in *The World We Have Gained: Histories of Population and Social Structure*, ed. Lloyd Bonfield, Richard M. Smith and Keith Wrightson (Oxford, 1986), 177–202; *idem*, 'Estates, Degrees, and Sorts: Changing Perspectives of Society in Tudor and Stuart England', *Language, History and Class*, ed. Penelope J. Corfield (Oxford, 1991), 30–52; *idem*, '"Sorts of People" in Tudor and Stuart England', in *The Middling Sort of People: Culture, Society and Politics in England, 1550–1800*, ed. Jonathan Barry and Christopher Brooks (Basingstoke, 1994), 28–51; and see also H. R. French, 'Social Status, Localism, and the "Middle Sort of People" in England, 1620–1750', *P&P* 166 (2000), 66–99; *idem*, *The Middle Sort of People in Provincial England, 1600–1750* (Oxford, 2007).

[14] The seminal revisionist article advocating continuity is Amanda Vickery, 'Golden Age

away from the traditional emphasis on the strictures of patriarchy and rather focused on the contingent and dynamic nature of social relations, in the process increasingly emphasising women's agency, strategies of negotiation, and informal roles. From this rather more optimistic perspective, even the deal struck between one Goodwife Watson and her parish officers in 1661, to leave the parish forever with one of her children while leaving behind her the other two to the parish overseers' care, could be presented as a triumph of negotiation.[15] While highlighting women's vital roles in community life, the significance of social structures and legal institutions in determining personal experiences has inevitably been played down.

The next section thus turns to present, however briefly, several contextual considerations concerning the parochial system of governance as it was manifested around the middle decades of the eighteenth century in East Hoathly and which also affected gender roles and relations. The following section examines more closely the ways in which gender and parish administration intersected in this eighteenth-century parish. Here our attention will shift to Peggy Turner and the Turner household. Lastly, focusing on Turner's service as an overseer of the poor in 1756–57, it will be possible to highlight both the importance of gender in matters relating to parish governance and the role of Mrs Turner.

II

Over the course of the early modern period, a powerful mechanism of parish rule had come into being in England. In each of England's *c*.9,000 parishes, local householders would assemble in parish vestries, approve taxation, discuss policies, and elect or select officers to execute the main business of the parish: namely, the relief and management of the poor. By the eighteenth century, as Eastwood explained, 'for most English people, their only contact with the world of officialdom and their only experience of political

to Separate Spheres: A Review of the Categories and Chronology of English Women's History', *HJ* 36 (1993), 384–414. See also *Women Privilege and Power: British Politics, 1750 to the Present*, ed. Amanda Vickery (Paolo Alto, 2001); *Women and Politics in Early Modern England*, ed. James Daybell (Aldershot, 2004). At the parish level, however, note Wrightson, 'Politics of the Parish'; Mark Goldie, 'The Unacknowledged Republic: Officeholding in Early Modern England', *The Politics of the Excluded, c.1500–1850*, ed. Tim Harris (Basingstoke, 2001), 153–94, p. 172; and important arguments in L. H. Lees, *The Solidarity of Strangers: The English Poor Laws and the People* (Cambridge, 1998), esp. chs 1–2; Amanda Flather, *Gender and Space in Early Modern England* (Woodbridge, 2006); Laura Gowing, *Common Bodies: Women, Touch and Power in Seventeenth-Century England* (New Haven, 2003); Hindle, *On the Parish?*; idem, '"Without the Cry of Any Neighbours: A Cumbrian Family and the Poor Law Authorities, c.1690–1730', in *The Family in Early Modern England*, ed. Helen Berry and Elizabeth Foyster (Cambridge, 2007), 126–57.
[15] Bernard Capp, *When Gossips Meet: Women, Family, and Neighbourhood in Early Modern England* (Oxford, 2003), 297.

authority' came through the parish officer and the 'parish state'.[16] The legal edifice that underpinned this mechanism remained in force from 1598 to 1834, and thus supported, with some amendments, what became a nation-ally co-ordinated system of local welfare. By the middle of the eighteenth century, however, important procedures had been adapted and historical circumstances had changed, which affected the operation of the system in East Hoathly and – in turn – gender roles and relations in the parish.

The first set of regulations that mattered in the parish, and are reflected in the events studied here, concerned the position of the overseers of the poor in relation to the parish vestry. Following legislation in 1691, the over-seers of the poor, who had always been accountable to the justice of the peace, had also been made accountable to the assembly of the parish vestry, which at that point was given the legal power to examine and approve all expenditure on poor relief alongside the JP. The aim was to restrain the parish officers, who 'frequently upon frivolous pretences (but chiefly for their owne private ends) give relief to what persons and number they think fitt'.[17] Each parish was thus to provide a book, where the names of all recipients were to be registered. The vestrymen were then obliged to assemble 'as often as it shall be thought convenient', or at the very least once a year, to review the book, and they were even empowered to call before them all recipients of relief to ascertain their claims.[18] The extent to which this stipulation took general effect is unclear, yet it evidently empowered our vestrymen in East Hoathly and underpinned their relationship with the overseers of the poor, including Thomas Turner. Following further legislation of 1744, the over-seer's legal accountability to the parish was moreover tightened, as he was made to give public notice of the parish rates in church, make them avail-able for inspection upon demand, and be personally responsible for promptly producing the accounts, when asked, as well as any supporting materials.[19] Tasks such as these were carefully undertaken and performed by Turner, as his diary and the parish documents reveal.

The second point of context concerns the operation of the vestry itself, that 'theatre in which the political life of the parish was forged'.[20] Although church meetings or town meetings in Tudor and early Stuart parishes are widely documented, 'the institution of vestries in many places have been

---

[16] Eastwood, *Government and Community*, 47; Steve Hindle, *The State and Social Change in Early Modern England, c.1550–1640* (Basingstoke, 2000); *idem, On the Parish?*
[17] 3 & 4 Will. & Mary c. 11–12 (1691). Cf. 43 Eliz. c. 2 (1601), where accounts were to be checked by JPs, and delivered by the outgoing officers to the incoming officers. See e.g. Hindle, *On the Parish?*, 405–6, emphasising the power of the JPs.
[18] 3 & 4 Will. & Mary c. 11 (1691).
[19] 17 Geo. II c. 3 (1744), esp. sections 1, 2, 3; 17 Geo. II c. 33 sections 1–2, 13. See Slack, *The English Poor Law*, 37; *An Abridgment of the Public Statutes now Forced in General Use from the Eleventh Year of George II to the Present* (1766), LXXII.
[20] Eastwood, *Government and Community*, 43.

delayed until after the Restoration or even later', as Hindle explains.[21] Yet by the eighteenth century the vestry took charge of 'the parish state'. To be sure, the size and constitution of vestries varied greatly. In the precarious economies of eighteenth-century England, moreover, the position of local oligarchies could never be secure: at least two of the men who ruled the fate of Ann and Lucy Braiser in East Hoathly in 1756 and 1757 found themselves within less than a decade among the recipients of parish relief, while one of the current recipients of dole, one Sam Jenner, had in the past himself been overseer of the poor.[22] Participation in the vestry and the bearing of public office, however, generally empowered the 'middling' and 'better sort' within the parish and continued through our period to define citizenship.[23] Following a general pattern, all ratepayers in East Hoathly had the right to assemble in public vestry meetings, deliberate, and vote.[24]

The third important feature of the system that crucially affected its operation in East Hoathly was mounting costs. The total expenditure on poor relief in England had risen from £400,000 in 1696 to £689,971 in 1748–50; by 1776 it had more than doubled, and had almost trebled by 1783–85.[25] The situation in East Hoathly was worse, with a near six-fold rise in parish expenditure on disbursements in the fifty years from 1712 to 1772 (see Figure 4.1). Legal costs on matters relating to settlement featured high on the parish's list of expenditure, as did the upkeep of families and children.[26] Rent, firewood, parish stock, and groceries were regularly provided to a number of females, including widows or elderly spinsters, unwed mothers, and deserted wives. A list of paupers, mostly male, were given a weekly dole

[21] Hindle, *State and Social Change*, 207–8. The word 'vestry' did not appear in the statute book until 1663: Sidney and Beatrice Webb, *English Local Government*, I: *The Parish and the County* (1906, rep. 1963), 37–9, n. 6. For the vestry, see Burn, *Justice of the Peace*, I, 195–6.

[22] ESRO, PAR 378/12/1–35; Naomi Tadmor, *Family and Friends in Eighteenth-Century England: Household, Kinship, and Patronage* (Cambridge, 2001), 209–10.

[23] See above, n. 13.

[24] Eastwood, *Government and Community*, 43; Burn, *Justice of the Peace*, I, e.g. 195–6, 202; II, 298–9. See also Joanna Innes, 'The "Mixed Economy of Welfare" in Early Modern England: Assessments of the Opinions from Hale to Malthus', in *Charity, Self-Interest and Welfare in the English Past*, ed. Martin Daunton (1996), 139–80. Until 1818, the poor had the legal right to attend vestry meetings.

[25] Slack, *The English Poor Law*, 22; G. R. Boyer, *An Economic History of the English Poor Law, 1750–1850* (Cambridge, 1990), esp. 23–9.

[26] ESRO, PAR 378/31/1; see also AMS 6093/7 (disbursements of overseers); PAR 378/12//2 (including arrangements for putting out children). Note also R. M. Smith, 'Ageing and Well-Being in Early Modern England: Pension Trends and Gender Preferences under the English Old Poor Law c.1650–1800', in *Old Age From Antiquity to Post-Modernity*, ed. Paul Johnson and Pat Thane (1998), 64–95. Although the present essay does not focus on ageing, the pattern in East Hoathly generally resembles that described by Smith for southern rural parishes c.1750, with no workhouse.

Figure 4.1. Expenditure on poor relief by overseers of the poor (corrected for inflation), East Hoathly, Sussex, 1711–79.

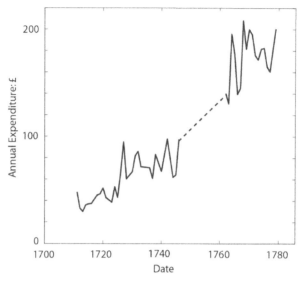

Source: East Sussex Record Office, PAR 378 AMS 6093/7 Disbursements of Overseers; PAR 378/31/12/1–35 Vestry Minutes 1711–47; PAR 378 31/1/1 Overseers' Account Book 1761–79.

of bread and beer and occasional charity.[27] Male and female householders received support for dependants, yet the children in such households were consistently at risk of being removed. At the same time, householders who took in pauper children were remunerated, whether on a weekly, monthly, or yearly basis. The clothing of pauper children often also fell to the parish, and bills for children's clothes and shoes regularly appear in the overseers' accounts. With added costs for fuel, work materials, medical care, and occasional legal bills, the keeping of children – as Karen Young calculated – was a major and long-term commitment for the parish.[28] The removal of pauper children was, moreover, employed, as already seen here, as a means of internally subsidising parish relief, since poor inhabitants were given children to foster and were paid for the task. By the same token, chief inhabitants received a supply of servants. Pauper children were expected to work: the older the child, the lower was the parish's pay to the new master. Overall,

[27] See ESRO, PAR 378 31/1/1 fol. 160; Diary, 11 January 1758, 7 February 1762, 13 February 1763(charitable bequest).
[28] The third highest number of surviving bills and vouchers from the parish are for paying parishioners for keeping children: Young, 'The Working of the Parish Office', based on ESRO, PAR 378/31/3/2–21 (1762–85). The overseers' account book, PAR 378/31/1/1, confirms the pattern of expenditure.

as Turner often commented in his diary, times were hard. When the annual dole was distributed before Christmas at the local mansion, hundreds queued at the gate, waiting for a piece of bread, a draught of beer, a small number of pennies, and for the overseers of the poor to record their names.[29] In view of all of this, it is hardly surprising that an eighteenth-century parish such as East Hoathly was conscious of the costs of the management of poor children and families.

The fourth set of regulations that affected the lives of paupers such as the Braiser family and the entire operation of the poor relief system in East Hoathly concerned the eligibility of inhabitants to be considered for poor relief, which, in turn, was rooted in the settlement legislation. In the 1690s, the regulations were cemented whereby settlement could be gained through rate payment, annual service, indentured apprenticeship, or one year's service in public office, as well as through marriage and descent and rental at a threshold of £10 *per annum*, which had been set in previous legislation. Rather than encouraging 'settlement by merit', these regulations frequently had the effect of making settlement hard to attain.[30] By the time that Ann, Lucy, and their father were facing the parish authorities, there was a large and growing number of paupers throughout the realm with derived and inherited settlement, whose ability to gain new parish settlement was circumscribed, and for whom parochial affiliation by descent or service (and in the case of wives by marriage) was of the utmost importance.[31] In East Hoathly, the division between settled inhabitants and unsettled poor – especially 'certificate men', as Turner called them; or 'certificate person' for a female – ran through the entire socio-economic fabric of the parish.[32] Whereas substantial farmers preferred to employ certified migrants, who tended to be young, single, and cheaper to hire than a local householder such as Master Braiser, overseers of the poor and parishioners kept a watchful eye on poor and labouring migrants to forestall any additional charge to the parish. These changing settlement regulations had an enormous impact on a parish such as East Hoathly and they were also swiftly absorbed into the negotiating strategies of the poor.

The question of settlement was particularly important in the management of pauper children. Since Master Braiser could not provide for his daughters, their position in his 'family' was deemed to have expired and

---

[29] Diary, 21 December 1759, 1761, 1762.
[30] See J. S. Taylor, 'The Impact of Pauper Settlement, 1691–1834', *P&P* 73 (1976), 42–74, p. 50. See also Philip Styles, 'The Evolution of the Laws of Settlement', in *idem*, *Studies in Seventeenth-Century West Midlands History* (Kineton, 1978), 175–204; Paul Slack, *Poverty and Policy in Tudor and Stuart England* (1988); Lees, *Solidarity of Strangers*, 28–33; Hindle, *On the Parish?*, esp. 300–25.
[31] See, e.g., new legislation aimed at dealing with the situation, 12 Ann. 1 c. 18 (1714); Burn, *Justice of the Peace*, II, 222–44, esp. 228; Lees, *Solidarity of Strangers*.
[32] Diary, 11 December 1762; 3 September 1757.

they passed to their parish's care as paupers in their own right.[33] The settlement of illegitimate children was of particular concern.[34] Evolving regulations clarified when the settlement of the bastard child was to follow the mother's, and how she was to care for the child during the age of nurture (traditionally defined as seven years).[35] This amended the Elizabethan legislation, by which the care of the bastard child fell on the parish of birth, and reinforced the Restoration legislation enabling the overseers of the poor to attach the assets of reputed fathers to cover costs.[36] The legal procedure for examining the mother's settlement was fixed in the reign of George II, as was the procedure for apprehending the reputed father and indemnifying the parish.[37] If the parish failed to follow the regulations, it immediately risked facing both expenses for child maintenance and legal costs. The overall effect of the legislation – as well as the growing burden of poor relief – was that the politics of procreation were at the forefront of the politics of parish governance.[38] Notably, the religious fervour that typified similar encounters in late sixteenth to mid-seventeenth-century Terling, as discussed by Wrightson and Levine, had subsided.[39] The main issues at stake in mid-eighteenth-century East Hoathly were cost and procedure.

This takes us to the last contextual consideration to be mentioned here, the increasing bureaucratisation of the 'parish state', manifested not least in the world of letters and print. The need for formal certification, according to the settlement legislation, directly affected the lives of labouring people in the parish, while an overseer of the poor such as Turner had to spend a great deal of time processing forms. The settlement certificate, for example,

---

[33] Burn, *Justice of the Peace*, II, 201, 216–19, 229, which explains when children are deemed to be 'of their father's family', and why a servant cannot be removed from the master so as not to dissolve a contract; 17 Geo. II c. 38 (1744), section 4. For contractual affiliation to the household-family, see Tadmor, *Family and Friends*, chs 1–2.

[34] For rising illegitimacy ratios, see Peter Laslett, 'Long-term Trends in Bastardy in England', in *idem*, *Family Life and Illicit Love in Earlier Generations* (Cambridge, 1977), 103–59. For the role of the rise in illegitimacy in the general population rise, see E. A. Wrigley, 'The Growth of the Population in Eighteenth-Century England: a Conundrum Resolved', *P&P* 98 (1983), 121–50, pp. 132–3; for the seventeenth century, see Keith Wrightson, 'The Nadir of English Illegitimacy in the Seventeenth-Century', *Bastardy and its Comparative History*, ed. Peter Laslett, Karla Oosterveen and Richard M. Smith (1980), 176–91.

[35] *An Abridgement of the Public Statutes*, LIII–IV section 7, sig. 6N (on 17 Geo. II c. 5, sections 7 and 25); Burn, *Justice of the Peace*, I, esp. 128–31; II, 212–16, 536–7, and references there to 5 Eliz. c. 5 (1563), section 12; 17 Geo. II c. 5 (1744), and other legislation; W. E. Tate, *The Parish Chest: A Study of the Records of Parochial Administration in England* (Cambridge, 1969), 216–17; Hindle, *The State and Social Change*, 160–2; Gowing, *Common Bodies*, 200–1.

[36] 13 & 14 Geo. II c. 22 (1742), section 19.

[37] 6 Geo. II c. 41 (1733), for mothers; Burn, *Justice of the Peace*, I, 128–31, 137–42.

[38] See also Lees, *Solidarity of Strangers*, 51, 57–60.

[39] Wrightson & Levine, *Terling*; esp. 126–34, 204, Wrightson, *ES*, esp. 84–6.

was by that time mass-produced, having been issued since around the start of the century in printed form, with slots for filling in the personal details and added spaces for the signatures required.[40] As well as that, there was the world of books and the expanding 'how to' genre aimed at men of the middle and upper ranks. One of the best-selling guidebooks of the eighteenth century, Burn's *The Justice of the Peace and the Parish Officer*, cited here, went through about thirty editions after its publication in 1755 and at least as many related imprints and abridgements. It was purchased almost immediately by Turner, who studied it, as is evident from his considerations, and relied greatly on its precedents.[41] In the seventeenth century, historians confirm, illiteracy was not a barrier to the fulfilment of parish office,[42] but by the eighteenth century, the situation had clearly changed. Reading and writing were fundamental requirements for the job, while an overseer of the poor such as Turner had to be able to handle correspondence, administration, and even legal research.[43] Tradesmen and established farmers were likely to be fully literate, and consistently more so than either women or labouring men, while some, like Turner, had specialised numeracy skills. The administrative print culture of East Hoathly, then, also reflected – and in turn reinforced – the social profiles of gender and rank.[44]

And so the 'parish state' continued to evolve as an oligarchic republic in miniature, with a designated local assembly, principles of enfranchisement, increasingly regulated and accountable offices, and facilities for social action and exclusion.[45] The system was rooted in two centuries of legislation and case law, yet its fully operative framework contained a number of contingent and evolving features. All the participants in the episodes narrated above were aware of the rules of the game, and did their best – from their respective points of view – to negotiate the system. The records of East Hoathly attest to the constant preoccupation of the parish with matters of the poor law, and particularly with settlement. The politics of procreation were of great concern for the parish. As Slack has shown, the emphasis at this point had shifted from the removal of the male vagabond, the crucial issue in the sixteenth century, to the management of families and of single women.[46] Poor householders were closely governed, single people with no solid means of support were watched, while single women were watched most closely

[40] See the standard formula in Burn, *Justice of the Peace*, II, 210–12; Steve Hindle, 'Technologies of Identification under the Old Poor Law', *The Local Historian* 36 (2006), 220–36.
[41] Diary, 6 February 1758.
[42] Goldie, 'Unacknowledged Republic', 165, and references there.
[43] ESRO, PAR 378/31/1/1.
[44] E.g. Wrightson, *ES*, 198–9, 207, 228–9. For Turner, see Tadmor, *Family and Friends*.
[45] See Goldie, 'Unacknowledged Republic'.
[46] Slack, *The English Poor Law*, 31.

of all. This takes us to the next section, and back to our opening question: 'where was Mrs Turner?'

III

'The ladies of the Restoration', as the pioneering historian Alice Clark concluded in 1919, 'were but shadows of the vigorous personalities of their grandmothers.'[47] The deterioration in their status was said to be mainly the result of economic change: home production had allegedly declined by the seventeenth century, leading to the exclusion of the wife from the farm-yard, the shop, and the workshop. At the same time, the increase in wealth permitted elite and middle-class women to withdraw from all connection with business. This developmental chronology, influenced by the work of Friedrich Engels, continued to echo in historical narratives well into the 1980s. Once its economic edifice was questioned and the 'decline and fall' model was generally challenged, the historiographical pendulum of women's history swung away from explanations of long-term change.[48] The working of the 'parish state' of East Hoathly invites us to revisit old debates about the social and economic experiences of eighteenth-century women, while reflecting on gender and rank, authority, dependency, and power.

One place where Peggy Turner was not to be found was the parish vestry. Following the age-old tradition, wives generally did not participate in local assemblies, nor carried parish office.[49] The handful of known exceptions demonstrate the rule.[50] The absence of women such as Peggy Turner from

[47] Alice Clark, *The Working Life of Women in the Seventeenth Century* [1919], ed. A.L. Erickson (1992), 41.

[48] See esp. Olwen Hufton, 'Women in History: Early Modern Europe', *P&P* 101 (1983), 125–57, p. 126; Judith Bennett, 'Medieval Women, Modern Women Across the Great Divide', in *Culture and History 1350–1600: Essays on Culture, Community, Identity and Writing*, ed. David Aers (1992), 147–75; Vickery, 'Golden Age', 402.

[49] No evidence for female office-bearing or attendance at the vestry can be found in the East Hoathly parish records. The shaky signature 'frances turner' was probably made by the blacksmith Francis Turner: ESRO, PAR 378/31/1, fol. 262.

[50] E.g. The National Archives, Home Office Domestic State Papers, no. 324, September 1819; Webb, *Parish and the County*, 158; Sara Mendelson and Patricia Crawford, *Women in Early Modern England* (Oxford, 1998), 52–8. Exceptions were made in the case of substantial widows, as French's study in the present volume shows. Burn approved the right of widows to take the oath required for public office but questioned its enforcement on wives, whose legal persona was subsumed by *coverture*. He ruled that women were not to serve as overseer of the poor: Burn, *Justice of the Peace*, II, 188. In places where an office was to be allocated by house row, he recommended the replacement of women by male deputies, as occurred frequently: Hindle, *The State and Social Change*, 214; Goldie, 'Unacknowledged Republic', 172, and references there. Note the structured roles for matrons in restricted legal contexts and the customary means of petitioning and protest, Capp, *When Gossips Meet*, ch. 7; Gowing, *Common Bodies*.

the 'organs of the parish' appears all the more conspicuous in light of their occasional inclusion among the lesser parish servants: whether as gaolers, sextons, nurses, etc.[51] The appointment of women to certain positions was allowed as long as public care was not a consideration. In 1739, for example, one female ratepayer was permitted to serve in the lowly office of parish sexton after the judge ruled that her position 'did not concern the public or the care and inspection of the morals of parishioners'.[52] The increasingly consolidated system of local governance offered women some employment opportunities, but no more than sporadic access to the formal structures of authority and power.

For a wife such as Peggy Turner, exclusion from the site of authority also meant limited access to the circuits of male sociability. This was all the more obvious since the parish's vestry meetings were typically held in the public house, and were accompanied by considerable consumption of food and drink in male company. Neither Peggy Turner nor any of her fellow matrons ever set foot in these meetings. Thomas Turner often noted specifically that his wife stayed and dined at home. The food eaten by the men on these occasions was typically superior to everyday domestic cooking and included choice joints of meat and rich pudding, whereas the daily menu at home was normally based on lesser cuts and leftovers. Indeed, the availability of lavish food and plentiful drink at the expense of the parish no doubt helped to raise attendance at the parish vestry. Conversely, Turner was quick to note when any of his neighbours hastened to leave the vestry meeting once the business was over, so as not to stay and drink at his own expense.[53] Both governance and sociability required time. It was not unusual for meetings to last well into the evening. On 19 April 1756, for example, when Turner was elected as an overseer of the poor, he had to return home briefly, but once he finished his business he immediately came back and continued to drink with the men. When summer arrived, the men played and watched cricket. When the May vestry meeting was due, one farmer suggested holding it at the 'cricketing' in the hope that 'if any more of the parish were there', they could come to a resolution concerning one pauper's affairs.[54] At numerous other times the parish men simply dropped in at the public house, had a drink, smoked a pipe, and conducted their affairs, or went travelling together on parish matters and on personal and business affairs.

The networks of male sociability, tied with the operation of the poor law, were also typified by friction; this, too, was largely beyond Peggy Turner's domain. Turner often complained about his quarrelsome and parsimonious

[51] Goldie, 'Unacknowledged Republic', 172; Capp, *When Gossips Meet*, 294–6. For 'the organs of the parish' and its 'servants', see Webb, *Parish and the County*, 17.
[52] *Report of the Adjudged Cases, etc., By Sir John Strange*, II (1795), 114.
[53] Diary, 19 October 1756.
[54] Diary, 24 May 1756; see also 30 August 1756.

neighbours, especially the wealthy tenant farmers, who did all they could to reduce the parish rates, and minimise expenditure on the poor, while at the same time driving wages down by employing migrants and 'certificate men' rather than local labourers. The most powerful among them, Mr French, regularly dominated the vestry meetings 'with Hoarse grating sound of his huge big Oaths' and interfered with the work of the parish officer, who was obliged to consult with his powerful neighbour on many matters, and often bit his tongue so as not to antagonise him. Although this particular domineering farmer, as Turner noted, could eventually be brought to good humour with the help of '2 or 3 drams of Old English Gin', the vestry men's regular consumption of alcohol also increased friction. One time when the butcher, the chandler, the blacksmith, the shoemaker, and several farmers assembled at the public house for a vestry meeting regarding 'the making [of] a poor book', 'some or most of them' were 'a little in Liquor' to the point they 'could not agree in some of there arguments'.[55] The parish meeting at the cricket game, mentioned above, was in fact strategically called to use the social gathering for smoothing over differences among the men.

While Peggy Turner did not partake in any such events, she was busy nurturing parallel social networks. Since her recent arrival in the parish as a young bride, this farmer's daughter had taken care to assist the social integration of her husband and herself. She befriended the wife of the active vestryman, the carpenter Mr John Vine Jr, and developed a close reciprocal relation with the wives of the butcher and the chandler. She also cultivated the acquaintance of a select group of local women distinctly above her station, such as Mrs Hannah Atkins, the well-to-do widow of the deceased steward of the local aristocratic estate, and the wife and daughters of the wealthy farmer Mr French. Occasionally she went to visit them and drank tea, and occasionally they called on her.[56] Children, relations, and household guests habitually participated in such visits. Peggy became popular among her neighbours and increasingly paid and received visits on her own. On 6 January 1756, for example, when Turner came home, he found two of the leading farmers and their wives in his house, drinking tea. When a female neighbour died, it was Peggy who attended the funeral.[57] Occasionally she went to a fair.[58] Generally, her social interactions took place indoors, and in the houses of her equals or betters, rather than in the arenas of popular culture. The only public events she regularly attended were the two Sunday services at the parish church.

[55] Diary, 18 March 1756. For Mr French, see esp. Diary, 1 May 1758. See also Hindle, *On the Parish?*, 369–71. For the dynamic between the neighbours and the distinction between them and 'friends', see Tadmor, *Family and Friends*, 172–4, 198–215.
[56] E.g. Diary, 8, 30 September; 22, 25, 30 November; 5, 11, 23 December 1755.
[57] Diary, 11 December 1755.
[58] E.g. Diary, 30 July 1755; 21, 27 May 1756. She was called back to enable Turner to visit a relation.

If the working of the parish vestry was lubricated by alcohol, then, Peggy Turner's social sphere was typified by tea. This once expensive luxury had become by the middle of the eighteenth century a polite amenity and was drunk by the middling women of East Hoathly and in mixed company.[59] Generally, Peggy Turner's social interaction was characterised by contemporary patterns of consumption and sociability. As a respectable wife, she cultivated her appearance and was – as her husband in retrospect recorded – 'remarkably Sweet & Cleanly'.[60] A dressmaker fitted her with a gown, altered two others, and the shoemaker provided pumps at the considerable cost of 3s 9d. When her husband sat down after a busy day, she enjoyed reading to him aloud sections from the contemporary best-seller *Clarissa*, or even from a political magazine.[61] Generally, she shared the reading of contemporary genres such as newspapers, sermons, novels, and plays together with her husband, with the maid, and often with any guests who happened to drop in. Together with the steward's widow, she invested in a lottery ticket.[62] She and her husband partook in the current culture of polite curiosity and went to the sea, to tour a castle, to visit a spa town, as well as to see friends and relations, and to hear a popular preacher. Together with a group of acquaintances, they once went to the nearby aristocratic estate to see turtles.[63] In the winter months the couple engaged in rounds of visits in the houses of local tradesmen and well-to-do farmers, where they had lavish meals and plenty of drink. Card games were invariably played. Occasionally polite engagement lapsed to revelling. When the visits ended, Peggy appropriately tipped the maid, Thomas the serving boy. Companionable home visits were at the centre of the middling sphere of the parish, which the Turners and their neighbours cultivated. This also stimulated trade: often clients and workers participated. Yet although Peggy engaged in many activities in female company, the female circles and mixed middling circle were often indistinguishable, which meant that while she had little share in her husband's sphere of governance, he habitually played a role in her social world and the two regularly spent time in company together.[64]

The result was social integration, which was undoubtedly important for both Peggy and Thomas Turner. Being young, and recently arrived migrants,

[59] Carole Shammas, *The Pre-Industrial Consumer in England and America* (Oxford, 1990).
[60] Diary, 23 June 1761; Tadmor, *Family and Friends*, 193. For cleanliness in dress, see John Styles, *The Dress of the People: Everyday Fashion in Eighteenth-Century England* (New Haven, 2007).
[61] Naomi Tadmor, '"In the Even My Wife Read to Me": Women, Reading and Family Life in Eighteenth-Century England', in *The Practice and Representation of Reading in England*, ed. James Raven, Helen Small, and Naomi Tadmor (Cambridge, 1996), 162–74.
[62] Diary, 3 September 1757.
[63] Diary, 7 August 1757. See visit to Pevensey, Diary, 8 January 1755; 15 August 1756.
[64] See, e.g., Vickery, 'Golden Age'; Lawrence E. Klein, 'Gender and the Public/Private Distinction in the Eighteenth Century: Some Questions about Evidence and Analytic Procedure', *Eighteenth-Century Studies* 29 (1995), 97–109.

their position in the parish was far from secure. Thomas had a share of a copyhold farm in Kent and was a customary tenant in another Sussex parish, but it was his mother who had a life interest in the property and his siblings who actually lived in it.[65] Being the son of a second marriage, his inheritance was disadvantaged, while his role as an elder brother had left him responsible for several relations.[66] About the time he undertook his parish office, he was striving to maximise his income by serving as a school teacher, personal tutor, occasional scrivener, and even undertaker.[67] Indeed, in East Hoathly, he was no more than a copyholder's tenant, and the house and shop, hired for £8 per annum, were below the settlement rental threshold; only with the rental of a warehouse did the total rise above the required level.[68] Both Turner and his wife were educated and well connected, and in possession of some funds; still, parish office must have been for them, too, a step towards integration and belonging. In this respect, Peggy's contribution was invaluable. The female and mixed social circles she cultivated served to complement the male sphere of governance, as well as to counterbalance it, and to contain its tensions and harmonise disputes while at the same time cementing neighbourliness and assisting trade.

The most important task that Mrs Turner undertook, however, and that filled most of her waking hours, was work.[69] The depiction of the middling eighteenth-century wife as idle and frivolous, advocated by pioneering historians such as Clark and indeed based on negative contemporary stereotypes, was far removed from the realities of Peggy Turner's life.[70] To begin with, the daily meals at home required a great deal of preparation and frugal ingenuity, to present economic yet respectable dishes. Peggy Turner laboured in the kitchen, together with her maid. There was an endless stream of clients, tradespeople, neighbours, relations, and friends who stopped in the house and shop and always had to be served. It was crucial to keep an orderly and hospitable household to establish credit. After Peggy recovered from a severe illness and the death of her only son she undertook to foster her husband's illegitimate nephew, a task for which the couple received pay, as well as the younger son of a half-sibling. The boys attended a small village school

65 ESRO, PBT 2/1/9 fol. 233 (John Turner's will); ADA 118, fols 13, 39–51 (manorial record). Thomas Turner was born in Groombridge, Kent, in 1729; his wife Peggy was four years younger.
66 John Turner's will; Tadmor, *Family and Friends*, 175–92.
67 Tadmor, *Family and Friends*, 175–7, 180–3, 222 and notes there; Julian Hoppit, *Risk and Failure in English Business, 1700–1800* (Cambridge, 1987).
68 Diary, 11 March, 6 May, 11 October 1755; Tadmor, *Family and Friends*. In the land tax assessment for 1763, for example, Turner paid 6s, while French paid £32 and was assessed for £160. ESRO, PAR 378/37/4/1 (land tax assessment, 1763).
69 See the working of the Turner household and kinship networks in Tadmor, *Family and Friends*.
70 Tadmor, 'In the Even My Wife Read to Me'; Amanda Vickery, *The Gentleman's Daughter* (New Haven, 1998), esp. ch. 4.

and were looked after at home.[71] Although, unlike her husband, Peggy (like all the women in her family) travelled little outside the parish and hardly ever went beyond it unaccompanied, she readily went on errands in East Hoathly: delivering messages and goods and handling many payments.[72] When a public reception was to be held in the local aristocratic mansion, she, her husband, and the maid went back and forth five times in one day, bringing supplies.[73] Goods were also made at home. Together with her husband, maid, and sister she laboured 'a making of Boulster & pillow Ticks & Bed Bottom' for the chandler.[74] She and a local wife worked together quilting.[75] Evenings were spent preparing tobacco for sale: one time she and Thomas worked through 20 parcels of tobacco, another through 70, 80, or 120, and even 240 with a total weight of 55lbs.[76] When her husband was commissioned to serve as an undertaker, it was she who worked the night before tying funeral 'favours'. When an audit was to be held, it was she who prepared the goods.[77] The shop was tended by Thomas, Peggy, the maid, and occasionally Turner's brother, as the need arose, and was always open to do business. On 23 March 1756, for instance, when Turner returned home, he found a fellow vestryman and officer, together with his wife and sister 'in the shop a Buying of Goods & who went in and Stayed ab[ou]t 2 Hours'.

IV

When Thomas Turner undertook parish office in 1756–57, then, it was the support of his wife that enabled him to meet the challenge and devote the time required for performing the office well; his brother and maid greatly assisted. Yet if we focus solely on the dynamics of social networks, consumption, and work we stand in danger of missing important social and legal structures. The pressures of parish governance not only required a great deal of work from the overseer of the poor and a great deal of support from his household, but also brought to the fore a host of issues relating to the 'lesser sort', thus making the politics of gender roles, to paraphrase Wrightson, inseparable from the politics of this parish's rule and the politics of privilege and poverty. Let us return, then, to the vestry of East Hoathly and to the parish men.

When it came to the administration of the poor law, the vestrymen of the parish closely managed the affairs of their pauper neighbours, which often

---

71 See discussions in Tadmor, *Family and Friends*, chs 1, 5.
72 See also *ibid.*, 185 n. 79.
73 Diary, 30 July, 10 August 1757. When one time she did not go, he was reproachful.
74 Diary, 30 July 1755.
75 Diary, 3–4 June, 5 September 1755.
76 Diary, 14 January, 3, 12 February, 5 March 1756; 19 August 1757.
77 Diary, 25 October 1757.

specifically involved matters relating to families and children. As relief was typically given in kind, they discussed the bushel of wheat given to a pauper wife, the exact amount of firewood to be doled out, whether to assist a local debtor, and the detailed upkeep arrangements for each pauper child.[78] On 27 March 1757 a special vestry meeting was called to debate whether to provide new clothing for a local girl about to be apprenticed and to assist her father. If this amounted to careful reckoning of the ratepayers' money (as the law stipulated), it was also a means of control. Even at the point of death the pensioners' goods were appropriated to reimburse the parish, including all personal belongings, to the disadvantage of the family.[79] It was over matters relating to women's fertility, however, that the closest surveillance was exercised to forestall any likely charge for child support. Focusing on Thomas Turner's work as an overseer of the poor during his year in office, April 1756 to April 1757, it is possible to see how critical these affairs were. This also serves to demonstrate how demanding the office of overseer of the poor was, and what support was required from Mrs Turner and the family.

In April 1756, when Turner took up his office, he immediately started dealing with the upkeep of Lucy and Ann Braiser, as discussed above, and then devoted a great deal of time to the affairs of a local debtor. By the start of July, it had been brought to his notice that a certain young woman in the parish was 'with Child'. He immediately set out to investigate the matter, together with the domineering farmer Mr French. As the two discovered, the young woman had managed to conceal her pregnancy for a very long time and had in fact 'not above 2 or 3 weeks more to go'; and so French and Turner carried her straight away to the county town, Lewes, to confirm her parish of settlement before a justice of the peace, and – as they very much hoped – extract from her along the way the name of the father, and thus charge him with the costs of the lying-in and the keeping of the child.[80] Although the men did all they could to 'prevail on her to confess the Father', the woman refused. Ten days later, she was found dead.[81] Turner and French suspected at that point that she may have been poisoned by her married lover, whose identity had by that time been revealed by assiduous neighbours. Both men attended the coroner's investigation, where, to their disappointment, no evidence for murder was found.[82] One week passed, and the two had to set out once more, since the same married lover had apparently defaulted on his payments to the parish towards the upkeep of another bastard child, whom he had fathered four years earlier.[83] Turner carefully studied the legal situation (most likely with the aid of Burn's, *The Justice of*

[78] E.g. Diary, 19 October 1756.
[79] See also Hindle, *On the Parish?*, 281–2.
[80] Diary, 2–3 July 1756.
[81] Diary, 13 July 1756.
[82] Diary, 15 July 1756.
[83] Diary, 23–24 July 1756.

the Peace and the Parish Officer), and found that the parish had at that time mistakenly obtained a personal bond from the father, thereby ignoring the recommended procedure and invalidating a previous order that would have had better force at law. Broader discussions then followed and legal counsel obtained.[84] No sooner had they procured a new warrant from the magistrate than another single woman was reported to be 'with Child'.[85] Once again, Turner and French went to question her, together with her master and mistress, to confirm her parish of settlement and the state of her pregnancy. After careful examination, Turner concluded that although she was indeed an inhabitant settled in the parish, she was probably not pregnant ('tho 'twas true', as the young woman testified, that 'she had deserved for it more than once or twice').[86]

Once these interviews were over, Turner and French travelled to the county town to continue their investigation of the disputed paternity bond. Before heading home, they stopped at a public house and dined on a piece of beef and greens, a roasted breast of veal and a butter pudding cake, all at the parish's expense.[87] Turner's remaining term as overseer of the poor included several similar affairs. The month of August 1756 was relatively quiet with no more than routine matters concerning settlement certificates, payments to local paupers, and the ongoing affair of a local debtor.[88] In the autumn more parish business was conducted and cricket played. October brought a new and demanding matter relating to the upkeep of a deserted wife, whose husband had absconded leaving a family of six. And so the vestrymen assembled immediately at the public house to allocate relief.[89] Turner was convinced that it was the lack of employment, owing to the preference of migrant labourers and 'certificate men' by the wealthy farmers, that broke the man's spirit and made him run away, but he kept such thoughts to himself and continued to co-operate with his powerful neighbours. The next major affair concerned a pregnant parishioner and her lover, himself a 'certificate man' from a neighbouring parish. Once the news reached Turner that the pregnant young woman was in the parish, he immediately took advice how 'to take the Man'.[90] The aim was simple: to change the pregnant parishioner's settlement by marriage, and thus dispose of her

---

[84] *Diary of Thomas Turner*, ed. Vaisey, 135, and note there. This was the point at which Dame Trill came to complain about Ann's Braiser's pay.

[85] Diary, 24, 29–31 July 1756.

[86] Diary, 31 July 1756.

[87] Diary, 31 July 1756.

[88] On 4 August Turner went to testify for a neighbour; a week later he made payments on the parish's account; and on 12 August he went to Lewes to get a certificate signed. Parish matters continued on 24, 27–28, 30 August.

[89] Diary, esp. 19–20 October 1756; 11 December 1761. See matters concerning removal, 24–25 January 1757.

[90] Diary, 18–19 February 1757. The consultation took place with the butcher, the chandler, and two farmers.

and her unborn child by removing them to the father's parish of settlement. Turner and the local shoemaker thus set out together to patrol the labourer's house and eventually apprehended him and kept him under watch (first in the public house, and then in the overseer's own home). By the next day, he was offered a deal by Mr French: £5, a ring valued at 10s, a wedding dinner, and the marriage licence fee, in return for marrying the pregnant woman. After intensive persuasion, the man agreed to marry, but by the next day he had changed his mind. Three days more under parish watch, and he relented. The farmer, the butcher, the rector, and the chandler witnessed the deal. The final settlement amounted to £6 10s, five stone of beef, as well as the ring, the formal marriage licence, and the wedding dinner. The marriage was immediately performed; and the overseer of the poor himself tolled the wedding bells. The next morning, the newly-weds were taken to the justice of the peace, the wife's new settlement was confirmed, and the couple, furnished with appropriate documents, were immediately escorted to the parish boundary and sent away.[91] Evidently, the parish was willing to go to enormous trouble and expense to free itself from illegitimate pauper children and nip in the bud potential claims for support from poor couples and families. Turner referred to the affair as 'troublesome'. Before the end of the next month, however, he and French went to chase yet another pregnant parishioner in the hope of marrying her to her reluctant lover, so that they could both be removed to the man's parish of settlement on the Isle of Wight, where eventually they were sent.[92]

The day after this last affair had been investigated, Turner noted in his diary: 'Oh how Pleasant has this day been for what some of the last past have, they being spent in hurry and Confusion but this at home in my business and in reading.' 'Oh! were I to chuse my way of Life it should be a retired recluse Life.'[93] The work of the parish office was evidently demanding and time consuming. The successful officer, to judge from the experience of Thomas Turner, had to be willing to drop all business at short notice, apply himself to his parish affairs day and night, disengage from his home and trade for hours, or even days, while having the economic independence required for dedicating himself to public service (and indeed even extending credit to the parish when needed).[94] In his year of office, briefly examined here, from April 1756 to April 1757, at least 108 days were reported by him in his diary as having included work on parish matters. When one demanding parish affair emerged after another, it was his wife and other members of his household and family who kept the house and shop going. Despite the shopkeeper's public role, the shop was always attended and business was carried

[91] Diary, 18 February–1 March 1757.
[92] Diary, 23 February 1757; 29–30 March.
[93] Diary, 2 April 1757.
[94] See ESRO, PAR 378/31/1?/1–35, e.g. 1712, 1714–15, 1738, 1744, 1747; Diary, 5 April 1763, recording a parish debt of £21 5s 3 ¼d.

out. And so on 24 May 1756, for example, while her husband was dealing with parish affairs, Peggy Turner took his horse to be sold and received 50s. At another time it was she who paid Dame Trill in his absence for the keeping of poor Ann Braiser. Evenings were spent preparing tobacco for sale, making goods, and regularly handling sums in payment, while battling with recurring illness. At the same time, she not only managed the house but showed hospitality to the neighbours. On three consecutive mornings in March 1757, breakfast was served to a total of eight guests and a generous dinner shared with two farmers and the chandler, who had just witnessed a shot-gun (or rather knobstick) wedding.[95] After her premature death, two maids, a hired shop assistant, and three siblings had to be brought in at times to support Thomas Turner's work and public office and fill the gaps.[96] Clearly, other wives in the parish were also active. In Mr French's household, accounts were handled not by the imposing farmer but by his wife, perhaps because he was so busy meddling in parish affairs and drinking at the public house.[97]

Far from it being the middling wife who withdrew from economic life, then, as pioneering historians argued, it was her husband, the middling parish officer and shopkeeper, who had to withdraw from business to perform his public role. As he hardly ever operated on his own and was regularly accompanied by other parishioners, who together spent a great deal of time on parish affairs while also socialising and drinking together, one can only extrapolate that the middling 'parish state' of East Hoathly relied to a very significant extent on the support and labour of wives and other members of their households. Yet while Mrs Turner worked to support her husband's parish office, her own social focus drifted away from the problems of the poor. When the work was over, she, her husband, and the steward's widow sat together, read a magazine, and drank a cup of tea.

V

To judge from the case of East Hoathly around the middle decades of the eighteenth century, the poor law influenced both women's roles and gender roles and relations. Middling women such as Mrs Turner were not included in parish governance, yet worked to support it, while labouring families and single women were closely managed by an assiduous male vestry. The relief of pauper families was a large and increasing drain on expenditure, and the vestrymen's most serious social problems were related to children and

[95] Diary, 29–31 March 1757.
[96] Naomi Tadmor, 'The Concept of the Household Family in Eighteenth-Century England', *P&P* 151 (1996), 111–40; *idem*, 'In the Even My Wife Read to Me'; *idem*, *Family and Friends*, esp. chs 1, 5.
[97] Diary, 3 April; 22 December 1756.

procreation. The participatory and accountable nature of the 'parish state' is noted by historians.[98] In East Hoathly, the structural disenfranchisement of women and wives was the reverse side of the very same pattern. The more the middling men of the parish invested time and energy in running their 'parish state', the more the power axis simply bypassed women, if only by default. To complicate matters still further, the social circles in which the middling women interacted generally had little to do with the politics of poverty, but were rather typified by contemporary patterns of consumption and polite sociability.

This power-balance was not the outcome of any 'decline and fall' process, nor the loss of a 'golden age' (an argument invoked by pioneering historians to explain women's exclusion from a 'public sphere', and currently confirmed as categorically and causally problematic). On the basis of the present study, one can surmise that the structured exclusion of women was from its very outset part and parcel of the 'parish state', which in many ways succeeded manorial institutions. Still, the historical patterns of disenfranchisement were not static. In the case of East Hoathly, the evolving legal and administrative regulations that empowered the vestrymen and subjected the overseers to the vestry, thus increasing accountability, also permitted them to intervene in the lives of paupers in adaptable ways (including micro-management not only by the overseers of the poor but by the entire vestry). By the early 1700s, this local scene was increasingly bureaucratic and standardised, an outcome which in turn highlighted profiles of social polarisation. With the mounting costs of poor relief and a stringent legal system, the politics of procreation were at the forefront of local politics, which immediately impacted on gender relations and roles. Social divisions rooted in the settlement legislation shot through the entire social and economic fabric of the parish. Virtually all labouring people were affected, from migrant workers and maidservants to poor local householders and many wives, and children, such as the Braiser girls, were caught in the system. The parties involved knew the rules of the game. By the time Ann, Lucy, and their father were facing their parish authorities, pressures were increasing, and all were involved in playing the system.

Governance of this sort was time consuming. Peggy Turner and her household, as seen here, had to work hard to enable Thomas to devote himself to parish work. It was not the middling wife who withdrew from business (as the old historiography would have us expect), but her husband, since the work required was both demanding and irregular. Time and time again the 'organs of the parish' sprung into action, swiftly responding to each case as it arose. The butcher, the chandler, the farmer, and the shopkeeper co-operated together, and spent a great deal of time managing their

Eastwood, *Government and Community*, 43; Slack, *The English Poor Law*, 48. Goldie, 'Unacknowledged Republic'; Hindle, *The State and Social Change*, 114.

little commonwealth, notwithstanding their evident personal differences. For them, the 'parish state' was cemented with male sociability, and lubricated in the key local institution, the public house, where food and drink were regularly consumed by the men at the parish's expense. Mrs Turner was not there; nor, however, was Master Braiser (let alone young Ann and Lucy).

The politics of parish governance (to paraphrase Wrightson) thus intersected with the politics of gender and rank in more than one way. Taking a 'Whiggish' bird's eye view, one can see that this local system of governance eventually gave way in the next century to allow formal female participation: by 1900, over one million propertied women were in possession of the local government vote.[99] In the course of the eighteenth century, moreover, middling women increasingly participated in associational life, particularly in urban settings, and of course continued to influence the networks of friendship and patronage. This snapshot from East Hoathly, however, highlights the structured yet dynamic aspects of governance. To judge from the case of East Hoathly, the complex and ambiguous role of gender in the processes of both class- and state-formation might be profitably analysed by further investigation of the structures and institutions of the 'parish state' and their change over time.

---

[99] Patricia Hollis, *Ladies Elect: Women in English Local Government, 1865–1914* (Oxford, 1987), 7.

5

Local Arithmetic: Information Cultures in Early Modern England

PAUL GRIFFITHS

Chester, 1626, and civic leaders had yet another problem to deal with. This time the cause was not a new wave of vagrants or unwelcome 'strangers' but one of their own. Gaps in the city records had come to light and the town clerk – Robert Brerewood – was the villain of the piece, although his 'underclerkes' also had to face the music. A string of complaints about 'uncivel' Brerewood claimed that he had been rude to a few mayors in a row and also to justices sitting at Chester's Quarter Sessions. He had not been doing his job by the book. In fact for three long years he had farmed out his 'office', lined his pockets, and created an administrative mess. Assembly orders had not been drawn up or written down in the book ever since he began to moonlight elsewhere, and names of juries went unrecorded. There was nothing left of the trust the city had once placed in its clerk. And to cap it all, word of new 'abuses' was brought to court: 'Imperfect orders' put down in records but not 'agreed on by the assembly'; 'accons' entered 'after a copie given out and baile put in by the defendant'; 'a declaracon and a record' both 'razed' and 'altered'; a 'judgement' 'blotted out'; another found after checking to be 'wrongfull'. '[O]ther misdemeanors' were not important enough to record but were important enough to 'hinder' justice and 'dishonor' the city. Troubled, aldermen looked through 'bookes of orders of assembly' and 'records of perticular cases complained of'. Little time was lost: Brerewood was sacked on the spot and a search started straight away for a 'fitting clerke' to take care of Chester's 'bookes and records'. Nothing mattered more it seemed than that Chester got its records back in 'good order'.[1]

Early modern magistrates depended on records, but on one day in Chester aldermen found that the city they knew was not the one in its records. It was hardly rare for pages to be ripped out of records or for a thick censo-

My thanks to Andy Wood and the editors for their very helpful suggestions.

[1]   Cheshire and Chester Record Office [CCRO], Z/AB/2, fol. 12v.

rious line to be drawn through entries. From the point of view of either expurgator or magistrate (and they were often one and the same), what records meant was a matter of real importance. This is understandable in governing cultures where the gathering and sorting of information became more vital for regulation as time passed. From the mid sixteenth century information was gathered and used by local governments on a scope and scale never seen before. Resulting records were essential for policy-making but they also had deep symbolic significance as representations of authority and legal status in times when it has been argued that writing and the written word were becoming more important to establish a case at law.[2] Also importantly, information was not just stored by single communities; it constantly circulated from place to place often across large distances to facilitate the understanding and regulation of problems far and wide. We tend to locate the development of sophisticated surveillance deep into the nineteenth century.[3] But if we go back to around 1600, we are not in a back-water before information was taken seriously. Far from it, policy-making and policing through collecting and counting was routine by then. Strategies to crack crime or other problems had more chance of success once those problems were understood through surveillance. What are archives for us now were working records four centuries ago, helping to regulate troubles that were felt to be on the rise, like urban sprawl, migrants slipping into a parish on the sly, or rigged weights and measures. Salisbury's justices made plans for a 'veywe' of the poor in 1613 to find out 'in what sorte they may be relyved'. Shortly before this magistrates in the same city asked constables to draw up a 'certificatt and information' of 'all newecomers', 'straungers', 'noysome watercourses', 'base borne children', and 'disordered houses' for the 'better government of this citie'.[4] By now gathering information and drawing up lists like this were daily social practices, standard and instinc-tive. John Graunt believed that 'knowledge' of the make-up of populations would make government 'more certain and regular'. But well before William Petty said that 'Political Arithmetic' ought to be an 'instrument of govern-ment', local governments all over England used 'local arithmetic' – counting and categorising – to think through tricky issues and make policies.[5]

[2] Adam Fox, *Oral and Literate Cultures in England, 1500–1700* (Oxford, 2000), ch. 5.
[3] See Daniel R. Headrick, *When Information Came of Age: Technologies of Knowledge in the Age of Reason and Revolution, 1700–1850* (Oxford, 2000); Edward Higgs, *The Information State in England: The Central Collection of Information on Citizens Since 1500* (Basingstoke, 2004). Cf. Paul Griffiths, *Lost Londons: Change, Crime, and Control in the Capital City, 1550–1660* (Cambridge, 2008), ch. 11; Paul Slack, 'Government and Information in Seventeenth-Century England', *P&P* 184 (2004), 33–68; Ann Blair, *Too Much to Know: Managing Scholarly Information Before the Modern Age* (New Haven, 2010).
[4] Wiltshire Record Office [WRO], G23/1/3, fols 231, 291v, 153v.
[5] John Graunt, *Natural and Political Observations ... Made Upon the Bills of Mortality* (1662), 100; Petty is quoted in Ted McCormick, *William Petty and the Ambitions of*

This proliferation and sophistication of information cultures were in large part the results of social change. The chronology of more widespread and polished information-gathering more or less mirrored sharpening social problems and resulting mentalities over the sixteenth and seventeenth centuries. In a nutshell, there was more to put down on paper. Nearly all of the concerns that were collected and collated in records resulted from sharper social strain, deepening social differentiation, and steeper regulation of more commercial markets.[6] England's population boom led to deeper divisions between the lucky 'haves' and down-on-luck 'have-nots'. The need to know England and its people better grew at the same time as numbers of poor soared, leading to more detailed recording of problems, including deep poverty, thinner resources, more migration, and crime-waves, real or imagined. Another consequence of changing social relations, the increasing role of 'middling' men in running local government, also had a pivotal part to play in developing information cultures. Increasingly able to read, write, and count, and often doing work that made these skills essential each day, 'middling' men who had most to lose if the parish peace or purse was threatened were the driving force behind collecting information.[7] They were men like Mathew Warren of Terling in Essex, who took on the time-consuming chore of answering a lengthy list of questions from county justices in 1630. 'A man of many parts', as a tailor, grocer, and one-time alehouse-keeper, '[h]e was well equipped to make the village report. Moreover, he could do it himself as he was literate. His lengthy reply to the justices' articles of enquiry with its careful penmanship, wayward phonetic spelling, and proud signature stands as a monument to his endeavour, to the pain it cost him, and to his sense of achievement.' Matthew doubtless got a pat on the back from his home pool of literate office-holders in this 'entirely agricultural village'.[8] Either in work where accuracy mattered or holding office, counting and recording became part and parcel of daily routine for 'middling' men like Matthew. In both arenas it helped to be precise. The men who kept business and household accounts, drew up inventories, and made wills were more often than not the same men who took steps to see that records were kept safely, recorded churchwardens' accounts, and walked around parishes noting people needing hand-outs. These were the 'most substantial inhabit-

---

Political Arithmetic (Oxford, 2009), 304. See also Joanna Innes, 'Power and Happiness: Empirical Social Enquiry in Britain from "Political Arithmetic" to "Moral Statistics"', in her *Inferior Politics: Social Problems and Social Policies in Eighteenth-Century Britain* (Oxford, 2009), 109–75.

6   See Wrightson, *ES*; Wrightson, *EN*, chs 4, 7, and 10.

7   Henry French, *The Middle Sort of People in Provincial England 1600–1750* (Oxford, 2007); Wrightson, *EN*, ch. 1. See also Keith Thomas, 'Numeracy in Early Modern England', *TRHS* 5th ser. 37 (1987), 103–32; Deborah Harkness, *The Jewel-House: Elizabethan London and the Scientific Revolution* (New Haven, 2007), ch. 3.

8   Wrightson & Levine, *Terling*, 142, 23.

ants' whose 'course of life', Edmund Wingate believed, 'may render them liable' to hold office.[9]

Authorities had been collecting information for centuries; the 'Domesday Book' (1086), after all, was the most spectacular example of nationwide counting before the first countrywide census (1801), and it is likely that long-standing practices of manorial record-keeping, including lengthy listings and surveys of holdings and other things, provided significant grounding for information-gathering in the early modern period.[10] But without question the potential for highly developed information cultures grew all over the country in the sixteenth and seventeenth centuries. Peter Burke calls attention to the 'paper state' or 'information state' at this time; this essay draws attention to local paper regimes.[11] It explores the domestic faces of discovery at a time when ships set sail to discover faraway lands and telescopes peered into outer space. A leading reason for England's spreading information cultures was the growing reach of the State into the provinces, most notably as a result of the Poor Law with its calls to count and classify people; legislation instructing parishes to keep registers of births, marriages, and deaths (1538); books of orders sent out to local authorities in times of plague and dearth (1578); settlement laws (from 1662 on); tax assessments; and countless articles of inquiry from Whitehall to all parts of the land.[12] It is still common to think of information flowing outwards from Westminster and Whitehall spearheaded by privy councillors or crown intelligence officers.[13] Yet we have a sizable body of evidence which shows that urban authorities had been counting and surveying paupers and other pressing problems for some time before the comprehensive 1598 Poor Law, so it would be a little misleading to always put central government in the driving seat of

[9] Thomas Forster, *The Lay-mans Lawyer: Or, the Second Part of the Practice of Law* (1654), 123; Edmund Wingate, *The Exact Constable With His Origin and Power in All Cases Belonging to His Office* (1677), fol. A4r. See also the essay by Henry French in this volume.

[10] See also O. Coleman, 'What Figures? Some Thoughts on the Use of Information by Medieval Governments', in *Trade, Government, and Economy in Pre-Industrial England*, ed. D. C. Coleman and A. H. John (1976), 96–112.

[11] Peter Burke, *A Social History of Knowledge From Gutenberg to Diderot* (Oxford, 2000), 117–19. See also Valentin Groebner, *Who Are You? Identification, Deceptions, and Surveillance in Early Modern Europe*, trans. M. Kyburz and J. Peck (New York, 2007), ch. 3; Norma Landau, 'The Laws of Settlement and the Surveillance of Immigration in Eighteenth-Century Kent', *C&C* 3 (1988), 391–420.

[12] See Michael J. Braddick, *State Formation in Early Modern England, c.1550–1700* (Cambridge, 2000); Steve Hindle, *The State and Social Change in Early Modern England, c.1550–1640* (Basingstoke, 2000); Paul Slack, 'Books of Orders: the Making of English Social Policy, 1577–1631', *TRHS* 5th ser. 30 (1980), 1–22.

[13] The classic statement remains G. R. Elton, 'Tudor Government: the Points of Contact', in his *Studies in Tudor and Stuart Politics and Government, III: Papers and Reviews 1973–1981* (Cambridge, 1983), 3–57.

England's developing information cultures without qualification.[14] Nonetheless, there were chronological overlaps between more wide-ranging information-gathering at central and local levels, not least because both were reacting to far-reaching social changes that altered the country for good. But the difference in this essay is that it takes attention away from the centre to examine information cultures from bottom up – improvements in uses of data at local levels – and the impacts of social change on collecting and applying information. My main argument is that local authorities developed their own information systems specific to local needs to a level of finesse and use over the seventeenth century that was distinctive.[15] They now more than ever before relied on information for government and policy and were also locked into information systems with other places near and far.

This period was also characterised by a developing formulation of authority in which public expression – processions, punishment, and other displays – while still vital was little by little starting to play second fiddle to private forms of discipline and government over the course of the seventeenth century. It is no coincidence that local information cultures became more highly developed over the same century (1600–1700) in which a nationwide system of incarceration inside houses of correction emerged with statutory backing and the scope and scale of punishing petty offenders in front of crowds was falling for the first time at significant rates. There was a shifting alignment in the day-to-day running of local-level government; it was a transitional time when formulations of authority were slowly but surely becoming more private and secretive while still keeping public faces. From around 1700 we no longer hear much in judicial records about ducking unruly women in water, carting wrongdoers, or locking others in stocks, and the focus for public whipping narrowed on the whole to flogging thieves. In addition, 'private' whipping is mentioned more often after 1650.[16] At a time when government was conducted more often in public – making appeals to the public, clamping down on loose talk, seizing writing – local government was ironically becoming more private and secretive and more dependent on information.[17] Authority was increasingly turning inwards, inside, and indoors. Local information systems in the hands of more literate

---

14 See, for example, Paul Slack, *From Reformation to Improvement: Public Welfare in Early Modern England* (Oxford, 1999), ch. 2.

15 Cf. Marjorie Keniston McIntosh, *Controlling Misbehaviour in England, 1370–1600* (Cambridge, 1998), esp. chs 1 and 3–4.

16 Joanna Innes, 'Prisons for the Poor: English Bridewells 1555–1800', in *Labour, Law, and Crime: A Historical Perspective*, ed. Francis Snyder and Douglas Hay (Oxford, 1987), 42–122; Paul Griffiths, 'Bodies and Souls in Norwich: Punishing Petty Crime, 1540–1700', in *Penal Practice and Culture, 1500–1900: Punishing the English*, ed. Simon Devereaux and Paul Griffiths (Basingstoke, 2004), 85–120.

17 Cf. *The Politics of the Public Sphere in Early Modern England*, ed. Peter Lake and Steve Pincus, (Manchester, 2007) and Paul Griffiths, 'Secrecy and Authority in Late Sixteenth- and Seventeenth-Century London', *HJ* 40 (1997), 925–51.

and numerate office-holders achieved new levels of significance and sophistication in times when far-reaching social changes and more private forms of government and institutions contributed to a surveillance-based frame of mind that shaped administrative responses. These systems will be examined in what follows through their greater use of counting, more careful record-keeping, growing resort to records for policy-making and prosecutions, information-sharing and contacts with other places, and also the deep unease felt by magistrates when information got into the wrong hands or became corrupted or out-of-date.

<h1 style="text-align:center">I</h1>

Exactitude and clarity were vital to information cultures. Magistrates called for 'true and perfect accompts' of anything to be counted, even if the results were sometimes a mixed bag. An East Sussex churchwarden was hauled over the coals for not handing in a 'true accompt'. Chester's Assembly complained at length about the 'want' of a 'perfect boucke' of accounts in 1567 that left 'many things' not 'perfectly knowne'. Winchester's leaders were also left in the dark as a 'carredge booke of cittie landes' had not been made for a 'longe tyme' and they had 'cleane forgotten' where most land was.[18] Sound government required clarity not incompleteness, ambiguity, nor doubt. The last order for governing Bridgnorth in 1587 stated that 'any contradiction, doubt or ambiguity' about the 'meanynge of these orders' would be cleared up by the 'bailiffs and xxiiii'. 'Doughts' coursed through Winchester in 1581 when someone realised that 'ancient usages and customes' had 'partlie growne out of memorie'.[19] A commitment to 'precysion' and its concomitant honesty was also a reason for clampdowns on deceits like disguise, perjury, forgery, 'false dice', 'false weights', 'false bills', breaking assizes of bread or ale, binding apprentices 'fraudulently', or any other 'deceavinge'.[20] Ideally, everything would be transparent, although records reveal countless exceptions to this rule. All over England magistrates became more concerned with precision, calculation, categorisation and their opposites, deception, ambiguity, and people who were said to be out of place.

Knowing that populations and problems were on the rise led to steps to plot them. Some guesses were wide of the mark. Many were couched in loaded language to convey a rising threat. Magistrates in Great Yarmouth bellyached in 1622 that 'the number of the poore' is 'of late yeares so greatly

---

[18] East Sussex Record Office [ESRO], Q1/EW2, fol. 15; CCRO Z/AB/1, fol. 119; Hampshire Record Office [HRO], Q1/1, fol. 44; W/B1/3, fol. 166v.

[19] Shropshire Record Office [SRO], BB/F/1/1/3, fol. 51; HRO, W/B1/3, fol. 27v.

[20] Lancashire Record Office [LRO], MBC/639, fols 173, 217; Gloucestershire Record Office [GRO], GBR/G/G3/SD/1, fol. 9; ESRO QI/EW2, fol. 19v; HRO, Q4/1, fol. 134; SRO, 3365/2430, fol. 62v; CCRO, QIB 2/7, fols 1v, 17, 68v.

increased and like to increase more and more'. The 'inummerable number of unnecesary alehouses' was on the minds of Chester justices in 1652. While in London, numbers of vagrants were 'extraordinary', 'excessive', and 'infinite'; numbers of 'foreign' workers without apprenticeships under their belts were 'vast'; and numbers of migrants squeezed into shabby alleys were 'unlimited'.[21] When anyone counted the people around them they tended to do so by rounding up numbers, like the men from the quick growing mining parish of Whickham (County Durham) who put the population at 100, 250, or over 500.[22] But it became necessary for local governments to be precise and learn the dimensions of something that needed sorting out. We have known for a while now about the growth in census taking after 1550, most famously the large-scale Census of the Poor compiled from house-to-house visitations in Norwich in 1570, but also notably in other towns like Salisbury, Canterbury, Poole, Worcester, Warwick, Ipswich, and others.[23] Local quantification was not just an urban phenomenon; we ought not to underestimate its role on county benches or in village administrations. Even the smallest village was asked to count something by justices from time to time, and villages like Cawston (not far from Norwich) launched their own inquiries when there were more needy people seeking charity to scrape by.[24] Urban counting was more pressing, however, as streams of migrants headed for towns. London and a number of East Anglian towns were in the front line of this law-and-order arithmetic. As in Norwich, censuses were conducted in times of trouble, and counting people led to finer tuned policies, better organised relief systems, the opening or reorganisation of bridewells, and clampdowns on vagrants and others singled out by shady lifestyles.[25]

Towns like Cambridge became inveterate counters as population grew, problems sharpened, and resources got thin on the ground. Articles issued by town governors at the start of the seventeenth century instructed 'surveyors' to 'diligently' and 'faithfully' collect and record the names and numbers of all people who had lived for less than three years in the town, along with 'poor persons able to gett theire living by labour', 'poor house-holders in everye parishe', inmates, anyone else who might need hand-outs, alehouse-keepers, and anyone giving room and board to beggars. Things got little better as time passed, as 'dewe and faythfull inquir[ies]' of inmates and divided tenements followed in 1623 and also in the next decade when

---

21 Norfolk Record Office [NRO], Y/C/19/5, fol. 266; CCRO, QJB/2/6, fol. 104v; Griffiths, Lost Londons, 39–40.

22 Levine & Wrightson, Whickham, 173.

23 Paul Slack, Poverty and Policy in Tudor and Stuart England (1988), 73–80.

24 Tim Wales, 'Poverty, Poor Relief, and the Life-cycle: Some Evidence from Seventeenth-Century Norfolk', in Land, Kinship and Life-Cycle, ed. Richard Smith (Cambridge, 1984), 351–404, esp. 368–9.

25 Paul Griffiths, 'Inhabitants', in Norwich Since 1550, ed. Carole Rawcliffe and Richard Wilson (2004), 63–88, esp. 63–75.

numbers of new-built houses and cottages and split tenements were worry-ingly high across the town.[26]

Magistrates spent more time counting and classifying paupers than on any other single issue. This regulatory arithmetic built up a real head of steam after 1570. A Chester parson picked up 6s for drafting a 'boke of all the names of the pore folke of the cittye' in 1572; children from hard-up families were added up in Great Yarmouth in 1574 and a 'viewe of all ye poore' took place two years later; child beggars on Ipswich's streets were counted in 1579 and 1582; the number of beggar 'boyes' in Great Yarmouth was noted in 1593; a Westminster parish reported in 1603 that it had fifty-two paupers who got weekly hand-outs (twelve were 'verie good' parish-ioners), 448 people likely to need hand-outs one day soon, ten landlords lodging migrants, and two 'oysterwives' ('or cryers of fishe').[27] Less spec-tacular than a large-scale census but still significant were counts of poverty-related issues like begging or numbers of pauper children living at home that were essential elements in planning policies. Again and again magistrates asked for names and numbers and they could get advice on counting and recording from treatises like *An Ease for Overseers of the Poore* (1601) and similar works that were aimed at parish officers.[28]

All over England people were counted and catalogued to an extent never seen before. A 'catalogue' of householders' names was handed to Chester's mayor in 1630. A lengthy list of Clitheroe's burgesses was drawn up in 1681 and similar lists were kept up-to-date in Gloucester and Marlborough (Wilt-shire). Constables in Great Yarmouth were given a week to produce 'true billes' of inhabitants in 1574. Names of Rye's householders were noted in a 'fayre booke' in 1593. The names of everyone living in Thetford were listed by constables in 1578 (lists of people in wards had been compiled a quarter of a century earlier). Winchester's leaders also collected inhabitants' names on a regular basis to get a better idea of the size of the city, for instance, or to get taxes paid on time. Inhabitants, apprentices, freeholders, copyholders, and taxpayers were added up everywhere.[29] The amount of counting in a single place was often impressive in both scope and scale. Preston's leaders

---

[26] Cambridge University Library [CUL], VC-CT-CUR 37.3, fols 218–23, 128–30, 131. See also Nigel Goose, 'Household Size and Structure in Early-Stuart Cambridge', *SH* 5 (1980), 347–85.

[27] CRO, TAR/1/14; NRO, Y/C/19/3, fols 91v, 138; Y/C/19/4, fol. 230; Suffolk Record Office Ipswich [SROI], C/4/3/1/1/2, fols 25, 50; Westminster Archives Centre [WAC], F6039; Guildhall Library, London [GL], MS 4524/1, fol. 91v. See also Griffiths, *Lost Londons*, ch. 11.

[28] *An Ease for Overseers of the Poore* (Cambridge, 1601). Other examples of instructions for local officers along the same lines include John Layer, *The Office and Dutie of Constables, Churchwardens and Other the Overseers of the Poor* (1641) and William Lambarde, *The Duties of Constables, Borsholders, Tyhtingmen and Such Other Low and Lay Ministers of the Peace* (1599).

[29] CRO, Z/AB/2, fol. 24v; LRO, MBC/639, fol. 225; GRO, GBR/F/4/5, fols 306–6v;

kept an eye on the state of the town after 1650 through counts of, amongst other things, out-of-work paupers, 'the poor to bee registered', people with no legal right to be in the town, burgesses who had not yet taken their oaths (as many as 100 in 1667), 'inmates, forreynors, and strangers and other enormities', people keeping 'great and unruly doggs' (twenty in 1665, including the mayor), unlicensed ale and beer sellers, irresponsible townspeople who did not turn up at the leet (ninety-five in one year), 'unnecessarie members', thoughtless people not clearing up 'middings' before their doors, and anyone making 'encroachments' on town lands. Trees in corporation woods were ordered to be 'numbered and marked' in 1708.[30] Information cultures were coming of age in England's provinces. When something irksome needed regulating magistrates were now more likely to count its dimensions and put it down on record. Drinking, selling without a licence, late night high spirits, empty seats in church, strangers lacking a toehold in the city, the marital standing of soldiers, hard-up boarders, Sunday sports, and the risk of something burning down to the ground and setting a city on fire, little escaped the quantifier's attention in seventeenth-century England.

Almost anything was counted and logged in records that became a basis for perceptions, policies, and prosecutions, including alehouse-keepers, brewers and malsters, inmates and vagrants (often on a weekly or monthly basis), officials and officers (like justices, collectors, jurymen, and watchmen), Quakers, 'persons popishly affected' and recusants (in lists that stretched to twenty pages or longer), servants, journeymen, 'mayds' who were 'out of service', workers, traders, trouble-makers not turning up at court, people who missed divine service, and seamen able to serve on board a royal ship.[31]

GBR/F/4/7, fols 5, 705; WRO, G22/1/20, fols 43–4, 176–7; G22/1/22, fols 178–9; NRO, Y/C/19/3, fol. 91v; Y/C/19/6, fols 39v, 109; ESRO, RYE 1/5, fol. 282.

[30] LRO, CNP 3/1/1, fol. 155v; CNP 3/1/3, fols 14v, 74v; CNP 3/2/1, fols 40, 87, 248, 297, 349, 416, 66, 84, 105, 131, 147, 241, 155–6, 296, 158, 169, 216–17, 391, 415, 111, 207, 95, 309.

[31] For instance, Northamptonshire Record Office [NORTHRO], NQS1, fol. 96v; 3/1, fols 54v, 303v; 3/2, fol. 8; DC/LR/A3/1, fol. 67; CUL, CUR 17.3 fols 71–2; LRO, MBC/639, fol. 191; Dorset History Centre [DHC], DC/DOB/8/1, fol. 190; SROI, C/4/3/1/1/3, fol. 210v; HD36/A/306; Cumbria Record Office Kendal [CROK], WQ/1/1, fols 4v, 54v; WQ/O/3, fol. 17v; GRO, GBR/F/4/5, fol. 411; GBR/B/3/2, fol. 590; HRO, BG/11/17/14, fol. 14; W/K5/4, fol. 33; W/D3/1, fols 22–4, 124–6; Q4/1, fols 118–22v; W/B2/1, fols 61v, 151; W/B1/4, fols 137v–8; ESRO, RYE 1/5, fols 48, 340, 360; QD/EW2, fols 6v–29; QD/EW7, fols 96–103v; QI/EW2, fols 35v–6; QI/EW5, fols 110–18v; Leicestershire Record Office [LERO], BRII/1/2, fol. 173; Southampton Record Office [SOUTHRO], SCA 6/1, fols 27, 30; CRO, Z/AB/1, fols 60, 232v, 252v; QJB 1/5, fols 30, 323, 530; QJB 2/6, fols 7–20v, 206–7v; ML/4/500; ML/3/478; Oxfordshire Record Office [ORO], C/FC/1/A1/02, fols 14, 53, 71v; WAC, E2416, fol. 134; NRO, Y/C/19/6, fols 39v, 78, 109; LMA, MJ/SBR/1, fols 67, 258, 310–11, 439, 560–2v; MJ/SBR/2, fols 121–2, 413–14; SRO, BB/C/7/5/1; EROC, JD/B5/SB4/1, fol. 1.

There was a cause-and-effect relationship between these lists and the labels increasingly used by local authorities to classify behaviour and status.

Paper lists sorted people into clear categories identifying inclusion and exclusion, respectability and lack of decorum, conformity and difference – householder, ratepayer, officer, citizen, someone with or without a licence, someone with or without residence rights, women living and working alone, or even well-behaved and restrained animals. In times when accelerating social differentiation led to more discrimination, lists of labels in records made definitions seem more fixed and stable. Listing labels after sorting information was an essential element of categorisation across all walks of life. Counting was the counterpart to the countrywide labelling of crimes and criminals. These quantitative and qualitative components of law and order shared common goals: precision, giving something not quite known a clearer form and identity, and, critically, categorisation. Anyone leafing through a quarter sessions order book or civic minute book can hardly fail to notice the counting and orderly listing of things vital to life and death: food, fuel, finances, war, and defence (muster rolls, for instance, tax rolls, grain and wood stocks, inventories of weapons and armour, bills of mortality, and so on). As the number of 'strangers' setting up home in England climbed, so too did the likelihood that they would end up as a statistic in a book, part of a population whose dimensions were now better known. One year before they added up their poor in 1570, Norwich's leaders counted 2,591 'strangers' in their midst, a number that soared to 3,925 in 1571. Most sizable East Anglian and south-eastern towns also added up their budding 'stranger' populations over the next few decades. Like policy more generally, counting was used and adapted to cope with emerging or emergency situations like harvest failure or epidemic disease, as when plague struck Great Yarmouth in 1590 and 'a trew note' of deaths was needed, and as in Ipswich in 1579 when beggars were quantified on paper and fourteen years later when names of recently arrived Londoners were collected.[32] Other matters singled out by counting might seem less significant but were in fact evidence of the extent to which quantification had become part and parcel of administration and also of the range of issues coming before local governments from houses about to topple down, 'criples', timber sales, and fire buckets to thatched roofs, 'lewd' wood-stealers, fishing boats, and 'noysome' 'chandlerhouses'.[33]

Local-level government depended on accurate books of records. One London parish asked its curate to 'make a perfecte booke' of the names of 'howseholders' and their wives, children, and servants in 1565. Governors in Winchelsea (East Sussex) instructed officers to 'serche out the lent of assize' and 'to make a perfect booke' of their findings. Hereford magistrates

32 NRO, Y/C/19/4, fol. 190v; SROI, C/4/3/1/1/2, fol. 25; C/4/3/1/1/3, fol. 34.
33 NRO, Y/C/19/5 fol. 265; Y/C/19/6, fol. 186v; CRO, Z/AB/1, fol. 123v; CUL, 17.3, fols 218–23; SOUTHRO, SCA 6/1, fol. 27; ESRO, RYE 1/5, fols 224, 260v–1, 351.

asked for an 'exact account' of the number of rogues who were whipped in 1682 as well as 'the names and surnames of all inmates'. Chester magistrates drew up 'a perfect list or callender' of Quakers locked up in prison in 1672.[34] 'Bookes' from all corners of the land covered the full range of policies and concerns including strangers, trades, hospitals, rents, orphans, musters, grain supplies, preaching, taxes, apprenticeship, cleaning streets, poverty, and vagrancy. Swallowfield's 'chief inhabitants' began 'a paper booke to regester all o[u]r doynges' in 1596. A 'booke of bastardy' was begun in Norwich in 1618. Names of prisoners were recorded in 'A paper booke for the gaole' in Gloucester. While St Michael-le-Belfry parish in York kept 'a booke for the 5th of November'.[35] When the post of Gloucester's mayor changed hands in 1613, the old mayor handed over to his successor an 'auncient ledger booke for inrollige leases', a 'boke of orphans', a 'great booke of the stew-ardes accompts', two 'booke[s] of common councell', a 'booke of survey', a 'paper booke of Mr maiors notes for corrections out of the sessions', an 'ancient booke of inrolement of deedes', 'dyvers bundles' of letters from the privy council, 'certen notes concerning the boothall', sessions rolls, and 'one great bundle of proclamacons'.[36] Information was also put on display in local communities in tables hung up for people to read 'dewties' and rules, as well as to pick up information on, amongst other things, apprentices, legacies, magistrates, benefactors, trades, weights, orphans, 'the sicknesse', fees, penal statutes, 'vestrie men', and pews. Like other places, one London parish kept a 'great table of the names of all the parishe' to check if people turned up for church on Sundays. A 'table' of the 'duties of pettie customes' was hung up in Southampton's 'owter audit howse' in 1616 in full 'publique viewe' so that there would no longer be any 'doubts' about them.[37]

'Bookes' held information vital to the running of government from one day to the next. Most of them were paginated to help the clerks flicking through them, and a name, case summary, or pointing finger in margins often let the reader find entries quickly. Records needed to be accessible. An 'inventory' of 'bookes and recordes remaining in the closett' in Norwich Guildhall was drawn up in 1609. A 'Register of the writings belonging to [St Martin-in-the-Fields] parish' (Westminster) was begun in 1685 and indexed all the way back to 1607.[38] It became common to index 'bookes' of records,

[34] GL, MS 6836, fol. 270; ESRO, Win/55, fol. 30; Herefordshire Record Office [HERO], BG11/17/1/5, fol. 67; CRO ML/3/486.

[35] HL, EL/6162, fol. 36; NRO, NMC 15, fol. 179; GRO, GBR/F/4/5, fol. 72v; York City Archives [YCA], YCA PR/Y/MB, fols 33, 60. See also Griffiths, *Lost Londons*, 412–13.

[36] GRO, GBR/G/G3/SO/1, fol. 29.

[37] GRO, GBR/F/4/5, fols 149v, 412; NRO, Y/C/19/5, fol. 166; SROI, C/2/2/2/1, fol. 36v; CROK, WSMB/K/1/5, 1596–97; GL, MSS 4524/1, fol. 37v; 4383/1, fol. 242; 2968/2, fol. 248v; 4385/1, fol. 233v; 4956/3, fols 28, 60; 4051/1, fol. 23; SOUTHRO, SCA 6/1, fol. 33.

[38] NRO, Assembly Book 5, fol. 385v; WAC, F2062.

a way to make information easier to find. Indexes were usually found at the back of books, as in Great Yarmouth's Assembly Book with subjects described in a few lines (1598–1625), Kendal's Order and Indictment Book (1685–1710), Lyme Regis's Orders of Mayor and Council (1594–1671), Chester's Assembly Books (1539–1624 and 1624–94), Winchester's 'Precedent Book' (1665), and Tewkesbury's Minute and Order Book (1608–90), which had an 'abstract of ordinances and constitucons' listed in sequence covering issues like 'hanging out lanternes in darke nights', 'not assisting officers', or 'revealing the towns secrets'.[39] Increasingly, names and contents were put in alphabetical order. John Taylor said that he listed towns in alphabetical order in his *Carriers Cosmographie* (1637) 'for the ease of the readers and speedier finding out' of each one.[40] Alphabetical lists of 'pentioners and orphans' (with payments noted down next to names) were made by St Martin-in-the-Fields parish (Westminster) after 1650. Gloucester's second oldest existing Common Council Minute Book (1632–56) has a twenty-two-page alphabetical index; the next one (1656–86) has an index at the front with big black letters cut into the sides of pages in neat alphabetical order. A Westminster parish compiled an 'alphabeticall book' of benefactors who gave money to 'inlarge' the church, and the same parish had an A–Z index at the back of its vestry book (1574–1640) listing subjects page-by-page including Bridewell, letters, perambulation, vagrants, records, the register, 'ticketts for poore people', and workhouses.[41] It was handy to have A–Z indexes of names in judicial records to track down recidivists. Names of prisoners and offenders are listed under the first letter of their last names in East Sussex's Sessions Indictment Books (1650–74) and Order Book (1673–79), Colchester's Book of Examinations and Recognizances (1600–19), Norwich's seven Sessions Search Books (1624–80), Herefordshire Sessions Order Book (1665–73), and Gloucester's Indictment Book (1638–53). 'The alphabet of the last sessions att Chichester and Lewes' was handed to justices in January 1661.[42] Some indexes stretched to twenty pages or even longer: those covering three successive Middlesex Sessions Process Register of Charges (1610–40) were thirty-nine, twenty-five, and twenty-nine folio pages long. A list of indicted recusants in Oxford diocese was seventeen pages long with names noted in alphabetical sequence and surnames highlighted in pink.[43]

39 CRO, Z/AB/1; Z/AB/2; NRO, Y/C/19/5; CROK, WSSMB/K/2/5; DHC, DC/LR/0/1/1; HRO, W/A6/1; GRO, TBR/A/1/2.
40 John Taylor, *The Carriers Cosmographie* (1637), fol. A3r.
41 WAC, F3348–3351; CRO, ML/3/486; GRO, GBR/B/3/2; GBR/B/3/3; WCA, F2001, fol. 163v.
42 ESRO, QI/EW2; QI/EW3; QI/EW4; QO/EW7; EROC, D/B5/SB2/6; GRO, GBR/G/G3/SIB/1; HERO, Q/SO/1; NRO, Norwich City Sessions Searchbooks 1–7; ESRO, QI/EW2, fol. 58v.
43 LMA, MJ/SB/P/001; MJ/SB/P/002; MJ/SB/P/003; HL, EL/2178.

There was growing confidence in records. It was important to say that something was backed up by records in times when written words were gaining importance as sources and emblems of authority: that it 'appeareth' 'by the booke', 'bill', 'recognizance' or 'noate', or that it was 'on record'. In one Great Yarmouth Audit Book a matter was cleared up as it 'appeared by the particulars thereof' from 'bookes beinge viewed and seene'.[44] Clerks cross-referenced between records, clinching something with data got from another page or book. Westminster churchwardens in 1601 asked that burial receipts 'bee examined and compared with the ministers register'. It was noted in Dorchester's Offenders Book that John Randall was presented on 4 February 1634 for swearing 'six oathes' and paid his fine thirteen days later. A long list of offenders' names in the same book has page references to the Mayor's Book next to each name to build cases. There are a string of page referrals in just one of Gloucester's Common Council Minute Books (covering 1632–56) on issues like catechising, 'gentlewomens seates in the colledge', sacking a coroner, meadows, brick, putting paupers to work, highways and prison repairs, 'forraigne butchers standings', the watch, cleaning streets, corn, hospitals, and pigs on the loose. Preston's records refer readers to other places to learn more about a wide range of issues including financial accounts, waste, town-lands, 'middings', crumbling walls, finding work for hard-up townspeople, court leet committals, and handing out 'swinemeate' to the needy.[45]

This is all to say that 'books' were very much working records, made to be consulted in courts, council chambers, and anywhere else where community matters were put on the table. Over and over again local authorities turned to records for guidance and validation, sometimes sending someone to search in other archives for 'evidens' or to have a word with someone else to help to clear something up. A Norwich clerk wrote in the margin of a sessions book in 1623: 'Remember to speake to Mr Alex Anguish about Mr Merricks sonne and for the evidences against Ann Hynds a prisoner'. In nearby Suffolk a quarter-of-a-century later magistrates got to the bottom of a riddle of a child left one day 'in an hayhowse in Croefield' when parish officials reported that 'it doth appeare by the register booke of Loddon that the child was there baptized' seven years ago.[46] Local records show their governments checking facts in charters, petitions, accounts, wills, parish registers, 'process', 'informacons', and depositions held in archives in hospitals, treasuries, schools, 'councell howses', assizes, and courts both in and outside their own patches. Likewise, parish records were consulted by magistrates sitting in civic courts, assizes, and quarter sessions to help settle disputes. London parishes consulted records held in archives at 'Chancerie', Exchequer, quarter

44 NRO, Y/C27/1, fol. 177.
45 WAC, F2001, fol. 96; DHC, DC/DOB/B/1, fol. 258v; GRO, GBR/B/3/2; LRO, CNP 3/1/3; CNP 3/2/1.
46 NRO, sessions book 1630–8, fol. 18v; SROI, B/105/2/1, fol. 98v.

sessions, sheriffs' prisons, the Mayor's Court, Star Chamber, other parishes, Christ's Hospital, the Tower, Parliament, Bridewell, the 'Prerogative Court', 'Capitall Office', 'Crowne Office', and in London's own Guildhall. Delegations travelled from further afield to trawl through records in London: for instance from Gloucester, Ipswich, Marlborough, Great Yarmouth, Chester, and Kendal.[47]

It is not far-fetched to think of England around 1600 in terms of interlocking networks of information systems in which places that were sometimes hundreds of miles apart kept in contact by letter, messenger, or emissary. Not much has been written about how provincial communities were linked by information pipelines heading not only in London's direction, but also to places near and far with which they had economic, judicial, or administrative connections. Gloucester, for instance, sent letters and envoys (or 'agents') to and from Bristol, Battle, Ludlow, Hereford, Stroud, Badminton, Taunton, Woodstock, Tewkesbury, Berkley, Oxford, Shrewsbury, Worcester, Exeter, Cirencester, Leicester, Manchester, Chester, Coventry, Ireland, the Council of the Marches, and royal, ecclesiastical, and parliamentary officials on issues that ranged from taxes, grain, elections, and customs duties to plague, wages, warrants, and writs.[48] Great Yarmouth was in constant touch with Whitehall and with nearby East Anglian towns like Norwich, King's Lynn, Beccles, Ipswich, Cambridge, Thetford, and Cromer. Kendal's contact sphere included Appleby, Carlisle, Lancaster, Manchester, York Assizes, and London, while the small parish of Walton-on-the-Hill in Lancashire paid for its administrators to ride to and from Liverpool, Preston, Warrington, Chorley, Crosby, Sefton, Kirkby, London, Tarbock, Lancaster for the assizes, Wigan 'for the inquisition', Prescot on a regular basis to bring presentments, Chester on religious matters for the most part, and Ormskirk to take prisoners and problems to quarter sessions.[49] In such ways, communities both large and small were bound up in networks with office-holders at the helm that were the building blocks of regional information cultures converging

---

[47] GRO, GBR/F/4/3, fol. 202v; GBR/B/3/2, fols 194, 554; GBR/B/3/3, fols 78, 283, 583; HERO, Q/SM/2, fol. 23; Q/SM/4, fol. 96v; SROI, C/4/3/1/1/3, fols 8, 52v, 106v; HRO, W/B1/4, fol. 46v; WRO, A1/160/1, Hil 1647, Mich 1646; G22/1/205/2, fols 26v, 99; LMA, MJ/SBR/1, fols 74, 138; MJ/SBR/5, fol. 345; WAC, WCB/2, fol. 121; EROC, D/B5/SB3/1, fols 35, 89; D/B5/Gb/1, fol. 30v; D/B5/SB3/1, fols 80, 81; LERO, 1D41/13/11/49a; 1D41/13/12/15a; NRO, Y/C/19/4, fol. 146; ORO, C/FC/1/A1/04, fol. 258v; Griffiths, *Lost Londons*, 414–15.

[48] GRO, GBR/F/4/3, fols 36v, 49v, 99v, 118, 168v, 238, 290, 411v; GBR/F/4/5, fols 13, 69v, 111, 220, 280v, 369v, 411, 487; GBR/F/4/6, fols 75, 87, 363, 444, 478; GBR/F/4/7, fol. 355; GBR/B/3/1, fol. 107v; GBR/B/3/2, fol. 751; GBR/B/3/3, fols 220, 260.

[49] NRO, Y/C/19/3, fols 6v, 40v, 83v, 105; Y/C/19/4, fols 8, 98v, 166, 199v, 220, 284; Y/C/19/5, fols 149, 328; Y/C/19/6, fols 45v, 85, 142, 216; CROK, WSMB/K/1/5, 1593–4, 1597–8, 1598–9, 1600–1, 1603–4, 1609–10, 1616–17; Esther M. E. Ramsay and Alison J. Maddock, eds, *The Churchwardens' Accounts of Walton-on-the-Hill, Lancashire, 1627–1667*, Lancashire and Cheshire Record Society 151 (2005).

on judicial, ecclesiastical, and economic focal points of contact, not least the capital city.

Six 'Great Letter Books' contain correspondence to and from Chester's mayors for almost two centuries after 1541, and they let us see how policing and policy could stretch over great distances, linking places in a common cause to bring troublemakers to justice. From these letters we learn for example that the lord chancellor knew that people suspected of 'burglarie and murther' in 1607 were lodging at 'Ye Signe of the Redd Lyon' in Chester (a 'descripcon' of their 'persons, ages, apparel, horses, and furniture' was put in the post); that Wigan's mayor knew that a thief on the run from his town was in a Chester lock-up in 1612; that a Warwickshire justice was tipped-off that a horse-thief who broke out of Warwick Prison in 1593 was under lock and key in Chester; and that Liverpool's mayor knew that a thief in Lancaster Prison was on the run from Chester in 1612.[50] Criminal business provided many reasons for communities to keep in touch through county-wide or countrywide hue-and-cries, for instance, sending information about crimes and criminals to one another, and taking suspects to prisons or courts in other places. Gloucester's civic accounts log fees paid to officers and officials for riding to Kingswood to bring back a 'preste' who killed a woman (1584), fetching 'Yearnolls wife' from Worcester by justice's order (1637), and sending one Newnham 'to make enquiry after the gent that was killed' (1658). Shrewsbury magistrates forked out 2s 'for Gods love' to hire a horse to fetch John Arude to give evidence against a suspected papist in 1580 and more money in 1585 to hire horses for 'ridinge aboute consernynge fellons'.[51] Physical descriptions of suspects that singled out build, distinctive marks, disabilities, hair, and colour and fabric of clothes followed them in hue-and-cries as they took flight, in the hope that they would end up in the authorities' net. Guidelines for hue-and-cries asked officials to provide a 'true description of the thieves and of the things taken'.[52] Some descriptions seem too short to have made a difference: a 'stranger' who caused trouble in Colchester in 1634 was said to be 'about 40 yeares of age, browne heyrd and somewhat grosse bodyed'; a carrier who had sex with a Dorchester woman in 1632 was described as being 'about 40 yeares and a short man with a whitish beard and blewish clothes'.[53] But other descriptions were more detailed: 'informacon' was passed around Norfolk in 1587 to round up a tall thief with a red beard who was wearing 'a broade russett hat with the verge buttened up', a 'blacke freise coate with a long dagger at his backe', and a gold ring on a finger; Chester's mayor was given instructions to track down

---

[50] CRO, ML/2/192; ML/2/254; ML/1/40; ML/6/85.

[51] GRO, GBR/F/4/3, fol. 232v; GBR/F/4/5, fol. 40; GBR/F/4/6, fol. 272; SRO, 3365/516; 3365/526.

[52] For example, Edmund Wingate, *Justice Revived Being the Whole Office of a Countrey Justice of the Peace* (1661), 112; *Compleat Justice* (1654), 135–6.

[53] EROC, D/B5/SB2/6, fol. 193v; DHC, DC/DOB/8/1, fol. 120v.

a light-fingered 'brode sett' man in 1604 who was said to have 'a reasonable bigg nose', was dressed in a green 'broad cloth' coat, and was said to be of 'middle stature' with a whitish beard 'shaven both sides' and a cut streaking across his forehead in a red line.[54]

Crime was another field of interest about which English communities passed information to a nearby town, neighbouring county, or somewhere further afield. We should think of information like news about current affairs criss-crossing the country. Letters crossed England long before the Post Office was launched in 1660, at 6d a letter in Marlborough in 1652 and 3d three years later in Gloucester (although rates varied).[55] Post-horses or 'hackney horses' carried 'post letters and proclamacons' along routes that were broken up by 'post-stages' in what was the quickest way to stay in touch, far faster than the time it took a 'footpost' to bring 'news from Dartmouth' to Gloucester in 1645. Winchester had 'fower posthorses in reddines' in 1590. Salisbury had horses ready to go into the 'west partes' at short notice.[56] Large sums were spent on the post network for 'busynes'. Marlborough spent £5 11s 4d on three post-horses in 1573, £8 for three more six years later, and £4 in annual salary to Richard Nash in 1600 'for kepinge of posthorses'. Gloucester's postmaster got a handsome quarterly salary of 50s in 1643.[57] Admittedly this postal service was not without faults: letters went missing, horses were not ready when needed, others were not returned to their owners, and saddles got lost.[58] But financial accounts from scores of places across England show how often the post-horse system was used and that it had strong backers, like Great Yarmouth's leaders in 1631 who were full of praise for a system in which letters went from their town to London by way of Ipswich that was 'very beneficiall' and by 'experience thought very necessary'.[59] All told, significant sums of money and effort were spent to make local paper regimes more effective.

With a book, information was accessible but also organised and hopefully controlled and protected. No wonder then that local governments tended to become more secretive; that orders were passed all over England in every conceivable jurisdiction making it a serious offence with steep fines (£5 in Leicester) to 'reveale secretts' of meetings of magistrates held 'in moste secret manner' or 'secret councell'.[60] Oxford's bailiffs moved their weekly meeting to the Audit House in 1637 as they could no longer 'consult' in

---

[54] NRO, Aylsham MS/181; CRO, ML/2/187. See also Griffiths, *Lost Londons*, 255–6.
[55] WRO, G22/1/205/2, fol. 101v; GRO, GBR/F/4/6, fol. 83.
[56] GRO, GBR/F/4/5, fol. 318v; GBR/F/4/6, fol. 86; SOUTHRO, SCA 6/1, fol. 19; HRO, W/B/2/2, fol. 9v; WRO, G23/1/3, fols 112v–13; CRO, ML/3/325.
[57] SRO, 3365/523; WRO, G22/1/205/2, fols 5v, 11v, 31v; GRO, GBR/B/3/2, fol. 255; GBR/F/4/3, fols 36v, 225v.
[58] ORO, C/FC/1/A1/03, fol. 68v.
[59] NRO, Y/C/19/6, fol. 192v.
[60] LERO, BRII/1/2, fol. 144; BRII/1/3, fol. 80; NRO, 3/1, fol. 103; NRO, NMC 8, fol.

'fitt and secret manner'.[61] Secrecy and protection went hand-in-hand and so magistrates took steps to take better care of records. In the middle of civil war, Bridgnorth's officials ordered the town clerk to make sure that 'writings' were kept 'safe in these dangerous tymes'.[62] Herefordshire's Sessions clerk was asked to keep a 'constant fire in the castle house' in 1688 to 'air' records that had become dangerously 'wett and damp' over the course of an 'extraordinary wett winter'. A Chester officer got 6s 8d for 'dustinge' records in 1614. People elsewhere picked up payments for covering, binding, stitching, cleaning, and 'repairinge' records. Oxford's 'red book' and 'litle white book' were sent to London to be 'transcribed in a faire and legible caracter' in 1663 because their 'greate antiquity' had made them 'obliterate and hardly to be read'.[63] Records were usually stored in strong-boxes: in a parish chest, 'boothall cheste', 'great iron chist', 'greate cheste', 'tresory chest', 'vestry chest', 'black chest', 'black boxe', 'great box', 'greate trunke', and (less impressively) a 'littell chest' or bag.[64] In order to keep sessions records 'safe in this time of danger' (1643), Wiltshire justices spent money on a 'stronge cheste' with two locks and keys. Government chests commonly had a number of locks with keys put in the hands of trusted officials. St Stephen Coleman Street parish (London) bought '2 padlocks and 4 keyes' for the 'great chest in the vestrie howse' in 1609.[65] Vestry houses are often mentioned as safe storage places for record chests, as well as the 'treasory', castle strong-room, gatehouse, 'armory', 'cowncell house' safe place, and 'hutch'.[66] In 1698 Preston's records were locked up in a strong-room lined with drawers that were 'marked with the letters of the alphabet', and magistrates also supplied a book that was kept in the same room with a guide to this filing system so that records could 'bee readily found by figure, letter, or reference in the said book'.[67]

584; NCQS, minute book 1571–81, fol. 13v; HRO, W/B1/5, fol. 105; W/B2/1, fol. 30v; GRO, TBR/A/1/2, fol. 36; EROC, D/B5/Gb1, fol. 9v; LRO, CNP 3/2/1, fol. 218.

[61] ORO, C/FC/1/A1/03, fol. 79.

[62] SRO, BB/C/1/1/1, fol. 45v.

[63] HERO, Q/SM/2, fol. 225v; CRO, TAB/1, fol. 30; TAR/1, fol. 22; ORO, C/FC/A1/03, fol. 311.

[64] E.g. ESRO, QO/EW3, fol. 34v; GRO, GBR/F/4/5, fols, 47, 74; Centre for Kentish Studies [CKS], Md/Can/1a, fol. 66; DHC, DC/LR/G/2/2, 1111671–72; NRO, Y/C/19/5, fol. 24; Norwich Clavors' Book 3, fol. 56; WAC, F2002, fol. 46; WILTRO, G23/1/3, fol. 289; HERO, BG/11/2315. See also Griffiths, 'Secrecy and Authority', 934–35.

[65] WRO, A1/160/1, Hil 1643; GL, MS 4457/2, fol. 120.

[66] E.g. GRO, GBR/F/4/3, fol. 151v; CKS, TE/S2, fol. 374; GL, MS 9680, fol. 119; NRO, Y/C/19/3, fol. 129; T/C1/2, fol. 211; Norwich Assembly Book 5, fol. 259v; North Devon Record Office [NDRO], Bi/3792, fol. 8; SROI, C/3/4/1/34, fol. 9; WAC, E2413, fol. 93; Wiltshire Record Office [WILTRO], G/22/1/205/2, fol. 74.

[67] LRO, CNP 3/1/1, fol. 14.

II

Chester's crooked clerk who began this essay revealed the potential for corruption and neglect in England's information cultures. The predicament was less deep but Mr Spooner who kept a key to Thetford's chest still caused problems in 1626 when he sheepishly owned up that he could not 'fynde it'.[68] Clerks were paid well on the whole and also picked up money on the side for drawing up documents: Hampshire's Sessions clerk was paid 363s in 1694 for 'writing 363 orders of sessions'.[69] But clerks made mistakes and also fell behind in writing up books. A Norwich clerk landed in trouble in 1608 for registering freemen in a book that had been 'discontynewed for many yeares'. Six decades later 'long neglect of takeing and auditing [treasurers] accompts' left Chester's finances in disarray. The 'want of yearly accompts' was enough to stir 'suspition of unfaithfull dealing' in Tewkesbury in 1618.[70] Not everything went according to plan all of the time. Lax officers forgot or failed to count as asked. Southampton's beadles were taken to task in 1604 for 'not presentinge' the 'names of all newcomers, inmates, and under-tenants' each week as they had been instructed to do by civic magistrates. A Westminster beadle also got on the wrong side of governors in 1659 for his 'greate neglecte' in not making a 'return of inmates'. Twenty-five years later a Westmorland constable ended up in court for not bringing in 'lists' of suspect poachers 'yt keepe guns and greyhoundes at home'.[71] Records also went missing, despite orders making it clear that they could not be copied or taken anywhere outside their storage places without prior permission.[72] In Great Yarmouth alone a fair number of inhabitants – officials for the most part – were ordered to hand over records to magistrates, including Mr Felton (1589), Mr Johnson (1588), Mr Thompson (1624), Mr Gryce and Mrs Bresely (1584), Widow Smith (1579), and the recorder's clerk who had 'cort rolls' with him at home in 1613 stretching all the way back to the 1580s. 'Divers persons' were asked to hand over 'town writings, records or rolles' at other times. Some had a stack of records at home and we must assume that at some point they had been given permission to keep them there. In 1621 the assembly happily reported that Mr Gray had 'brought in these court rolls' – '8 Eliz, 8 Jac, 13 Jac, 14 Jac, 15 Jac, 16 Jac, 17 Jac' – a few months after he was first asked to do so, but unhappily it was also noted that he still had 'rolles of two yeres with him at home, 15 Eliz, 22 Eliz'.[73] Also

---

[68] NRO, T/C1/4, fol. 37.
[69] HRO, Q3/3, fol. 97.
[70] NRO, NCQS minute book 1603–25, fol. 107; CRO, Z/AB/2, fol. 148v; GRO, TBR/A/1/2, fol. 22.
[71] SOUTHRO, 6/1, fol. 28; WAC, F2003, fol. 203; CROK, WQ/O/3, fol. 48.
[72] ORO, C/FC/1/A1/03, fol. 103v; NRO, T/C1/2, fol. 211; NRO, 3/1, fol. 207v.
[73] NRO, Y/C/19/3, fol. 82; Y/C/19/4, fols 1, 83v, 158v, 176; Y/C/19/5, fols 20, 83, 122, 220v, 238, 306v; Y/C/19/6, fol. 86v.

tiresome were people who did not bring records to magistrates when asked to do so, like the three Norwich dyers who were put on trial in 1640 'for refuseinge to shew the book of their company [to aldermen] and refuseing to tell wher it is'.[74]

Information and records were always at risk of tampering or worse, although magistrates thinking first and foremost of what was 'prejudiciall' or 'superflouse' also removed or 'rectified' orders after reviewing which of them were 'meetest to be observed' and which 'growen out of use and voide' or how many were 'fitt to be repealed' or 'needful' to 'be added or amended'.[75] Magistrates also cut entries that were damaging or when someone who was once a valued member of a community caused offence, like William Malama whose name was 'taken oute' of Clitheroe's records in 1628 when he was stripped of his 'burgesse' status for bad behaviour. Joseph Venables was 'struck out' of a Shropshire 'freeholders book' because word arrived that he was a dissenter. A London parish paid 4d to take 'a mans name out of the register' but we do not know why. In 1655 Gloucester's leaders ordered that 'words' were 'to be blotted out of the 39th article of the ordinances of ye hospitalls'. In Preston in 1655 Henry Chorley (bailiff) was up in arms after it was put down on civic record that his accounts failed to balance. It took five long years before he could finally 'cleare himselfe', at which point magistrates said it was 'unreasonable' that his 'presentment' 'should stand on record' and ordered it to be immediately 'expunged' and 'obliterated'.[76] Thick lines or squiggles also crossed out entries that were no longer in effect: baptism and burial registrations, for instance, cases of 'uttering scornefull words' against a deputy steward and 'breakinge the assize of ale and beere' in Loughborough, and another from Ashby-de-la-Zouch about a payment 'for maimed soldiers and prisoners as appears by an acquittance May 5 1631'.[77]

Local authorities also took care to keep a sharp eye on what might have been inserted in their records without permission – blank spaces in record books were sometimes filled in to try to prevent later additions – and on any attempt to deface or blot entries by someone who did not have authority to do so. Now and then a clerk opened a book and found that some of its pages had been torn out or entries blotted out without word from anyone in government. In Thetford, Norfolk, at the start of the seventeenth century, the town clerk grew anxious as he leafed through the 'Towne Booke' and found to his dismay that pages were missing: 'the foregoing tenn leaves were lost before I had the booke', he wrote in the same book: someone else ripped

[74] NRO, NCQS minute book 1639–54, fol. 12v.
[75] HRO, W/B21, fols 2v, 91; W/B1/1, fol. 99; CRO, Z/AB/1, fol. 178; GRO, GBR/B/3/2, fol. 136; GBR/B/3/3, fol. 25v; NRO, Y/C/19/4, fol. 25v; Ramsay and Maddock, *Churchwardens' Accounts*, 52.
[76] LRO, MCB/172; SRO, QS 1/3, fol. 30; GL, MS 4241/1, fol. 313; GRO, GBR/B/3/2, fol. 845; LRO, CNP/3/2/1, fol. 139.
[77] HL, HAM Box 26, folder 12, folder 22; HAM Misc Box 12.

them out, not me. He probably felt that his job was on the line and that he needed to do something to save his own skin and also to make sure that Thetford was not harmed in any way by its lost leaves. A distressed Westmorland Sessions clerk who was tracking back through a sessions book found that four pages had been ripped out, and, shortly after, he saw that two more pages were missing from the same book.[78] A record book was the nucleus of information cultures and its pages were sacrosanct inscriptions of authority, not to be tampered with unless magistrates said so. That some people did the exact opposite is a further testament to the power of records in early modern England. It is unclear why information in Thetford and Westmorland books was wiped out, except to say that almost certainly it was done by someone with self-preservation in mind.

At other times self-interest was a reason for gaps and blotches in records. Winchester's recorder 'scandalously' called the mayor-elect 'a drunkard and swearer' in 1657; this was only the latest in a string of abuses that stretched back over more than five years of his term in office, and still strong in memories was the 'evil council' he gave the mayor in his second year in office that led to the 'eras[ing] and oblterat[ing]' of 'orders in the assembly booke'.[79] Other 'obliterations' were evidently cover-ups when panicky people scratched out presentments, prosecutions, or payments. A Cheshire tenant complained to 'gentlemen' in his parish in 1648 after hearing that 'one Hodgkinson' had 'altered and corrupted' the 'churchbooke' to raise his annual rent and he was doubtless relieved when 'the booke was recti-fied againe'. Two Herefordshire grand jurymen stood in the dock rather than the jury box in 1666 after it emerged that 'without the privity and consent of fellow jurors' they had 'cutt off' 'a parte of the parchment' on which constables' presentments were written down, no doubt to spare a friend from embarrassment. An East Sussex 'defacer' 'blotted out present-ment bills after they had been 'sworne and signed' by a justice; another ended up in hot water 'for altering and strikeing out certaine figures in the poore booke'; and one more ended up on trial after he was caught 'blotting out and defaceing' court leet 'presentments'.[80] There are also cases when nervous people who needed to hide something from scrutiny raided chests to remove incriminating papers. When a set of churchwardens' accounts was found to be 'unjust and unreasonable' in Stratford-on-Avon in 1696, the offending churchwardens tried to cover up their tracks by 'privately tak[ing] awaye' the records in question. It came to light at the Somerset Quarter Sessions in 1612 that the recently deceased Humphrey Quick of West Monkton had 'imbeseled' 'wrytings and evydencs' that detailed 'the

[78] NRO, T/C1/6, fol. 11; CROK, WQ/I/3, fols 143, 150, 161–4.
[79] HRO, W/B1/5, fols 119v–20v.
[80] CRO, QJB 1/6, fol. 241; HERO, Q/SO/1, fol. 39; ESRO, QI/EW6, fol. 55; QI/EW7, fols 152v, 154v.

ordering and governynge' of the town's almshouse, possibly in an attempt to influence the election of the 'howse' governor.[81]

III

By seeking information on a wide range of social, economic, and administrative matters, central government (and the Church also) had a large helping hand in shaping local information networks across sixteenth- and seventeenth-century England. This level of central government information collection drew local communities up and down the land into an embryonic countrywide information network that grew in scope and scale as central government worked hand-in-hand with local authorities to cope with sharp social strains after 1550 associated with the impact of population growth from the mid sixteenth century. In this two-way process local governments received encouragement and direction from Whitehall, but we must never forget that towns in particular took leading roles in collecting information about their people and problems, and that local-level surveillance had its own self-generating priorities and processes.

Up to now, however, we have tended to follow a top-down point of view to this question of information collection, leaning towards the impetus and requirements of central government. But this essay has been all about local arithmetic and how information was generated and communicated within and between local communities who used data day after day to try to make government more effective. A fair amount of local information went to Whitehall, but more of it was collected for needs that were specific to events and predicaments in particular communities. Salisbury's 'straungers', Ipswich's child beggars, Preston's 'great and unruly doggs', Northampton's 'maides', Southampton's 'hedgebreakers', and Gloucester's 'criples' were all local matters that were verified by local information, irrespective of the fact that they cropped up across the length and breadth of the country. Communities 'surveyed' themselves, but they also took advantage of contact spheres to exchange information with places far and near. Whether seeking statistics and solutions on their own home patch or swapping information with another town or village, local governments were more often than not trying to cope with issues that were the direct results of social change and differentiation and discrimination: crime, for instance, policing, migration, settlement, vagrancy, hardship, hygiene, inmates, land, beliefs, and many more besides. Information cultures were rooted in social change both in terms of responding to tough challenges and in terms of the rising potential for local-

[81] *The Vestry Minute Book of the Parish of Stratford-on-Avon, From 1617 to 1699 A.D.* (1899), 151; E. H. Bates, ed., *Quarter Sessions Records From the County of Somerset,* I: *James 1, 1607–1625,* Somerset Record Society (1907), 89.

level surveillance that resulted from more private forms of government and the roles and duties of middling men in office who were by and large more adept at reading and writing and had greater mathematical competence.

Information-gathering and record-keeping on a wide scale became part and parcel of everyday local government and social practice in early modern England. Information cultures were still in the making and far from being foolproof or without flaws, but unquestionably and irrevocably information cultures fanning out across England became more highly developed at local levels. This should make us rethink chronologies of the development of polished local-level surveillance over time, so that the early modern period no longer looks like a deficient stage on the road to modern information systems, but more accurately like a time in its own right when important improvements and innovations were made in the collection and handling of information. Also importantly, reconfigurations of social relations can be examined and understood through information and records that categorised populations and problems. This is all to say that the choices prioritised by local authorities when it came to gathering information, along with the resulting sorting of information in their records, mirrored, encouraged, and also helped to define growing social polarisation (deeper splits between people in and around the lower, middle, and upper rungs of the social ladder that have long been essential elements in Keith Wrightson's body of work). Like labelling crime, or any other situation or perception in which magistrates defined behaviour or social relations, information collation that was very deliberate and ideologically driven made and remade English society but only as local authorities saw fit. For us, but also for people in power in early modern times, each one of the communities that together made up English society is imagined by the information in its records. For a long while now local arithmetic has had a leading role in defining and cataloguing English society.

6

Intoxicants and the Early Modern City

PHIL WITHINGTON

In early 1629 Elizabeth Sanderson sued Alice Wilkinson for defamation in the church courts. Both women ran alehouses in Stonegate, York, with their respective husbands (William Wilkinson and Ralph Sanderson). Elizabeth Sanderson's main witness was her cousin, Anthony Carthorne. He deposed that in August 1628, Alice Wilkinson had sent for him at her alehouse, ostensibly about money he owed her but really to challenge him over her husband's recent arrest 'at the suit of Ralph Sanderson'. Thomas Prainge, a shoemaker then 'drinking two pots of ale', described how Alice Wilkinson told Carthorne 'you have now gotten your desire, for you have gotten my husband laid in the low gaol'. When Carthorne 'answered and swore that he did not know of the arrest', Alice retorted that 'your drunken wey-necked Jade your cousin [Elizabeth Sanderson] hath caused it to be done, her neighbours take notice of her drunkenness'.[1] It was these menacing words, spoken in anger before witnesses, which gave Elizabeth Sanderson the chance to initiate legal proceedings against Alice Wilkinson.

That Sanderson decided to act on the opportunity is unsurprising. Thanks in large part to Keith Wrightson and other practitioners of the 'new social history' it has long been appreciated that one striking – indeed defining – characteristic of early modern England was the increasing willingness of ordinary men and women to appropriate legal institutions to resolve interpersonal conflict.[2] In this respect Ralph and Elizabeth Sanderson

This essay was researched and written with the help of an ESRC Research Fellowship.

[1] Borthwick Institute of Historical Research [BI], CPH 1823 (1629), *Sanderson* v. *Wilkinson*, depositions of Anthony Carthorne, Thomas Prainge.

[2] See Wrightson & Levine, *Terling*, 119–20; C. W. Brooks, 'Interpersonal Conflict and Social Tension: Civil Litigation in England, 1640–1830', in *The First Modern Society: Essays in English History in Honour of Lawrence Stone*, ed. A. L. Beier, David Cannadine, and J. M. Rosenheim (Cambridge, 1989), 357–99; Laura Gowing, *Domestic Dangers: Women, Words and Sex in Early Modern London* (Oxford, 1996), 30–58; Steve Hindle, 'The Keeping of the Public Peace', in *The Experience of Authority in Early Modern England*, ed. Paul Griffiths, Adam Fox, and Steve Hindle (Basingstoke, 1996), 213–48; Craig Muldrew, 'The Culture of Reconciliation: Community and the Settlement of

were archetypal. Nor is it unexpected that it was an attack on Elizabeth's public reputation which precipitated the suit. It is now historical orthodoxy that notions of 'credit', 'fame', and 'repute' carried enormous significance not merely for England's landed and political elites but for all sections of society; that as far as ordinary people were concerned, status, wealth, and moral standing were inextricable; and that the basis and behaviour upon which personal reputations were constructed were changing during the early modern period.[3] However, it is a third feature of this everyday and ostensibly unremarkable incident which this article addresses: namely what it suggests about the centrality of drink to the lives of these Stonegate neighbours. The Wilkinsons and Sandersons were both 'tiplers': keepers of alehouses in which people like Prainge consumed 'pots of ale'. Likewise the main slur on Elizabeth Sanderson was 'drunkenness'. According to Alice Wilkinson, Elizabeth's drinking made her garrulous ('wey-necked'), sexually incontinent ('Jade'), and vulnerable to neighbourly sanction. Moreover, Alice's threat (that 'her neighbours take notice of her drunkenness') suggests such sanction need not be limited to gossiping, tutting, and raised eyebrows. Rather, the prevailing juridical culture of early seventeenth-century England meant that, in York as elsewhere, the 'notice' of neighbours could quickly lead to a jury presentment at the quarter sessions, exposure to the wrath of magistrates, formal punishment, and for tiplers the rescinding or 'discharge' of their licence. Whatever the 'real' reasons behind this feud, it was in Elizabeth's interests to clear her name of drunkenness.[4]

If drinking figured prominently in the lives of these Stonegate neighbours, it is likewise central to Wrightson's conception of social relations in the later sixteenth and seventeenth centuries. As he explains, 'it can be asserted without exaggeration that at the level of the local community, the struggle over the alehouses was one of the most significant social dramas of the age'.[5] This was a drama in which the litigious proclivities and status obsessions of men and women were driving forces. On one hand, alehouses stood at the heart of parish neighbourhoods: 'the centres *par excellence* of the social lives of the common people'. On the other, from the mid sixteenth century they became foci for the reformatory energies of 'moralists and magistrates'.

Economic Disputes in Early Modern England', *HJ* 39 (1996), 915–42; and the essay by Tim Stretton in this collection.

[3] See Wrightson, ES, 222–8; Anna Bryson, *From Courtesy to Civility: Changing Codes of Conduct in Early Modern England* (Oxford, 1998), esp. 43–74; Craig Muldrew, *The Economy of Obligation: The Culture of Credit and Social Relations in Early Modern England* (Basingstoke, 1998), 148–73; Alexandra Shepard, 'Manhood, Credit and Patriarchy in Early Modern England, 1580–1640', *P&P* 167 (2000), 75–106; Phil Withington, *The Politics of Commonwealth: Citizens and Freemen in Early Modern England* (Cambridge, 2005), 124–55.

[4] Wrightson & Levine, *Terling*, 135–6.

[5] Wrightson, ES, 167.

A raft of parliamentary legislation, with compulsory licensing at its centre, empowered local governors to prevent the 'hurts and troubles … abuses and disorders' that these establishments housed. These laws were initially 'widely ignored' by communities, local office-holders preferring to sanction misdemeanours rather than reform manners. From the 1610s, however, there was a momentous attitudinal change: 'parish and village officers also began to turn against the previously tolerated activities of their ale-sellers'. It was here that the real significance of the drama lay. By 'attacking the major centres of popular sociability', local office-holders 'were dissociating themselves from the customary behaviour of their neighbourhoods and aligning themselves with a definition of good order and social discipline derived from their social superiors'.[6] They forsook, in other words, one concept of order for another.[7] In this way the struggle over alehouses and behaviour associated with them encapsulated a pivotal development of the early modern era. This is the emergence of cultural distinctions – in 'education, religion, attitudes, beliefs and manners' – that reinforced 'the polarising effects of demographic and economic development' and facilitated 'the dissociation of polite and plebeian cultures' within local societies.[8]

The travails of York householders might seem to corroborate this compelling narrative of the relationship between drinking and social change. From 1610, influential sections of the York citizenry used civic offices to police drinking habits and places – and punish perceived excesses – on an unprecedented scale. One consequence of these intermittent but intense campaigns was that by the later 1620s 'drunkenness' belonged to the wider vocabulary of insult and defamation within the city: a person's relationship to drink constituted their 'credit' and 'fame' to a greater extent than in previous or indeed subsequent decades.[9] Yet in other respects there are obvious differences between circumstances in York and the prolonged social drama Wrightson identifies. To stay with the Stonegate feud: the depositions reveal not so much tiplers at their neighbours' mercy as tiplers policing

---

6   *Ibid.*, 168–9; see also Keith Wrightson, 'Alehouses, Order and Reformation in Rural England, 1590–1660', in *Popular Culture and Class Conflict 1590–1914: Explorations in the History of Labour and Leisure*, ed. Eileen Yeo and Stephen Yeo (Brighton, 1981), 1–25; Wrightson & Levine, *Terling*, 136–41.

7   Keith Wrightson, 'Two Concepts of Order: Justices, Constables and Jurymen in Seventeenth-Century England', in *An Ungovernable People: the English and their Law in the Seventeenth and Eighteenth Centuries*, ed. John Brewer and John Styles (1980), 21–46.

8   Wrightson, *ES*, 13–14. This narrative is also found in Norbert Elias, *The Civilizing Process: Sociogenetic and Psychogenetic Investigations*, trans. by Edmund Jephcott (Oxford, 2000); Jan de Vries, *The Industrious Revolution: Consumer Behaviour and the Household Economy, 1650 to the Present* (Cambridge, 2008); Max Weber, *The Protestant Ethic and the Spirit of Capitalism* (1992 edn).

9   Based on comparing defamatory language reported in the church courts the 1590s with the 1620s. See Phil Withington, 'Intoxicants and Society in Early Modern England', *HJ* 54 (2011), 631–57.

each others' drinking. Nor did the feud pit 'rich' against 'poor': both families belonged to the same moderately prosperous milieu of urban freemen. Ralph Sanderson was listed as a ratepayer in 1632, paying 1d per week in poor relief; a William Wilkinson with close connections to the drinks trade was assessed to pay 4d per week to the parish of North Street the same year (suggesting the Wilkinsons may have moved neighbourhood after the dispute); and Alice Wilkinson was prosperous enough to lend money to Carthorne in 1628.[10]

More intriguingly, although drunkenness could be a dangerous reputation to acquire in seventeenth-century York – especially for women – subsequent depositions dissecting Carthorne's character suggest it was a more normal feature of city life than Alice Wilkinson's threat implies, at least for men. A number of deponents were called by the Wilkinsons to show why Carthorne was 'a man of small credit and estimation amongst his neighbours'.[11] A recurring reason was that he was 'much addicted to drunkenness and to haunt and frequent alehouses very disorderly'; that he was 'noted and defamed for a common drunkard within the city of York'.[12] Thomas Martin explained that Carthorne

> was and is such a person as is termed a good fellow, and such as one will keep company and spend his money with his friends, the which he endeavours to refrain as much as he can but that he is drawn away some time by his friends and wits and is such as one as used to go to alehouses and drink hard sometimes, in so much that … he hath sometimes been so overtaken with drink, as that he was not fit to keep company any longer.

To illustrate the point, Martin told a story of Carthorne 'drinking in the house of Mr Whalley within the parish of St Sampson's with some company at which time a wager was laid, about the striking the top of the house or chamber where they were with their feet'. Carthorne succeeded and

> demanded the wager, whereupon some quarrel cross betwixt him and some of the said company which was with him, and being moved onto the street they began to fight, whereupon the constable of that parish [George Brownless] came and set both him and the rest of the company in the stocks in the Thursday Market.[13]

Other neighbours called to testify by the Sandersons contested this depiction of Carthorne, arguing that whatever his excesses he was 'an honest

---

10 York City Archives [YCA], E70 (1632).
11 BI, CPH 1823, *Sanderson v. Wilkinson*, deposition of John Clarke. For an account of this procedure see Alexandra Shepard, 'Poverty, Labour and the Language of Social Description in Early Modern England', *P&P* 201 (2008), 51–95.
12 BI, CPH 1823, *Sanderson v. Wilkinson*, charges against Carthorne.
13 *Ibid.*, deposition of Thomas Martin.

man and person of good credit and estimation'. They also observed that Martin was hardly a model of sobriety. Thomas Harrison, a twenty-six-year-old 'labourer' who had worked as a servant to Ralph Sanderson, described Martin in the same terms as others had Carthorne: as 'a very poor man and man of small credit ... given to excessive drinking'. He recalled one occasion when Martin 'was so overtaken with excessive drinking that he was forced to lie down upon a bed in the house of Ralph Sanderson ... and was not able to help himself but lay sleeping there for five hours'. When Martin's wife arrived Harrison heard her explain 'that her husband had been drinking wine that morning'.[14]

These stories are striking for a number of reasons. However vividly neighbours painted these anecdotes with moral gloss, the behaviour described was evidently quotidian and normative for sections of the male urban populace.[15] Carthorne and Martin were not like John Clark of Terling, who developed an impressive portfolio of bad behaviour at the turn of the sixteenth century and was, as Wrightson shows, legally harassed for his lifestyle.[16] The company which culminated with Carthorne in the stocks was an example of habitual behaviour gone wrong, with boundaries between 'good fellowship' and drunkenness blurred. Martin could stereotype it as the company of 'good fellows', 'friends', and 'wits'.[17] Its punishment was, in turn, a reactive, pragmatic, and quite possibly frequent strategy on the constable's part which as far as can be told did not lead to more formal proceedings. Furthermore, Martin himself did not feel impelled to start defamation proceedings about his rumoured intoxication; nor does he seem to have suffered especial stigmatisation because of it. Nor were Carthorne and Martin 'poor' in any straightforward sense. Carthorne was a cloth-weaver then employed as a bailiff by the Council of the North, which was housed in the King's Manor, close to Stonegate: he was a minor state official whose duties, and apparent zeal in fulfilling them, made him not only unpopular with householders he arrested but equally capable of affording 'hard' drinking sessions himself. Although Martin described himself as a 'labourer', he signed his name with an educated hand and could afford to drink wine in the morning. He was not listed as a ratepayer of the parish of St Wilfred, where he lived, but a compulsory and extensive assessment for church repairs in 1639 taxed

14 *Ibid.*, depositions of William Rockliffe, Thomas Harrison.
15 Phil Withington, 'Company and Sociability in Early Modern England', *SH* 32 (2007), 291–307; Alexandra Shepard, '"Swil-bolls and Tos-pots": Drink Culture and Male Bonding in England, 1560–1640', in *Love, Friendship and Faith in Europe, 1300–1800*, ed. Laura Gowing, Michael Hunter, and Miri Rubin (Basingstoke, 2005), 110–30.
16 Wrightson & Levine, *Terling*, 110–11.
17 For good fellowship see Mark Hailwood, 'Sociability, Work and Labouring Identity in Seventeenth-Century England', *Cultural and Social History* 8:1 (2011), 9–29; for 'wit' see Phil Withington, '"Tumbled in the Dirt": Wit and Incivility in Early Modern England', *Journal of Historical Pragmatics* (forthcoming 2012).

him 12*d* (in the bottom third of contributors but by no means in the basement).[18] Moreover, if neither man fits easily into the (rural) social structures Wrightson described, then the urban alehouse invoked in the depositions also sits uneasily with their reputation as institutions run, in Peter Clark's words, 'by the poor for the poor'.[19] The Sandersons and Wilkinsons were ratepayers who ran their houses as businesses; likewise the house in St Sampson's where Carthorne and company started their fight was owned by Mr Whalley. Carthorne and Martin did not resort to these houses from necessity or poverty; as far as can be discerned they did so by choice and for reasons of 'pleasure' and 'taste' (in the complicated sociological sense of those terms).[20] As importantly, they could do so because they had, however temporarily, the requisite cash or credit.

All of which begs questions of the story told by Wrightson about the *rural* alehouse. This article aims to respond to some of these questions from an *urban* perspective which is relatively absent from Wrightson's account of English society. It does so not to deny either the centrality of alehouses to local communal life or the impact of the reformation of manners in seventeenth-century English society. Rather it argues that this particular drama was one dimension of a more expansive, multifaceted story of intoxicants and social change, the full extent of which is as yet unrecognised.[21] This story becomes more apparent once the complexities of urban living are appreciated. What follows examines an early modern city, not a village, using the kind of detailed community study which Wrightson has done so much to develop.[22] In so doing it considers the drama surrounding alehouse licensing as part of a broader economy of intoxication – one where ale and beer were two of several commodities increasingly available to consumers; where wholesalers, producers, consumers, and retailers lived cheek-by-jowl; where various kinds of authority looked to regulate and profit from the trade; where 'Puritanism' was an important but by no means singular agent of social change; and where 'companies' frequenting drinking establishments were many, diverse, and not easily reduced to a single social class.[23] The argument divides into two sections: the first outlines the kind of urbanism

---

[18] BI, Y/MB 34, Churchwardens Accounts for Michael le Belfrey, July 1939.

[19] Peter Clark, 'The Alehouse and the Alternative Society', in *Puritans and Revolutionaries: Essays in Seventeenth-Century History Presented to Christopher Hill*, ed. Donald Pennington and Keith Thomas (Oxford, 1978), 47–72, pp. 48, 52–7.

[20] Pierre Bourdieu, *Distinction: A Social Critique of the Judgment of Taste*, translated by Richard Nice (Cambridge MA, 1984).

[21] For an important step in the right direction see Beat Kumin, *Drinking Matters: Public Houses and Social Exchange in Early Modern Central Europe* (Basingstoke, 2007).

[22] For insights shed on early modern drinking practices by community studies, see B. Ann Tlusty, *Bacchus and the Civic Order: the Culture of Drink in Early Modern Germany* (Virginia, 2001); James R. Brown, 'The Landscape of Drink: Inns, Taverns and Alehouses in Early Modern Southampton' (unpublished University of Warwick Ph.D., 2008).

[23] Withington, 'Company', 293–6.

characterising early seventeenth-century York; the second unpacks another fraught conversation in Stonegate to highlight some central features of the city's economy of intoxication.

I

Cities and towns come in all shapes and sizes. As a provincial capital York served as a semi-autonomous community of citizens in its own right and an urban centre for its immediate hinterland (the Vale of York), the three Yorkshire Ridings, and, in certain respects, 'the north' more generally.[24] Its urbanism depended both on the institutions and services located in the city and their ongoing connections with the metropolis.[25] The assizes were a case in point. Twice yearly, judges from London trailed the urban circuits, their presence a catalyst for the 'country' to descend on the town. Likewise the economic services drawing people to the city – and also connecting York to its local urban system of market towns and smaller townships – were provided through trading networks with London and north-western Europe via the port of Kingston-upon-Hull. In these respects York was no different from other provincial centres like Bristol, Norwich, Chester, or Carlisle; and in terms of their basic patterning these provincial, metropolitan, and international relationships were a medieval inheritance.[26]

One defining feature of the early modern city is that fifteenth-century economic decline was followed by gradual and ultimately unprecedented resurgence after c.1550.[27] In York at least this was based less on manufacturing – which had already gravitated to Leeds and the West Riding – than on its accentuated role as an urban centre: a process which saw the revitalisation of the city's metropolitan and international commerce in conjunction with a renewed provincial appetite for urban services.[28] These developments were not, however, reflected demographically. Whereas Norwich and Bristol

---

[24] Charles Phythian-Adams, 'An Agenda for English Local History', in *Societies, Cultures and Kinship, 1580–1850*, ed. Charles Phythian-Adams (Leicester, 1993), 1–23, pp. 17–18; Paul Slack, 'Great and Good Towns, 1540–1700', in *The Cambridge Urban History of Britain*, I: *1540–1840*, ed. Peter Clark (Cambridge, 2000), 347–76, pp. 347–8; David Palliser, *Tudor York* (Oxford, 1979), 185; Chris Galley, *The Demography of Early Modern Towns: York in the Sixteenth and Seventeenth Centuries* (Liverpool, 1998), 41.

[25] Jan de Vries, *European Urbanisation 1500–1800* (1984), 10–17.

[26] Jenny Kermode, *Medieval Merchants: York, Beverley and Hull in the Later Middle-Ages* (Cambridge, 1998), 159–90.

[27] Kermode, *Medieval Merchants*, 188–9, 318–19; D. M. Palliser, 'York under the Tudors: the Trading Life of the Northern Capital', in *Perspectives in English Urban History*, ed. Alan Everitt (Basingstoke, 1973), 39–59; Wrightson, *EN*, 171–81; Muldrew, *Economy of Obligation*, 15–36; Withington, *Politics of Commonwealth*, 16–50.

[28] Palliser, 'York under the Tudors', 56–8; Kermode, *Medieval Merchants*, 315–17; Galley, *Demography*, 36–8.

more than doubled in size between 1525 and 1695, and London exploded from 60,000 to 600,000 inhabitants in the same period, York's population only rose from 8,000 in 1524 to possibly 10,000 by 1671: as Chris Galley notes, York's demography was characterised by diachronic stability, especially during the seventeenth century.[29] Urban regeneration was apparent, however, in the provision of hostelries. Alan Everitt long ago noted that, on the evidence of the (albeit patchy) national survey of 1577, York 'may well have contained more inns than any other provincial town at this date'.[30] Certainly the 'just certificate' of 86 inns, 11 taverns, and 171 alehouses returned for York and the Ainsty (the extra-mural wapentake the corporation administered) dwarfed the infrastructure recorded in provincial capitals like Carlisle (12 inns, 3 taverns, 60 alehouses) and Canterbury (12 inns, 4 taverns, 24 alehouses), a county town like Northampton (5 taverns, 17 inns, 40 alehouses), and even the fourteen Cinque Ports along the southern coast (28 inns, 18 taverns, 123 alehouses).[31] A century later a more comprehensive (though less informative) national survey counted 483 guest-rooms in York and stabling for 800 horses. Much the most capacious town in Yorkshire, York had a capacity greater than Canterbury (236 rooms; 467 stabling); comparable with Carlisle (413; 522) and Chester (514; 803); slightly smaller than the more populous Norwich (550; 930); although much diminished in comparison to Bristol (1,019; 1,377).[32]

York thus provides a contrasting perspective on early modern English drinking to that Wrightson developed in his study of rural communities in Essex and Lancashire. Terling, for example, had an estimated population in 1525 of 330 inhabitants, which had risen to 580 by 1671 – half the size of York's most populous parish (see below). Although the number of seventeenth-century alehouses in Terling is unclear, by the 1700s it was reduced to one, an outcome consistent with the village's emergence as 'a near classic example of the carefully regulated "closed parish"'.[33] The contemporaneous trajectory of York was very different. A shining exemplar of what Peter Borsay termed the eighteenth-century 'urban renaissance', whereby cities and towns served as fulcrums of provincial gentility and sociability, it also became a Victorian byword for urban deprivation and inequality – a space for two kinds of world in which intoxicants were prominent as social lubricants and palliatives.[34] There is, of course, nothing surprising about the

---

[29] Galley, *Demography*, 43.
[30] Alan Everitt, 'The English Urban Inn, 1560–1760', in *Perspectives*, ed. Everitt, 91–138, p. 93; Peter Clark, *The English Alehouse: a Social History 1200–1830* (1983), 47–8.
[31] The National Archives [TNA], SP 12/117, fols 88–9; SP12/118, fol. 3; SP 12/118, fol. 77; SP12/116, fols 185–7.
[32] TNA, WO/30/48.
[33] Wrightson & Levine, *Terling*, 45, 183–4.
[34] Peter Borsay, *The English Urban Renaissance: Culture and Society in the Provincial*

disjunction between the stories of Terling and York: Wrightson is better aware than most that 'England has many histories'.[35] However, there are at least two reasons why the tale told about Terling became a kind of surrogate national narrative. First, Wrightson helped make it so. Insofar as alehouses emblematise a process of social stratification and cultural dissociation then the particular history of Terling reflected 'a general trend in much of rural England'.[36] Although Wrightson stresses that Terling is only 'one example, one variant' of 'a larger story', it is nevertheless the variant foregrounded in *English Society*.[37] Second, as Wrightson notes, urban historians and historians of the alehouse told much the same story.[38] Until recently historiographical orthodoxy held that Elizabethan and early Stuart townsmen faced unprecedented problems of poverty, crisis, and disorder to which the overwhelming responses were oligarchy and Puritanism.[39] In this bleak environment the urban alehouse, like its rural equivalent, became at once a sanctuary for the poor and a target for the authorities.[40] It was only post-1660 that towns suddenly and somewhat miraculously became the integrative, convivial, and intoxicating places of the urban renaissance and alehouses became respectable. Yet the urban renaissance becomes much more explicable once the invigoration of urban centres within provincial, metropolitan, and international networks *before* 1660 is appreciated.[41] Indeed Wrightson has amply demonstrated that the emergence of 'the poor' as a social class was inextricable from the intensification of trade and commerce and the formation of a market economy – one in which erstwhile neighbours exploited economic and educational opportunities even as others were unable to do so.[42] The key point is that it was more pervasive and sharper *differentials* in wealth

Town, 1660–1770 (Oxford, 1989); B. S. Rowntree, *Poverty: a Study of Town Life* (1901). Rowntree's estimates of poverty in late nineteenth-century York are endorsed in Ian Gazeley and Andrew Newell, 'Poverty in Britain: an early social survey rediscovered', PRUS Working Paper no. 38, www.sussex.ac.uk/Units/PRU/wps/wp38.pdf.

[35] Wrightson & Levine, *Terling*, 1.

[36] Wrightson, 'Alehouses', 20.

[37] Wrightson & Levine, *Terling*, 218; Wrightson, *ES*, 227.

[38] Wrightson & Levine, *Terling*, 212.

[39] See Peter Clark and Paul Slack, 'Introduction', in *Crisis and Order in English Towns: Essays in Urban History*, ed. Peter Clark and Paul Slack (1972), 1–56; Peter Clark and Paul Slack, *English Towns in Transition 1500–1700* (Oxford, 1976); Robert Tittler, *Architecture and Power: the Town Hall and the English Urban Community, 1500–1640* (Oxford, 1991).

[40] Clark, 'The Alehouse', 52–3; Clark, *English Alehouse*, 76–8, 166–8.

[41] See Phil Withington, 'Two Renaissances: Urban Political Culture in Post-Reformation England Reconsidered', *HJ* 44 (2001), 239–67; and *idem*, 'Citizens, Community and Political Culture', in *Communities in Early Modern England*, ed. Alexandra Shepard and Phil Withington (Manchester, 2000), 134–55, pp. 134–7.

[42] Wrightson, *EN*, 198–201.

rather than poverty per se which characterised the period: alongside impov-
erishment there was conspicuous affluence in early modern England.[43]

This was never more so than in commercial and service centres like York.
The city had a typical pre-industrial topography – a populous and crowded
centre merging into a rural periphery of orchards and closes, occasional
mansions, and 'strays' of common land restricted to the use of freemen.[44]
Mapped onto this were four quarters, or wards, centred on the four main
thoroughfares into the city (Map 6.1): Walmgate, Monk, and Bootham on
the east bank of the River Ouse, Micklegate to the west. These wards subdi-
vided into parishes, serving as civic as well as religious units. Map 6.2 shows
how population was concentrated in Bootham and the inner parishes of
Walmgate, Monk, and Micklegate. This central area was bordered by the
cathedral precinct and King's Manor in Bootham and by York Castle (the
centre of county government) and Fosse Bridge along Walmgate. It encompassed the markets in All Sts Pavement and St Sampson (Thursday Market),
the city quay and riverside warehouses, and the civic buildings on Coney
Street and Ouse Bridge; it also extended along Micklegate, the city's main
processional route. [45] The social profile of these inner-city neighbourhoods
reflected the trades and services located in them. Merchants congregated
in All Sts Pavement, St John Ousegate, and the bottom of Micklegate; the
leather and malting industries were based in North Street in Micklegate and
beyond the Fosse; civil and common lawyers inhabited Coney Street and St
Michael le Belfrey; butchers, St Sampson; mercers, grocers, and manufac-
turers, Stonegate, Belfrey, Christ's, and Crux. Drinking places also agglom-
erated although, as is shown below, they did so in various parts of the city.

The clustering of occupations had obvious implications for the distribution of wealth and poverty. All neighbourhoods contained rich and poor
households and in most parishes the majority of households neither contributed to the poor assessment nor received relief. For example, in 1638 the
Stonegate overseers counted 22 rate-payers, 6 recipients of relief, and around
79 households which neither gave nor took from the poor rate – it was one
of several parishes notable for its social mixing.[46] Other especially 'mixed'
parishes included All Saints North Street in Micklegate (where ratepayers

---

[43] Muldrew, *Economy of Obligation*, 31–2.
[44] Galley, *Demography*, 70–4; Phil Withington, 'Views from the Bridge: Revolution and
Restoration in Seventeenth-Century York', *P&P* 170 (2001), 121–51, pp. 127, 132–3.
[45] Population estimated from the maximum number of households per parish, counted by
Chris Galley from hearth tax returns of the 1660s and 1670s. These have been multiplied
by 4.5, the figure used by Levine and Wrightson in their study of Terling. The figures may
be slightly conservative, especially for inner parishes. Parochial wealth is represented by
the difference between the annual amount of poor relief raised and distributed in each
parish. Although amounts could vary annually, the basic redistributive structure was
constant until at least the 1680s. This data is from 1656. *Sources:* Galley, *Demography*,
45; YCA, E70 (1656).
[46] YCA, E70 (1638).

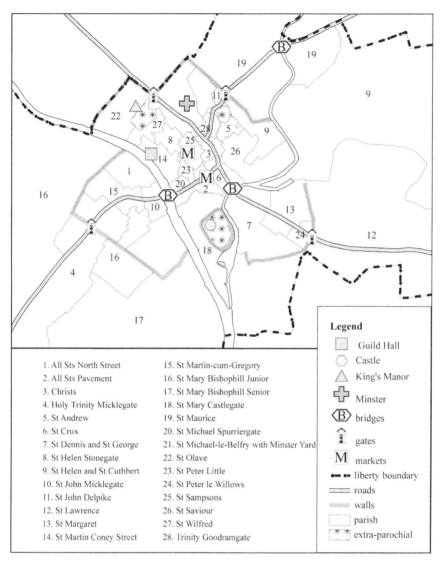

Map 6.1. Early modern York: institutions and parishes.

Legend

- Guild Hall
- Castle
- King's Manor
- Minster
- bridges
- gates
- markets
- liberty boundary
- roads
- walls
- parish
- extra-parochial

1. All Sts North Street
2. All Sts Pavement
3. Christs
4. Holy Trinity Micklegate
5. St Andrew
6. St Crux
7. St Dennis and St George
8. St Helen Stonegate
9. St Helen and St Cuthbert
10. St John Micklegate
11. St John Delpike
12. St Lawrence
13. St Margaret
14. St Martin Coney Street
15. St Martin-cum-Gregory
16. St Mary Bishophill Junior
17. St Mary Bishophill Senior
18. St Mary Castlegate
19. St Maurice
20. St Michael Spurriergate
21. St Michael-le-Belfry with Minster Yard
22. St Olave
23. St Peter Little
24. St Peter le Willows
25. St Sampsons
26. St Saviour
27. St Wilfred
28. Trinity Goodramgate

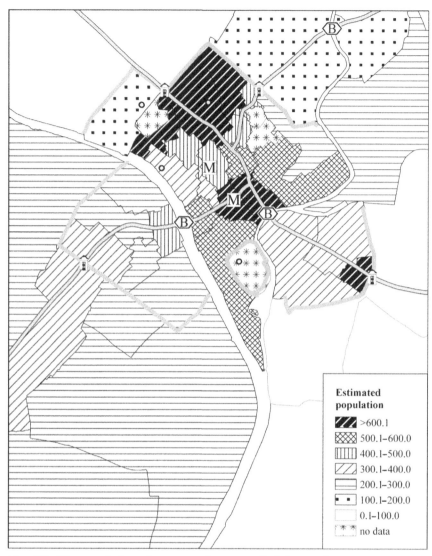

Map 6.2. The population of seventeenth-century York by parish.

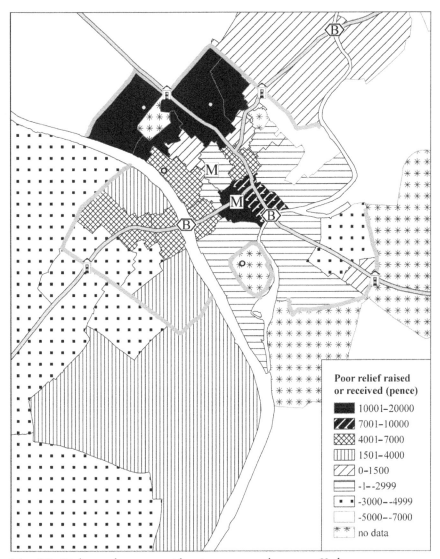

Map 6.3. Richer and poorer parishes in seventeenth-century York.

could still afford 'their' poor) as well as St Mary Castlegate in Walmgate and the two Monk parishes of St Sampson and St Saviour (where they could not). Likewise in Trinity Goodramgate the money raised for poor relief in 1656 exactly balanced the amount expended. Elsewhere, however, the difference between richer and poorer neighbourhoods was starker. As Map 6.3 shows, by the mid seventeenth century the mural parishes of Monk, Walmgate, and Micklegate expended considerably more in poor relief than was raised, relying on weekly payments from wealthier parishes to meet the shortfall.[47] From the 1620s, when the procedure was systematised, the redistribution of parochial rates institutionalised the dependency of the poorer suburbs on the wealthy inner-city. In 1656, for example, the overseers of All Sts Pavement paid only £4 0s 8d to their parish poor; they collected (and passed on) £451 6s 8d. The ratepayers of St Michael le Belfrey relieved the poor of St Helen and St Cuthbert; the poor of St Mary Bishophill Junior depended on householders in St Martin-cum-Gregory and St John Ousegate; ratepayers in St Crux supported the poor in St Margaret; and so on. If the number of poor grew in the city then so, too, did the capacity to relieve them.

II

It is with this dynamic social topography in mind that in 1640, twelve years after Alice Wilkinson accused Elizabeth Sanderson of drunkenness, we find a company of middle-aged York householders 'drinking a pint of wine in the house of Mrs Mary Secker widow situated in the parish of St Helens in Stonegate'.[48] It was the Lent Assize and the city was packed with visitors, the more so because of the perilous national situation. Whether it was politics that was bothering the merchant Richard Knight is hard to tell; but something clearly was. The tailor Richard Atkinson, one of those enjoying 'a cup of wine', deposed that 'Knight having (as it seemed) been in some other company, came into the room where this examinant and his said company were and behaved himself very uncivilly in words to divers of the company'. John Calvert, a forty-two-year-old baker, recalled that Knight initially 'began to abuse' his fellow merchant, Mr Christopher Brearey; when George Robinson asked Knight 'in a fair and friendly manner' to 'forbear such ill language' Knight replied in 'an angry and jeering manner': 'Thou, well thou hast got thy means by indirect ways and light weights', adding that Robinson was a 'dishonest and incontinent man and whoremaster'.[49] It was these words which prompted Robinson to initiate defamation proceed-

[47] YCA, E70 (1656).
[48] BI, CPH 2345, *George Robinson* v. *Robert Knight* (1640), deposition of Richard Atkinson.
[49] *Ibid.*, depositions of Richard Atkinson, John Calvert, Christopher Brearey.

ings against Knight in the Consistory Court. The resulting depositions reveal seven men drinking in company (eight if Knight is included), none of whom lived in Stonegate. Four of the company dwelt across Ouse Bridge in Micklegate (Calvert and Samuel Brearey inhabited St Martin-cum-Gregory; Christopher Brearey, St John; Christopher Waide, Trinity); Knight lived closer, in the parish of St Michael Spurriergate; and Atkinson, Robinson, and Richard Coltman were a few streets from home in the Bootham parishes of St Martin Coney Street and St Michael le Belfrey. This was not, then, a company of 'neighbours' in the sense of spatial propinquity: it took time and effort to walk from Micklegate to Stonegate. The men had much in common nonetheless. Like Ralph Sanderson and William Wilkinson all were freemen and citizens: householders permitted to trade in the city in return for their active participation in civic life. With the exception of Waide, a tipler in Trinity Micklegate, all were substantial parish ratepayers; and all but Waide had acquired the title 'Mr' (which, when claimed by York citizens, intimated that they had served as chamberlain, the most junior office in the Corporation's *cursus honorum*). That Mary Secker claimed 'Mrs' suggests she was a widow with close civic ties; certainly she was among the twenty-two ratepayers in the parish. These were, in short, affluent house-holders of a certain age. What insights do the profile and experience of this company disclose about the city's economy of intoxication?

Most obviously, this economy was not limited to ale and beer. The company shared 'a pint of wine'; Mary Secker was one of at least twenty licensed vintners in the city; and two of the company, the Breareys, made part of their living from importing wine. The experiences of Thomas Martin likewise suggest that, for those who could afford it, wine was a prominent intoxicant in York in the first decades of the seventeenth century. Other evidence indicates, in fact, that it was much more than this: that the 1620s and 1630s – important decades in the war on alehouses and drunk-enness – also witnessed an astonishing increase in the English market. W. B. Stephens estimated that annual wine imports into England in the first half of the sixteenth century averaged between 9,403 and 9,820 tuns. Port books show that by 1623 the figure was 20,708 tuns and that by 1638 it had risen to 49,446 tuns, dropping to 29,363 tuns in 1641. Aside from the later 1680s, when imports reached 38,700 tuns per annum, in the second half of the seventeenth century annual wine imports were less than half those of the 1630s.[50] Put slightly differently, between 1623 and 1638 the national consumption of wine rose from 3.8 litres per capita to 8.6 litres per capita, reverting to the lower figure after 1660.[51] Moreover, imports through

[50] W. B. Stephens, 'English Wine Imports c. 1603–40, with Special Reference to the Devon Ports', in *Tudor and Stuart Devon*, ed. Todd Gray et al. (Exeter, 1992), 141–72, p. 141.
[51] Stephens, 'English Wine Imports'; E. A. Wrigley and R. S. Schofield, *The Population History of England, 1541–1871: A Reconstruction* (1981), 528.

Kingston-upon-Hull surged far ahead of this national increase. In 1609 there were four notable cargoes, all from Bordeaux, total imports for the year amounting to 378 tuns, 35 hogsheads, 2 tierce, 7 pipes of French wine, and 76 butts of Spanish ('some Rhenish wine' was also recorded).[52] By 1637 this trickle was a flood. The year saw 32 shipments, most from Bordeaux but also from Rotterdam (4), Amsterdam and Calais (2 each), Hamburg and Middleburg. The amount of French wine imported was 2,095 tuns, 348 hogsheads, 10 tierce, and 13 pipes; Spanish wine amounted to 495 butts, 15 pipes, 2 hogsheads, 2 tierce.[53] Not only was this a dramatic increase in imports over the previous three decades; it was significantly more wine than at the height of the medieval trade before the fifteenth-century slump, when an average of 1,000 tuns per annum were imported into Hull.[54] The proportion of York merchants involved in the wine trade likewise increased. In 1609 they included William Brearey (Christopher and Samuel's father), Christopher Dickinson, William Robinson, and Simon Martin (whether a relation of Thomas is difficult to establish), with Robinson claiming more tuns than any other merchant. Together they accounted for 13 per cent of wine imports through Hull that year. By 1637 York merchants numbered 18 (16 per cent of all merchants bringing wine through the port), accounting for 49 per cent of the market share. The largest importer was the Hull burgess – and future regicide – Peregrine Pelham: between December 1636 and December 1637 he shifted 247 tuns, 12 hogsheads, 75 butts. However, the next two largest traffickers were York citizens: Henry Thomson imported 194 tuns; Henry Simpson 186 tuns, 8 hogsheads, 19 butts. Christopher and Samuel Brearey, William's sons, were part of the following pack, moving 55 and 48 tuns respectively.

The potential ramifications of this intensification in traffic are remarkable. In 1609 the amount of wine passing annually through the hands of York merchants equated to 5.6 litres per capita of the city population. By 1639 that figure had risen to 118.3 litres per capita (though not all wine would have been sold in the city). It is hardly surprising that the number of vintners licensed in York rose from the statutory eight to the corporation's preferred figure of twenty. The profits this entailed are evident from the high rate of poor relief assessment made on the wine merchants – all paid 3d or more per week in 1638 and eight were in the three highest assessment bands (paying 8d or more per week). There was, moreover, a strong correlation between the wine trade and civic power. In 1609 three of the four traders sat on the aldermanic bench. In 1637 four of the nineteen wine merchants were aldermen, one was a sheriff, and a further six became aldermen over the next two decades (as in other cities aldermen were also justices of the

52 TNA, E190/312/6.
53 TNA, E190/318/1B.
54 Kermode, *Medieval Merchants*, 179.

peace). Indeed it is no exaggeration to claim that the three most powerful civic dynasties in seventeenth-century York – the Robinsons, Thomsons, and another family of Thompsons – owed their fortunes in large part to hogsheads.

This rapidly expanding market was by no means the only dynamic feature of the city's economy of intoxicants. Companies not only imbibed claret in Mary Secker's house; they 'drank' tobacco. Indeed Richard Knight made money from the new tobacco traffic, York's vinous flood coinciding with the full assimilation of 'the holy herb' into the local diet.[55] The timing of this process is straightforward to gauge nationally. Joan Thirsk has shown how enterprising merchants and farmers in London and the south-west anticipated the commercial viability of domestic cultivation in the 1610s. Their potentially lucrative 'projects' were criminalised after lobbying from the Virginia Company and the crown's decision to take direct responsibility for the American colony in the early 1620s.[56] There was clearly a market for tobacco, which had been debated, fetishized, and commodified long before it was available for popular consumption; with the crown's monopoly enforced, imports increased rapidly – from about 60,000lbs per annum in 1622 (0.012lbs per capita) to 2,000,000lbs per annum in 1638 (0.39lbs per capita).[57] While the wine trade orientated York towards Bordeaux and the Dutch ports, tobacco pulled it towards London and the Atlantic: arriving from Virginia via the metropolis, tobacco reached York first through the annual trading fairs and latterly through coastal shipping (see below). The impact on the local market was, in turn, transformative. By the time Knight harangued Brearey and Robinson in 1640 there were 126 licensed retailers in York, unknown numbers selling illicitly.[58]

Mapping the distribution of these retailers reveals a number of features about the city's economy of intoxication. First, the vast majority of tobacco suppliers were also involved in the drinks trade. Of the 126 licensees, 35 (21 per cent) described themselves as innholders, 56 (45 per cent) as tiplers, 19 (15 per cent) as vintners. No matter that tobacco was officially justified as a medical panacea, 88 per cent of licensed retailers sold it in drinking establishments. Of the remaining 15 licences, 5 were held by cooks and victuallers (4 per cent); a mercer, tailor, and barber had one each; 3 were held by 'widows' (there were 15 female licensed retailers altogether); and, interestingly, the city gaoler and warden of the castle were both licensed.[59] That

---

[55] TNA, E178/5793, deposition of John Fisher.
[56] Joan Thirsk, 'New Crops and their Diffusion: Tobacco-Growing in Seventeenth-Century England', in *Rural Change and Urban Growth 1500–1800: Essays in English Regional History in Honour of W. G. Hoskins*, ed. C. W. Chalklin and M. A. Havinden (1974), 76–103.
[57] Wrightson, *EN*, 180, 238; Muldrew, *Economy of Obligation*, 54–5.
[58] TNA, E178/5793.
[59] Three occupational descriptors are ineligible.

Table 6.1. Tobacco retailers and the streets of York in 1638

Street	Ward	Tiplers	Vintners	Innholders	Total
Blake Street	Bootham	1	0	0	1
Bootham Bar	Bootham	4	5	1	10
Coney Street	Bootham	3	4	3	10
Petergate	Bootham	3	2	1	6
Stonegate	Bootham	6	2	2	10
Mural Bootham	Bootham	7	0	0	7
Minster Yard	Bootham	4	0	0	4
		28	13	7	48
Castlegate	Walmgate	0	3	5	8
Water Lane	Walmgate	2	0	7	9
Fossgate	Walmgate	3	0	4	7
		5	3	16	24
Colliergate	Monk	2	1	1	4
Goodramgate	Monk	1	0	3	4
Peaseholme	Monk	2	0	1	3
Thursday Market	Monk	5	0	5	10
		10	1	10	21
Micklegate Bar	Micklegate	6	1	0	7
Micklegate	Micklegate	7	1	2	10
		13	2	2	17
Total		56	19	35	110

Source: TNA, E 178/5793

innholders, vintners, and tiplers applied for licences suggests that smoking was already perceived to be an important accoutrement to their hospitality – part of the services they offered – and one means of making their houses attractive to customers; that they operated, in effect, in a commercial market. Certainly the grocer Thomas Green told the licensing commission how he had seen 'the servant of Andrew Corney of Petergate innholder at several times bring papers of Tobacco to his guests and receive money for the same, which he thinks was for their said masters' use'.[60] Corney

---

[60] TNA, E178/5793, deposition of Thomas Green.

was a prominent innholder who had served as master of the Company of Innholders as recently as 1636.[61] However, most of tobacco retailers were tiplers, suggesting that alehouses were quite as susceptible to commercial considerations as inns and taverns.

The distribution of all inns, taverns, and alehouses licensed to sell tobacco accordingly reveals not simply the most likely places in York to smoke in 1638 but also the neighbourhoods most associated with the drinks trade. Table 6.1 and Map 6.4 show that Stonegate was one such neighbourhood; indeed the cramped Bootham streets – proximate to the Minster, Council of the North, and Guildhall and teeming with shopkeepers, clergy, lawyers, and the visitors they attracted – contained by far the highest proportion of tiplers and vintners selling tobacco.

Aside from the wealthy Bootham parishes, licensed retailers were concentred in the two 'mixed' parishes of St Mary Castlegate (adjacent to the castle and encompassing the narrow Water Lanes leading to the river) and St Sampson (with the busy Thursday Market at its centre). Across the river tobacco was abundant around Micklegate Bar – in the 'poor' parish of Trinity – and the more prosperous Micklegate thoroughfare, though the latter encompassed a much larger area than the Bootham streets or Castlegate and Thursday Market. Thus although most householders were in striking distance of a pipe's worth there was a close correlation between tobacco licences and the services and institutions clustered around the inner-city and main city gates. As notably, no licensee was 'poor' in the institutional sense of the term. Rather, in Bootham and Micklegate just under half were ratepayers, in Walmgate a third, in Monk a seventh. The remaining retailers did not pay poor rate but neither did they receive relief.

In Stonegate, Mary Secker was one of six tobacco retailers paying rates, tobacco retailers forming over a quarter of all ratepaying parishioners. Indeed her fellow vintner, Mr William Bradley, paid more than any other householder. Neither were licensee ratepayers invariably innholders and vintners. Stonegate tiplers like Thomas Maskall and Thomas Nelson were substantial enough to be taxed; and even those tiplers who did not pay poor relief were eligible for the church assessment.[62]

Tobacco was good for business, its local adoption supplementing and stimulating the market not only for wine but also for ale and beer. The commercialisation of the latter had a long history – one involving at least two of the company in Mrs Secker's house.[63] Waide and Robinson were both licensed to sell malt in the city – a lucrative privilege which, like the wine trade,

[61] BI, MTA 17/1, fol. 9.
[62] YCA, E70 (1638).
[63] Judith M. Bennett, *Ale, Beer and Brewsters in England: Women's Work in a Changing World 1300–1600* (Oxford, 1996), 84–92; Clark, *English Alehouse*, 114–15; Richard W. Unger, *Beer in the Middle Ages and the Renaissance* (Philadelphia, 2004), 97–103.

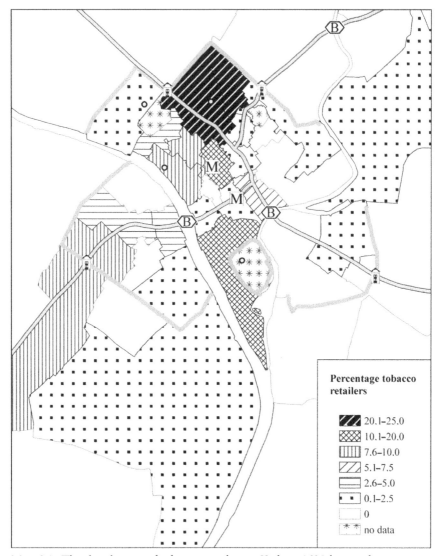

Percentage tobacco retailers

20.1–25.0
10.1–20.0
7.6–10.0
5.1–7.5
2.6–5.0
0.1–2.5
0
no data

Map 6.4. The distribution of tobacco retailers in York in 1638 by parish (percentage).

made for wealthy freemen.[64] That the licence was so profitable confirms the vibrancy of the brewing and beer-retailing industry in the period. It also explains why the power to license became such a contentious and destabilising issue in the decades before 1640 – not simply for the governed but also for different sorts of governor. York maltsters were usually licensed by the corporation: as well as enriching the licensee, licences were an important source of civic patronage, income, and regulatory power. During the 1630s, however, the citizenry spent much time and energy combating attempts by royal monopolists to sequester their licensing powers; when the city's power to license maltsters was finally confirmed by charter in 1638, fifty inhabitants were fined in quarter sessions for brewing without authority.[65] The saga reminds us that licensing was part of a wider regulative culture in which citizens protected their trades on three fronts: from unauthorised producers and retailers; from other companies of tradesmen; and from alternative sources of authority, such as monopolists and county gentry. Intoxicants were subject to especial control because of both their problematic social consequences and their potential profitability: contests over the wine trade were even more long-running than alehouses, and on occasions politically explosive. Tobacco was likewise a political incendiary, though in York the magistrates co-operated with, rather than opposed, licensing commissioners: indeed wine merchant Henry Thomson sat on the local commission in 1638.[66] Alehouse licensing was further complicated by the role of alehouses as an economic makeshift for the poorer members of communities, magistrates in both town and country recognising licensing as a powerful tool of paternalism, patronage, and poor relief.[67] Thus while alehouse licensing could certainly be implicated in the struggle to reform manners, and occasionally hijacked to pursue that agenda, licensing campaigns also reflected the protection and extension of urban 'freedoms' and 'liberties' in a rapidly expanding market economy. When aldermen observed in 1612 that the

---

[64] YCA, K68: 3.

[65] YCA, B35, fols 346r, 347, 348r, 350, 352; B36, fols 5, 17; C22, fol. 7.

[66] Anne Crawford, *A History of the Vintners' Company* (1977), 121–25; Phil Withington, 'Public Discourse, Corporate Citizenship and State Formation in Early Modern England', *AHR* 112 (2007), 1016–18; Withington, 'Citizens, Community and Political Culture', 147–50; Hugh Murray, A *Directory of York Pubs 1455–2004* (2004), ix. For tobacco see Thirsk, 'New Crops', 92–7; M. W. Beresford, 'The Beginning of Retail Tobacco Licenses, 1632–41', in *Time and Place: Collected Essays*, ed. M. W. Beresford (1984), 227–42; Thomas Cogswell, '"In the Power of the State": Mr Anys's Project and the Tobacco Colonies, 1626–1628', *English Historical Review* 123 [500] (2008), 35–64.

[67] Wrightson, 'Alehouses', 3; Anthony Fletcher, *Reform of the Provinces: the Government of Stuart England* (New Haven, 1986), 237–41; Stephen K. Roberts, 'Alehouses, Brewing and Government Under the Early Stuarts', *Southern History* 2 (1980), 45–71. For discussion of the complexity of official and 'popular' attitudes, see Mark Hailwood, 'Alehouses and Sociability in Seventeenth-Century England' (unpublished University of Warwick Ph.D., 2010), ch. 2.

'reformation' of unlicensed alehouses was 'at this present a great labour to the magistrates of this city' they had political economy as well as social reformation in mind.[68]

The immediate fruits of this labour are elusive because York quarter session records are missing for the first three decades of the seventeenth century. What do survive, at least for certain years before 1640, are lists of fines (recording money received rather than the number of fines issued). These confirm that policing alehouses was a significant, sometimes obsessive, concern of city jurors and magistrates. They also suggest that fines were much more likely for inhabitants keeping alehouses by 'their own authority' (unlicensed by the civic magistracy) than for those providing a home for 'evil' company and behaviour.[69] In 1627, for example, 99 per cent of all fines were alehouse related. Of these, 55 were for unlicensed alehouses and brewing, only one for behaviour within the house. In 1621 – a year when civic licensing powers were directly challenged by royal monopoly – 41 (85 per cent) of all fines were for unlicensed alehouses and brewing, only 3 per cent for the kind of company kept. In other years the enforcement of licensing regulations, while still notable, was less intense.[70]

The determination to retain alehouses under civic regulation was one of a number of means by which citizens looked to profit from the burgeoning trade in intoxicants while alleviating market pressures. That only freemen and women of the city could keep alehouses was constantly reiterated; moreover the power to bestow freedom was taken from individual trading companies and centralised with the corporation. It was on this basis that John Brice, master of the Company of Innholders in 1613, collaborated with common councillors (including the wine merchants William Brearey, William Robinson, and a young Henry Thomson) to reform the organisation of his trade. The skills and resources requisite of innholders were now specified in an ordinary; the company assumed greater regulative powers and procedures; those innholders unable to meet the new criteria were 'discharged from keeping any Inns' by 'all his company together'; and accounts and meetings were recorded for posterity.[71] Not only was innholding now reserved for a certain sort of citizen; the custom of men becoming innholders (and so freemen) merely to keep alehouses was curtailed.

Brewers and tiplers were also encouraged to form their own company.[72] Alehouse-keepers proved unwilling, however, to serve as searchers and officers in the proposed company, perhaps because a significant proportion of alehouses were makeshift rather than commercial concerns. Certainly

68 YCA, B33, fol. 294r.
69 YCA, B33, fol. 321, 16 Dec 1611. Crimes not punished by fines – some of which were associated with drunkenness – are unrepresented in the sample.
70 Figures from YCA, Series C (Chamberlains Accounts), years specified.
71 YCA, B34, fol. 3; BI, MTA 17/1.
72 YCA, B34, fols 2, 26r, 27, 39.

beer-brewers are absent from the list of company searchers made in 1618.[73] It was nevertheless on the back of these negotiations that the basic principle of civic licensing seems to have been accepted, however reluctantly, by the larger body of freemen. In the absence of a formal company of tiplers and brewers to regulate the trade, licensing served as the primary means of civic governance. In this it was well-suited, endowing the licenser with significant discretionary powers.[74] In the same breath, for example, that George Johnson and Ann Hutton were granted licenses because they 'hath no occupation' (and had petitioned city magistrates before selling ale) William Ward, Wilfred Browne, and Marmaduke White were bound 'not to keep any alehouse hereafter' because they had previously kept alehouses 'out of their own authorities'.[75] It also compelled licensees to produce three sureties for good behaviour, making tiplers as obligated to neighbours, friends, and kin who provided them with credit as they were to the civic magistracy. In this way household, communal, and civic authority were transposed onto each other. That neighbours were also jurors presenting unsuitable tiplers for prosecution only accentuated the participatory basis and discretionary nature of regulation. It was for precisely these reasons that Alice Wilkinson's allegations were so materially dangerous to the Sandersons.

IV

All of this suggests that York's economy of intoxication was, as elsewhere, paradoxical. When Richard Knight assailed George Robinson in March 1640 York was awash with more intoxicants than ever, and at least five of the eight citizens at Mrs Secker's house profited from wine, tobacco, or ale and beer. The market this implies is consistent with York's role as a centre of consumption, with the bemoaning of contemporary commentators, and with the diverse drinking habits glimpsed in legal depositions – the self-conscious 'civility' of the Brearey brothers and their fellow citizens; Knight's angry drinking; Thomas Martin's morning dissipation; the hard drinking of Anthony Carthorne and his company. More depositions would doubtless reveal more kinds of company. In the meantime, however, the city had witnessed an unprecedented period of regulative activity whereby the citizenry competed (mostly successfully) with royal monopolists and county magistrates to police urban drinking and control its provision and profits. This they did as individuals and as a corporate body. Much of this regulation, or at least more than is usually acknowledged, was accorded with corporate governance more generally: it can be understood in terms of the

[73] YCA, B34, fol. 32; C16, fol. 72.
[74] Cynthia Herrup, *The Common Peace: Participation and the Criminal Law in Seventeenth-Century England* (Cambridge, 1987), 195; Hindle, 'Keeping the Peace', 218–19.
[75] YCA, B33, fol. 29r.

consolidation of urban freedoms in a rapidly expanding market economy. The licence provided access to those profits, especially for vintners, tobacco retailers, innkeepers, and keepers of established alehouses. In the case of alehouses it also served as a source of relief for impoverished freemen and women. These related functions are indicated by Mr William Atkinson, a successful innkeeper between the 1630s and 1660s. On one hand, Atkinson made enough to contribute regularly to poor relief and to play an active role in the lower echelons of civic government. On the other, in 1663 he stood surety to no fewer than twenty-eight alehouse licensees, all operating at the bottom end of the drinking economy. He did so not as a private individual but in his capacity as officer to Walmgate Ward, to which he had been elected the previous year. In effect, the corporation guaranteed the behaviour of its own licensees.[76]

That is not to deny that many citizens (humble as well as influential) were fired by reformatory zeal or that the most intense moments of licensing and prosecution coincided with the political ascendency of 'godly' factions. They were and they did: it was such zeal which prompted the wealthy vintner, John Kilvington, to berate the lord mayor, John Vaux, with charges of corruption after Vaux prosecuted a jury for not indicting Kilvington for keeping disorderly company in his house in 1638.[77] Vaux was renowned as 'extreme against drunkards'; the following year the tailor James Marshall called him 'Puritane' and 'Rogue' and threatened to 'set him in the stocks as he hath done me being a Justice' (perhaps for hard drinking like Carthorne).[78] It is here that the paradox surrounding intoxication is most apparent. The early seventeenth-century city not only witnessed marked reformatory energy; it was energy directed at the very commodities and practices upon which urban economies like that of York had grown to depend, and to which many reformers owed their livelihoods. In a way that should resonate with modern readers (and taxpayers), intoxication and its reformation were two sides of the same coin.

This is neatly demonstrated by the 1656 survey of York's licensed drinking places.[79] An annual survey was instituted in 1625 and went hand-in-hand with the development of other kinds of civic surveillance such as 'views of the poor'; copies survive for 1646–63. The 1656 survey was unusual for four reasons. It included inns and taverns as well as alehouses; it coincided with the presence of Cromwell's major generals in York; it had an unambiguous puritan dynamic; and, as well as licensees, it listed retailers 'discharged' from selling alcohol. The result is the most comprehensive depiction of the city's

---

[76] YCA, K68: 10; B36, fol. 181.

[77] YCA, F7, fol. 26.

[78] 'The Life of Master John Shaw', in Charles Jackson, ed., *Yorkshire Diaries and Autobiographies in the Seventeenth and Eighteenth Centuries*, Surtees Society (Durham, 1877), 129; YCA, F7, fol. 40.

[79] YCA, K68: 8.

drinking topography before modern censuses – one that clearly illuminates how the contradictions of early modern intoxication were intensified by the mid-century conflict.

On one side, the sheer scale of 'discharges' nicely demonstrates the social impact of regulation when combined with reformatory zeal and political necessity: across the city 157 householders were banned from retailing intoxicants; all but 13 of these kept alehouse. The ideology driving this policy was emblazoned on the survey itself – beside the column of licenses and discharges for St Michael le Belfrey, the parish with the highest number of drinking establishments, the copyist has enclosed the opening of the Lord's Prayer in a tiny shield.[80] The doodler may even have been the wine merchant Henry Thomson, one of the presiding aldermen. Alehouses rather than taverns or inns were the targets of reformation in this instance: 133 tiplers and 24 innholders were discharged, compared to 141 alehouses and 95 inns or taverns licensed.[81] Beyond that, however, comparison of the house-holders Thomson helped license and those he discharged does not reveal obvious sociological differences. A slightly higher proportion of licensees were women (22 per cent compared to 17 per cent female discharges) and slightly more licensees were 'Mr' or 'Mrs' (8 per cent compared to 5 per cent). A somewhat higher proportion of licensed tiplers and brewers were ratepayers (26 per cent compared to 21 per cent of those discharged) and a negligible proportion (around 1 per cent) of both licensees and discharges received poor relief. Ten per cent of licensed tiplers or brewers served as overseers of the poor or jurymen in the mid 1650s; this compared with 5 per cent of their discharged equivalents. By each comparator the proportional difference is 5 per cent at most. There was, in effect, no simple correlation between wealth and licensing in 1656, although it is perhaps telling that by far the highest number of discharges was in the parish of St Mary Castle-gate. This was a socially mixed neighbourhood at once dominated by the drinks trade and susceptible to high levels of poverty (in 1656 a significant proportion of its poor were maintained by ratepayers in St Michael Spurrier-gate). As importantly, the proximity of the castle, gaol, and quay meant the neighbourhood was also notorious for 'sojourners', 'vagabonds', and (in the context of the 1650s) political malcontents. It was also the parish where, unusually for such a prominent merchant, Henry Thomson lived.

The particular circumstances of 1656 allowed Thomson, with Major General Robert Lilburne looking over his shoulder, to give full expression to his reformatory zeal. On the other hand, the survey demonstrates that, far from slaking the city's thirst, the war had made it thirstier, both merchants and retailers profiting as a result. The number of freemen securing a licence

---

[80] YCA, K68: 8, unfoliated.
[81] 'Innholders' includes freemen appearing in the Company of Innholders minutes and additional individuals listed as innholder in licensing records.

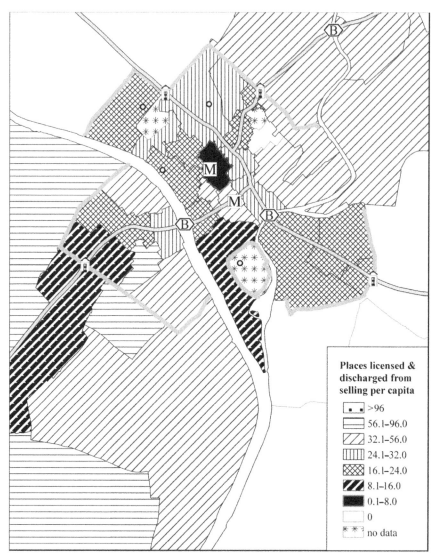

Map 6.5. Drinking places per capita in York in 1656.

in 1656 was 235, approximately one licensed house per 41 inhabitants. This was a much higher number of licensed retailers than in the 1640s (in 1646 one house served 87 people) and only slightly lower than 1663, when 264 licensees equated with one retailer per 37 people (almost exactly the same proportion of retailers to population as in 1577). Clearly the concentration of licensed alehouses in York in 1656 was high: a port like Southampton, which had an extensive 'landscape of drink' on account of its marine traffic, averaged one drinking place per 61 inhabitants at the beginning of the seventeenth century; and Beat Kumin estimates a national average of one licensee to 84 inhabitants in 1700 (Kumin suggests that English drinking places were, in turn, much denser per capita than those in central Europe).[82] However, it is when the number of licensees in 1656 is combined with the number discharged from retailing that the potential size of York's drinking topography – licensed and illicit – becomes visible. This made for 392 retailers or 25 persons per drinking place. Map 6.5 shows, moreover, that in parishes closely identified with the drinks trade the proportion of retailers per head of population was even lower – 23 people per house in Bootham parishes, 14 per house in St Mary Castlegate, and a remarkable 7 people per house in St Sampson, the parish where Carthorne drank with his company of 'good-fellows'.[83]

It is perhaps ironic that a civil war fought partly – if indirectly – to reform England's drinking culture should expand rather than diminish numbers of alehouses. But it is hardly surprising. Wars are fought by armies and armies drink, usually where they are garrisoned. In the meantime, the disruption of trade may well have encouraged more householders than usual to supplement their incomes by retailing ale. Moreover the political ascendency of militant Puritanism was accompanied neither by cultural hegemony nor economic quiescence, even among parliamentarians: Angela McShane has convincingly demonstrated the politicisation of drinking, especially heavy drinking, in the light of royalist defeat.[84] Certainly the market and taste for intoxicants so evident before 1640 continued apace thereafter. This final point is nicely illustrated by snapshots of Hull's coastal trade between the 1630s and 1660s – the goods reaching Yorkshire from London and other provincial ports. The trade had insured a diverse supply of commodities to the region since the medieval era, and by the 1630s at least this traffic

---

[82] Brown, 'Landscape of drink', 25; Kumin, *Drinking Matters*, 29.

[83] YCA, K68: 8. Wilfrids counted with Michael le Belfrey; John Delpike with Trinity Goodramgate; Peter Le Willows with St Margaret; Peter Little with All Sts Pavement.

[84] Angela McShane Jones, 'Roaring Royalists and Ranters', in *A Pleasing Sinne: Drink and Conviviality in Seventeenth-Century England*, ed. Adam Smyth (Woodbridge, 2004), 69–88; *idem*, 'The Extraordinary Case of the Flesh Eating and Blood Drinking Cavaliers', in *The Extraordinary and the Everyday in Early Modern England*, ed. Angela McShane and Garthine Walker (Basingstoke, 2010), 192–210.

included goods associated with the drinks trade.[85] In the first three month of 1636, for example, merchants imported 2 hampers of spirits, 109 lasts of barley, 11 lasts of malt, 24 bags of hops, 100lbs of tobacco, a batch of pipes, and 31,504 litres of Spanish wine. By 1645 the traffic had expanded dramatically. Between January and March alone 5,047 litres of spirits, 18,240 litres of beer, 164 bags of hops, 167 lasts of barley, 97 lasts of malt, over 50,000lbs of tobacco, thousands of pipes, and approximately 25,619 litres of wine entered the port.[86] While much of this business came from London, the region's garrisons also provided an expanded market for commercial farmers in East Anglia and Essex. By 1655 the demand for southern beer and its ingredients had returned to pre-war levels. The traffic in tobacco, however, remained intense, as it did for Spanish wine, spirits, and unspecified cargoes of 'drugs'.[87] By 1663 drugs, Spanish wine, tobacco, spirits, and ingredients for beer were all important commodities in the region's coastal trade.[88] War had telescoped, it seems, the general trajectory of market growth.

Thirty years earlier the humanist and future royalist martyr Sir Henry Slingsby lamented that, as 'in former times amongst the Romans', cities had become a place of 'abuse and excess' in which not 'the nobility only, but even other *honours gratis*, must imitate even beyond which their abilities will afford'. As a result, 'our own markets are too mean to afford them that which curious appetites would have; but they must send beyond sea and make the trade of Merchants, only intended for public commodity, now at last serve their private ends of vain glory'.[89] Slingsby was a Yorkshire gentleman who knew York and its citizenry well: while the pejorative gloss was clearly his own, he could nevertheless claim first-hand experience of the city's economy. His observations corroborate the preceding discussion. The boon in American tobacco; the rejuvenation of the French and Spanish wine trades; the ascendancy of Dutch beer-brewing techniques over traditional ale production: these were long-term trends which converged in York during the 1620s and 1630s, and which pose obvious problems for stories of a 'consumer revolution' beginning c.1650.[90] The economic opportunities provided by national, continental, and colonial commerce enabled the social proliferation of 'curious appetites' in an English provincial capital; they also facilitated, and were encouraged by, the 'private ends' of urban citizens. Whether for merchants like Henry Thomson or retailers like Mary

---

[85] T. S. Willan, *The Inland Trade* (Manchester, 1976), 26–41; Kermode, *Medieval Merchants*, 186–9.

[86] TNA, E190/317/14; E190/318/2. One last equals approximately 4,000lbs weight.

[87] TNA, E190/319/4.

[88] TNA, E190/319/13.

[89] *The Diary of Sir Henry Slingsby of Scriven*, ed. Reverend D. Parsons (1836), 24–5.

[90] For a useful critique of this narrative see Sara Pennell, 'Consumption and Consumerism in Early Modern England', *HJ* 42 (1999), 549–64, pp. 557–9. For its recent restatement see De Vries, *Industrious Revolution*, *passim*.

Secker, the profits to be gained from intoxicants were clearly significant. This trade was, in turn, inextricable from modern rituals of consumption and company among the wider populace: indeed it was the valorisation and pursuit of intoxication, rather than the market for intoxicants, which drove contemporary moralists into print.[91] One of Wrightson's many achievements has been to show how this discursive polemic animated, in a very real way, the politics of drinking in local rural communities. Absent from his account is the commercialisation of consumption which so perturbed Slingsby and the apparently normative power of 'abuse and excess' for large sections of the population, the affluent included. Social reformation was a defining characteristic of English early modernity. So, too, was the urban market for intoxicants.

---

[91] Hailwood, 'Sociability, Work and Labouring Identity'; Withington, 'Intoxicants and Society'.

7

Food, Drink and Social Distinction
in Early Modern England

ADAM FOX

In almost all human societies, access to the resources necessary to sustain life is one of the defining expressions of rank. The extent to which individuals and groups are able to satisfy their most basic requirements for food and drink are as sure an indication as any of their place within the hierarchy of wealth and esteem. In many communities, both the quantity and the quality of essential consumption serve not only to express but also to create those fine grains of distinction and difference upon which caste systems or class structures are built.[1]

In early modern England the food and drink that people ingested provided resonant markers in the expression of worth and the articulation of status. This essay seeks to explore some of the social significance invested in these forms of consumption between the late sixteenth and early eighteenth centuries. As Keith Wrightson has demonstrated, however, this was a period in which the constitution of English society and the texture of relations between its inhabitants were evolving and diversifying in important ways. Thanks to Wrightson's work we have a much more vivid sense not only of the manner in which economic distinctions between the 'poorer sorts', 'middle sorts' and 'better sorts' of people were being reconfigured in these generations, but also of the new forms of social identity that this bequeathed.[2] One reflection of contemporary changes in economy and society was the introduction of novel foodstuffs and the revision of established attitudes towards old ones. A closer examination of these developments serves as a vehicle through which to explore an aspect of the ever more complex forms of status differentiation in early modern England of which Wrightson has made us aware.

---

[1] On this subject see, for example, Pierre Bourdieu, *Distinction* (1984), 177–200; Jack Goody, *Cooking, Cuisine and Class* (Cambridge, 1982); Stephen Mennell, Anne Murcott and Anneke H. van Otterloo, *The Sociology of Food* (1992).

[2] Wrightson, *ES*, chs 1–2; *idem, EN; idem,* '"Sorts of People" in Tudor and Stuart England', in *The Middling Sort of People*, ed. Jonathan Barry and Christopher Brooks (Basingstoke, 1994), 28–51.

I

In early modern society it was a basic assumption that diet was a fundamental expression of social place. A cluster of medical theories, cultural assumptions and social prejudices contributed to the way in which this type of consumption was perceived and explained. Galenic physiology, revived during the Renaissance, affirmed that the constitutions of the different sorts of people in society suited them to contrasting dietary regimes.[3] In sixteenth- and early seventeenth-century England, it was often observed that certain kinds of food agreed with the humoural balance of those accustomed to a life of leisure while others were more appropriate for those conditioned to the world of work. Thus, small and delicate produce was naturally thought 'fit for fine complexions, idle citizens, [and] tender persons', while other 'more gross, tough, and hard' fare was apt for 'country persons and hard labourers'.[4] Astringent vegetables such as onions, leeks and garlic were synonymous with the dirty and smelly bodies of the vulgar. Indeed, when searching for a foodstuff that symbolised the lowest of the low it was generally garlic for which contemporaries reached, and 'garlic-eaters' served as a ready euphemism with which to describe and denigrate the plebs.[5]

The 'meaner sorts' were commonly affirmed to have 'stomackes like ostriges, that can digest hard iron', and therefore their constitutions were adapted to 'gross' foods such as hard cheese and brown bread. 'For grosse meat is meete for grosse men', affirmed Thomas Cogan in Elizabeth's reign when disparaging the leeks, beans and peas consumed by 'rustickes' and the salt bacon eaten by 'labouring men'. 'Husbandmen, and such as labour', agreed Robert Burton soon after, 'can eat fat bacon, salt gross meat, hard cheese, etc … [what tough insides have these mowers!], coarse bread at all times, go to bed and labour upon a full stomach, which to some idle persons would be present death'.[6]

Moreover, it was not only that the bodies of the different social ranks were accustomed by usage to different types of fare, but also that their mental and physical characteristics were actually determined by them. Light foods and dainty dishes contributed to the refined minds and delicate equilibrium of the 'better sort', while the dull spirits and hard flesh of the common people were no less the product of their 'unwholesome' staples and crude offal.

[3] Piero Camporesi, *Bread of Dreams* (Cambridge, 1989), 103–4, 120–1, 169–70; Ken Albala, *Eating Right in the Renaissance* (Berkeley, 2002), 184–216; Sheila McTighe, 'Foods and the Body in Italian Genre Painting, about 1580: Campi, Passarotti and Carracci', *Art Bulletin* 86 (2004), 301–23.

[4] Thomas Muffett, *Healths Improvement*, ed. Christopher Bennet (1655), 31–2.

[5] William Shakespeare, *Coriolanus*, IV, vi, 102; *idem*, *1 Henry IV*, III, i, 158; John Houghton, *England's Great Happiness* (1677), 18.

[6] Thomas Cogan, *The Haven of Health* (1612), 57, 117; Robert Burton, *The Anatomy of Melancholy*, ed. Holbrook Jackson, 3 vols (1932), I, 232.

'What makes the peasant grovel in his muck, humbling his crooked soul, but that he eats bread just in colour like it?', a character in one of William Cartwright's plays asked. 'Courage ne'er vouchsaf'd to dwell a minute where a sullen pair of brown loaves darken'd the dirty table ... You never knew a solemn son of bag-pudding and pottage made a commander, or a tripe-eater become a tyrant.'[7]

Contemporary humoural theory thus implied that people were what they ate in a much more profound sense than is understood by the later cliché to that effect. Inhabitants of the north Wiltshire 'cheese country', for example, were said to have a largely dairy diet that 'cooles their brains too much, and hurts their inventions', making them 'melancholy, contemplative and malicious'. At the same time, consumption of the 'sowre and austere plants, as sorrel' growing in the region 'makes their humours sowre, and fixes their spirits'. In Glamorganshire the 'oaten bread and small drink' diet of upland dwellers was said to make them a 'tall, mighty and active people' of 'tractable and pleasant behaviour' compared with their lowland neighbours whose 'bread made of wheat' and drink of 'ale and beer' gave them a 'more boisterous crabbed nature'.[8]

By the later seventeenth century the first systematic attempts were being made to quantify in terms of expenditure the differences in diet across the social order that were thought to be as obvious and inevitable as they were natural and biological. In the early 1670s, Sir William Petty estimated that 'the table of great men is but 1/3 of their expence, but of artisans & laborers tis above 2/3 of ye whole'.[9] A generation later Gregory King went further in trying to calculate with more precision both the absolute sums and the proportions of their total annual outgoings that people in England, 'according to the severall degrees of living', spent on food and drink. He found that

> the poorest sort, whose general expence was but 3*li*. p[er] head p[er] an[num] or 2*d*. p[er] diem, spent 2 thirds, or somwhat above 5 farthings p[er] diem in dyet. The middle sort whose general expence was 7*li*. p[er] head, spent 4*li*. p[er] an[num] in dyet. And the better sort whose general expense was above 50*li*. p[er] head p[er] an[num] spent less than a third in dyet.

7 Cogan, *Haven of Health*, 113; Muffett, *Healths Improvement*, 249–50; Carl Bridenbaugh, *Vexed and Troubled Englishmen 1590–1642* (New York, 1967), 92.

8 John Aubrey, *The Natural History of Wiltshire*, ed. John Britton (1847), 11; Rupert H. Morris, ed., 'Parochialia', *Archaeologia Cambrensis* (3 pts in 1, 1909–11), iii, 116–17; and cf. Margaret Pelling, 'Food, Status and Knowledge: Attitudes to Diet in Early Modern England', in *idem, The Common Lot: Sickness, Medical Occupations and the Urban Poor* (1998), 38–62, pp. 47–8.

9 British Library [BL], Additional MS, 72865, fol. 39v; Marquis of Lansdowne, ed., *The Petty Papers*, 2 vols (1927), II, 236.

Table 7.1. Gregory King's calculations of annual expenditure on food and drink in late seventeenth-century England, categorised according to social group

Number of people in social group	Percentage of national population	Annual expenditure per head on diet	Annual expenditure of group on diet	Percentage of national expenditure on diet
900	0.02%	£120	£108,000	0.52%
9,000	0.16%	£30	£270,000	1.30%
40,000	0.73%	£20	£800,000	3.85%
80,000	1.45%	£15	£1,200,000	5.78%
120,000	2.18%	£10	£1,200,000	5.78%
200,000	3.64%	£8	£1,600,000	7.70%
300,000	5.45%	£6	£1,800,000	8.66%
500,000	9.09%	£5	£2,500,000	12.03%
800,000	14.55%	£4	£3,200,000	15.40%
1,200,000	21.82%	£3	£3,600,000	17.33%
2,250,000	40.91%	£2	£4,500,000	21.65%
5,499,900	100.00%		£20,778,000	100.00%

Source: Gregory King, 'The LCC Burns Journal', in Peter Laslett (ed.), The Earliest Classics: John Graunt and Gregory King (London, 1973), 210.

The 'better sort' thus spent on average about eight times as much as the 'poorest sort' on provisioning while employing a far smaller proportion of their resources to do so (Table 7.1).[10] Elsewhere, King elaborated and in an ambitious calculation sought to break down the population more precisely 'into classes' and to compute both the absolute sums and the percentage of their income that each one spent on foodstuffs:

> I considerd how this answer'd the general product of the land. The revenue of Excise gave a light into the quantity of malt and drink; others had given us account of the wine imported; a due allowance of bread and corn was to be made; the milk, butter, and cheese depended on the stock of kine, and that stock upon the proportion of pasture and of other cattle; the allowance of flesh depended on the stock of cattle for food in general; fish, fowl, eggs, fruit and garden stuff, salt, oyl, pickles, spices, grocery, confectionary wares and the like, required a due consideration.

For eleven different socio-economic classes, King gave a precise figure for their expenditure on each of eight food and drink groups, thus providing a quite finely graded distribution of the total of something under £21 million that he reckoned the nation as a whole spent on comestibles in a year (Table 7.2).[11]

King's figures amount to a detailed contemporary picture of the relation-ship between social status and consumption in late seventeenth-century England. They reveal that his 'poorest sort', who needed to spend £2 per annum, or two-thirds of their total income, on food amounted to 41 per cent of the population. This group laid out fully 50 per cent of its dietary budget simply on bread and other grain-based foods, and a further 7.5 per cent on malt drinks. Their next most significant outgoing was on dairy produce, accounting for some 18.75 per cent of expenses on subsistence. By contrast they devoted only 8.75 per cent of their meagre outgoings in this direction on fruit and vegetables, and just 6.25 per cent on meat products.

Predictably enough, the proportion of dietary expenditure devoted to bread and other grain staples diminished by degrees at the higher levels of society. Thus those who spent £8 per head per annum on diet, who might be considered at the top end of the 'middle sort' and whose outgoings were exceeded by no more than 4.5 per cent of the population, consumed only one-fifth of their food budget on this item. In the case of the very wealth-iest few in society, daily bread represented a miniscule one-fortieth of their

---

[10] National Library of Australia, MS 1458, 15; Joan Thirsk and J. P. Cooper, eds, *Seventeenth-Century Economic Documents* (Oxford, 1972), 795.

[11] *Ibid*.; Gregory King, 'The LCC Burns Journal', in *The Earliest Classics*, ed. Peter Laslett (1973), 210; and cf. the pioneering breakdown of King's own household expenditure, 250.

Table 7.2. Gregory King's calculations of annual expenditure per head on specified items of food and drink, classified according to social group

Number of people in social group	Bread, breadcorn, cakes and meal		Corn, flesh, venison, hares and conies		Butter, cheese, milk and cream		Malt drinks		Beer, wine, spirits and strong liquors		Fish, fowl and eggs		Fruit and vegetables		Salt, oil, pickles, spices, confectionery and jellies	
	£ s d	% of total	£ s d	% of total	£ s d	% of total	£ s d	% of total	£ s d	% of total	£ s d	% of total	£ s d	% of total	£ s d	% of total
900	3 0 0	2.50	20 0 0	16.67	7 0 0	5.83	10 0 0	8.33	25 0 0	20.83	15 0 0	12.50	10 0 0	8.33	10 0 0	8.33
9,000	2 5 6	7.58	5 0 0	16.67	3 5 0	10.83	4 0 0	13.33	4 0 0	13.33	5 0 0	16.67	2 10 0	8.33	3 0 0	10.00
40,000	2 0 0	10.00	3 0 0	15.00	3 0 0	15.00	3 0 0	15.00	3 0 0	15.00	3 0 0	15.00	2 0 0	10.00	2 0 0	10.00
80,000	1 16 6	12.17	2 5 0	15.00	2 2 6	14.17	2 8 0	16.00	1 11 0	10.33	2 1 0	13.67	1 9 0	9.67	1 7 0	9.00
120,000	1 13 6	16.75	1 10 0	15.00	1 6 0	13.00	1 14 6	17.25	1 1 0	10.50	1 2 0	11.00	0 19 0	9.50	0 14 0	7.00
200,000	1 12 0	20.00	1 6 6	16.56	1 6 0	16.25	1 8 0	17.50	0 16 0	10.00	0 15 6	9.69	0 14 0	8.75	0 10 0	6.25
300,000	1 9 6	29.58	0 18 0	15.00	0 15 0	12.50	1 0 0	16.67	0 10 6	8.75	0 10 0	8.75	0 10 0	8.33	0 7 0	5.83
500,000	1 8 0	28.00	0 14 6	14.50	0 13 0	13.00	0 15 6	15.50	0 7 6	7.50	0 8 0	8.00	0 8 0	8.00	0 5 6	5.50
800,000	1 5 0	31.25	0 10 6	13.12	0 11 6	14.37	0 11 0	13.75	0 5 0	6.25	0 6 0	7.50	0 6 6	8.12	0 4 0	5.00
1,200,000	1 3 0	38.33	0 6 6	10.83	0 9 6	15.83	0 7 0	11.67	0 2 6	4.17	0 4 0	6.67	0 5 0	8.33	0 2 6	4.17
2,250,000	1 0 0	50.00	0 2 6	6.25	0 7 6	18.75	0 3 0	7.50	0 0 6	1.25	0 2 0	5.00	0 3 6	8.75	0 1 0	2.50

Source: as in Table 7.1

grocery bill. For the top one-fifth of the population, the proportion of total provisioning expenditure dedicated to meat was within a relatively narrow range of between roughly 13 and 16.5 per cent. In absolute sums this represented the difference between 10s 6d per head per annum in the case of those at the lower end of the 'middle sort' spending £4 in total, up to £1 1s 6d for those at the top end of the middling range spending £8, and to £5 annually for those at the wealthier end of the 'better sort' each spending £30 a year on food overall. Among the wealthiest, the expenditure on luxury items became proportionally greater. So, for example, all of the 4.5 per cent of the population at the apex of the economic and social pyramid devoted more than 10 per cent of their outlay in this context to strong drink and the very richest few as much as 20 per cent.

In the early 1730s, Jacob Vanderlint performed similar calculations among the population of the capital city, comparing the breakdown of necessary expenditure for 'a labouring man and his family in London' with that of 'a family in the middling station of life'. He also found that the 'labouring' class consumed two-thirds of their disposable income on diet, whereas this source accounted for between one-third and one-half of the expense of his 'middling' rank. In absolute sums, those in the former group laid out less than half as much per head per week on food and drink as the latter. Whereas the weekly expenditure per head on bread was equal between the two groups, labourers and their families spent only 40 per cent of what the 'middle sort' spent on meat, only one-third of what they spent on butter, and 55 per cent of what they spent on beer.[12]

II

While the ancient assumptions of Renaissance physiology reveal the properties attributed to certain foodstuffs and the detailed calculations of political arithmetic provide a snapshot of expenditure on them slanted towards the urban consumer, such evidence betrays neither the social meanings of these products in a particular context nor the extent to which these changed over time. Generalisations about the relationship between eating habits and social class remain notoriously fraught with difficulty, undermined as they are by the myriad local particularities, shifts in fashion, and individual

---

[12] Jacob Vanderlint, *Money Answers All Things* (1734), 75–6, 141–2, tabulated and discussed in Peter Earle, *The Making of the English Middle Class* (1989), 271–2, 280–1. Recent research on other evidence broadly confirms these contemporary calculations: Carole Shammas, 'Food Expenditures and Economic Well-Being in Early Modern England', *Journal of Economic History* 63 (1983), 89–100, p. 93; idem, *The Pre-industrial Consumer in England and America* (Oxford, 1990), 123–30.

circumstances that can defy attempts to impose patterns on the evidence.[13] Nevertheless, it is possible to identify certain basic and enduring structures that characterise the contemporary sociology of food, as well as to high-light some important developments that reflect the broader course of social change in early modern England.

One conspicuous manifestation of status in this society was the kind of bread that people ate. The nobility and gentry enjoyed white 'manchet' in which wheat flour was combined with eggs, butter and milk and baked into little 'roules', either in their households or by commercial bakers. This contrasted markedly with the 'great loaves' of the lower orders made from inferior grains or mixtures of grains and pulses. In their very names – 'yeoman's bread', 'francklin's bread', 'carter's bread' – these cheaper varieties proclaimed their intended markets.[14]

In Cornwall it was barley bread upon which 'the poore' were 'princi-pally relieued, and the labourers also fed', as were 'the poor people and the hinds of north Wiltshire before the Civil Wars and the 'poorer sort' in Staffordshire. Across Shropshire, on the eastern sands of Suffolk or in the Vale of York, among other places, it was rye that made the bread of the lower orders.[15] Meanwhile in Pembrokeshire, the indigenous Welsh were distinguished from their anglicised neighbours by their oaten husbandry. In Lancashire the bread eaten 'by the nobility and gentry is made of wheat', it was said, 'but by other persons generally of oates'. Equally, in Cumberland and Westmorland, oats, or 'harbers' as they were called, and 'bigg', a coarse variety of barley, were the main cereals and from these 'the mountainers and dalesmen generally make all their bread'.[16]

On the one hand, the 'better sort', accustomed to white wheaten bread, despised the associations as well as the taste of the dark and hard varieties of the multitude. So the well-to-do 'south-country man' Thomas Baskerville found the homemade rye bread in Restoration York 'so coarse and black you will care not to eat any of it'. Equally the genteel traveller Celia Fiennes was at an inn just over the Scottish border at the end of the seventeenth century and 'finding they had noe wheaten bread', was forced to tell the

[13] See the excellent discussion in Joan Thirsk, *Food in Early Modern England* (2006).

[14] William Harrison, *The Description of England*, ed. Georges Edelen (Ithaca, 1968), 133–5; Muffett, *Healths Improvement*, 241; F. G. Emmison, *Tudor Food and Pastimes* (1964), 37–8; Sir William Ashley, *The Bread of our Forefathers* (Oxford, 1928), 35.

[15] Richard Carew, *The Survey of Cornwall* (1602), fol. 20r; Royal Society MS 92, 288; Robert Plot, *The Natural History of Stafford-Shire* (Oxford, 1686), 205; Joan Thirsk, 'Farming Techniques', in *The Agrarian History of England and Wales*, IV: *1500–1640*, ed. *idem* (Cambridge, 1967), 161–99, pp. 169–71.

[16] George Owen, *The Description of Pembrokeshire*, ed. Dillwyn Miles (Llandysul, 1994), 62, 64; Cumbria Record Office Carlisle [CROC], D/Lons/L12/2/18, 3; CROC, D&C/ Machell MS 1, 65.

landlady that she just 'could not eat their clapt oat bread'.[17] On the other hand, however, husbandmen were said positively to esteem their various brown breads 'as abiding longer in the stomack, and not so soone digested with their labour'. The 'poor folkes' of the East Riding before the Civil War regarded their loaf made from a mixture of rye and peas as a 'hearty breade'. Later in the century 'the common inhabitants' of Derbyshire were observed 'to prefer oates, for delight and strength, above any other grain'.[18]

Consumption of fresh meat was a no less graphic index of wealth and status. Gregory King calculated in the 1690s that just under half the population could afford to eat fresh meat every day, consuming a daily average of 6.4 ounces per head. Meanwhile, roughly one-third of the nation were unable to have it more than twice a week, 'by reason of their poverty', and something over one-fifth of people 'eat not flesh above once a week'.[19] At the same time quality was as important as quantity. In London, civic dignitaries, substantial merchants and distinguished professionals enjoyed a standard of flesh which, William Harrison thought in the 1570s, was 'often comparable herein to the nobility of the land'. They rejected anything from the city butchers, sourcing instead 'all manner of delicate meats from every quarter of the country'. Below this level, 'the artificer and husbandman makes greatest account of such meat as they may soonest come by and have it quickest ready', and this 'consisteth principally in beef and such meat as the butcher selleth, that is to say, mutton, veal, lamb, pork, etc'. By the end of the seventeenth century 'the middling sort of people' in the capital were said to have 'ten or twelve sorts of meats' taking turns at their tables that could be as fine as those of any gentleman or wealthy citizen.[20] As for the lower orders, they had to make do with whatever was left over. One observer noted around 1700 that at the fag end of the day in Smithfield market all that remained were 'some Welsh runts and Scotch carrion, which wait for the coming of Shoreditch butchers, who buy 'em up for the Spittle-fields weavers, and the poorer sort of Huguenots, who have taken possession

[17] 'Thomas Baskerville's Journey in England', in HMC, *Thirteenth Report, Appendix, Part II* (1893), 312; *The Journeys of Celia Fiennes*, ed. Christopher Morris (1947), 188, 193–4, 205.

[18] Fynes Moryson, *An Itinerary Containing his Ten Yeeres Travell*, 4 vols (Glasgow, 1907–08), IV, 171; *The Farming and Memorandum Books of Henry Best of Elmswell, 1642*, ed. Donald Woodward (1984), 109; Philip Kinder, 'Historie of Darby-Shire', ed. W. G. D. Fletcher, *The Reliquary* 22 (1881–82), 21; and cf. William Ellis, *The Country Housewife's Family Companion* (1750), 12.

[19] Laslett, ed., *The Earliest Classics*, 213; Thirsk and Cooper, eds, *Seventeenth-Century Economic Documents*, 783–4.

[20] Harrison, *The Description of England*, 129, 131; A. L. Simon, *The Star Chamber Dinner Accounts* (1959); Andrew B. Appleby, 'Diet in Sixteenth-Century England: Sources, Problems, Possibilities', in *Health, Medicine and Mortality in the Sixteenth Century*, ed. Charles Webster (Cambridge, 1979), 97–116, pp. 99–105; Henri Misson, M. *Misson's Memoirs and Observations in his Travels over England*, trans. John Ozell (1719), 314.

of that part of the town'. Inmates of the city's poor houses and hospitals were typically served up '6 ounces of beefe boyled without bones' or 'halfe a pound of boyled mutton', while the 'carriers and drovers' who frequented the hundreds of cheap cookshops across the capital had to be content with 'measly pork and neck-beef'.[21]

In the countryside, a table groaning with prodigious quantities of best meat was one of the ways in which the aristocracy and gentry proclaimed their status.[22] The fact that a haunch of venison was so often given as a gift between the wealthy spoke volumes about the symbolic importance of prestigious foods.[23] As for the prosperous middle ranks, Thomas Fuller depicted the Kentish yeoman's table in the 1640s as bearing 'as many joints as dishes', while the Essex clergyman Ralph Josselin was variously buying mutton, pork and beef for his family, even in the hungry year of 1649. For most households at this social level, however, lesser cuts clearly provided the usual daily fare, with more expensive flesh confined to high days and holidays. In Jacobean Berkshire, for example, the thriving farmer Robert Loder normally ate pork from his own pigs, supplemented only by beef from his cattle on special occasions. A century later in Lancashire Richard Latham also relied on his own home-bred pork, confining his purchases in the market to offcuts such as heads and plucks and only indulging in beef at Christmas.[24]

Household servants could expect a diet that in some ways reflected the status of their masters and mistresses. Retainers of the aristocracy and gentry had to be content with 'maslin' bread and second quality beer but they seem to have regarded a daily allowance of cuttings from the roast as entitlements. In the late seventeenth century Richard Baxter was probably right to think

---

[21] Ned Ward, *The London Spy*, ed. Arthur Heywood (1927), 88, 94; Ian W. Archer, *The Pursuit of Stability: Social Relations in Elizabethan London* (Cambridge, 1991), 116–17, 190–1; J. C. Drummond and Anne Wilbraham, *The Englishman's Food* (1939), 126; Shammas, 'Food Expenditures', 97–9.

[22] For example, Lawrence Stone, *The Crisis of the Aristocracy, 1558–1641* (Oxford, 1965), 555–62 and Appendix XXIV; *Selections from the Household Account Books of the Lord William Howard of Naworth Castle*, ed. George Ornsby, Surtees Society 68 (Durham, 1878), lxxv; Gladys Scott Thomson, *Life in a Noble Household 1641–1700* (1937), 131–2; Emmison, *Tudor Food*, 40–53; J. T. Cliffe, *The Yorkshire Gentry from the Reformation to the Civil War* (1969), 114.

[23] For example, Scott Thomson, *Life in a Noble Household*, 235; *The Diary of John Evelyn*, ed. E. S. de Beer, 6 vols (Oxford, 1955), IV, 171, 220; Linda Levy Peck, *Consuming Splendor* (Cambridge, 2005), 26, 174; Susan E. Whyman, *Sociability and Power in Late-Stuart England* (Oxford, 1999), 23–33; D. R. Hainsworth and Cherry Walker, eds, *The Correspondence of Lord Fitzwilliam of Milton and Francis Guybon, his Steward 1697–1709* (Northampton, 1990), *passim*.

[24] Mildred Campbell, *The English Yeoman under Elizabeth and the Early Stuarts* (1960), 244; Alan Macfarlane, *The Family Life of Ralph Josselin, a Seventeenth-Century Clergyman* (Cambridge, 1970), 75; *Robert Loder's Farm Accounts 1610–1620*, ed. G. E. Fussell, Camden Society, 3rd ser. 53 (1936), xxvii, xxx; *The Account Book of Richard Latham 1724–1767*, ed. Lorna Weatherill (Oxford, 1990), xix, xxiii.

that even the 'poorest household servants of lords, knights and gentlemen' who 'feed on the variety of flesh and fish that come from their masters tables' were far better off than the 'poore tenants' of these landlords.[25] Meanwhile, the domestics of the urban middling sort, or that 40 per cent of the rural labour force that were employed as servants in husbandry, felt it their due to benefit from cooked meat regularly provided for the whole 'family'.[26] Even the remuneration of hired workers on estates and farms included meals in which meat was a usual, if not an expected, component.[27]

For small cottagers and independent craftsmen, landless labourers and the poor, whose provisioning was dependent upon their own resources, the lowest status foods most often defined their existence. These were the people whom Baxter thought 'glad of a piece of hanged bacon once a week, and some few that can kill a bull eate now and then a bit of hanged biefe, enough to trie the stomack of an ostrige'. Among such, 'he is a rich man that can afford to eat a joint of fresh meate (biefe, mutton or veale) once in a month or fortnight. If their sow pigge or their hens breed chickens, they cannot afford to eate them, but must sell them to make their rent.' In regions where pigs were plentiful, a flitch of salt bacon might sustain a poor family for many months. So in Elizabethan Suffolk it was said to 'liberally furnisheth the meaner sort the greatest part of the year', while in Leicestershire the common diet of 'beans and bacon' was renowned.[28]

Throughout rural England an important part of the popular diet comprised those creatures that could be snared from the air, trapped on common land or fished from rivers. Such animals were enjoyed by all classes but for some they were more of a mainstay than for others. Rabbits, for example, were

[25] 'The Reverend Richard Baxter's Last Treatise', ed. Frederick J. Powicke, *Bulletin of the John Rylands Library* 10 (1926), 183, 184. See, for example, Stone, *Crisis of the Aristocracy*, 558; Emmison, *Tudor Food*, 40; 'The Diary of John Greene (1635–57)', ed. E. M. Symonds, *English Historical Review* 43 (1928), 600; F. P. and M. M. Verney, *Memoirs of the Verney Family*, 4 vols (1892), II, 225; J. Jean Hecht, *The Domestic Servant in Eighteenth-Century England* (1980), 109–15.

[26] Earle, *The Making of the English Middle Class*, 279–80; Tim Meldrum, *Domestic Service and Gender, 1660–1750* (2000), 196–9; Ann Kussmaul, *Servants in Husbandry in Early Modern England* (Cambridge, 1985), 40–2; John Walter, 'The Social Economy of Dearth in Early Modern England', in *Famine, Disease and the Social Order in Early Modern Society*, ed. John Walter and Roger Schofield (Cambridge, 1989), 75–128, pp. 97–8; Naomi Tadmor, *Family and Friends in Eighteenth-Century England: Household, Kinship, and Patronage* (Cambridge, 2001), 25–6.

[27] *The Farming and Memorandum Books of Henry Best*, 98, 121, 144; Thomas Tusser, *Five Hundred Points of Good Husbandry*, ed. Geoffrey Grigson (Oxford, 1984), 267–8; Michael Roberts, '"Waiting upon Chance": English Hiring Fairs and their Meanings from the 14th to the 20th Century', *Journal of Historical Sociology* 1 (1988), 119–60, pp. 137–8.

[28] 'The Reverend Richard Baxter's Last Treatise', 183; Lord Francis Hervey, ed., *Suffolk in the XVIIth Century* (1902), 37; Joan Thirsk, 'The Farming Regions of England', in *Agrarian History*, IV, ed. *idem*, 91; Alan Everitt, 'The Marketing of Agricultural Produce', in *Agrarian History*, IV, ed. Thirsk, 415–16, 451–2.

plentiful in areas of sandy heathland soil or on coastal plains where they were easily caught or bought inexpensively from managed warrens.²⁹ Jugged hares, roasted hedgehogs and fried squirrels were all familiar fare to country people. Blackbirds and thrushes, ravens and swallows also provided valuable meat supplements. Rooks, if parboiled and then 'well ro[a]sted or baked', were said to be 'good meate for poore folkes', while during the siege of Exeter in 1645 the only things that prevented starvation among the inhabitants were the larks taken on the sea side of the city.³⁰

While the wealthy enjoyed the most prestigious fruits of the sea such as salmon, sturgeon or ling, these were mostly beyond the reach of the majority, especially in areas far inland. Only in shoreline communities did the common people seem regularly to enjoy fish, especially the shellfish which could be readily gleaned or cheaply bought. On the north Yorkshire coast women trapped lobsters and crabs in the tide or picked up mussels on the beaches, and 'this maketh them content yf they have wherwith to live'. At Cockerham in Lancashire, on the Isle of Purbeck in Dorset and by Selsey in West Sussex cockles were said to be collected by the 'poorer sort' without hindrance or charge. In Essex oysters were dredged along the River Colne from Brightlingsea, while in Colchester sprats were so common that they were known as 'weaver's beef'. Down on the Cornish coast oysters were very often 'in such great plenty that the poor may gather them on the shores in great abundance, especially at a spring tide'.³¹

The other great staple with which the common people were associated was dairy produce. In the sixteenth and early seventeenth centuries, so-called 'white meats' were 'reputed as food appertinent only to the inferior sort'. For many, these were supplied by the family cow. The inventories of poor tenant farmers, sampled for the period 1560–1640, indicate that in the north of England about three-quarters of them owned a cow or two, in the east of the country around 70 per cent did so, while in the Midlands the figure was 60 per cent and in the west 55 per cent. The best of a cow's yield was too valuable not to sell, but the skimmed milk left once the precious cream had been removed, or the buttermilk remaining after the churning

²⁹ Hervey, ed., *Suffolk in the XVIIth Century*, 35; Thirsk, 'Farming Techniques', 195; B. A. Holderness, 'East Anglia and the Fens', in *The Agrarian History of England and Wales, V: 1640–1750, I: Regional Farming Systems*, ed. Joan Thirsk (Cambridge, 1984), 237; Thirsk, *Food*, 242–3.
³⁰ Muffett, *Healths Improvement*, 75–8, 90–106; *Cavalier: Letters of William Blundell to his Friends, 1620–1698*, ed. Margaret Blundell (1933), 59; Richard Blome, *Britannia* (1673), 80; Cogan, *Haven of Health*, 122; C. Anne Wilson, *Food and Drink in Britain* (1973), 127.
³¹ John Gough Nichols, ed., *The Topographer and Genealogist*, 3 vols (1846–58), II, 409, 415, 418; *Diary of the Rev. John Ward*, ed. Charles Severn (1839), 125; Beinecke Library, Osborn MS, b. 314, ur, bbr, 119, 189–90.

process, together with the more solid curds, and the whey deposited by cheese making, all provided a mainstay of the peasant diet in many places.[32]

Thus in areas of 'wastes, mountaines, and heathes', people were given to 'liuing very hardly with oaten bread, sowre whay, and gotes milke'. In the pastoral country of north Wiltshire, where 'they only milk the cowes and make cheese, they feed chiefly on milke meates'. The inferior quality hard cheese of Suffolk provided 'at all times so ready a dish' for the local inhabitants, 'especially of the meaner sort'. The poor tenants of the west Midlands had to sell the best of their butter and cheese, leaving only 'skimd cheese and skimd milke and whey curds' for them and their families. Meanwhile in the 'sad little hutts' of the Cumbrian fells 'clap bread and butter and cheese and a cup of beer' was all one would find. In the mid eighteenth century a lad from the 'remote mountainous parts' around Pendle in Lancashire could still tell one visitor that 'oat-cake and butter-milk was their common food', although 'on a festival day they had a piece of meat and a pye-pudding'.[33]

Across the country these residual and inferior dairy products went into a variety of regional dishes, all of them cheap but hearty. Thin milk or water mixed with sprouted barley or oatmeal made a range of porridges and puddings: 'frumenty', 'flummery', 'crowdie' and 'hasty-pudding' among them. In Westmorland 'thickgulls' was a 'haisty pudding made with oatmeal and milk'; in Lancashire 'brawiser' a dish 'made of meal soked in ye fat scumed of ye porridge pot'. Another Lancastrian staple was a concoction known as 'braughwham' made from 'cheese, eggs, clap-bread and butter boiled together'. In Lincolnshire and the East Riding curd cheese tart was a popular favourite.[34]

Together with their dependence on brown bread and 'white meats', it was their consumption of roots and leaves that distinguished the diet of the lower orders in the countryside and helped in some way to define their inferiority. The crudest of it grew wild and, as contemporaries put it, cost nothing but the labour to gather. 'Our poor country-people feed for the most part on hard cheese, milk and roots', observed the preacher John Downame at the beginning of the seventeenth century. At the end of it, Gregory King could still note that many of 'the country people and poorer sort' lived 'in

---

[32] Harrison, *The Description of England*, 126; Alan Everitt, 'Farm Labourers', in *Agrarian History*, IV, ed. Thirsk, 413–15.

[33] John Norden, *The Surveyors Dialogue* (1607), 107; Aubrey, *Natural History of Wiltshire*, 11; Hervey, ed., *Suffolk in the XVIIth Century*, 41; 'The Reverend Richard Baxter's Last Treatise', 183; *Journeys of Celia Fiennes*, 196; *The Travels through England of Dr. Richard Pococke*, ed. J. J. Cartwright, 2 vols, Camden Society, new ser. xlii–xliv (1888–89), I, 203–4.

[34] Wilson, *Food and Drink*, 210–14; Jane M. Ewbank ed., *Antiquary on Horseback* (Kendal, 1963), 127; Folger Shakespeare Library, MS V.a.232, part II; John Ray, *A Collection of English Words, Not Generally Used*, 2nd edn (1691), 11; Thirsk, *Food*, 93, 201, 209.

a manner wholly upon roots or plants with ye help of oatmeal and rye or barley bread'.[35]

'Pottage', a watery soup to which almost any root vegetable or leguminous plant could be added, was on occasion taken by everyone, but for the poor it was a stand-by. A meal in itself, it was also a good way to soften stale bread or thin porridge. Cabbage leaves, colewort, or kale, as it was variously known, were commonplace, 'not a village without them', and were such a staple of pottage that they gave their name to the dish in some places: 'Good keal is half a meal', went the popular saying. Another basic ingredient was leeks, which were equally easy to grow and plentiful, such that 'few thinke any good pottage can be made without them'. In the Midland counties peas were an important crop and here 'pease porridge', or 'peas pottage', sometimes flavoured with bacon or onions and thickened with barley, was a foundation of the popular regimen.[36]

Much edible vegetation grew by hedgerows and along riverbanks, on common lands or in forests, and was gathered by country people as a matter of routine. As one authority put it, 'every hedge affords a sallet', if the yield was properly dressed. Thus, lady's thistle, found 'upon waste and common places by high waies', had leaves thought very wholesome once the prickles were removed and they had been peeled and soaked. Young nettles, burdock leaves and the stalks of alexanders could both be eaten raw with vinegar or boiled as a vegetable. Comfrey, goat's beard and the tops of marsh mallows, all found in boggy ground, were equally nourishing when cooked, while watercress, goosegrass and elder-buds did perfectly well in pottage.[37] A kind of asparagus, 'small and bitter, and not comparable to the cultivated', might be found 'growing wild both in Lincolnshire and in other places'. Ramsons, or wild garlic, flourished in wooded areas: 'Eat leekes in Lide [March], and ramsins in May,/ And all the yeare after physitians may play', as 'the vulgar in the west of England' were wont to say.[38]

Equally, fruits, berries and nuts that could be gathered freely were important supplements in the diets of the 'poorer sort' according to the varieties of season and region. In Worcestershire there was said to be such a 'great aboundance of fruits, that even the hedgerows and high-wayes are

[35] Keith Thomas, *Man and the Natural World* (1983), 26; Laslett, ed., *The Earliest Classics*, 213.
[36] John Worlidge, *Systema Horti-Culturae*, 3rd edn (1688), 169, 175–6; Royal Society, MS 92, 291; BL, Additional MS, 1033, fol. 207r; Muffett, *Healths Improvement*, 222; Cicely Howell, *Land, Family and Inheritance in Transition* (Cambridge, 1983), 164–5.
[37] John Evelyn, *Acetaria. A Discourse of Sallets* (1699), 5; William Coles, *The Art of Simpling* (1656), 48–9; Thomas Tryon, *The Way to Save Wealth* (1695), 17–21; Geoffrey Grigson, *The Englishman's Flora* (1958), 417–18, 255–7, 414–15, 229, 302–3, 422, 110, 70–1, 368–9, 378.
[38] *Diary and Correspondence of John Evelyn, F.R.S.*, ed. William Bray (1906), 635; John Gerarde, *The Herball or Generall Historie of Plantes*, ed. Thomas Johnson (1633), 179–80; BL, Lansdowne MS, 231, fol. 104v.

beset therewith, which are common to all passengers'. In Herefordshire, as in Gloucestershire, it was reported that 'the very hedges in the country are planted with apple trees'.[39] Throughout the country it was a commonplace that youngsters would scrump, or 'plash', the fruit in orchards.[40] During the season blackberries were gratefully collected in most places: 'how the poor live upon them, daily experience sheweth'. Forests and woods afforded strawberries, wimberries, bilberries, massards and nuts at various times of the year.[41] From such bounty the poor were said to make shift even in periods 'of great scarcity or famine', while in farmers' houses 'scarce a day passes without apple pyes or pear pyes (and damson pyes in season)'.[42]

Finally, while household servants and labouring people had to be content to wash down such fare with ale made from malted barley, 'small beer', or even water, conventionally regarded as being detrimental to health, the more prosperous middle ranks brewed hopped beer and distilled aqua vita, while the wealthiest supplemented these with the full variety of wines and spirits that could be imported from abroad.[43] So it was that at the end of the seventeenth century Richard Baxter could draw such a sharp contrast between the 'coarse fare' of poor 'tenants' and 'husbandmen' and 'all the varieties and fullnes of flesh and wines and strong drinkes' consumed by 'idle, gluttonous and voluptuous rich men'. The diet of the former he summed up in a short list: 'brown bread and milk, and pease pies and apple pies, and puddings and pancakes, and gruel and flummery and furmety, yea dry bread and butter and cheese, and cabbages and turnips, and parsnips and carrots, and onions and potatoes, and whey and buttermilk, and small drinke'.[44]

[39] Blome, *Britannia*, 244; [John Macky], *A Journey through England*, 2 vols (1724), II, 129; Moryson, *An Itinerary*, IV, 148.
[40] Cogan, *Haven of Health*, 88; Sir William Brereton, *Travels in Holland, The United Provinces, England, Scotland and Ireland 1634–1635*, ed. Edward Hawkins, Chetham Society 1 (1844), 170; John Bunyan, *The Pilgrim's Progress*, ed. J. B. Wharey and Roger Sharrock (Oxford, 1960), 194; *Blundell's Diary and Letter Book 1702–1728*, ed. Margaret Blundell (Liverpool, 1952), 91.
[41] Muffett, *Healths Improvement*, 217; Cyril Hart, *The Forest of Dean* (1995), 172; Aubrey, *Natural History of Wiltshire*, 50; *Memoirs of Lady Fanshawe* (1829), 54–5; *Journeys of Celia Fiennes*, 165; Thomas Denton, *A Perambulation of Cumberland 1687–1688*, ed. A. J. L. Winchester and Mary Wane, Surtees Society 207 (Woodbridge, 2003), 135.
[42] Laslett, ed., *The Earliest Classics*, 213.
[43] Richard Short, *Peri Psychroposias, of Drinking Water* (1656); Gervase Markham, *The English House-Wife* (1631), 243–8; A. L. Simon, *The History of the Wine Trade in England*, 3 vols (1906; rep. 1964).
[44] 'The Reverend Richard Baxter's Last Treatise', 180.

III

In early modern England there was thus a hierarchy of foods and drinks which was determined by the cluster of ideological and cultural assumptions surrounding them, as well as by their simple price and availability. Few of these comestibles were entirely exclusive to any one class, but for the most part the 'inferior sort' ate what was commonplace and cheap and such things were inevitably tainted with vulgar associations and sometimes attributed detrimental qualities. The 'better sort', meanwhile, overindulged in certain esteemed products, even when medics advised against their supposedly deleterious effects, and recoiled from others in a context where prestige was more important than utility. During the seventeenth century, however, there were a number of developments that significantly altered the dietary regimes and eating habits of various groups of people within English society. Taken together they served to reconfigure in important ways some of the patterns and characteristics in the contemporary sociology of food.

The first of these was the expansion of wheat growing in large parts of the country. The basic assumption that the 'better sort' enjoyed white bread while the 'poorer sort' ate brown was substantially undermined, across southern counties in particular, during this period. The century after 1600 saw 24 per cent of the land mass of England enclosed and, alongside this, sustained attempts to enrich poorer soils with crop rotations and new fertilisers.[45] Thousands of acres hitherto unsuitable for wheat cultivation were thus 'improved' with the result that, according to one calculation, output of this grain in Hampshire, Herefordshire, Lincolnshire, Norfolk and Suffolk combined rose by 39 per cent during the seventeenth century. In the 1690s Gregory King put the nation's total annual production of wheat at 12 million bushels; by the 1760s Charles Smith reckoned that it had increased to 30 million at a time when population size remained broadly constant. Consequently, while the price of wheat varied greatly both between regions and over time, the general trend was downward during these years. Its average, aggregated across the country, which had been 43.88s per quarter in the decade 1640–49, fell by one-third to 28.98s by 1740–49.[46]

As a result, more and more country people in certain regions became accustomed to white bread. John Aubrey commented in the 1680s that,

[45] J. R. Wordie, 'The Chronology of English Enclosure, 1500–1914', *EcHR* 2nd ser. 36 (1983), 483–505; *The Agrarian History of England and Wales, V: 1640–1750, II: Agrarian Change*, ed. Joan Thirsk (Cambridge, 1985).

[46] M. K. Bennett, 'British Wheat Yield per Acre for Seven Centuries', in *Essays in Agrarian History*, ed. W. E. Minchinton, 2 vols (1978), I, 69; Mark Overton, *Agricultural Revolution in England* (Cambridge, 1996), 86; Thirsk and Cooper, eds, *Seventeenth-Century Economic Documents*, 782; Ashley, *Bread of our Forefathers*, 8; Peter J. Bowden, 'Agricultural Prices, Wages, Farm Profits and Rents', in *Agrarian History*, V, II, ed. Thirsk, 9; *idem*, 'Appendix III: Statistics', in *Agrarian History*, V, II, ed. Thirsk, 849 (table 7).

thanks to the shift from barley to wheat in north Wiltshire within living memory, 'all the labourers and poor people ate wheaten bread' and thought the old barley bread to be 'very hard fare'. Edward Lhwyd observed a similar change from oats to wheat, and so from brown bread to white, in upland Glamorgan, where the inhabitants began 'imitating ye low countrey in fare and fashion' and living 'more delicately and easily'. By the mid eighteenth century the wealthy Essex miller Charles Smith could calculate that wheat contributed almost 90 per cent of all the grain used to produce bread in the counties of the south-east including East Anglia, three-quarters of it in the West Country, and about two-thirds in the Midlands and Welsh borders. Only in northern counties was brown bread still dominant.[47]

A second commonplace about the diet of the inferior sort, that it was dominated by 'white meats', was also substantially dissipated by the agrarian changes of the seventeenth century. Enclosure encouraged the decline of the agricultural smallholder and contributed to an evident reduction in that ownership of cattle among poor cottagers that had been so high in the century before 1640. A sample of the inventories of such people indicates that their possession of a cow had fallen to just 6.7 per cent in the fielden areas of the Midlands by 1720; it had declined to 20 per cent in the south-eastern counties and a mere 16.7 per cent in the west during the period 1700–29. Only in the northern counties where the extent of agrarian change was more limited does ownership appear to have remained high. As a result many lost immediate access to one of the traditional mainstays of their nourishment. Sometimes the by-products of dairying were given away to them by the larger herdsmen but when Defoe visited the Wiltshire cheese country in the early eighteenth century he found that farmers simply threw out what skimmed milk and whey could not be fed to their pigs.[48]

The reciprocal of this decline in the cow-owning smallholder was the rise of the larger dairy farmer producing ever greater amounts of higher quality produce for regional, national and even international markets. This development was both cause and effect of the growing prestige accorded to white foods during the period. It gradually became fashionable among the gentry to drink fresh milk. The milkmaid selling her wares by the tankard emerged as a familiar sight in London markets and places of genteel resort.[49] As the quality of butter improved, the most renowned coming from East Anglia,

[47] Royal Society, MS 92, 288; Morris, ed., 'Parochialia', 117; Ashley, *Bread of our Forefathers*, 6–8.

[48] Carole Shammas, 'The Eighteenth-Century English Diet and Economic Change', *Explorations in Economic History* 21 (1984), 254–69, pp. 262–4; *idem*, *Pre-industrial Consumer*, 140–5; Daniel Defoe, *A Tour through the Whole Island of Great Britain*, ed. G. D. H. Cole, 2 vols (1927), II, 284.

[49] Thirsk, *Food*, 270–4; Sean Shesgreen, ed., *The Criers and Hawkers of London* (Aldershot, 1990), 120–21; *The Diary of Samuel Pepys*, ed. Robert Latham and William Matthews, 11 vols (1970–83), VIII, 339; IX, 175, 184, 224, 533–4.

the habit of spreading it on bread became commonplace; it was popular to melt it into a sauce for pouring on vegetables and use it as an ingredient in the puff pastry beloved of the affluent.[50] Finally, cheese experienced a similar reversal of fortunes after the Civil War. Cheshire cheese began to be shipped to London in great quantities. City merchants were soon employing factors at Malmesbury in Wiltshire and Tetbury in Gloucestershire to source the best 'Cheddars' from the west of England. Finest Red Leicester from the rich pastures of the Vale of Belvoir was now being sent up to the capital, and in the late seventeenth century Stilton, originating from Melton Mowbray, also made its debut on the metropolitan market.[51]

If it was becoming harder by this time automatically to identify the common people with brown breads and dairy products, it was also becoming less easy to see them as the principal consumers of fruit and vegetables. The expansion of market gardening in England from the late sixteenth century had much to do with a greater acceptance of 'greens' and 'sallets' on the tables of the social elite. New varieties were introduced and improved strains nurtured in the carefully tended beds and 'hot houses' around London and other urban centres. French beans and new garden peas became delicacies. In refined form, carrots and turnips shed their reputation as animal fodder and found a place at the best tables alongside novel root vegetables such as beetroot. Globe artichokes and asparagus, cauliflowers and new varieties of cabbage became some of the most desirable groceries.[52]

This transformation in the variety and quality of 'garden stuff' helped engender new attitudes towards it. As the dominant humoural theory of the Renaissance became less prevalent, some of the prejudices about vegetables receded. More commentators began to argue for the positive benefits to health of a leguminous diet and from the mid seventeenth century full-blown vegetarianism found its first ideologues. Suspicion of some produce may have remained: Samuel Pepys heard of two people who were alleged to have died from eating cucumbers, but he was quite happy to enjoy new peas or buttered asparagus on occasion.[53] Thus Gregory King could calculate that by the 1690s the English were spending £1.2 million per annum on 'fruit, roots, and garden stuff', and out of this the contribution of the wealthiest 4.5 per cent of the population was fully 86 per cent.[54] The household accounts of the aristocracy and gentry confirm this steady purchase of

[50] Thirsk, *Food*, 274–8.
[51] Charles F. Foster, *Cheshire Cheese and Farming in the North West in the 17th & 18th Centuries* (Northwich, 1998), 6–9; Aubrey, *Natural History of Wiltshire*, 105, 115; Gordon Mingay, 'The East Midlands', in *Agrarian History*, V, I, ed. Thirsk, 99.
[52] Malcolm Thick, 'Market Gardening in England and Wales', in *Agrarian History*, V, II, ed. Thirsk, 503–32.
[53] Thomas, *Man and the Natural World*, 290–2; *Diary of Samuel Pepys*, IV, 285; III, 69, 75, 91; X, 146.
[54] Laslett, ed., *The Earliest Classics*, 67, 213.

green groceries of all sorts in the later seventeenth century.[55] Meanwhile the manuscript recipe books kept by well-to-do ladies reveal the ways in which they were being integrated into the diets of their families.[56] After the Civil War, the rise of the kitchen garden among the provincial gentry emphasised this desire for a ready supply of fresh and high quality greens.[57]

At the same time, a new interest in the cultivation of fruit bushes and the planting of private orchards was indicative of a similar change in attitudes and tastes among the upper ranks of society.[58] This fashion was not merely confined to those in the traditional fruit-growing regions of the south of England. 'Gardens, such as belong to noblemen and persons of distinction are very much improved, since the time of the late civil wars', reported Hugh Todd from the diocese of Carlisle in the 1690s. 'A kind year will gratify the generous improver with melons, apricocks, peaches, nectarines, mulberries, cherries, and apples of the best kinds, in a great plenty, and perfect maturity.'[59]

In sum, the effect of these improvements in both agriculture and horticulture was to undermine the extent to which certain foodstuffs acted as social markers and to redefine the ways in which others did so. Above all, the enhancement and refinement of so much produce created a more variegated spectrum of quality and choice, and a marketplace in which the price mechanism reflected more finely grained distinctions. Those regularly employed labourers, urban artisans and diverse members of the 'middling sort' whose real earnings were improving quite palpably over the course of

[55] For example, Scott Thomson, *Life in a Noble Household*, 144–7; J. R. Magrath, ed., *The Flemings in Oxford*, 3 vols (Oxford, 1904–24), *passim*; *The Household Account Book of Sarah Fell of Swarthmoor Hall*, ed. Norman Penney (Cambridge, 1920), xx, 5, 57, 141, 155, 257; *Selections from the Disbursements Book (1691–1709) of Sir Thomas Haggerston, Bart*, ed. Ann M. C. Forster, Surtees Society 180 (Gateshead, 1969), ix, 5, 25, 33, 42, 48, 49, 72.

[56] For example, BL, Egerton MS, 2,415, fol. 9r; BL, Additional MS, 27,466, fol. 122v; BL, Additional MS, 28,327, fol. 182; BL, Additional MS, 34,722, fol. 50r; BL, Additional MS, 56,248, fol. 31v; BL, Additional MS, 57,944, fols 15v, 30r, 33, 44v, 48v, 57v, 63v, 64v, 68r, 112v, 157r, 160r; and cf. BL, Additional MS, 78,340, fol. 20v; BL, Additional MS, 78,341, fol. 6r.

[57] For example, *Memoirs of Sir John Reresby*, ed. Andrew Browning (Glasgow, 1936), 73; Verney and Verney, *Memoirs of the Verney Family*, I, 8; III, 114; IV, 403–4; *The Estate and Household Accounts of Sir Daniel Fleming*, ed. Blake Tyson (Kendal, 2001), 171, 215; *Blundell's Diary and Letter Book*, 55, 133, 237–8, 243; *A Diary of the Journey through the North of England made by William and John Blathwayt*, ed. Nora Hardwick (Bristol, 1977), 23.

[58] For example, *A Royalist's Notebook*, ed. Francis Bamford (1936), 95; T. E. Gibson, ed., *Crosby Records* (1880), 157; *The Garden Book of Sir Thomas Hanmer Bart*, ed. E. S. Rohde (1933), 152–6; John Evelyn, *Elysium Britannicum*, ed. John E. Ingram (Philadelphia, 2001), 317–34; *Journeys of Celia Fiennes*, 110, 165, 176.

[59] Hugh Todd, *Account of the City and Diocese of Carlisle*, ed. R. S. Ferguson (Kendal, 1890), 32; and cf. Denton, *A Perambulation of Cumberland*, 157, 189, 296, 353.

the late seventeenth and early eighteenth centuries found themselves in a position to benefit to varying extents from these trends.[60] When the likes of King and Vanderlint came to compare their expenditure with that of the 'poorer sort' it was more in the nature of what they bought than in the basic quantity that the most telling difference was now to be found.

As for the 'better sort', they had the opportunity, as well as the ability, to seek out ever more rare and expensive dainties in order to reposition their consumption and distinguish themselves in more conspicuous ways from those beneath. In this they were helped by developments in transport and the emergence of a more integrated national economy that allowed the finest produce to be delivered, at a price, to the discerning customer around the country. With the advent of 'potting', for example, delicacies such as lampreys, caught on the River Severn near Gloucester, or char, the 'golden alpine trout' of Lake Windermere, could now be preserved and sent long distances. In season, salmon caught on the River Derwent was ridden post haste through the night from Carlisle to London where some were prepared to pay between 2s 6d and 4s per pound for it in the early eighteenth century.[61]

At the same time the transformation of overseas trade in this period enormously increased the range of exotic and exclusive foodstuffs arriving in England to satisfy the refining tastes and vanity of the rich. Among fruits, prunes and figs came from southern Europe and rhubarb from the East Indies. Almost eleven million oranges and lemons were being imported annually from the Mediterranean by the late seventeenth century, and lime juice was shipped in barrels from Jamaica by the 1680s. Other costly novelties included bananas, mangos and pineapples. Meanwhile, in high class grocers at the Royal Exchange and New Exchange the wealthy could find rare morsels such as olives and vanilla pods, or anchovies and caviar. They could flavour their dishes with new spices such as 'guinea pepper' or 'chyan', and 'Jamaica pepper' or 'allspice', while it was observed in 1680 that 'now we have a new sawce called Catch-up, from East-India, sold at a guiney a bottle'. They could indulge a sweet tooth with sugar sold by the loaf, or candied fruits, or patronise the new breed of French chocolatier beginning to appear on the London landscape.[62]

These trends were no less reflected in the supply of and demand for drinks. Developments in internal communication brought the first bottles of

[60] Wrightson, *EN*, 230–1, 296–300, 316–17.
[61] Wilson, *Food and Drink*, 57; *The Memoirs of Sir Daniel Fleming*, ed. R. E. Porter and W. G. Collingwood (Kendal, 1928), 83–4; *Journeys of Celia Fiennes*, 191–2, 235; Defoe, *A Tour through the Whole Island of Great Britain*, II, 269, 274–5.
[62] BL, Additional MS, 72890, fols 26–41; Donald F. Bond, ed., *The Spectator*, 5 vols (Oxford, 1965), I, 295–6; Wilson, *Food and Drink*, 292–3, 295, 299–301, 345, 347, 357; Jane Grigson, *Jane Grigson's Fruit Book* (1982), 48, 229, 335; Earle, *The Making of the English Middle Class*, 274–5; [William Petyt], *Britannia Languens* (1680), 285.

famous 'Hull ale' to London in 1623. It would be joined by the best beers of towns along the River Trent, or that of Sandbach in Cheshire, and the celebrated 'Northdown' from Margate in Kent, among the many strong brews that sold at the 'bottle-beer shop in the Strand' and select establishments for 12d a piece.[63] After the Civil War, cider began to be sent from the West Country up to the capital where bottles made from the finest Herefordshire redstreak apples would fetch 1s 6d each.[64] Meanwhile the first tea imported into England by the East India Company in 1664 was prohibitively expensive; six years later the Duke of Rutland paid 10s for half a pound to be brought to Belvoir Castle. Coffee too was costly, powdered beans selling for as much a 6s per pound by 1693, although the proliferation of the coffee-house made this beverage more widely available. Another novelty, cocoa, remained dear, and chocolate houses were among the most exclusive resorts in late seventeenth- and early eighteenth-century London.[65] As for wine, both the quantity and the quality arriving into the country were transformed in these years. Some offerings were new: Champagne made its debut after the Restoration and Port began arriving in the 1670s, while Château Haut-Brion became the first individual property to be famed in England. Clarets and Sauternes from Bordeaux, 'Shably' from Burgundy, Hermitage from the Rhone Valley and the pure 'Rhenish' of Hockenheim were just some of the most prestigious wines to be now more clearly itemised both in the customs accounts of ports and the cellar books of gentlemen. They explain the fact that Gregory King would find the richest in society allocating fully one-fifth of their provisioning expenditure to alcoholic drinks.[66]

These luxury foods and drinks added new levels of sophistication to the tables of the social elite in town and country. They were accompanied by refinements of the whole culinary experience in high society, which in the later seventeenth century included telling changes in the timing of dinner and the division of meals into separate courses, alongside the cultivation of ever more elaborate table manners and the adoption of a new material culture of dining.[67] The developing taste for French 'haute cuisine' with

[63] Peter Mathias, *The Brewing Industry in England 1700–1830* (Cambridge, 1959), 150, 174–5; [Lorenzo Magalotti], *Travels of Cosmo the Third* (1821), 403; Guy Miege, *The New State of England* (1691), I, 56; *Diary of Samuel Pepys*, I, 211.

[64] Thick, 'Market gardening', 303; Beinecke Library, Osborn MS, b. 314, 272–3.

[65] Wilson, *Food and Drink*, 406–14; Thirsk, *Food*, 129, 136–7, 308–9; Simon, *History of the Wine Trade*, III, 249–52.

[66] *Ibid.*, III, chs 9–13; Scott Thomson, *Life in a Noble Household*, 190–201; Bodleian Library, Ashmole MS 1820b, fol. 7; A. L. Simon, *Bottlescrew Days* (1926), 153–5.

[67] On each of these changes, see R. N. K. Rees and Charles Fenby, 'Meals and Meal-Times', in *Englishmen at Rest and Play*, ed. Reginald Lennard (Oxford, 1931), 214–17, 232; Norbert Elias, *The Civilizing Process*, rev. edn (Oxford, 2000), 72–108; Anna Bryson, *From Courtesy to Civility* (Oxford, 1998), 80–1, 91–3, 98–100; Jean-Louis Flandrin, 'Distinction through Taste', in *A History of Private Life: Passions of the Renaissance*, ed. Roger Chartier (Cambridge MA, 1989), 265–307.

its 'bisques', 'ragouts' and 'fricassees', its wine infused sauces and desserts such as syllabub and 'coulis', was another manifestation of the tendency to invent fresh forms of discrimination. At this time, it was still something for the metropolitan 'beau monde' rather than the bluff aristocracy, provincial squirearchy or sturdy yeomanry who tended to despise such outlandish 'kick-shaws'.[68] Nevertheless, a growing number of domestic French chefs among a section of the elite, and the rise after the Restoration of the 'French ordinary' on London's commercial dining scene, pointed the way to the future.[69]

IV

The consumption of meat and drink was a powerful expression of worth and status in early modern England. Attitudes towards foodstuffs were clearly altering in significant ways during this period, however, and these provide a prism through which to view broader developments in contemporary society. Between the late sixteenth and early eighteenth century, England underwent dramatic commercial expansion, the market economy became ever more integrated, and London emerged at its head as an international metropolis. National income increased rapidly and levels of personal wealth among certain groups rose markedly. New forms of production and fresh sources of supply made available a novel range and improved standard of all manner of goods. The extent to which people were able to acquire such products increasingly came to reflect both their individual identity and their social place. As Keith Wrightson has observed, consumption 'is a form of self-fashioning, a way of assuring oneself that one possesses certain attributes and tastes. But it is not simply self-directed, for the adoption of a particular pattern of material life also inevitably imparts messages to a larger social audience.'[70]

For the top 4.5 per cent of society – those aristocrats, gentlefolk, large merchants and wealthy professionals whom Gregory King collectively labelled 'the better sort' – the average of perhaps £16 per head that they spent yearly on gastronomy came to be bestowed on an ever greater array

[68] Stephen Mennell, *All Manners of Food* (Oxford, 1985), 83–101; Felicity Heal, *Hospitality in Early Modern England* (Oxford, 1990), 116–17; Samuel Sorbiere, *A Voyage to England* (1709), 61–2; [Magalotti], *Travels of Cosmo the Third*, 464. On the 'middling sort' antipathy to foreign 'sauces', see Thomas Fuller, *The Holy State* (Cambridge, 1642), 117; *The Diary of the Rev. Henry Newcome*, ed. Thomas Haywood, Chetham Society 18 (Manchester, 1849), 146; *The Autobiography of William Stout of Lancaster 1665–1752*, ed. J. D. Marshall (Manchester, 1967), 227, 237.
[69] Robert May, *The Accomplisht Cook* (1660), sig. A6; *Diary of Samuel Pepys* (on French domestic dining) I, 269; IV, 341; VI, 2, 112; VIII, 251; IX, 78, 423–4; X, 148; (on eating out) VIII, 211; IX, 82, 115, 172, 206, 317; X, 427; Simon, *History of the Wine Trade*, III, ch. 8; Bryant Lillywhite, *London Coffee Houses* (1963), 137, 450 2, 730.
[70] Wrightson, *EN*, 299.

of finer quality and more exotic produce. Among these ranks, eating and drinking had never been so varied, so rich, or so refined. Never had the opportunity to use meals and beverages in order to make social statements contained such attractions and offered such possibilities. As for that diverse range of peoples who made up the 'middling sort', comprising in King's estimation more than half the population and each spending an annual mean of about £4 on foodstuffs, most were able to benefit to some degree from the commercial changes that defined the era. In better joints of meat more often bought, in green groceries nicely cultivated and foreign spices increasingly affordable, in occasional luxuries to supplement the 'decencies' of life, such groups positioned themselves in the shifting hierarchies of the social order. It was the two-fifths of the population at the bottom of the ladder, King's 'poorer sort' with no more than £2 to sustain themselves for a twelve month, amongst whom these developments made least impact. Some were able to swap their rustic bread for pure wheaten, and a few their 'white meats' for fresh dairy, but lack of surplus income limited their engagement with the elaborating world of goods. Most struggled to make ends meet as they had always done, spending two-thirds of their earnings simply on keeping body and soul together. Theirs were still the residual by-products of provisioning the more affluent, the gleanings from nature's bounty and the leavings in the market at the end of the day. They were by no means immune from the improvements in quality and choice, but they were substantially insulated from them.

Thus the distinctions between the lifestyles of the 'better', 'middle' and 'poorer' sorts of people were becoming more sophisticated in these generations and the divisions between them more pronounced. The tendency of the market economy to disaggregate more sharply and differentiate more subtly is confirmed by the evidence of the early modern period. The consumption of food and drink sheds light upon one aspect of this remaking of English society.

8

Written Obligations, Litigation and Neighbourliness, 1580–1680

TIM STRETTON

Elizabethans and Jacobeans living through the most dramatic per capita increase in litigation levels in English history lamented the weakening of personal and community relations that growing litigiousness both produced and embodied. In 1576 a parliamentary bill complained of the 'multitude of contentions which for lack of charity rise upon the smallest occasions between neighbours', while in 1626 Walter Cary identified the 'infinite number of suits' at law as one of the three ills of the age that had grown dramatically over his lifetime.[1] To those observers who regarded rising prices for foodstuffs and a growing tendency for creditors to charge interest on loans as expressions of greed, rather than as responses to economic change and rising demand, the expansion of litigation was simply a further manifestation of 'the replacement of the values of the commonwealth with those of commodity and covetousness'.[2] As Robert Burton reflected in *The Anatomy of Melancholy* (1621), 'now for every toy and trifle they goe to law … ready to pull out one anothers throats, and for matters of commodity, to squise blood … out of their brothers heart'.[3]

Neighbourly relations, it seems, were under attack from all sides. Torrents of insults flying back and forth in fields and on doorsteps produced an unprecedented surge of defamation suits in the church courts.[4] In many regions

---

[1] C. W. Brooks, *Pettyfoggers and Vipers of the Commonwealth: The Lower Branch of the Legal Profession in Early Modern England* (Cambridge, 1986), 133; Walter Cary, *The Present State of England* (1626), 3.

[2] Steve Hindle, 'A Sense of Place? Becoming and Belonging in the Rural Parish, c.1550–1650', in *Communities in Early Modern England: Networks: Place, Rhetoric*, ed. Alexandra Shepard and Phil Withington (Manchester, 2000), 96–114, p. 97.

[3] Robert Burton, *The Anatomy of Melancholy* (1621), 32

[4] J. A. Sharpe, *Defamation and Sexual Slander in Early Modern England: The Church Courts at York* (York, 1980); Martin Ingram, *Church Courts, Sex and Marriage in England, 1570–1640* (Cambridge, 1987); Laura Gowing, *Domestic Dangers: Women, Words, and Sex in Early Modern London* (Oxford, 1996).

criminal prosecutions were also rising, including those for the new statutory crimes of witchcraft and infanticide, and pamphlets publicised infamous murders and bemoaned growing social disobedience and religious dissension.[5] Meanwhile *habeas corpus* and other prerogative writs complained of unwarranted imprisonment or unfair litigation.[6] The world was out of joint, especially for those living in 'swarming' London, and authors often listed the values associated with neighbourliness as among the first casualties.[7] In Robert Wilson's comedy *The Three Ladies of London* (1581–82) the character Lady Lucre gets the better of Lady Love and Lady Conscience; the trio of Fraud, Simony and Usury dupe Simplicity and Sincerity; and Usury murders Hospitality. The lawyer in the play, a colleague of Fraud and Dissimulation, keeps men in law ten years or more and honest dealing is rare. The play's satirical critique of an emerging materialism and of souring interpersonal relations appears to have touched a nerve with its London audiences and in 1588–89 Wilson penned a sequel.[8]

Such epitaphs for the passing of a simpler, more honest and charitable age were common in late Elizabethan England, yet current scholars tend to downplay them as nostalgic yearnings for a largely mythical golden past. The consensus seems to be that the economic, religious and political transformations of the period recalibrated hierarchies of wealth and contributed to ongoing tensions, but produced little in the way of lasting changes to community relations and values, except for a decline of hospitality and a hardening of attitudes to the poor.[9] As Keith Wrightson observes, most of today's historians stress that social relations were negotiated, contested and often in flux, but seem reluctant to identify clear or consistent change over time.[10] This chapter questions these assertions of relative continuity through an analysis of the social effects of lawsuits over bonds and promises during the expansion of central court litigation that gained momentum in

---

[5]   J. A Sharpe, *Crime in Early Modern England* (Harlow, 1999), 70–88, 244–5; Frances E. Dolan, *Dangerous Familiars: Representations of Domestic Crime in England 1550–1700* (Ithaca, 1994), 2–3; Ian Archer, *The Pursuit of Stability: Social Relations in Elizabethan London* (Cambridge, 1991), 204–5.

[6]   Paul D. Halliday, *Habeas Corpus: From England to Empire* (Cambridge MA, 2010).

[7]   Paul Griffiths, *Lost Londons: Change, Crime and Control in the Capital City 1550–1660* (Cambridge, 2008), esp. 433–7; Archer, *Pursuit of Stability*, 1–17.

[8]   Lloyd Edward Kermode, ed., *Three Renaissance Usury Plays* (Manchester, 2009), 30, 79–163.

[9]   See, for example, Naomi Tadmor's insightful analysis of the historiography of kinship, in Naomi Tadmor, 'Early Modern English Kinship in the Long Run: Reflections on Continuity and Change', *C&C* 25 (2010), 15–48; Felicity Heal, *Hospitality in Early Modern England* (Oxford, 1990).

[10]   Keith Wrightson, 'Mutualities and Obligations: Changing Social Relationships in Early Modern England', *Proceedings of the British Academy* 139 (2006), 157–94, esp. 158.

the 1580s and persisted (with minor interruptions in the 1620s and 1640s) until the 1670s.[11]

In the 1970s Lawrence Stone concluded that in sixteenth- and seventeenth-century England 'tempers were short, and both casual violence and venomous and mutually exhausting litigation against neighbours were extremely common'.[12] Since the 1980s, however, scholars have hurried to the defence of English men and women and their values, rejecting sweeping master narratives of change and taking a more utilitarian view of the expansion of litigation in the century after 1580.[13] Many point to the reluctance of litigants to sue each other and how few cases proceeded to a final decision (even though completion rates were almost identical to today's), and suggest that many parties initiated legal proceedings to encourage amicable settlement outside of the courtroom.[14] Recent research has confirmed that debt-related lawsuits accounted for the bulk of the growth in litigation, leading scholars to regard them as a relatively straightforward symptom of the expansion of marketing and of other economic activities resulting from growing population and demand, an increasingly integrated economy and a breathtaking reliance on credit.[15] Put simply, a rise in the number and complexity of economic transactions led to a corresponding rise in defaults, exacerbated by chains of credit that were only as strong as their weakest links. That prosperity was the cause of soaring litigation was one of the few things that Edward Coke and Francis Bacon agreed on, Coke reflecting that 'peace is the mother of plenty—and plenty the nurse of suits'.[16] Examinations of local, urban and regional court records suggest that the ability of merchants, traders, shopkeepers and their neighbours to survive and prosper

---

[11] C. W. Brooks, *Lawyers, Litigation and English Society since 1450* (1998), 29–32, 66, 68.

[12] Lawrence Stone, *The Family, Sex and Marriage in England, 1500–1800* (1977), 99.

[13] See, for example, Alan Macfarlane, *The Justice and the Mare's Ale: Law and Disorder in Seventeenth-Century England* (Cambridge, 1981), esp. 184–99.

[14] Brooks, *Pettyfoggers*, 76, n. 9; J. A. Sharpe, '"Such Disagreement Betwyx Neighbours"; Litigation and Human Relations in Early Modern England', in *Disputes and Settlements: Law and Human Relations in the West*, ed. John Bossy (Cambridge, 1983), 167–88; J. A. Sharpe, 'The People and the Law', in *Popular Culture in Seventeenth Century England*, ed. Barry Reay (1985), 244–70; Martin Ingram, 'Communities and Courts: Law and Disorder in Early Seventeenth-Century Wiltshire', in *Crime in England, 1550–1800*, ed. J. S. Cockburn (1977), 110–34.

[15] Craig Muldrew, 'Credit and the Courts: Debt Litigation in a Seventeenth-Century Urban Community', *EcHR* 2nd ser. 46 (1993), 23–38; Craig Muldrew, *The Economy of Obligation: The Culture of Credit and Social Relations in Early Modern England* (Basingstoke, 1998); Brooks, *Lawyers, Litigation and English Society*, chs 2, 4, 5; W. A. Champion, 'Recourse to Law and the Meaning of the Great Litigation Decline, 1650–1750', in *Communities and Courts in Britain 1150–1900*, ed. C. W. Brooks and Michael Lobban (1997), 179–98.

[16] As quoted in Christopher Hill, *The Intellectual Origins of the English Revolution Revisited* (Oxford, 1997), 203; Francis Bacon, *The Elements of the Common Lawes of England* (1630), sig. A3v.

in these changing economic conditions depended on maintaining a reputation for honest dealing—on having credit in both senses of the word. This implies that the unprecedented levels of indebtedness resulting from these market conditions and a shortage of specie actually helped tie communities together.[17] Lawsuits were unwelcome, but becoming increasingly accepted as the most appropriate means of settling differences and restoring harmony, and the English embraced them on such a scale that historians now place litigation, legal institutions and a growing belief in the rule of law at the centre of explanations of state formation.[18]

Diary evidence nonetheless reveals that at least a few neighbours fretted over the negative consequences of legal confrontations. Complaints about vindictive or vexatious litigation were particularly strident and numerous, it is argued, not because such litigation was common, but because it went against and therefore endangered social harmony. So, while surging litigation levels placed immense strain on values of neighbourliness and community, and refigured them in a more utilitarian form, those values held fast and remained a cherished ideal for decades to come.[19] The older contention that a more instrumental and self-interested world characterised by contractual thinking was displacing a traditional world of face-to-face associations and shared customs and values has largely been dismissed as a myth.[20] Viewed from these various perspectives, debt-related litigation becomes less a sign of eroding personal relations than a measure of the heat generated by a robust economy within an increasingly sophisticated society served by an expanding and centralising state.[21]

This chapter seeks to darken this surprisingly positive vision of the meaning and effect of rising interpersonal conflict and to join Keith Wrightson in questioning optimistic interpretations that recognise the significance of economic change but nonetheless stress relative social continuity.[22] For while historians are right to conclude that the explosion of

[17] Craig Muldrew, 'Interpreting the Market: The Ethics of Credit and Community Relations in Early Modern England', *SH* 18 (1993), 163–83, p. 169.

[18] Lawrence Stone, *The Crisis of the Aristocracy 1558–1641* (Oxford, 1965), 240; Steve Hindle, *The State and Social Change in Early Modern England, c.1550–1640* (Basingstoke, 2000); C. W. Brooks, *Law, Politics and Society in Early Modern England* (Cambridge, 2008).

[19] Craig Muldrew, 'The Culture of Reconciliation: Community and the Settlement of Economic Disputes in Early Modern England', *HJ* 39 (1996), 915–42; Brooks, *Law, Politics and Society*; Archer, *Pursuit of Stability*, 74–82.

[20] Craig Muldrew, 'From a "Light Cloak" to an "Iron Cage": Historical Changes in the Relation Between Community and Individualism', in *Communities*, ed. Shepard and Withington, 156–77; Alexandra Shepard and Phil Withington, 'Introduction', in *Communities*, ed. Shepard and Withington, 1–15. Cf. Hindle, *The State and Social Change*, 54–8.

[21] For a rare dissenting voice, see Hindle, *The State and Social Change*, 78–87, 90–3.

[22] Wrightson, 'Mutualities and Obligations', 157–94.

litigation was not caused by a decline in values of neighbourliness, they are arguably wrong to assume the opposite, that the eruption of litigation did not erode neighbourly relations, for it seems almost certain that it did. Nowhere is this more apparent than in litigation over conditional bonds.

Whereas local court records from the period reveal a growing reliance on informal oral promises underpinned by personal reputation, central court records indicate an unprecedented reliance on formal legal agreements, such as deeds and indentures, statutes staple and especially bonds.[23] Conditional or penal bonds (or 'bands' or bills obligatory) had been in use for centuries, but in the later sixteenth century individuals and institutions put them to a dizzying array of uses. Crown officials used them to ensure the performance of their orders or the appearance of offenders at assizes and to bind over individuals to good behaviour or to keep the peace. Ecclesiastical officials used them to give force to orders of alimony and to ensure honest diligence in the administering of deceased persons' estates. Ordinary citizens used them to arrange and secure marriage promises, the sale of goods and above all loans of money, with Thomas Wentworth noting in his manual for executors that 'the greatest number of debts' are 'debts due by specialty, viz. bond or bill'.[24] Their use became so widespread that authors employed penal bonds and the language of conditions, forbearance, forfeitures and penalties as metaphors to describe God's grace, love, marriage, justice and even a witch's covenant.[25]

In the central common law courts of King's Bench and Common Pleas, the number of lawsuits over debt proceeding beyond initial stages rose from 3,161 a year in 1560 to 16,260 in 1606, and made up 60, rising to 70, per cent of all actions in those courts. The majority of these actions, around 90 per cent, involved bonds or other written obligations, and between 1560 and 1640 suits over bonds increased by almost 800 per cent.[26] Penal bonds supplied security because they brought simplicity to contractual arrangements, replacing bilateral commitments – such as a promise to supply barley and a promise to pay for that barley – with a unilateral obligation to pay a fixed penalty. Suing on a bond at common law was straightforward and offered

---

[23] In the borough court of King's Lynn, only 11 per cent of suits involved bonds or other sealed instruments; Muldrew, 'Culture of Reconciliation', 925, n. 36.

[24] Thomas Wentworth, *The Office and Dutie of Executors* (1641), sig. Bbbv. And see Brooks, *Pettyfoggers*, 68.

[25] Thomas Cranmer, *An Aunswere by the Reverend Father in God Thomas Archbyshop of Canterbury* (1580), 81; Thomas Dekker, *Blurt Master-Constable. Or the Spaniards Night-Walke* (1602), sig. F1v; George Wilkins, *The Miseries of Inforst Mariage* (1607), sig. K2; Robert Parsons, *A Quiet and Sober Reckoning with M. Thomas Morton* (1609), 654; Anon, *The Famous & Renowned History of Morindos a King of Spain who Maryed with Miracola a Spanish Witch* (1609), sig. B (and see B3).

[26] My calculations based on Brooks' figures. In Common Pleas by 1606, over 80 per cent of cases in advanced stages were debt suits involving a bond or other form of written obligation, rising to 88 per cent by 1640; Brooks, *Pettyfoggers*, 67, 69.

a number of advantages over the alternative methods of settling disputes over promises, such as wager of law or actions of covenant or *assumpsit*.[27] For all their flexibility, however, penal bonds proved to be surprisingly clumsy instruments that could encourage behaviour that was decidedly un-neighbourly. Most bonds included penalties for default of around 100 per cent of the value of the money loaned or the goods purchased, even for debts or transactions of short duration.[28] In a society that had only recently come to terms with interest rates of 10 per cent per annum, returns on defaulted bonds equivalent to 400 per cent or more provided incentives for uncharitable dealing and 'corrupt and indirect practyce to receyve gret gayne' that many found difficult to resist.[29]

The equity courts of Chancery and Requests also experienced a dramatic expansion of lawsuits beginning in the final decades of the sixteenth century, the lion's share of which related to debts and bonds.[30] However, a growing proportion of these lawsuits were counter-suits launched in response to legal process initiated at common law, as plaintiffs sought injunctions staying or halting actions on bonds running against them in other courts.[31] Most historians have failed to realise that the single largest category of litigation in these prerogative courts was effectively appeals against common law actions, although most were initiated before, rather than after, judgment given in their sister courts.[32] The resulting barrage of injunctions created tensions between the equity and common law jurisdictions (helping to spur James I's notorious intervention on the side of equity in 1616), but pleadings from these cases also lay bare fundamental disagreements between litigants about the force of written promises and the nature of personal trust.

A number of common law defendants who hurried as complainants to Chancery and Requests made claims for equitable intervention that all but the staunchest defenders of the common law accepted. They conceded that the suits against them were legally sufficient – that they were bound by obligations, had failed to satisfy the terms of those obligations and so were liable to pay the stated penalties – but pleaded mitigating circumstances.

---

[27] A. W. B. Simpson, 'The Penal Bond with Conditional Defeasance', *Law Quarterly Review* (1966), 392–422.

[28] See Nathanael Homes, *Usury is Injury* (1640), 20.

[29] *White v. Elam*, The National Archives [TNA], REQ 2/164/176, Bill.

[30] Tim Stretton, *Women Waging Law in Elizabethan England* (Cambridge, 1998), ch. 3; W. J. Jones, *The Elizabethan Court of Chancery* (Oxford, 1967).

[31] Up until the 1590s counsel requesting injunctions in Chancery staying debt actions in King's Bench did so by questioning the Bill of Middlesex procedure that evaded Chancery writs (and fees); N. Jones, 'The Bill of Middlesex and the Chancery', *Journal of Legal History* 22 (2001), 1–20.

[32] Most historians downplay the extent and significance of collateral actions and vexatious litigation: Brooks, *Pettyfoggers*, 111; Brooks, *Law, Politics and Society*; Champion, 'Recourse to Law'; Ingram, 'Communities and Courts'. Cf. Jones, *Chancery*, 314–15, 418; Hindle, *The State and Social Change*, 82–3.

Debtors, for example, suggested that they had been ready to settle debts on due dates but had been unable to do so, owing to sickness, misunderstanding, or an inability to locate their creditors.[33] Others said they had paid most of the amount due, or had tried to make payment within hours or days of lapsed deadlines, so that to suffer the full penalty was unduly harsh.[34] In each instance they either hoped that their creditors would see reason and settle for the repayment of the principal plus something 'for forbearance', or suggested that the lure of a high penalty had induced their opponents to ignore accepted standards of neighbourliness and compassion.[35]

Of greater significance is the far larger number of litigants who did not concede the sufficiency of the common law suits running against them, arguing instead that they were against conscience or even fraudulent. A small proportion of these centred around questions of fact, such as whether 'bisket bread' assured to be of good quality was 'corrupt, rotten & naghtye bredd not meate for any person to eate' or whether a colt had been cured as promised 'of a dangerous hurt the sayd coult had in one of his eyes'.[36] More commonly plaintiffs asserted that they had fully satisfied their obligations, yet their opponents were nevertheless trying to profit from the agreed penalty, in what amounted to double or triple charging.[37] The common law permitted such actions because a bond was a sealed instrument and so considered unsatisfied at law unless it was cancelled, by physically defacing or destroying it or through the provision of a sealed written acquittance.[38] As the maxim put it, 'specialty must be met with specialty' and to accept otherwise would have made money lending, mercantile trade and economic life in general impossibly uncertain, and amounted to a return to the very world of one person's word against another's that bondholders sought to escape.[39] It followed, from a common law standpoint, that most plaintiffs in Chancery and Requests bond suits were dishonestly vexing opponents or attempting to evade their obligations and responsibilities.

Litigants in equity courts provided a staggering range of explanations for why satisfied bonds remained uncancelled. Some described how their bonds had indeed been returned to them after settlement or else left in the safekeeping of third parties. All was right with the world until the bonds fell into the wrong hands, as a result of theft, collusion, or the death of

---

[33] TNA, C33/87, fol. 29v–30.

[34] *Seller v. Blackman*, TNA, REQ 2/271/20.

[35] *Barker v. van Lore*, TNA, C2/Eliz/B9/9; *Allen v. Marron*, TNA, REQ 21, 102.

[36] *Franklyn v. Rose and Rose*, TNA, REQ 1/35A, fol. 184; *Androwe v. Denys*, TNA, C2 Eliz/A1/19, m. 4. Cf. the essay by Adam Fox in this volume.

[37] *Clark v. Weekes*, TNA, REQ 1/21, 228; Jones, *Chancery*, 444.

[38] Simpson, 'The Penal Bond', 416.

[39] Robert Atkyns, *An Enquiry into the Jurisdiction of the Chancery in Causes in Equity* (1696), 36–9; Mark Fortier, *The Culture of Equity in Early Modern England* (Aldershot, 2005), 63–4.

the bondholders, and ended up in suit at common law.[40] Others alleged that they had settled their obligations without seeing their original bonds cancelled or returned, or asking for written acquittances.[41] The realities of economic life meant that individuals often did not have their bonds about them at the time of settlement, and calling for a bond to be returned, or even asking for a legally acceptable acquittance, could smack of distrust and risk souring a good professional relationship among those who believed that 'an honest person held to his word and did not demand written proof'.[42] In other cases plaintiffs argued that their original written agreements were subject to unwritten understandings or oral terms or that a newer bond superseded an older one, even though the original remained uncancelled.[43] To common lawyers these represented invitations to perjury, raising the daunting possibility that bare words could undermine sealed written instruments, or as Christopher St German expressed it, 'that every man by a nude parol and by a bare averment should avoid an obligation'.[44]

The longevity of bonds was one of their virtues, but could cause problems when they came into the hands of individuals who had not been parties to the original agreements. In 1640, after William Ireland's widow had remarried and joined her husband in putting in suit a thirty-year-old bond, the Masters of Requests ordered the couple to deliver up the bond for cancelling 'in regard it did not appear that the said William Heather in his life tyme or the said William Ireland after his death made any demand of any thinge to be done upon the said bond'.[45] Executors and administrators were under a legal obligation to put in suit uncancelled bonds possessed by the deceased, but for others the lure of the penalty encouraged lawsuits over long-settled agreements.[46] In these and other instances the nature of bonds and 'the strict course of the common law' in relation to sealed instruments created opportunities for harsh dealing that would be difficult to imagine

---

[40] *Feilder v. Feilder*, TNA, REQ 1/26, 322–3; *Bishop v. Bishop*, TNA, REQ 1/15, fol. 29v; *Thompson and Thompson v. Bradley and Pound*, TNA REQ 2/276/33; *Hill v. Horne and Winniffe*, TNA, REQ 2/217/34.

[41] *Wright and Wright v. Wolley*; *Lowe and Reade v. Playse and Playse*, TNA, REQ 1/21, 82–3, 98–99; Jones, *Chancery*, 444.

[42] M. T. Clanchy, *From Memory to Written Record: England 1066–1307*, 2nd edn (Oxford, 1993), 193.

[43] *Bird v. Prior*; *Manley v. Cade et al.*; *Duryvall v. Sutton*; TNA, REQ 1/21, 86–7, 90, 314–15; *Buswell v. Buswell*, TNA, REQ 2/115/29; *Dunford v. Dunford*, TNA, REQ 1/34, 183; *Freer v. Freer*, TNA, C2 Eliz/F/F/3/23, m. 1; *Albright v. Reve*, TNA, C2 Eliz/A1/7. For earlier examples see W. T. Barbour, 'The History of Contract in Early English Equity', *Oxford Studies in Social and Legal History*, IV, ed. Paul Vinogradoff (Oxford, 1914; repr. 1974), 84–97, 172–234

[44] Christopher Saint German, *The Dialogue in English betweene a Doctor of Divinitie and a Student of the Lawes of England* (1593), fol. 22v.

[45] *Cole v. Harrison and Harrison*, TNA, REQ 1/36B, fols 25–6.

[46] Thomas Wentworth, *The Office and Dutie of Executors* (1641), sig. Eee.

with oral agreements. For example, when bond conditions named the day of repayment but neglected to name the place, unscrupulous creditors went into hiding to prevent repayment and so induce forfeiture.[47]

Bonds could also draw into the net of simple agreements a wide supporting cast of individuals acting as sureties. When bonds went unsatisfied sureties could find themselves put in execution for outstanding penalties.[48] The Cheshire gentleman Sir Richard Grosvenor spent most of the 1630s imprisoned under just these circumstances, while the character Antonio in George Chapman's *Two Wise Men and All the Rest Fooles* (1619) not only has a surety arrested, but boasts to the hapless debtor 'it joies me much, that either he shall die in prison, or I shall have that monie'.[49] Another problem with bonds was that technically they were not transferable except at death, a fact that made chains of credit particularly inflexible and prone to serial collapse. However, the archives of Requests and Chancery are full of allegations that individuals purchased bonds from executors, paid to have them cancelled or else gained letters of attorney authorising them to sue on other people's bonds.[50] Once again, the temptation to profit from penalties, or to use the threat of them to provide advantage in entirely different transactions, proved too strong for those who increasingly came to view bonds as commodities, even though at common law they had no intrinsic value (for example if stolen) and under ecclesiastical law were valued according to the amount of the loan, sale or condition, rather than of the penalty.[51]

Plaintiffs consistently alleged that defendants were seeking to profit from the penalties in bonds to which they had no moral right or that were out of all proportion to the loss sustained or the harm caused. When Richard Chappell could not pay Johane Yearde all of the rent due for a tenement, orchard and garden in Dorset in 1590 she allegedly agreed to forbear the outstanding 20s for a week, but when he went to pay she 'refused to accept the same' and 'puposethe and threatneth' to put the bond in suit to claim the penalty of £100.[52] In 1579 William Constantyne complained that his new son-in-law John Collier was ignoring his solemn vow and 'faythefull promise' to return a bond for cancelling, and he 'mynded rather the spoile

---

[47] *Cooke v. Wattes*, TNA, C2/Eliz/C10/9, m. 1.

[48] *Cutler v. Hanford*, TNA, C2/Eliz/C8/24, mm. 1, 2; Muldrew, *Economy of Obligation*, 160–1.

[49] *The Papers of Sir Richard Grosvenor, 1st Bart. (1585–1645)*, ed. Richard Cust, Record Society of Lancashire and Cheshire 134 (Stroud, 1996), xi, xiii, xix; 60–1; George Chapman, *Two Wise Men and All the Rest Fooles* (1619), 60–1.

[50] *Barker v. van Lore*, TNA, C2/Eliz/B9/9; *Cowper v. Toftewoode and Toftewood*, TNA C2/Eliz/C17/9, m. 1.

[51] William Blackstone, *Commentaries on the Laws of England* (Oxford, 1765–69), IV, 234; Wentworth, *Office and Dutie of Executors*, 56.

[52] Yearde alleged Chappell had broken a series of covenants relating to maintaining the property; *Chappell v. Yearde*, TNA, C2/Eliz/C8/32, mm. 2, 4.

and utter undoynge' of Constantyne and 'his poore wife and children' by claiming the £200 penalty.[53]

From succumbing to the temptation of claiming a large penalty it was a short step for bondholders to engage in murkier practices that flirted with outright fraud (which was defined more broadly in equity than at common law).[54] An infamous example of enrichment through the exploitation of legal instruments is the case of *Courtney* v. *Glanvill* in King's Bench that reached its conclusion in 1616, a key suit in the clash between common law and equity jurisdictions that resulted in the personal intervention of King James. Richard Glanvill had sold jewels to Francis Courtney for £460 with payment secured by a bond for £600, and managed by devious means to procure a successful suit on this bond at common law. As if a court order to pay this £600 penalty was not injury enough, Courtney then learned that one of the jewels was worth only £20, not £360 as Glanvill had assured him. In Chancery, the Master of the Rolls ignored the common law judgment and ordered Glanvill to accept back the jewel and to make sure that Courtney suffered no financial loss from the offending bond, and then imprisoned him for contempt when he refused to oblige, prompting a string of *habeas corpus* writs demanding his release.[55] John Baker has reflected that it was 'unfortunate' that the issue of gaining relief after judgment 'was raised in a case so devoid of merit', but Glanvill's behaviour was not untypical.[56] In a 1613 case 'yt appeared playnely' to the Masters of Requests 'that the complainant was cercumvented and deceaved' and 'there was great lykelihood that the defendants were not cleere from the participacion in the frawde'.[57] In another case Edward Clovill accused the London scrivener Richard Evans of working upon his 'tender age and unskilfullnes in worldy affaires' to furnish him with a watch, a sword and other goods and to draw him 'into severall bonds with great penalties for payment of the said prices upon the said wares' valuing them at 'more then treble their true values', bonds that Evans now 'violently prosecuteth … intending thereby to recover the penalty'.[58]

To take one final example, in 1583 when Henry Gates became bound to the London goldsmith Giles Sympson in two obligations totalling £300 for the payment of £157 10s, the barber surgeon John Barney bound himself

[53] Collier countered with his own account of abused trust and the 'leude unnatural and unhonest practise and devise' of Constantyne in 'craftelie and deceitfullie' tricking him, 'being within age', into signing a release for his wife's legacies; *Constantyne* v. *Collier*, TNA, C2/Eliz/C8/23, mm. 1, 2.
[54] D. M. Kerly, *A Historical Sketch of the Equitable Jurisdiction of the Court of Chancery* (Cambridge, 1890), 145–6.
[55] *English Reports*, 176 vols (Edinburgh, 1907), LXXIX, 294–5; Halliday, *Habeas Corpus*, 90–1.
[56] J. H. Baker, 'The Common Lawyers and the Chancery: 1616', *The Irish Jurist* (1969), 369–93, p. 375.
[57] *Neave* v. *Wright et al.*, TNA, REQ 1/26, fols 388–9 [or 382–3].
[58] *Clovill* v. *Evans and Johnson*, TNA, REQ 1/35A, fol. 145v.

as surety. Barney became concerned that Gates 'would not keepe his day', leaving himself liable as surety for the bond penalty, so weeks before the repayment date he met Sympson to discuss supplying the funds himself. Sympson allegedly assured him that he would never 'sewe, impleade or vexe' Barney 'being but a suarty', but he seemed 'very loathe and unwillinge that the bondes should be saved by performing the condicion'. In their conversation it became clear that Sympson actively wanted Gates to forfeit his bond 'for that he would be revenged against the said Gates by the forfeiture' for £60 that Gates owed him upon an 'older reckoninge'.[59] Thanks to Sympson's 'craft, disceyte & subtylty' Gates duly forfeited his bond, but despite his former assurances Sympson threatened suit against Barney for the penalty. Litigants in other cases made similar charges against Sympson, one accusing him of having sought a penalty despite having received the principal as well as interest that exceeded the amount of the original loan, 'as usurers are seldome satisfyed with any reason'.[60] Accused of usury, of preying on a surety and of using a forfeited bond to gain vengeance against a despised enemy, Sympson was a veritable Shylock.

The hardening of attitudes that was occurring is reflected in equity court officials' diminishing sympathy for victims' tales of hardship and unconscionable behaviour and their growing tendency to hold complainants responsible for their own behaviour. In Chancery, for example, Sir Thomas Egerton narrowed the grounds on which equitable relief was available, expressing his reluctance to relieve complainants' negligence or folly.[61] Numerous equity cases arguably had little merit and were initiated to evade obligations or to delay valid proceedings at common law. In one bond case heard in Chancery, for example, the injunction staying suit at common law lapsed after the widow complainant refused to attend a commission, using the excuse that she regarded the meeting place in a London tavern as 'unseemly'.[62] In Requests a note in the decree book for 1610 states that King James was 'often troubled with manie peticions preferred by bad debters against their creditors', in which the debtors 'presuming upon the charitable inclynacion' of the Requests Masters 'have many tymes of purpose by vexacion of sute' obtained process 'to call in their creditors from divers remote places of this kingdome in hope to gett favourable composicions for the payment of their debts'. This was 'contrary to the common justice of this land, many of the said creditors being as poore or poorer then the debters' and the Masters made orders to deter this behaviour.[63] The Privy Council also complained

---

[59] 'Revenged' replaces the crossed out word 'releved'; Barney v Sympson TNA C2/Eliz/B11/31, m.1.

[60] *Cade and Hatton v. Sympson*, TNA, REQ 2/120/46, m. 2.

[61] W. H. Bryson, *Cases Concerning Equity and the Courts of Equity 1550–1660* (2001), I, 314, 334–5.

[62] TNA C33/121, fols 632v–633.

[63] TNA REQ 1/25, 103.

on occasion about false or unconscionable debt claims in Chancery and Requests, yet when considered alongside complaints about harsh or fraudulent bond suits at common law, these allegations of questionable equity suits only add to the sense that community members were at each other's throats and purses in late sixteenth- and early seventeenth-century England.[64]

Despite equity justices' apparent reluctance to offer relief on bonds, it is telling that they nevertheless issued an increasing number of injunctions. In 1562 the Masters of Requests did not issue a single injunction staying process at common law, yet by 1603 Requests and Chancery Masters were issuing, or threatening to issue, over 100 injunctions a year staying bond suits.[65] By 1612 this had risen to over 100 injunctions in Hilary term alone and by 1637 to over 400 in this term.[66] The number of Chancery injunctions continued at high levels in the 1650s and beyond, partly because of the closure of the Court of Requests in 1642, although the less passionate language of the decision books, and the court's growing willingness to leave the decision to take out injunctions to complainants, suggests a slight lowering of the temperature of debates as suitors became accustomed to new ways of doing business.[67]

Suits on bonds at common law allowed vindictive creditors to exact revenge on their opponents by having them imprisoned for debt. If a debtor could not repay the outstanding principal by the due date, how then, in the absence of sureties, were they supposed to come up with the penalty of double that amount?[68] Arrests on bonds were common enough for Dromio in Shakespeare's *The Comedy of Errors* (c.1593) to quip that 'the Serjeant of the Band' is 'he that brings any man to answer it that breakes his Band', and it became almost proverbial wisdom in the seventeenth century that 'every Creditor falls upon the poor man when he is once arested'.[69] Some unscrupulous debtors went to prison to escape their obligations, leading Henry Smith to condemn 'those Foxes which have wealth enough to pay their debts and yet lie in prison because they would defraud their Creditors'.[70] However, miserly creditors actively sought to punish debtors' bodies

---

[64] *Calendar of State Papers Domestic Addenda 1580–1625* (1872), 88; the Privy Council also aided harassed debtors: TNA, PC 2/17, fols 839v, 847v.

[65] TNA, REQ 1/11; REQ 1/21.

[66] TNA, C33/123; C33/124; REQ 1/26; C33/171A; C33/171B; REQ 1/35A.

[67] TNA, C33/195; C33/196; C33/199.

[68] Stone, *Crisis of the Aristocracy*, 518.

[69] *The Comedie of Errors* 4.3.28–9 in William Shakespeare, *First Folio* (1623), 94; Richard Young, *The Prevention of Poverty* (1655), 23.

[70] Henry Smith, *A Preparative to Marriage ... Whereunto is Annexed a Treatise of the Lord's Supper and Another of Usury* (1591), sig. E8v. And see John Taylor, *The Praise and Vertue of a Jayle and Jaylers* (1623), sig. A7v; Thomas Lupton, *The Second Part and Knitting Up of the Boke Entitled Too Good to be True* (1581), sigs Aa1v–Aa2v; Roger Lee Brown, *A History of the Fleet Prison: The Anatomy of the Fleet* (Lewiston, Queenston and Lampeter, 1996), x.

rather than their purses: as a character in Thomas Middleton's play *Michaelmas Terme* (1607) puts it, 'should you offer him mony, goods or lands now, hee'd rather have your body in prison'.[71] In July 1637, for example, Court of Requests commissioners certified William Savage 'to be cruell and unconscionable & very refractory, intending to oppress the complainant, and that he will spend £1000 but that he wil undoe her & lay her in prison till shee rott & will provide a box for her bones'.[72] Their words echo those of the poet George Whetstone who described how a defendant caught up in conditional bonds 'In prison vile, of force must lye and rott, / Till they have paid, their debt and cost God wott'.[73] Little wonder that John Smith of Nibley in Gloucestershire referred to Westminster Hall as 'our cockpitt of revenge'.[74]

The rising flood of imprisoned debtors shifted the primary population of the Fleet prison in London from alleged enemies of public order to debtors and prompted anxious responses from social commentators.[75] The character Omen, in Thomas Lupton's 1581 utopian dialogue about the 'wonderfull lawes' of the 'people of Mauqsun', is astonished to learn of English prisons 'that are for indebted persons' and are full of 'pore decayed prisoners'. In response he asks, 'What uncharitable men are their Creditors that wil suffer them to lye there, being not able to pay them'? Surely, he reasons, 'by being abroad, they might in time be able to pay them, either part or all: but by lying in prison they bring them to povertie, their wives to penurie, and their children to miserie'.[76] In 1622 Thomas Scott described how in the United Provinces if a debtor 'be cast into prison' the creditor 'shall be forced to keep him there at his owne charge', unlike 'the mercilesse man' in England 'who with us sayth He will make Dice of his bones'.[77] Petitions to Parliament complaining about imprisonment for debt became common in the seventeenth century, one from 1621 alleging that nine-tenths of the debts that led to imprisonment were 'usurious and corrupt loanes and contracts, or forfeitures upon penall bonds and engagements', while another from 1628 estimated that 10,000 people were imprisoned for debt.[78] In 1645 inmates in the Fleet drew up and signed 'A Declaration and Appeal' on behalf of the 8,000 debtors they believed were imprisoned in England and Wales, complaining of the unfairness of confinement for debt and questioning

---

[71] Thomas Middleton, *Michaelmas Terme* (1607), sig. F3v.

[72] *Hammond v. Savage*, TNA, REQ 1/35A, fols 122–124.

[73] George Whetstone, *The Rocke of Regarde Divided into Foure Parts* (1576), 76.

[74] As quoted in Stone, *Crisis of the Aristocracy*, 240 (and see 238). See also Thomas Tusser, *Five Hundred Points of Good Husbandry* (Oxford, 1984), 21.

[75] Brown, *History of the Fleet Prison*, x–xi.

[76] Lupton, *The Second Part … of the Boke Entitled Too Good to be True*, sigs Z4v–Aav.

[77] Thomas Scott, *The Belgicke Pismire Stinging the Slothfull Sleeper* (1622), 87.

[78] David Hawkes, *The Culture of Usury in Renaissance England* (New York, 2010), 152–3.

its legality.[79] The 'Large Petition' of 1648 demanded 'to have considered many thousands that are ruined by perpetual Imprisonment for Debt, and Provided for their enlargement' and in 1691 Moses Pitt published *The Cry of the Oppressed: Being a True and Tragical Account of the Unparalleled Sufferings of Multitudes of Poor Imprisoned Debtors.*[80] These pleas fell on deaf ears and debtors' prisons remained a prominent feature of the urban English landscape until the nineteenth century, a testament not just to economic misfortune but also to the uncharitable spirit of creditors.[81]

Adversarial litigation invariably involves exaggerated complaints about opponents, but further evidence for a hardening of attitudes can be found in printed treatments of usury. Historians argue that attitudes to usury – charging to lend money without risk to the lender – underwent a clear and significant transformation beginning in the sixteenth century. Biblically inspired condemnations of usury, which often invoked Aristotle's position that it was against nature for the barren metal of coins to breed more coins, gradually gave way to an acceptance that it was reasonable to charge a fee for the use of money.[82] This change from regarding lending at interest (in the modern sense) as 'gainful idleness' to seeing it as an essential means for supplying capital and liquidity to a burgeoning economy was supposedly under way by 1571, when Parliament passed the Statute Against Usury, and was all but complete by 1612 when Francis Bacon defended usury as necessary.[83] Yet over this same period writings on usury became more, rather than less, common and they continued to appear throughout the seventeenth century.[84] Some religious writers stuck doggedly to older prohibitions against charging interest without risk, while others moved to condemn 'the charging of an *excessive* rate of interest', but what is striking is how many authors and dramatists focused their attention not on interest per se, but on unconscionable or exploitative practices that depended on bonds.[85]

---

[79] Walter Cunningham, *The Growth of English Industry and Commerce in Modern Times* (repr. New York, 1968), 191.

[80] Bulstrode Whitlocke, *Memorials of the English Affairs* (1732), 399 (and see 336, 398, 405, 410, 415, 418, 423, 531, 537, 555).

[81] Joanna Innes, *Inferior Politics* (Oxford, 2009), 227–78; Brooks, *Lawyers, Litigation and English Society*, 88, n. 113.

[82] Norman Jones, *God and the Moneylenders: Usury and Law in Early Modern England* (Oxford, 1989). As Eric Kerridge has pointed out, legitimate interest covering the loss or cost of making a loan (not our modern meaning of a charge for the benefit of a loan) was always legal and usury was always illegal. The key element that distinguished the two was risk: Eric Kerridge, *Usury, Interest and the Reformation* (Aldershot, 2002), 5–21.

[83] Jones, *Moneylenders*, 145–74; Kermode, ed., *Three Renaissance Usury Plays*, 10; Francis Bacon, 'Usury and the Use Thereof', in *The Works of Francis Bacon*, ed. J. Spedding (1857–74), IX, 325.

[84] Hawkes, *Culture of Usury*; Kermode, ed., *Three Renaissance Usury Plays*, 1–16; Arthur Bivens Stonex, 'The Usurer in Elizabethan Drama', *PMLA* 31 (1916), 190–210.

[85] Wrightson, *EN*, 207.

Early printed examinations of the exploitation of bonds concentrated on how usurers and brokers used them to deprive 'thriftelesse enherytors and wasteful gentlemen' of their lands, but these soon expanded to include losses of money sustained by rich and poor alike.[86] In sermons published in 1591 Henry Smith described how some 'will take no Usurie, but they will take a pawne which is better than the money which they lende' to be forfeited if the money is not repaid on the agreed day 'which daye the Usurer knoweth that the poore man is not able to keepe'. Quoting the prohibitions against usury in Leviticus 25, Smith was adamant that 'thou shalt not take the forfeiture; for then thou takest vauntage, when thou takest more than thou lendeth'.[87] Richard Carew described in his *Survey of Cornwall* (1602) how unscrupulous creditors dealt in tin rather than money to evade the Statute Against Usury, and their 'cutthroate and abominable dealing' netted them 'above fiftie in the hundred'. Having delivered the wares the trick was to wrap or bind 'the poore wretch' in 'Darbyes bonds' to secure the deal. [88] Darby appears to have been a notorious sixteenth-century usurer and references to Darby's bonds, or bands, abound.[89] In 1641 Gerrard Winstanley was 'cheated by false spirited men' upon fraudulent bonds securing £700 worth of textiles, possibly inspiring his 1649 reflection that 'Men that are guided by principles of fair dealing void of deceit knowe not this day how to live, but they will be cheated and cosened'.[90]

John Taylor confirmed in 1622 that the mere charging of interest – by the usurer, who 'for a hundred's use doth take but ten' – was less destructive than the taking of forfeitures by the extortioner, or pawnbroker, who 'for ten a hundred takes agen'.[91] In Nicholas Breton's words:

> Extortioners are Monsters in all nations,
> All their Conditions turne to Obligations,
> Waxe is their shot, and writing pens their Guns,
> Their powder is the inke that from them runs.
> And this dank powder hath blowne up more men
> In one year, then gunpowder hath in ten.[92]

---

[86] These bonds were underwritten by statutes staple, a form of registered specialty that used land as collateral; Thomas Bastard, *Chrestoleros Seven Bookes of Epigrames* (1598), 38; Robert Greene, *The Defence of Conny Catching* (1592), sigs. Bv–B3v.

[87] Smith, *A Preparative to Marriage*, sig. C5 (and see C5v); Miles Mosse, *The Arraignment and Conviction of Usurie* (1595), 24.

[88] Richard Carew, *The Survey of Cornwall* (1602), sigs E3r–v.

[89] *Oxford English Dictionary*, 'Father Derby's or Darby's bands'. Francis Marbury, *A New and Pleasaunt Enterlude* (1570), sig. Di; Whetstone, *The Rocke of Regarde*, 76.

[90] J. D. Alsop, 'Gerrard Winstanley: The Experience of Fraud 1641', *HJ* 34 (1991), 973–84, pp. 973, 975.

[91] John Taylor, *The Water Cormorant His Complaint Against a Brood of Land-Cormorants* (1622), sigs C3v–C4.

[92] Nicholas Breton, *Wits Private Wealth* (1612), sig. B4v.

From this perspective, it was bonds themselves that made possible unneighbourly behaviour through the lawsuits they precipitated. Hence, Samuel Rowlands' comic Monsieur Usurie chews 'the cud in contemplation of Bandes and Billes' as he walks, and in Robert Greene's *The Blacke Booke Messenger* (1592) disreputable Londoners 'doe nothing but walke up & downe Paules' with 'budgets of writings under their armes'.[93] These rogues are keen to 'talke with any man about their sutes in lawe, and discourse unto them how these and these mens bonds they have for money' and 'complaine that they cannot get one penny'. The bonds, in Greene's world of cutpurses and connycatchers, are counterfeit, but the victims are far from innocent, grabbing at the chance to recover loans or penalties, hoping 'by one clause or other' to defeat the bondholder 'of all that he hath'.[94] Here forfeited bonds resemble winning lottery tickets, virtually guaranteeing lucrative risk-free gains.

Dozens of authors pointed out how hard-nosed creditors were ready to pounce 'if you breake but your daye'.[95] In Anthony Copley's *Wits, Fittes and Fancies* (1595) a man who could not repay his debt to a merchant 'shifted away all his goods and fled the Countrey'. Far from being upset, the merchant 'was heartily glad' that the debtor 'had forfeyted his band' for now he could 'take the benefite of the double'.[96] In *The Raven's Almanacke* (1609) Thomas Dekker describes a usurer who changed the time on his clock to lead a hapless debtor to miss his payment and so 'stande to the forfeit of the bands'.[97] It is revealing that the most famous dramatic treatment of failing to make a day of payment, Shakespeare's *The Merchant of Venice* (c.1597), involves an agreement not between a creditor and a debtor (Shylock and Bassanio) but between a creditor and a debtor's surety (Shylock and Antonio) and features Shylock lending money without charging any interest. There is no usury involved in this transaction, as the risk remains that Antonio will repay the loan on time, leaving Shylock with nothing. As Thomas Wilson explained of such an agreement, 'ther was no bargaine for any overplus to be had for the receipt of that money if it were paid at the daye, but onely a forfeyture of a bond'.[98] Everything therefore centres round the bond forfeiture and its gruesome penalty of a pound of Antonio's flesh. Shakespeare's treatment of this theme inspired others, and a failed bond lies at the heart of Day, Rowley and Wilkins' play *The Travailes of the Three English Brothers* (1607) and of Massinger's *The City Madam* (1632), while an unsuspecting surety suffers on

---

[93] Samuel Rowlands, *Diogene Lanthorne* (1615), sigs A3v–A4.

[94] Robert Greene, *The Blacke Bookes Messenger* (1592), sig. Dv.

[95] See, for example, Robert Greene, *A Quip For an Upstart Courtier* (1592), sig. C2.

[96] Anthony Copley, *Wits, Fittes and Fancies* (1595), 121; and see Joseph Hall, *Characters of Vertues and Vices* (1608), 121.

[97] Thomas Dekker, *The Raven's Almanacke* (1609), sigs Fr–v.

[98] Thomas Wilson, *A Discourse Upon Usury*, ed. R. H. Tawney (1925: repr. 1963), 264.

behalf of a debtor in Thomas Middleton's *Michaelmas Terme* (1607).[99] The motive of revenge also recurs in writing on bonds of all kinds.[100]

Stage usurers are obviously fictional, but it is difficult to overlook the clear appeal that these characters, and the numerous pamphlets decrying usury, held for their audiences.[101] Furthermore, many authors clearly drew upon personal experience. When Thomas Wilson reported a range of devious practices involving bonds in his *Discourse Uppon Usurye* (1572) he had been hearing similar allegations for a decade as a Master of the Court of Requests. In his dedicatory epistle to the Gentlemen of the Inns of Court in *An Alarum against Usurers* (1584) Thomas Lodge railed against the worldly abuses not just of 'those monsters' usurers 'but also such devouring caterpillars, who not onely have fatted their fingers with many rich forfaitures, but also spread their venim among some private Gentlemen of your profession'.[102] Francis Bacon spoke as an experienced lawyer when he flattered his queen by suggesting that the 'royal policy of your Majesty' had both limited the growth of lawsuits 'whereof a great part are alwaies unjust' and restricted 'the indirect courses and practices to abuse law and justice', particularly 'frauds in contracts, bargaines and assurances'. He went on to advocate 'a generall amendment of the states of your lawes' that would see 'the swarving penalties that lye upon many subjects removed'.[103] Charles Ross has highlighted how changes to the law of fraudulent conveyance inspired an Elizabethan literary focus on defaulting debtors, but I would argue that unconscionable creditors, and the threat they posed to civil society, loomed just as large, or larger, in the literary imagination.[104]

In smaller communities honest broking was essential to maintaining trust and credit. But in an economy so dependent on financial credit, beggars could not always be choosers. When Henry Smith condemned usury from the pulpit he condemned predatory creditors but not debtors 'in that necessitie and extremitie which I can imagine', who ask 'may I borrowe money of these Usurers to save my life, or my credite, or my living, seeing no man will lend mee freelie'?[105] Many of the sharp practices complained of in equity

---

[99]   John Day, William Rowley and George Wilkins, *The Travailes of the Three English Brothers* (1607), sigs E3v, F; Philip Massinger, *The City-Madam* (1659); Middleton, *Michaelmas Terme*.

[100]   Robert Greene, *The Defence of Conny Catching* (1592), sigs Bv–B3v.

[101]   Hawkes, *Culture of Usury*, esp. 1–6, 16–17.

[102]   Thomas Lodge, *An Alarum Against Usurers* (1584), sig. A2.

[103]   Swarving means choking: Francis Bacon, *The Elements of the Common Lavves of England* (1630), sig. A4. Lord Burleigh and Sir Thomas Egerton had also discussed reforms in 1585: Brooks, *Lawyers, Litigation and English Society*, 88, n. 113; see also Gerard Malynes, *England's View, in the Unmasking of Two Paradoxes* (1603), 158–9; Scott, *The Belgicke Pismire*, 86–7.

[104]   Charles Stanley Ross, *Elizabethan Literature and the Law of Fraudulent Conveyance: Sidney, Spenser, and Shakespeare* (Aldershot, 2003).

[105]   Smith, *A Preparative to Marriage*, sig. E7.

suits were technically legal and probably born of opportunity rather than
of malice aforethought. Bondholders could therefore justify their actions
to neighbours and live on to seal more bonds in the future. At the same
time the new economic realities appear to have fostered a growing cynicism
or stoicism about the diminishing ethics of the marketplace. Thomas Bell
marvelled in 1596 at those who 'blush not with brasen face' to defend 'the
filthy lucre of usurie' and to 'term it a lawfull contract', while John Norden
observed in 1632 that 'riche men are called good men' because 'a man will
take thy band for a hundred pounds before thy neighbours for a hundred
pence' even if this 'honest poore' neighbour's word 'is as good as thy band'.
As he went on to ask, 'doth any man trust another in these dayes because
he is an *honest* man'?[106]

In Massachusetts lawmakers succeeded in making it illegal to imprison
for debt, but reform in England, when it came, took a different shape.[107]
Beginning in the 1670s, common law justices began moving from the strict
enforcement of bond penalties to awarding compensation for losses actually sustained, a development that was given statutory force in 1696/97
and 1705.[108] By adopting an approach similar to Chancery's, common law
courts diminished the need for the counter-suits that have been the subject
of this chapter.[109] As petitioners had complained in the 1640s, 'it seems
much against equity that if the defendant shall by Answer confess the whole
Debt to be paid to suffer him to go to trial at Law, which will be but a vain
Expense to the Parties, and only profitable to Lawyers'.[110] While the ability
of creditors to exploit the rigidity of the law relating to bonds acted as a catalyst for reform, the rise in popularity of the action of *assumpsit* for enforcing
informal promises created its own set of problems, helping to prompt the
passing of the Statute of Frauds in 1677.[111] Lawmakers believed that too
many plaintiffs were falsely claiming the existence or contents of oral promises and leaving juries to determine their merits, in a system that barred
defendants (and plaintiffs) from testifying and in which jurors lacked direct
knowledge of essentially private bargains. The solution provided by this
'Act for prevention of Frauds and Perjuryes' was to demand that all significant transactions be in writing, to provide juries with tangible evidence of

---

106 Thomas Bell, *The Speculation of Usurie* (1596), dedicatory epistle; John Norden, A
Good Companion for a Christian (1632), 27–8.
107 Hill, *Intellectual Origins of the English Revolution*, 234.
108 8 & 9 Will. 3 c. 11 s. 8; 4 & 5 Ann. c. 3 ss. 12, 13.
109 Mike McNair, 'Common Law and Statutory Imitations of Equitable Relief under
the Later Stuarts', in *Communities and Courts*, ed. Brooks and Lobban, 115–31; Tim
Stretton, 'Contract, Debt Litigation and Shakespeare's *The Merchant of Venice*', *Adelaide
Law Review* 31 (2010), 111–26, pp. 123–4; Atkyns, *Enquiry into the Jurisdiction of the
Chancery*, 36–9.
110 Whitlocke, *Memorials*, 624.
111 29 Car. II c. 3 (1677).

their terms. This 'very un-English piece of legislation' failed to achieve most of its aims, but it provides striking evidence of lawmakers' fears that English men and women could not be trusted to keep their word, or English jurors to reach just verdicts.[112]

Most historians take it for granted that it was the spectre of fraud that led to an increased reliance on written obligations. The pleadings from Requests and Chancery suggest that the opposite was also true—that the proliferation of bonds was serving to undermine traditional forms of trust and to increase incentives to engage in unethical financial practices. The form of bonds placed a heightened focus on the literal meaning of the impersonal 'harde and stricte' conditions they contained, rather than on the personal promises they represented. For example, when Reynold Boothe entered a bond with a penalty of £200 promising to marry Anne Blackthorne by May of 1587 or pay her £100, he assumed default could only arise if he failed to marry Anne. Imagine his surprise when default arose 'uppon her refusal to marye' him.[113]

As suing on bonds became more common it became more acceptable, with victims of harsh bond suits becoming less hesitant to bring such suits themselves. In 1637, while Sir Richard Grosvenor was in prison as surety for his brother-in-law's unpaid debts, George Glegg accused him of threatening to put in suit a bond for £2,400 'upon pretence of some small breach of the saide articles', intending to 'take the forfeiture thereof, being of soe great a penalty'.[114] Such suits also became the target of satire, with the character Luke in Massinger's *The City Madam* (1632) marvelling at the generosity that Sir John Frugal showed to debtors, in marked contrast to habitual bond penalty claimers who 'are born only for themselvs, and live so'.[115] The impersonal nature of bonds also tempted the unscrupulous to engage in newer kinds of extortion, with Thomas Wright alleging that in 1629 the merchant Henry More had lured him to a tavern in St Katherine's and held him over a trapdoor above the Thames until he sealed a bond with a penalty of £7,000 with nothing in consideration.[116] Bond suits suggest that some litigants were coming to view litigation not as a means to settle disputes and restore harmony, but as a way to maximise gains, presaging our

---

[112] K. M. Teeven, 'Seventeenth-Century Evidentiary Concerns and the Statute of Frauds', *Adelaide Law Review* 9 (1983), 252–66, p. 252.

[113] Anne naturally provided a different version of events; *Boothe v. Blackborne*, TNA, C2/Eliz/B13/52, mm. 1, 3.

[114] TNA, C33/171, fols 91v–92: *Papers of Sir Richard Grosvenor*, xi, xiii, xix.

[115] Massinger, *The City-Madam*, 14, 16, 73; Middleton, *Michaelmas Terme*, sig. D.

[116] The incident sparked two decades of litigation and a pamphlet protesting More's innocence; Edmund Leach, *Deceptio Intelectus & Visus. Or the Lawyers Wiles Unmasked* (1652), 10–11.

modern, dispassionate contractual world of *caveat emptor* and a fear of fine print.[117]

The seventeenth century seems to have had a greater share than the sixteenth of men and women 'born only for themselves' who went to law for personal gain. The claiming of penalties on forfeited bonds provides the best example, but there are others. Attention paid to the dramatic expansion of defamation suits in Elizabethan church courts has masked the 'tidal wave' of defamed individuals who instead sought relief at common law. While success in a defamation action resulted in the ritual penance of the defamer, a successful slander action achieved the payment of damages, and litigant demand for this more lucrative outcome grew dramatically.[118] K. J. Kesselring has shown the gains that profit-takers made from criminal forfeitures, and how quickly neighbours descended on the property of convicted felons. As she concludes, 'once we look at forfeitures, we find people interested in personal profit more than the common peace'.[119] Distraint of goods, sequestration of lands and informing for a reward were also on the rise, while the general suspicion that paid oath-takers were committing perjury undermined the ancient defence of wager of law.[120] Gains were not always financial, and in the 1630s Sir Richard Grosvenor warned that requests by warring neighbours for recognizances to keep the peace had become 'too common a way of revenge upon the least unkindness'.[121]

Prescriptive literature, spiritual diaries, charges to juries and the rhetoric of equity pleadings all reveal the enduring strength of a Christian belief in neighbourliness and abhorrence of quarrelling, but plays, sermons and the details in tens of thousands of legal pleadings reveal how often individuals fell short of this ideal, providing corroboration for the literature of social complaint. When Miles Mosse bemoaned in 1595 that 'this taking of forfeitures is a grinding of the faces of the poor too common in this uncharitable age, and it is a kind of gain which our fathers in former ages scarce knew, but seldom or never practised' he was not engaging in a naive and misplaced nostalgia, but remarking on actual social change.[122] Legal pleadings drafted by lawyers naturally drip heavy with outlandish rhetorical flourishes and tit-for-tat accusations, but whether or not the mud-flinging was sincere or contrived, the astonishing quantity of mud that was flung had an effect. English men and women were becoming increasingly accustomed to hard dealing, days in court and a growing tendency to rely on, or to hide behind, the strict letter of legal instruments. Sir Richard Grosvenor repeatedly

[117] On the corrosive nature of litigation see Hindle, *The State and Social Change*, 82–9.
[118] Brooks, *Law, Society and Culture*, 392–6.
[119] K. J. Kesselring, 'Felony Forfeiture and the Profits of Crime in Early Modern England', *HJ* 53 (2010), 271–88.
[120] Baker, *Introduction to English Law*, 5–6, 74, 326, 348.
[121] As quoted in Hindle, *The State and Social Change*, 111.
[122] Mosse, *Arraignment and Conviction of Usurie*, 24.

counselled his son to be honest and 'not prone to fale att odds with your neighbours', yet he warned him that 'Theire are many of soe bad & ungodly dispositions that (if they observe a gentlman to distast a neighboure) are ready to add fuell to the fire' and fill his ears 'with false & fained tales' so as 'to sett them att a further distance'. As he lamented on another occasion, 'itt is proper to base spirrits to seke to glutt themselves in revenge and to delight in the miseryes of theire neighbours'.[123]

The bitter disputes over forfeited bonds that raged from the 1580s to the 1670s represent more than the inevitable result of growing economic activity in an increasingly commercial society and should be seen as a cause as well as a symptom of change.[124] As Keith Wrightson observes, in the 'more commercialised, competitive and insecure environment' of later sixteenth- and seventeenth-century England, 'in which institutions that previously provided a modicum of stability were being eroded', neighbours became increasingly suspicious of each other's intentions.[125] Interpersonal conflict was obviously not new, but for most English men and women it now played out against a world view that was becoming more utilitarian and contractual and that increasingly depended on the intervention or assistance of external authority, a world view Thomas Hobbes would describe in chilling terms only a few years later.[126] The anxieties litigants and commentators expressed should not be read simply as the teething problems accompanying adjustment to new economic realities that subsided as litigation levels fell after the 1670s. They marked a transformation of economic relations as the exchange value of money eclipsed its use value, a transformation that made those relations colder, harder and less personal or neighbourly.[127] Confirmation that litigation may have been one of the causes of this corrosion of personal relations can be found in its precipitous decline after the 1670s, as more and more individuals lost faith in lawsuits as the best means of resolving conflicts. In the realm of conditional bonds in particular, it appears that 'commodity' was indeed displacing 'community', or to borrow John Lane's phrase, 'Charitie which is the band of peace / Is turned to a Scriveners scribling band'.[128] Some observers (then as now) might regard this as a small price to pay for growing national prosperity, but it was a price paid nonetheless.

---

[123] Grosvenor also referred to litigants as 'men of froward dispositions and turbulent spirritts' and described extortion as a fault that 'hath thriven much of late dayes'; *Papers of Sir Richard Grosvenor*, xxiv, xxvii, 13, 33–7 (and see 39–40, 41).
[124] Muldrew, 'Culture of Reconciliation', 920, 939–40.
[125] Wrightson, 'Mutualities and Obligations', 120.
[126] Muldrew, 'Culture of Reconciliation', 921; Muldrew, *Economy of Obligation*, 318, 321–2, 327.
[127] Hawkes, *Culture of Usury*, 37.
[128] John Lane, *Tom Tel-Troths Message and His Pen's Complaint* (1600), 38.

9

Witchcraft and Neighbourliness in Early Modern England

MALCOLM GASKILL

The history of witchcraft as a crime in England maps roughly onto the early modern period as a whole. Exactly how many suspected witches were pros-ecuted between 1542 and 1736 is unknown; we can only extrapolate from where records are most complete. An estimated 1,000 trials, spread over two centuries and 9,000 parishes, suggests that it would have been rare to experience one directly. Some places, notably in Essex, indicted scores of witches; many more did not. Despite the persistent notion that villagers routinely used accusations to explain misfortunes and attack enemies, the numbers speak for themselves.[1] Perhaps, then, witchcraft has attracted more attention than it deserves. And yet it is justified as a historical subject by more than quantification alone. Case-studies have revealed fine details of social activity and change: the interplay of learned and plebeian ideas, shifting attitudes to gender, popular legal activity, and so on. Witchcraft has been profitably studied from *above* as ideology and policy; from *below* as an expression of socio-economic conflict; and from *within* as a spyhole on early modern subjectivity, fantasy and psychological meaning. It is a point of entry, not an end in itself.[2]

Unanswered questions nonetheless remain. The political dimension in local society deserves more attention: how did particular personalities and affiliations permit (or inhibit) the development of suspicions into accusa-tions? Fresh connections might also be made by historians of medicine, law and art, likewise by theologians and philologists. Intellectual and cultural linkages between witch-trials in England and America, and with continental Europe, could be further explored. Furthermore, compared to our knowledge

I am grateful to Andy Wood and the editors for their comments.

[1]   C. L'Estrange Ewen, *Witch Hunting and Witch Trials* (1929), 111–13.
[2]   *Witchcraft Historiography*, ed. Jonathan Barry and Owen Davies (Basingstoke, 2007); Malcolm Gaskill, 'The Pursuit of Reality: Recent Research into the History of Witch-craft', *HJ* 51 (2008), 1069–88.

of the causes and dynamics of accusations, we understand little about public reactions: most sources relate the immediate facts of a case rather than its ramifications. This also explains why historians have tended to concentrate on a few principal players rather than the supporting cast. Yet as witnesses and spectators, spreaders of gossip and consumers of news, dozens of people inhabited the penumbra around the spotlight of each accusation. We might ask, then, what did prosecutions mean to them?

The main theme of this essay is neighbourliness – not just the physical context of neighbourhood, but its moral and emotional abstraction seen through the lens of witchcraft.³ Clergymen derived lessons from witch-trials, sometimes publishing them as pamphlets; usually the message was simple: avoid sin or be judged. But the representation and reception of accusations went beyond their objectification as cautionary tragedies, or even as entertainment. It is implausible that the experience of all readers or listeners was entirely detached, vicarious or voyeuristic. Instead, we should think of witchcraft stories being internalised, like community morality plays performed in the round. They were involving, challenging and cathartic.⁴ The various stages of a prosecution, witnessed first-hand or received as news, invited people to clarify ambivalent feelings and to confront their own failings as Christians and neighbours. More broadly, witches offered a salutary means of coming to terms with social, economic and cultural change.

People in Jacobean England expressed nostalgia for the days when charity, hospitality and sociability had been unforced effusions of parochial amity.⁵ This vision was partly religious, evoking a pre-Reformation culture of festivals and rituals; but its substance was economic. Dramatic population growth led to shortages, high prices and marked differentiation in wealth and status. Landowners consolidated estates to increase profits, tenants were evicted, common land was privatised and traditional rights abrogated; customary bonds were strained. The ranks of the poor multiplied, their immiseration increased, and pessimism and fear deepened.

This was the changing world described by Keith Wrightson in *English Society*. 'The quarrels which triggered suspicions of *maleficium*', we learn, 'were commonly the result of breaches of charity or neighbourliness – the turning away of an old woman who had come to beg or borrow from a neighbour being a common pattern.'⁶ Wrightson's source was a study by Alan Macfarlane, who in 1970 had analysed evidence from Essex using anthro-

---

³ Keith Wrightson, 'The "Decline of Neighbourliness" Revisited', in *Local Identities in Late Medieval and Early Modern England*, ed. Norman L. Jones and Daniel Woolf (Basingstoke, 2007), 19–49.

⁴ Marion Gibson, *Reading Witchcraft: Stories of Early English Witches* (1999), chs 2–4; Andrew Cambers, 'Demonic Possession, Literacy and "Superstition" in Early Modern England', *P&P* 202 (2009), 3–35.

⁵ Cf. the essays by Andy Wood and Tim Stretton in this volume.

⁶ Wrightson, *ES*, 203. See also Wrightson & Levine, *Terling*.

pological models. Macfarlane argued that economic change had widened the gap between richer and poorer neighbours, provoking confrontations. Neighbours resented both giving alms *and* paying the parish rate, but felt guilty for shirking traditional obligations. If a beggar had a dubious reputation, and a refusing householder was afflicted by misfortune, suspicions of witchcraft might develop. Witches were victims of adverse economic conditions; but more specifically they were victims of their neighbours' selfishness.[7]

Macfarlane's book, though a county study, has often been made to stand for the entire English experience. A year after its publication, the nationally framed *Religion and the Decline of Magic*, by Macfarlane's mentor Keith Thomas, described essentially the same dynamic of accusation, there being no study comparable to Macfarlane's in 1971, or even a decade later when Wrightson wrote *English Society*.[8] No county was as well documented as Essex, but still plenty of evidence did not fit Macfarlane's model. Other places experienced similar changes but generated far fewer trials. Furthermore, although most accusations involved competition for authority and resources, not all show the 'charity-refused' pattern.[9] Finally, Macfarlane saw a 'functionalist' purpose in witch-trials: they vented social pressures and restored community equilibrium.[10]

Cultural historians have reacted against deterministic theories that overlook contingency, ambiguity and the influence of emotional states by investigating these issues using legal testimony. Textual analysis and speculation about the psycho-dynamics of prosecutions have raised witchcraft studies to another level, offering interpretations that are controversial, but from which there can be no retreat.[11] Wrightson's warning against dismissing witchcraft as 'a fantasy world of a deluded minority' has matured into a field of depth and sophistication where witch-beliefs are treated as social reality.[12] One drawback of the 'cultural turn', however, has been the habit of privileging the meanings of particular situations over a bigger picture of causation and change. Although witch-trials are important manifestations

---

[7] Alan Macfarlane, *Witchcraft in Tudor and Stuart England: A Regional and Comparative Study* (1970).

[8] Keith Thomas, *Religion and the Decline of Magic* (1971).

[9] Malcolm Gaskill, 'Witchcraft in Tudor and Stuart Kent: Stereotypes and the Background to Accusations', in *Witchcraft in Early Modern Europe: Studies in Culture and Belief*, ed. Jonathan Barry, Marianne Hester and Gareth Roberts (Cambridge, 1996), 257–87.

[10] Cf. Max Marwick, 'Witchcraft as a Social Strain-Gauge', *Australian Journal of Science* 26 (1964), 263–8. For a critique of functionalism, see T. G. Ashplant and Adrian Wilson, 'Present-Centred History and the Problem of Historical Knowledge', *HJ* 31 (1988), 257–60.

[11] For instance: Lyndal Roper, *Witch Craze: Terror and Fantasy in Baroque Germany* (New Haven, 2004); *Languages of Witchcraft: Narrative, Ideology and Meaning in Early Modern Culture*, ed. Stuart Clark (Basingstoke, 2001).

[12] Wrightson, *ES*, 203–4.

of anxiety in an era of transformation, they are a crude index of crisis. Even when all Macfarlane's causal factors coincided, only occasionally did they lead to prosecutions. Witch-beliefs were endemic, poor women were legion, all neighbours competed, and many used the law. Macfarlane explained why accusations occurred, but failed to show why more often they did not.[13]

We might look to *indirect* experience of witch-trials, where intellectual history – witchcraft as ideology – meets both the 'new social history' and the 'new cultural history'. Witchcraft accusations are vivid specimens of social exchange, thickly plotted dramas involving diverse affinities and opinions. A typical prosecution was not a hysterical outburst, but the peculiar outcome of chance, opportunity and pragmatism[14]. As such, it was unlike Evans-Pritchard's functionalist analysis of the Azande (a major influence on Macfarlane), but a perfect example of Keith Wrightson's 'politics of the parish' – a fluid matrix of authority and decision-making.[15] In the 1670s the Wiltshire magnate Sir James Long had a witch tried simply because she was scaring off his tenants. When the judge ordered her neighbours to pay weekly gaol fees of 2s 1d, Long offered to keep her on his estate for 7d less. This episode was not some unilateral action of victim against suspect: it was plain politics.[16] The archives are full of surprising situations. An impecunious old woman petitioned Norwich magistrates in the 1650s, alleging that her neighbours were conspiring to bewitch *her*. [17]

Whereas usually we see only accuser-versus-accused, behind the scenes supportive neighbours might cluster round both parties. Onlookers not directly involved in accusations, but still affected by them, were influential. Their participation in a mesh of social relations shaped and guided communities, a network of which comprised the early modern state. Witchcraft accusations were diffuse experiences, involving complex emotions. The accuser's rage we understand; but what of doubt and remorse, pity and redemption? Here the moral lodestone of neighbourliness is instructive. There seems little point dissecting Macfarlane's thesis, especially his idea that accusations signified nascent individualism, not least because he

---

[13] Illuminating studies include: Robin Briggs, *Witches and Neighbours: The Social and Cultural Context of Witchcraft* (1996); Brian P. Levack, *Witch-Hunting in Scotland: Law, Politics and Religion* (2008).

[14] Clive Holmes, 'Popular Culture? Witches, Magistrates and Divines in Early Modern England', in *Understanding Popular Culture*, ed. Steven L. Kaplan (Berlin, 1984), 85–111; Annabel Gregory, 'Witchcraft, Politics and "Good Neighbourhood" in Early Seventeenth-Century Rye', *P&P* 133 (1991), 31–66; Anne Reiber DeWindt, 'Witchcraft and Conflicting Visions of the Ideal Village Community', *JBS* 34 (1995), 427–63.

[15] E. E. Evans-Pritchard, *Witchcraft, Oracles and Magic among the Azande* (Oxford, 1937); Keith Wrightson, 'The Politics of the Parish in Early Modern England', in *The Experience of Authority in Early Modern England*, ed. Paul Griffiths, Adam Fox and Steve Hindle (Basingstoke, 1996), 10–46.

[16] Augustus Jessopp, ed., *The Lives of the Norths*, 3 vols (1890), I, 168.

[17] Norfolk Record Office, C/S 2/1, pp. 121, 253, 405 (Mary Childerhouse).

himself has recanted.[18] Instead, we might consider the wider community's role in suspicion and accusation, and how its values were affected. Witchcraft stories not only sated appetites for sensationalism, but forced reflection upon honour, charity, hospitality, compassion and moderation, which from the later sixteenth century were perceived to be increasingly threatened.

This essay will argue that reactions to declining neighbourliness were divided between those who saw witches as the problem and those who blamed accusers. Some individuals wavered in feeling, especially over individual cases. Stories about witches were received as a source of moral instruction, inviting people to search their hearts for a sense of vindication, but sometimes also pity at the plight of the accused. Protestant tales of repentance, mercy and redemption provide an important context: in death, condemned witches could become virtuous and a source of wonder. In the seventeenth century the balance gradually tipped in favour of the accused. As scepticism became more entrenched, so the constituency of suspects became the epitome of deserving pauperism. And with that, their persecutors seemed not just disorderly or ignorant, but symbols of failed neighbourliness, and at a time when fears for the social and moral integrity of communities were intensifying. Hence witchcraft drew an axis along which attitudes to the poor turned in early modern England.

I

Tudor thinkers were fully aware of England's transformation and its political challenges. Concern was heightened by the fact that commonwealth ideology, against which change was measured, was schematic and prescriptive.[19] Its ties were respect, responsibility and reciprocal love – a 'tree of commonwealth', rooted in concord, nurtured by obedience and bearing 'the fruite of profytable tranquilitie necessarie for the commynaltie'.[20] Sever the ties and chaos would ensue. 'Worldy policie qualifyed with charitie, is therby converted into christen civilitie', advised Thomas Starkey, 'one without the other can not longe endure'.[21] Charity was fundamental, its absence alarming; if neighbourhoods failed, what hope for the state? When people lived only for themselves, as by the later sixteenth century some felt they did, order suffered. The growth of litigiousness was seen as both cause and

---

[18] Alan Macfarlane, *The Origins of English Individualism* (Oxford, 1978), 1–2, 59–61; *idem, The Culture of Capitalism* (Oxford, 1987), ch. 5.

[19] Arthur B. Ferguson, 'The Tudor Commonweal and the Sense of Change', *JBS* 3 (1963), 11–35; Whitney R. D. Jones, *The Tree of Commonwealth, 1450–1793* (2000), chs 1–3.

[20] Edmund Dudley, *The Tree of Commonwealth*, ed. D. M. Brodie (Cambridge, 1948), 87–94, 100–5, quotation at 105.

[21] Thomas Starkey, *A Preface to the Kynges Hyghnes* (1536), 40.

effect of moral decline. Sir Thomas Smith scorned those 'lovers of trouble' who desired only 'to vex their neighbours, and to live alwaies in disquiet'.[22]

Advocates of colonisation argued that overpopulation hurt the common-wealth. Emigration was an act of Christian charity 'in respect of our poore sorte, whiche are verie many amongst us, livyng altogether unprofitable, and often tymes to the great disquiet of the better sorte'.[23] In 1609 Robert Gray looked fondly on 'those times when our Country was not pestered with multitude, nor overcharged with swarmes of people'. Scarcity bred crime which caused national insecurity.[24] Litigation was blamed. In 1622 one promoter asked: 'was there ever more suits in law, more envie, contempt and reproch then now adaies?' It was impossible to set up a trade, he added, without falling out with neighbours, so fierce was competition; towns were full of unemployed artisans, while beggars roamed the countryside and England 'groaneth under so many close-fisted and unmercifull men'.[25] John Winthrop's exodus to Massachusetts was one response. 'We must love brotherly without dissimulation', he wrote in A Model of Christian Charity, 'we must love one another with a pure heart fervently. We must bear one another's burthen.'[26]

Some echoed Winthrop's yearning for old English ways. A ballad from 1629 described a world where 'All friendship now decayes', 'Pride hath banisht all' and the Christmas custom where 'Neighbours were friendly bidden' in prosperous homes had vanished. It ended by asking God to punish those who deny the poor alms.[27] In the same decade Michael Sparke described a commonwealth decayed by poverty and pitilessness, blaming landowners who seize land, exploit casual labour and oppress the commons. Even modest householders shun poor men, he lamented, and would rather hang them than find them work.[28] Another ballad told of a pauper who accepted the devil's charity after 'churlish' farmers refused him bread and milk. The intervention of a wealthy neighbour suggested there might be some Christian charity left in England; but not much.[29]

Alan Macfarlane was not the first to link declining neighbourliness with witchcraft accusations. In 1584 Reginald Scot pitied widows who 'go from house to house, and from doore to doore, for a pot full of milke, yest, drinke, pottage, or some such releefe, without the which they could hardlie live'.

---

[22] Thomas Smith, De Republica Anglorum (1583), 91.

[23] Christopher Carleill, A Breef and Sommarie Discourse upon the Entended Voyage to the Hethermoste Partes of America (1583), sig. B1v.

[24] Robert Gray, A Good Speed to Virginia (1609), sigs B2–B4.

[25] William Bradford, Of Plymouth Plantation (1622), 70–1.

[26] The Puritans in America: A Narrative Anthology, ed. Alan Heimert and Andrew Delbanco (Cambridge MA, 1985), 90.

[27] [Martin Parker], Times Alteration, or the Old Mans Rehearsall (1629).

[28] Michael Sparke, Greevous Grones for the Poore (1621), 11–15, 18–19.

[29] A New Ballad, Shewing the Great Misery Sustained by a Poore Man in Essex (1640).

People feared them because they were 'leane and deformed, shewing melan-cholie in their faces, to the horror of all that see them'. Those who refused a witch she cursed.[30] George Gifford, an Essex clergyman, was more credu-lous than Scot about the consequences. 'Forth shee calleth her spirite, and willeth him to plague such a man ... [who] doth thinke himselfe unhappy that he was so foolish to displease her.'[31] The idea remained current a century later. In 1688 the bishop of Norwich told of a gentlewoman whose blighted life was attributed to her servant having refused 'a poore begging woman' who 'went away Grumbling'.[32]

Macfarlane's thesis may have limited applicability outside Essex, but some resonances are striking in England and on the Continent.[33] Norbert Schindler has referred to 'the origins of heartlessness' in Salzburg, connected to a witch-hunt of 1675–90. Economic crisis undermined Christian duty, inciting middling society to attack paupers 'because it could no longer bear the sight of those who negated its way of life'.[34] This does not imply that witchcraft accusations were cynically deployed, rather that conflicting feel-ings of resentment and guilt were projected unconsciously. Perhaps accusa-tions made middling sorts feel cleansed and united: self-redefinition through the exercise of common interest and deliberate social distinction. But the lower orders, too, were hostile to witches. In the later seventeenth century, Roger North recalled an incident where some women – all 'very old, decrepit, and impotent' – were arraigned 'with as much noise and fury of the rabble against them as could be shewed on any occasion'. Revolutions, he said, had begun with less urgency and commotion.[35] Dangerous passions found an outlet. In the 1640s the swimming of Kentish witches seemed out of control, and parishes in Ipswich and Cambridge paid witchfinders out of poor receipts – acts of charity to save the community.[36]

What satisfied some worried others. Lynch-mobs did not mend the worn fabric of society: they tore it asunder. Gossiping, backbiting and spreading rumours, themselves symptoms of malaise, made things worse. The more hysterical the stories, the more indiscriminate the accusations – a tendency despised in the common people by sceptics and believers. Puritans thought it both uncharitable and impious to blame all disasters on witches, believing

[30] Reginald Scot, *The Discoverie of Witchcraft* (1584), 7–8.
[31] George Gifford, A *Discourse of the Subtill Practises of Devilles by Witches and Sorcerers* (1587), sig. G3.
[32] Bodleian Library, Oxford, Tanner MS 28, fol. 162.
[33] Cf. Jonathan B. Durrant, *Witchcraft, Gender and Society in Early Modern Germany* (Leiden, 2007), 30–1, 245–6; Wolfgang Behringer, *Witchcraft Persecutions in Bavaria* (Cambridge, 1997), 11–13.
[34] Norbert Schindler, *Rebellion, Community and Custom in Early Modern Germany* (Cambridge, 2002), ch. 6, quotation at 292.
[35] Jessopp, ed., *Lives of the Norths*, I, 130.
[36] *Perfect Occurrences of Both Houses of Parliament* (14–21 Aug. 1646), sig. Ii3; East Suffolk Record Office, C/5/3/2/3/2; Cambridgeshire Record Office, P30/11/1.

that the experience of bewitchment 'ought to be internalized and made the occasion of a spiritual transaction between the individual (or the community) and God'.[37] Irreligion and aggression were signs of the times. 'The fables of Witchcraft have taken so fast hold and deepe root in the heart of man', wrote Scot, 'that fewe or none can (nowadaies) with patience indure the hand and correction of God.'[38] Gifford noticed how people rushed to threaten suspects when friends fell ill, when they 'should runne only unto God by a lively faith, true repentance and hartie prayer, to have the devill remooved'.[39]

Some believed the antidote to witchcraft lay not in the confrontational arena of the courtroom but, like its causes, in the spiritual life of the community. In the 1580s when Richard Greenham, rector of Dry Drayton (Cambridgeshire) tried to quell his flock's terror of witches, he noticed an unfortunate legacy of the Reformation. 'Many having escaped out of the gulf of superstition', he observed, 'are now far too plagued and swallowed up of prophainess'; they underestimated God's power while exaggerating the devil's. Greenham's remedy was pastoral care, protecting the parish by ministering to the 'bewitched'. Satan did nothing without divine permission, he said, so people should contemplate God and themselves before adopting sinister explanations.[40] Collective rituals banished evil. Early seventeenth-century recommendations included making suspects touch the Bible and repeat Scripture at the font, while the preacher declared himself 'a swifte witnesse against witches'. Next they would renounce sin as the charges were read, followed by a climactic sermon. The method was patient and holistic. The objective: redemption.[41]

The same principle guided the ecclesiastical courts: unorthodoxy was an error to be corrected so repentant sinners could re-enter the fold. Here witchcraft usually meant sorcery: incorrect worship not apostasy. Some suspected sorcerers committed other offences, including absence from church and failing to take communion.[42] Church courts also dealt with more hostile people, without mentioning witchcraft. These included a Cambridgeshire woman known as 'A comon and A notorious blasphemer of godes holy name by sweareinge' and 'an abominable curser of any man or other creature that do in anywyse offend her'. Alice Skilling of Mepal in the same county was presented in 1608 'for useing the Minister & Churchwardens in irreverent

[37] Stuart Clark, *Thinking with Demons: The Idea of Witchcraft in Early Modern Europe* (Oxford, 1997), 449.
[38] Scot, *Discoverie of Witchcraft*, 1.
[39] Gifford, *Discourse*, sig. H3.
[40] John Rylands Library, Manchester, English MS 524, quotation at fol. 9.
[41] British Library [BL], Royal MS 17 C.XXIII.
[42] See, e.g., Canterbury Cathedral Diocesan Record Office [CCDRO], DCb/X.1.8, fol. 153v; *The Letter Book of John Parkhurst ... 1571–5*, ed. R. A. Houlbrooke (Norwich, 1974–75), 259.

termes as thus wisheinge the meats & drinke they eate might goe up & downe theire bellies as men goe to harrowe'.[43] To most parishioners, these people were infinitely worse than cunning folk because they were sowers of discord and enemies to charity.

In other cases malevolent witchcraft was explicitly stated. *Maleficium* appeared at the Canterbury church courts prior to the 1563 Witchcraft Act, suggesting that popular pressure may have helped initiate it. In 1560 people at Sutton Valence (Kent) turned on Alice Forest who 'knoweth well that she by her words have hurte & harmed things'. Five years later they presented Goodwife Young as 'a virie comon scolde And a trobler of all o[u]r neighbors' and a harmful witch; she was, they said, 'a poore woman and both she and hir husband lyveth by the charitie of o[u]r p[ar]ishe'.[44] Charges this serious demanded secular intervention, which suited divines like William Perkins who wanted harsher penalties than ecclesiastical courts could inflict. In a book of 1590, Richard Greenham's disciple Henry Holland expressed disgust at 'the continuall trafficke and market which the rude people have with witches'.[45] Cunning folk, like Catholic priests, fed off the impiety of the weak. In 1609 a London preacher condemned those 'who, when God smites them, they fly unto a witch or an Inchauntresse, and call for succour'; like Saul consulting the Witch of Endor they turn from God and lose his favour. The 'good witch' was more wretched than the 'hurting witch' because she appears saintly as she lures clients to the devil.[46]

Cunning folk also catalysed accusations. In 1575 when William Delman of Marden (Kent) charged Widow Fowseden 'openly in the church before the chefest p[a]rt of ye p[ar]ishe' with bewitching his cattle, she stood up and 'dyd desyre the people there p[re]sent to forgyve her'. However, Delman had consulted diviners, for which he was censured.[47] On the advice of a witch imprisoned at Canterbury, a man denounced a woman for stealing his wife's purse, 'to the great dysquyetinge of his honest quyet neighbours'.[48] Healers and soothsayers offended the godly, but they also encroached upon social authority by imparting knowledge and making decisions. The more one Kentish woman was rebuked by her minister for visiting witches, the more 'she sayd she would do it in desspyte of hym that should saye naye'.[49] Such reports led some to suppose that Protestant Christians were afflicted, even deeply flawed, both as individuals and as communities.

---

[43] Cambridge University Library [CUL], EDR B/2/14, fol. 65; B/2/29, fol. 139.

[44] CCDRO, DCb/Y.2.24, fol. 24; X.1.7, fol. 35v.

[45] William Perkins, A *Discourse of the Damned Art of Witchcraft* (Cambridge, 1608), 255–7; Henry Holland, A *Treatise against Witchcraft* (Cambridge, 1590), sig. B1.

[46] George Benson, A *Sermon Preached at Paules Crosse* (1609), 72.

[47] CCDRO, DCb/X.1.12, fols 131–131v.

[48] Ewen, *Witch Hunting*, 282; CCDRO, DCb/X.1.10, fol. 6.

[49] CCDRO, DCb/X.1.12, fol. 28.

II

Although church courts punished cunning folk into the seventeenth century, *maleficium* became the preserve of the secular authorities. Establishing the supremacy of statute belonged to the wider formalisation of state procedures, the success of which relied on people reporting crime and abandoning customary sanctions. At first, even the godly were unsure. Suffolk puritans meeting in 1588 debated what to do with witches, some suggesting body searches, others believing this 'to be fancy in the people easilie conceiving such a thing and to be reproved in them'. Finally, the rector of Erwarton declared witchcraft a matter for a magistrate.[50] His view became orthodox, and obedient subjects required to shun counter-magic and ordeals. One Elizabethan pamphleteer urged anyone suspecting witchcraft to put a lawful stop to it, 'for Charitie to thy Christian brother, and tender regard of thine own state'.[51] Prosecution was a last resort, but from the 1570s indictments rose steadily, peaking in the 1580s and not significantly subsiding until after 1600.[52]

Clerical opinion varied. Whereas some, like William Perkins, believed in the efficacy of the law, others saw there the plague of litigiousness. Ministers lambasted congregations for witch-hunting not only because it inhibited contemplation of sinfulness, but because it exacerbated conflict. George Gifford regarded accusations as a device by which Satan divided neighbours, with the worst witchmongers themselves possessed by demons: 'It is of a mad rage, and not of a good zeale that the most are carried withall against witches, which ought to teach men wisedome, discreation & warines.' In the 1620s the Somerset preacher Richard Bernard, an advocate of legal sanctions, recognised that witnesses against witches might be 'so transported with rage and uncharitable desire of revenge ... that they will over diligently gather matter to strengthen their suspicions'. This even the witchfinder John Stearne conceded.[53]

Outside the village, the consequences of such zeal could be serious. Gifford described how rumours solidified into legal truth:

Wel, mother W doth begin to bee very odious & terrible unto many [of] her neighbours, dare say nothing but yet in their heartes they wish shee were hanged. Shortly after an other falleth sicke and doth pine, hee can have no stomacke

---

[50] Vincent B. Redstone, *Memorials of Old Suffolk* (1908), 267.

[51] *A Detection of Damnable Driftes, practized by three Witches* (1579), sig. A3v.

[52] James Sharpe, 'England', in *Encyclopedia of Witchcraft*, ed. Richard M. Golden, 4 vols (Santa Barbara CA, 2006), II, 312.

[53] Gifford, *Discourse*, sig. I1v; Richard Bernard, *A Guide to Grand-Jury Men* (1627), 194–6, quotation at 196; John Stearne, *A Confirmation and Discovery of Witch Craft* (1648), 34.

unto his meate, nor hee can not sleepe. The neighbours come to visit him. Well neighbour, sayeth one, do ye not suspect some naughty dealing: did yee never anger mother W? truly neighbour (sayeth he) I have not liked the woman a long tyme.

When the dying man recalls asking the suspect to keep her chickens out of his yard, the parish makes up its mind, and she is tried and convicted. At the gallows she pleads innocence, and indeed 'doubtles some are put to death not beyng gylty'. This made murderers of the jurors, who act on ignorant assertions, especially when cunning folk were consulted, which was like asking the devil to identify his work. Perkins accepted more risk, believing witches to be skilled actors, but even he advised jurors 'not to condemne any partie supected upon bare presumptions without sound and sufficient proofes that they be not guiltie through their owne rashnesse of shedding innocent blood'.[54] How to achieve this was unclear. In 1621 a judge advised a hesitant foreman to 'Doe in it as God shall put in your hearts.'[55]

The action of conscience upon an accuser or juror was only as reliable as his ability to hear God rather than the devil. People erred: fear trumped reason and spite was detected where none existed. Even Christian neighbourliness might be misinterpreted if proffered by a suspicious person, for example gestures of seasonal goodwill. On Christmas morning 1566 a Kent woman visited a neighbour's sick child, 'and tooke the same childe by the hand & said god blesse the childe'; shortly afterwards she was accused of witchcraft.[56] A Yorkshireman fell ill in 1648 after attending a yuletide hog-roast where a neighbour 'sate her downe next unto him & said shee Loved him and all at his howse very well, & gave him a Little Clappe with her hand on his knee'.[57] Not all gifts were gratefully received. When Mary Wade was accused of bewitching Sir John Mallory's daughter, a witness deposed that the woman had made a sarcastic remark about a Christmas dole of bread. This case also involved *reciprocal* kindness. Wade recalled that when 'my Lady & children came downe to her howse about 3: or 4: yeares since y[a]t she gave them a dish of nuts among them'. The result, however, was not amity but more suspicion.[58]

Witch-suspects gave food to neighbours who then became ill. Such episodes fit conventional narratives about witchcraft; but they can also be seen as neighbourliness gone wrong, even reversals of Macfarlane's paradigm. The suspect tries to be kind, against the prevailing meanness of the times, but the recipient cannot accept it. A Kent woman who offered

---

54 Gifford, *Discourse*, sigs G4–G4v; Perkins, *Discourse*, 218–19.
55 Henry Goodcole, *The wonderfull Discoverie of Elizabeth Sawyer a Witch* (1621), sig. B2v.
56 CCDRO, DCb/X.1.8, fol. 107.
57 The National Archives [TNA], ASSI 45/3/1/243.
58 TNA, ASSI 45/5/3/133v, 135.

friendly advice about a sick cow was told pointedly that they had 'ill neighbors'.[59] This may have been true, but, some contemporaries argued, the 'ill neighbors' were not necessarily the witches. Witchcraft accusations thrived on bad fellowship, and might lead to the censure of either party. In 1667 magistrates in Connecticut told a plaintiff that he 'did greatly Sin in Harboureing such Jealousies in his Breast of his Neighboure who … hath beane a Loveing & Beneficiall Neighboure to him in affoardeing them what help shee could'.[60] Some suspected witches were cunning folk, their victims former clients who had sought help from the accused, not the other way round. Conflict between John Tatterson and Ann Green at Gargreave (Yorkshire) in 1656 began when she scorned him for not trusting her as she diagnosed his earache. Patients harmed had *asked* to be treated.[61]

Many cases involved unneighbourly hard bargains. A Yorkshire woman was accused after complaining 'thatt it was a pittiful Case that such a Cake shold be att a penny'. A Newcastle huckster was blamed for bewitching a customer who queried the price of her cherries. Employment, too, was contentious. In 1672 a man reported 'a p[er]son of an evill Life and Conversac[i]on and suspected to have done many Injuries to her Nighbour[s]' after she refused to pay him for ploughing her field.[62] Some saw the devil at work here, but not as accusers imagined. Perhaps *they* were the instruments of Satan, whereas the accused were the blameless poor – images of Christ. The truth turned on the question of proof. Most agreed that wicked witches deserved death, but how could they be identified? This was crucial: the guilty person was the most reviled creature; the innocent, the most deserving of pity. An anonymous writer from around 1630 declared his belief in witches *and* his scepticism about evidence, calling for 'Greate warines'. Many blame misfortunes on witches, he argued, from malice or ignorance and inability to accept providence, advising that 'a Christian moderation must be had in passinge uncharitable termes uppon the persons of witches & wizards &c'. Witches were pitiful creatures, an object-lesson to all Christians. 'Therefore lett us beholde in them a spectacle of mans misery … & to be moved w[i]th compassion to pray for theire conversion.'[63]

Pamphlets about witch-trials were meant to be exciting and edifying, but there are undertones of pity. Vengeance belonged to God alone, and however wicked the crime, a hanging was a time for solemn reflection, even empathy. In 1566 Agnes Waterhouse died well at Chelmsford, demonstrating God's grace. 'She yelded up her sowle', it was reported, 'trusting to be in joye with Christe her saviour, whiche dearely had bought her with

[59] CCDRO, DCb/Z.4.12, fol. 18.
[60] Helen Schatvet Ullmann, ed., *Hartford County, Connecticut, County Court Minutes, Volumes 3 and 4, 1663–1687, 1697* (Boston MA, 2005), 71.
[61] TNA, ASSI 45/5/1/32.
[62] TNA, ASSI 45/4/2/13; ASSI 45/7/1/7; ASSI 45/10/2/80.
[63] Beinecke Library, Yale University, Osborn fb 224.

his most precious bloudde.' In life she was the picture of evil; in death, a paragon of Protestant virtue.[64] A pamphlet of 1612 described the execution of Helen Jenkinson at Northampton. 'Thus ended this woman her miserable life', concluded the author, 'after she had lived many years poor, wretched, scorned and forsaken of the world.' By off-setting disgust with pity, he urged readers to save their hypocrisy and to appreciate the pathetic state of the sinner.[65] Anne Bodenham's defiant death at Salisbury in 1653 elicited mixed feelings. Edmond Bower described her preparations – including a farewell to her husband – with some sensitivity, and his account of her humiliation in prison must have offended some, if only because her treatment flouted proper procedure.[66] It is telling that witnesses against Bodenham were subsequently charged with consulting her as a cunning woman.[67]

Muted triumphalism over vanquished witches can be traced back to uneasiness in the neighbourhood. The efficacy of the 'strain gauge' – accusations made communities feel better – is unproven. As prosecutions were more often concatenations of circumstance than calculated initiatives, consensus about guilt was elusive. When Anne Symes of Littleport (Cambridgeshire) was indicted in 1639 she was poor in every way: indigent, sick, disreputable and friendless. Five years earlier the vicar had accused her of killing his daughter as revenge for his moving her pew. Opinion may have turned against Symes, but we have no more evidence of this than evidence that she inspired sympathy. What we do know is that the jury listened to the witnesses then acquitted her. Symes was tried again in 1646. A pathetic figure, she pleaded 'to her knowledg[e] that shee is no witch and that to her knowledg[e] she never bewitcht the boddie of any man, women, or Child, or horses, Beastes, or Cattell'. This is what judge and jury decided was most likely to be true and, as in 1639, Symes was acquitted.[68]

Trials were difficult, sometimes dangerous. Parishes were at least as likely to turn against someone who made unsubstantiated accusations of witchcraft as against accused witches. In 1614 a woman was accused in Star Chamber, having 'troubled manie of her neighbours some by chargeing them of Comon Sorcery hagges and wiches and did call their names in question and could not make anie due prooffe thereof'.[69] Authority figures might discourage prosecutions – a respectable Yorkshire woman warned a servant that 'she hoped she had a bett[e]r faith then to feare either witch or devill' –

[64] 'The ende and last confession of mother Waterhouse at her death', in *The Examination and Confession of Certaine Wytches at Chensforde* (1566).
[65] *The Witches of Northamptonshire* (1612), *Witchcraft in England, 1558–1618*, ed. Barbara Rosen (Amherst MA, 1969), 354.
[66] Malcolm Gaskill, 'Witchcraft, Politics and Memory in Seventeenth-Century England', *HJ* 50 (2007), 289–308.
[67] TNA, ASSI 24/22, fol. 12v.
[68] CUL, EDR, E11 Informations 1639, box ii, fols 17–20; E11 (Anne Symes, 1639).
[69] TNA, STAC 8/151/7, m. 2.

but the disincentives were plain enough: expense, humiliation and counter-suit.[70] In 1687 Joan Walker, widow of Bicester (Oxfordshire), complained to JPs about a malicious accusation, declaring she had 'ever lived in good fame credit and reputation, carrying and behaving herselfe as a very honest sober and civill person living virtuously justly and uprightly without any wrong or injury to any person or persons whatever'. She successfully requested that her persecutors be sworn to good behaviour.[71]

Occasionally records disclose the scale of community disagreement over a suspect's guilt. Controversy followed factional or ideological lines, or might be a simple reaction to perceived injustice. In 1651, 230 people petitioned judges on behalf of Mary Hickington, a condemned prisoner at York, stating that she and her husband 'did behave themselves honestly and innocently among their Neighbours, nor did we ever heare or could observe that she the said Mary was in the least wise suspected to be guilty of sorcery or witch-craft'. When Susanna and Joseph Hinchcliffe of Denby (Yorkshire) were denounced in 1674, over fifty people said it was the accuser who was at fault, 'but that we judge Recrimination to be but an indirect way of Clearing the Innocent'. Goodwife Hinchcliffe was 'of good example and very Helpfull and usefull in the Neighborhood, according to her poore ability'.[72] Clergy and gentry took sides. Around 1590 Reverend Thomas Grey of Pulham (Norfolk) interviewed parishioners about an accused witch, then reported to a JP the good name they gave her; a prominent local man endorsed a petition in her favour. In 1641 Henry Oxinden of Barham (Kent) gave Goodwife Gilnot a letter addressed to his brother-in-law, a magistrate, praising her character. She stood accused of bewitching sheep by farmers who 'will not with patience endure the hand and correction of God'. Gilnot had brought up her children as pious Christians, Oxinden affirmed, but her cry of innocence 'though it reach to heaven is scarce heard heere uppon earth'.[73]

Such entreaties were effective. When in 1577 Alice Rumbold was cited for witchcraft at a Cambridgeshire church court, she 'did exhibite a tr[u]e testimoniall under the hands of diverse honest and credyble p[er]sones of Sawston, wherein yt was signifyed that they thinke and beleve she is no such mann[er] of woman as she ys pr[esen]ted to be'. A magistrate upheld the claim. Another Cambridge suspect presented a statement by neighbours at

---

[70] TNA, ASSI 45/4/2/13.

[71] M. Sturge Gretton, ed., *Oxfordshire Justices of the Peace in the Seventeenth Century*, Oxfordshire Record Society 16 (1934), 38–9.

[72] TNA, ASSI 47/20/1, fols 512–513v; ASSI 45/1/1/90–3. See also: James Sharpe, *Instruments of Darkness: Witchcraft in England, 1550–1750* (1996), 165–7; Malcolm Gaskill, *Crime and Mentalities in Early Modern England* (Cambridge, 2000), 51–4.

[73] Historical Manuscripts Commission (HMC), *Report on Manuscripts in Various Collections*, 8 vols (1901–13), II, 243–4; *The Oxinden Letters, 1607–1642*, ed. Dorothy Gardiner (1933), 220–2.

Horningsea and was discharged.[74] In 1606 fifteen people from South Perrott (Dorset) successfully petitioned the Court of Exchequer that Joan Guppy had never done 'hurte or damage to any p[er]son or p[er]sons whatsoever by waye of enchauntmente Sorcerye or witchcrafte'.[75] Even pardons were not unusual. The patent rolls for 1581–82 alone, for example, record seven acts of mercy to witches from five counties.[76] A campaign on behalf of Christian Weech of Mendham (Norfolk) led to her conviction being quashed in 1604. Norfolk JPs backed a petition to the earl of Salisbury and informed the Lord Chancellor that ratification of a royal pardon had been delayed 'by the sinister means of her enemies'. Weech was 'a gentlewomen verie aunciently decended, and for the greatest parte of her life to have lived without any manner of note or suspition of exercizinge of the devilishe and detestable practize of witchcrafte'.[77]

III

Far from being simple actions of subject (the united community) upon object (the isolated witch) witchcraft accusations were capricious and contested, which explains why so many never reached the courts. Increasingly in the seventeenth century, witchcraft divided opinion, prised open existing social fissures and caused doubt about how best to promote charity and defend order. Public denunciation exposed accuser as well as accused, and it was never certain who would be vilified or exonerated. Even the basic agreements needed to initiate prosecutions unravelled easily. People who had followed the inner voice of conscience, or succumbed to peer pressure, changed their minds or had them changed for them. Around 1600 Margaret Francis of Holkham (Norfolk) was imprisoned by the sheriff of Norfolk. A gentleman requested her release, explaining that she suffered from a 'disease called the Mother' and that the people who had complained were 'only proceedinge of ignorance or malice' and now felt ashamed. Some deposed that a 'victim', Joan Harvey, had faked her fits. Francis was freed and returned to Holkham, although things did not calm down. Harvey attacked the old woman and she died.[78]

Others who encouraged witchcraft accusations, through gossip or passive consent, later regretted what they had or had not done. Emotion rather than reason gave witch-trials momentum – and often dissipated. Doubts crept in. When in 1586 Joan Cason was tried at Faversham (Kent), one

[74] CUL, EDR, D/2/10, fols 4v, 22, 37, 51v, 77v; EDR, B/2/13, fols 18v, 25v.
[75] TNA, E 163/17/5; STAC 8/149/24, quotation at m. 4.
[76] *Calendar of Patent Rolls, Elizabeth I, IX, 1580–1582* (1986), 69, 214, 236, 255.
[77] TNA, SP 38/7, Docquet, 16 Apr. 1604; SP 38/10, Docquet, 3 Apr. 1610; HMC, *Salisbury Manuscripts*, XXIV, Addenda (1976), 109–11.
[78] BL, Add. MSS 28223, fol. 15; Egerton MSS 2714, fol. 104.

account described her accusers as 'all very poor people' given credit 'for that they were her near neighbours and her offence very odious'. Cason blamed the 'malicious dealings of her adversaries', admitting only that a rat-spirit had visited her. One of her relatives claimed that Cason knew a spell whereby 'she would be even with those that angered her' and accused her of hurting a child. The jury acquitted her of murder, but not of conjuration and she was condemned. The mood at the gallows was restless. Cason confessed her sins and 'therewithal made so godly and penitent an end, that many now lamented her death which were her utter enemies'. All Faversham's uncharitableness, briefly fixed upon one woman, now shrank back to its source: the hearts and minds of the neighbourhood.[79] The maidservant responsible for the downfall of Anne Bodenham in 1653 begged the judge to spare the witch's life, a cry of conscience which ironically only confirmed the girl's piety and reliability as a witness.[80]

Enthusiasm for witch-panics was rare, and considered eccentric or rebarbative. Reactions to the witch-hunt of 1645–47 demonstrate this.[81] Assaults upon witches disturbed the peace and usurped state authority. When a suspect was beaten to death in Rotherham in 1663, neighbours spoke fondly of her and denounced her killer.[82] The pamphlet about the Northampton witches failed to mention their harsh treatment, described elsewhere, perhaps to avoid eliciting sympathy.[83] Witnesses from Heptonstall (Yorkshire) weakened their case in 1646 by admitting abusing a woman who told magistrates that she 'did confess unto them what they required in hope to be freed from further blowes'.[84] Her defence would have seemed as reasonable then as it does now. And by the later seventeenth century, when it was harder to prove witchcraft by any means, the plight of such unfortunates seemed all the more piteous, their neighbours' spite the more reprehensible. In 1694 fourteen people from Overhilton and Middlehilton in Lancashire swore that Henry Baron had killed the elderly Ann Crook. One related how he 'tooke her up in his arms & threw her violently down like a log of wood'. Baron had boasted that no one could be hanged for killing a witch, but he was proved wrong. About the suspicion of witchcraft, Crook's neighbours said nothing.[85]

[79] Raphael Holinshed, *Chronicles of England, Scotland and Ireland*, 6 vols (London, 1586; 1808 edn), III, 1560–1, quotation at 1561; Centre for Kentish Studies, Fa/JQs 1 (bdl. 104); Fa/JQs 23 (bdl. 128).
[80] John Heydon, *Psonthonphanchia* (1664), 144.
[81] Notably John Gaule, *Select Cases of Conscience Touching Witches and Witchcrafts* (1646).
[82] TNA, ASSI 45/6/3/154–5.
[83] *Witches of Northamptonshire*, 344–56. Cf. BL, Sloane MSS 972, fol. 7.
[84] TNA, ASSI 45/1/5/38A.
[85] TNA, PL 27/2 Pt. 1 (unfol.), informations against Henry Baron, 1694.

Intellectual scepticism contributed to changing attitudes, yet belief in witchcraft coexisted with doubts about evidence. Many throughout the seventeenth century would have agreed with the Jacobean writer who condemned 'the beggerly rabble of witches, charmers, imposters, and such like cozeners that regard more to get monie than to helpe for charitie'.[86] Others, by contrast, argued that witches' righteous but hypocritical neighbours must share the blame. Witchcraft was a crime of the poor, wrote Michael Sparke, because God-fearing people did too little to prevent it. Selfishness and toleration of idleness engendered all sorts of blasphemy, slander, dispute and drunkenness. All vagrants, not just witches, said Sparke, were 'the verie perfect pictures of Sathan'. After 1650 it became harder to ignore the effects of poverty and hostility to the poor. John Brinsley understood that cunning folk were 'forced to fall upon the honest plainness of the common people ... [to] patch up the breaches of their Fortune'.[87]

Even maleficent witches received sympathy. Henry More appreciated their predicament, arguing in 1653 that witchcraft arose from 'extreme Poverty, irksome old Age, want of Friends, the Contempt, Injury and Hard-heartednesse of evil Neighbours, working upon a Soul low sunk into the body and wholy devoid of the Divine life'. The most avid witchmongers are those who made them 'and have no more goodnesse nor true piety than these they so willingly prosecute'.[88] Brinsley agreed: 'a small matter will beget suspicion, and upon this multitudes of Proofs shall be muster'd up, and so by a ready Climax, the poor people are hurried up to the Gallows it self'. Those who brood about witches, he observed, are their most likely victims. Insanity, in both accuser and accused, was cited. In 1655 Thomas Ady attributed witch-beliefs to fancy, madness, drunkenness, gossip and spite. Hearing rumours, many surrender reason and 'joyn their hand with the rest in persecuting blindly without due consideration'.[89] Confessions were dubious. In 1655 Méric Casaubon, a cleric who believed in witchcraft, said no woman should die just because 'she should tell many strange things of her self'. In the 1670s the physician John Webster cast doubt on all testimony, mocking the notion that witches should be flown to sabbats, only to be sent back 'ragged and tattered, begging their bread from door to door'.[90]

By this time witch-trials drew attention not only to the inadequacies of evidence, but to the specific problems of elderly and poor people. The 1651 edition of Scot's *Discoverie of Witchcraft* justified republication 'for the undeceiving of Judges, Justices, and Juries, and for the preservation of poor,

---

[86] Edmund Gardiner, *The Triall of Tabacco* (1610), 49.
[87] Sparke, *Greevous Grones*, 2, 6–8, quotation at 8; John Brinsley, *A Discovery of the Impostures of Witches and Astrologers* (1680), sigs A4–A4v.
[88] Henry More, *An Antidote Against Atheisme* (1653), 147; Brinsley, *Discovery*, 20–1, 25.
[89] Thomas Ady, *A Candle in the Dark* (1655), 168.
[90] Méric Casaubon, *A Treatise Concerning Enthusiasme* (1655), 90; John Webster, *The Displaying of Supposed Witchcraft* (1677), 68.

aged, deformed, ignorant people; frequently taken, arraigned, condemned and executed for Witches, when according to a right understanding, and a good conscience, Physick, Food, and necessaries should be administered to them'. The editor reviled 'the lewd unchristian practises of Witchmongers, upon aged, melancholy, ignorant, and superstitious people', adding that unlike the anti-Christian practices of witches, their persecutors' inhumanity was easily proved. 'Witches' did not break charity with their neighbours: it was the other way round. Scot himself had argued that 'manie of these poore wretches had more need to be releeved than chastised', and would be better served by doctors than gaolers or executioners. Yet still people treated beggars with 'unnaturall & uncivill discourtisie', 'cancred and spitefull malice' and 'outragious and barbarous crueltie'.[91] In 1671 the Royal Society received a letter from a French doctor describing witches tried at Rouen, 'poor, mad people who mislead others after having been themselves misled'.[92] Shifting attitudes reached the stage. In a play of 1681, the witch is a defenceless victim of popish enthusiasm.[93]

This idea reached fruition in the next century, when English witch-trials ceased. In 1718 Francis Hutchinson conclusively demonstrated how parishes created their own witches. 'When some Poor Old Creature, through Poverty, and old Age, and bad Diet, and want of convenient Linnen, is grown Nasty, may she not have some Rank Unsavoury Smell, that may grow to an Antipathy against those that have fall'n into Fits by their Fear at the Sight of her?' The neighbourhood, rather than the old woman, was at fault. Jane Wenham, the last person convicted under the Witchcraft Act, in 1712, was, Hutchinson insisted, utterly blameless; it was simply her misfortune to live in 'a barbarous Parish'.[94] Notions of a Christian commonwealth in crisis may have seemed old fashioned by then, but the kind of charity and neighbourliness that upheld civility, decency and the rule of law remained a cherished ideal into the age of commerce and politeness.[95]

V

The decline of witch-trials did not follow a straight path from ignorance to enlightenment, pre-modernity to modernity. The concept of witchcraft, as philosophical proposition and provable crime, had always been fragile.

---

91 Reginald Scot, *The Discoverie of Witchcraft* (1651); *ibid.* (1584 edn), sig. B2v, 17.

92 *The Correspondence of Henry Oldenburg*, ed. A. Rupert Hall and Marie Boas Hall, 12 vols (Philadelphia, 1965–86), VIII, 329.

93 Thomas Shadwell, *The Lancashire-Witches, and Tegue o Divelly the Irish-Priest*, ed. Judith Bailey Slagle (New York, 1991). For another sympathetic dramatisation, see Rowley, Dekker and Ford's *The Witch of Edmonton* (1621).

94 Francis Hutchinson, *An Historical Essay Concerning Witchcraft* (1718), 3, 131.

95 Owen Davies, *Witchcraft, Magic and Culture, 1736–1951* (Manchester, 1991), ch. 1.

Even in 1600, guilty verdicts arose from sectional support for charges that were just plausible, rather than from consensual attitudes and unanimous decisions. 'Witchcraft trials were generated within a multicausal matrix of extreme complexity', argues Robin Briggs, 'whose outcome in particular cases could never be reliably predicted.'[96] In its envy and aggression, witchcraft was inherently conflictual; but so were accusations, and ultimately contempt for the latter surpassed fear of the former. After 1650 concerns about injustice done to suspects, and pity for the poor from whose ranks they came, terminated the legal viability of witchcraft. Although witchbeliefs endured, the tormentor of witches replaced the witch as a symbol of unneighbourliness, and the witch-stereotype came to represent the impotent poor and the need to relieve them. We assume trials declined because magistrates and judges no longer countenanced them; but perhaps villagers' willingness to victimise also diminished.

From the 1560s, when witch-trials began, accusations invited greater reflection not just about diabolic influence on neighbours but about the neighbourhood itself: its coherence, values, purpose – all apparently threatened by social change. Seventeenth-century commentators were so voluble about 'good fellowship' not because it was normal but because it was a precious but impossible ideal. 'The very insistence with which the rhetoric was pressed', Ian Archer suggests, 'may in itself be a sign of the failure to measure up to its demands.'[97] To people within and without its immediate arena, a witchcraft accusation activated fears about the spiritual and material welfare of parish and commonwealth. And to those of tender conscience, it indicated that the malice concentrated in the witch actually existed all around, perhaps especially in persecutors' hearts. Even clergy hostile to witchcraft understood that by looking accusingly at a witch one might see reflected one's own depraved self and society.

This did not mean that communities really were in decline, or that some golden age of neighbourliness had ever existed, however much contemporaries mourned its passing.[98] 'Community' is as hard to define as 'decline' is to detect and measure.[99] And the debate about the 'real nature' of early modern communities – peaceful hives of mutual regard and respect,

---

[96] Robin Briggs, *The Witches of Lorraine* (Oxford, 2007), 377.

[97] Ian W. Archer, *The Pursuit of Stability: Social Relations in Elizabethan London* (Cambridge, 1991), 84.

[98] Richard M. Smith, '"Modernisation" and the Corporate Medieval Village Community in England: Some Sceptical Reflections', in *Explorations in Historical Geography*, ed. Alan R. H. Baker and Derek Gregory (Cambridge, 1984), 140–79; Christopher Dyer, 'The English Medieval Village Community and its Decline', *JBS* 33 (1994), 407–29.

[99] Jeremy Boulton, *Neighbourhood and Society: A London Suburb in the Seventeenth Century* (Cambridge, 1987), ch. 9.

or hotbeds of dissension and malice – has been mostly sterile.[100] Keith Wrightson has described community less as a concrete entity than 'a quality in social relations which is, in some respects, occasional and temporary, and which needs periodic stimulation and reaffirmation if it is to survive the inevitable tensions which arise in local society'.[101] To this end, witch-stories *stimulated* and *reaffirmed* collective values amid turbulent transitions. The spread of literacy was crucial. Cheap print illustrated temptation, providence and grace, but also emphasised the importance of tolerance and compassion if society was to keep reconstituting itself, and so maintain stability.

This essay has worked some of the interests of new cultural historians, especially mentalities and emotions, into the new social history agenda – a politically engaged history, rooted in the locality and concerned with change. The story of early modern England is fundamentally one of increased social stratification, of poverty and prosperity, authority and hegemony, alienation and resistance. Neighbourliness, like custom and commonwealth, seemed embattled; but perhaps the very fact that people worried about it ensured its survival. Things about witches that people saw and heard were food for thought, not just about spiritual jeopardy and the ontology of witch-craft, but about social responsibility. All three issues concerned Reginald Scot's contemporaries, but by the later seventeenth century the latter predominated. The reflex to blame others for misfortune became more firmly restrained by a sense that this was wrong, not least because the usual suspects were so abject. To position oneself fairly and decently in relation to neighbours may have kept the heart of a community beating, even when the pulse felt weak. While many feared the worst for society, in the end it mattered more that they hoped for the best and continued to profit from each other's company.

Early modern people belonged to political milieux and processes contin-ually 'forged anew in the crucible of change'.[102] Even if economic indi-vidualism *was* a characteristic of early modernity, it did not grow at the expense of community. As Craig Muldrew has shown, had this been so England would have descended into 'a state of constant Hobbesian civil war', whereas its social institutions in fact grew better at channelling and

---

[100] J. A. Sharpe and Lawrence Stone, 'The History of Violence in England', *P&P* 108 (1985), 206–24; Steve Hindle, *The State and Social Change in Early Modern England, c. 1550–1640* (Basingstoke, 2000), 94–7. Keith Wrightson reconceptualises this in 'Mutualities and Obligations: Changing Social Relationships in Early Modern England', *Proceedings of the British Academy*, 139 (2006), 157–94.

[101] Wrightson, *ES*, 62.

[102] Patrick Collinson, *De Republica Anglorum: Or, History with the Politics Put Back* (Cambridge, 1990), 17–18; quotation from Steve Hindle, 'A Sense of Place? Becoming and Belonging in the Rural Parish, c. 1550–1650', in *Communities in Early Modern England: Networks, Place, Rhetoric*, ed. Alexandra Shepard and Phil Withington (Manchester, 2000), 96–114, p. 98.

absorbing conflict. Litigiousness may have been a symptom of deteriorating relations, but governors and governed preferred it to violent feuding.[103] Yet by 1700 communities were held together by hierarchy and power exercised through law, as much as by faith and charity. The poor were not perse-cuted but neither were they loved: they became objects of bureaucracy as poor relief was secularised, its social relationships cooler and more formal. The humanist romance of commonwealth was deadened by policy and prac-tice.[104] When in 1598 a Kentish labourer said that 'yf the Queene did putt downe begginge she is worse than Nan Bennett', an executed witch who 'forsooke God and all the world', he conflated royal will and diabolism as affronts to neighbourliness.[105]

The elusive quality of modernity in 'early modernity' can be found in witchcraft, but not in the triumph of enlightened ideas or civil government. Historians and anthropologists have seen witchcraft prosecutions as a birth-pang of social, economic, religious, political and legal change.[106] Modernity may have banished witch-trials, but first it made them possible: anger from below, law from above and the administration of justice in between.[107] Here we should distinguish between 'modernisation' and 'modernity': the former a process, the latter an experience. Like community, modernity 'is not one moment or age, but a set of relations that are constantly being made and remade, contested and reconfigured'.[108] The fact that criminal witchcraft remained in limbo for so long, inconclusive but credible, disproves 'modern-isation theory'.[109] Change happened at different speeds and times, and in contexts – custom, jurisprudence, theology, philosophy, fashion – that did not necessarily merge or overlap.[110] Witchcraft accusations demonstrate that

---

[103] Craig Muldrew, 'From a "Light Cloak" to an "Iron Cage": Historical Changes in the Relation between Community and Individualism', in *Communities*, ed. Shepard and Withington, 156–77, p. 159.

[104] Jones, *Tree of Commonwealth*, ch. 4; Ferguson, 'Tudor Commonweal', 34.

[105] J. S. Cockburn, ed., *Calendar of Assize Records: Kent Indictments, Elizabeth I* (1979), 71, 423.

[106] Peter Geschiere, *The Modernity of Witchcraft, Politics and the Occult in Postcolonial Africa* (Charlottesville VA, 1997); Monica Hunter, *Reaction to Conquest: Effects of Contact with Europeans on the Pondo of South Africa* (1936), chs 6, 13.

[107] The classic example is Paul Boyer and Stephen Nissenbaum, *Salem Possessed: The Social Origins of Witchcraft* (Cambridge MA, 1974). For a critique, see Richard Latner, 'Salem Witchcraft, Factionalism, and Social Change Reconsidered', *William and Mary Quarterly* 65 (2008), 423–48.

[108] Kathleen Wilson, 'Citizenship, Empire and Modernity in the English Provinces, *c.* 1720–1790', *Eighteenth Century Studies* 29 (1995), 69–96, p. 71.

[109] See: Garthine Walker, 'Modernization', in *Writing Early Modern History*, ed. Garthine Walker (2005), 25–48; Phil Withington, *Society in Early Modern England: the Vernacular Origins of Some Powerful Ideas* (Cambridge, 2010).

[110] Miles Ogborn, *Spaces of Modernity: London's Geographies, 1680–1780* (New York, 1998), 9–12.

ideas were deeply and obscurely embedded in social relations, cultural norms and the messy micro-politics of the parish.

Wrightson is surely right that change 'presents itself to the historian as a series of localized social dramas', not least because this is how early modern people experienced it themselves: sometimes seismic but typically episodic, cushioned by continuities of family and lifecycle, by a persistent sense of the ordinary.[111] Eighteenth-century England perhaps grew more accustomed to the vicissitudes of economic life: insecurity in work, trade and tenure was painful but normal. In this world of old and new things, expressions of nostalgia for charity, hospitality and neighbourliness became, for some, 'a rhetorical weapon to challenge the dominance of the market-place in their own culture by a return to a mythical past of open generosity'.[112] For the losers this rhetoric vainly resisted change; for the winners it palliated it, paying lip-service to common interests while personal ambitions were pursued. If witchcraft accusations *were* rooted in the guilt of nascent middling sorts, as Macfarlane once suggested, it was an anxiety assuaged by class, prosperity and consumption, and the self-justifying creation myths of modern English society.

[111] Wrightson, *ES*, 222.
[112] Felicity Heal, *Hospitality in Early Modern England* (Oxford, 1990), 403.

10

Deference, Paternalism and Popular Memory in Early Modern England

ANDY WOOD

The poetry of John Clare, the most articulate voice of the rural working class of early nineteenth-century England, can be read as a meditation upon the relationship between memory and social relations. Clare drew upon the local traditions with which he had been brought up, setting them as golden memories against the harshness of the social conditions of the time at which he was writing.[1] Within Clare's vision of agrarian history, parliamentary enclosure had fractured a distinct set of social relations, one characterised by paternalism, decency and kindness. In *The Shepherd's Calendar*, Clare conjures up a lost world of social harmony, when masters drank and socialised with their workers. Clare shows us an old farm labourer working with his younger workmates:

> ... in some threshing floor
> There they wi scraps of songs & laugh and [t]ale
> Lighten their an[n]ual toils while merry ale
> Goes round & gladdens old mens hearts to praise
> The thread bare customs of old farmers days
> Who while the sturting sheep wi trembling fears
> Lies neath the snipping of his harmless sheers
> Recalls full many a thing by bards unsung
> & pride forgot – that reign[e]d when he was young[2]

The research upon which this article is based was supported by grants from the Arts and Humanities Research Council and the Leverhulme Trust. I am grateful to the editors and to Malcolm Gaskill and Claire Langhamer for their comments on this piece.

[1] George Deacon, *John Clare and the Folk Tradition* (London, 1983).
[2] *John Clare: Poems of the Middle Period, 1822–1837*, ed. Eric Robinson, David Powell and P. M. S. Dawson, 2 vols (Oxford, 1996), I, 79. For an anonymous memoir of the Warwickshire villages of Arlescote and Warmington before parliamentary enclosure which conjures up a similar picture, see Warwickshire Record Office, DR666/20.

The last two generations of early modern social historians have demonstrated that, whatever else they were, English villages before large-scale
parliamentary enclosure were not rural idylls; yet Clare's poetry routinely
presents them as such. If the task of the historian lies in the search for
unmediated, objective truth, then Clare's work might easily be dismissed as
nostalgic retrospection. But for the concerns addressed in this chapter – the
relationship between collective memory and social relations – his poetry
comprises a uniquely rich archive. The memories evoked in Clare's poetry
are set within a strong sense of place, landscape and environment; drawing
upon local folklore, they demonstrate the embedding of collective mentalities within the small-scale world of the village; they are full of an awareness of power relations; and, critically, they are defined by a particular sense
of historical rupture, separating Clare's past from his present.[3] In all these
respects, Clare's poetry illuminates broader processes of collective remembering, in which messy historical realities are reduced to a set of basic characteristics, producing a body of memories that maintain social identities
and construct collective meaning.[4] The latter half of this chapter pursues
these insights more fully, dealing with popular memories of paternalism as
they were invoked in the sixteenth and seventeenth centuries. The first half
of the chapter is concerned with the social logic of deference and paternalism.[5] In the conclusion, we will see that there are certain similarities
between early modern popular memories of lordship and those evoked by
John Clare; but that there are fundamental dissimilarities too. These reflect
broader shifts in social relations and class formation that were taking place
in the early nineteenth century. Throughout, I present paternalism as one

[3] John Barrell, *The Idea of Landscape and the Sense of Place, 1730–1840: An Approach to the Poetry of John Clare* (Cambridge, 1972).
[4] James Fentress and C. J. Wickham, *Social Memory* (Oxford, 1992); Barbara A. Misztal, *Theories of Social Remembering* (Maidenhead, 2003).
[5] Here, I sketch some similarities within otherwise different modes of paternalism. These do not always correspond to strict criteria, for which see N. Abercrombie and S. Hill, 'Paternalism and Patronage', *British Journal of Sociology* 27 (1976), 413–29. The following have influenced my thinking: David Roberts, *Paternalism in Victorian England* (New Brunswick NJ, 1979); Eric R. Wolf, 'Kinship, Friendship and Patron–Client relations in Complex Societies', in *The Social Anthropology of Complex Societies*, ed. Michael Bainton (1966), 1–22; Michael Kenny, 'Parallel Power Structures in Castile: the Patron–Client Balance', in *Contributions to Mediterranean Sociology: Mediterranean Rural Communities and Social Change*, ed. J. G. Peristiany (Paris, 1968), 155–62; Patrick Joyce, *Work, Society and Politics: the Culture of the Factory in Later Victorian England* (1980); J. A. Pitt-Rivers, *The People of the Sierra* (1954); J. G. A. Pocock, 'The Classical Theory of Deference', AHR 81 (1976), 516–23; J. Corbin, 'Social Class and Patron-Clientage in Andalusia: Some Problems of Comparing ethnologies', *Anthropological Quarterly* 52 (1979), 99–114; Howard Newby, *The Deferential Worker: A Study of Farm Workers in East Anglia* (1977).

of the defining characteristics of early modern social relations, the product of a historically specific class structure.

A strong sense of the historical specificity of early modern social relations runs through Keith Wrightson's work, defined as it is by a profound awareness of social dynamics. Within the core period with which his work has been concerned, there is a similar concern to address fundamental processes of change, most notably social polarisation. But at the same time, Wrightson has a clear sense of what is distinct about the sixteenth and seventeenth centuries. His writing on the subject shifts between synchronic and diachronic modes and has three outstanding features: an attention to the embedding of social relations within fundamental structural inequalities of wealth and power; an awareness of the difficulty of capturing the multifaceted complexity of early modern social relations within any simple interpretive formula; and a constant attention to tangled, everyday social complexity. All three concerns are apparent throughout his most influential publication, *English Society, 1580–1680*. In that book, Wrightson elegantly navigated his way past one of the then determining questions in early modern social history. For some historians at the time at which *English Society* was published, early modern society was based upon class struggle. For others, the notion of class was an anathema: to them, Tudor and Stuart England was a traditional hierarchy built upon the universal acceptance of clientage, reciprocity, paternalism and deference.[6] In contrast to this dichotomy, Wrightson rejected the view 'that the forms of social alignment that we label hierarchy and class are somehow mutually exclusive'. Instead, he suggested that 'hierarchical or class alignments ... may coexist in time in different places and different circumstances. They may even coexist in time in single minds as alternative responses.'[7]

Contemporaries did not possess any single, unitary vision of the early modern social order. Rather, they were capable of describing their social worlds in very different terms, from Sir Thomas Elyot's analogy between social, natural and divine hierarchy to Gerrard Winstanley's depiction of mid-seventeenth-century England as a world of conflict and oppression. Differing models of social relations were routinely articulated in legal

[6] See for instance M. E. James, *Family, Lineage and Civil Society: a Study of Society, Politics and Mentality in the Durham Region, 1500–1640* (Oxford, 1974), 27, 38. The confrontation between Boris Porschnev and Roland Mousnier set the parameters for later debate. See *France in Crisis, 1620–1675*, ed. P. J. Coveney (Totawa NJ, 1977), best read alongside Armand Arriaza, 'Mousnier and Barber: the Theoretical Underpinning of the "Society of Orders" in Early Modern Europe', *P&P* 89 (1980), 39–57.

[7] Keith Wrightson, 'The Social Order of Early Modern England: Three Approaches', in *The World We Have Gained: Histories of Population and Social Structure* ed. Lloyd Bonfield, Richard M. Smith and Keith Wrightson (Oxford, 1986), 177–202, p. 198. See also F. W. Kent '"Be Rather Loved than Feared": Class Relations in Quattrocento Florence', in *Society and Individual in Renaissance Florence*, ed. William J. Connell (Berkeley, 2002), 13–50.

disputes, in which each side sought to stereotype the other as riotous, dispu-
tatious, seditious, disorderly or irreligious. Thus the Court of Star Chamber
heard a complaint concerning a breach of social norms at Culpho (Suffolk)
on the night of 8 August 1604. The complainant, a gentleman called
Thomas Hall, described an obscene slight to his dignity. He claimed that a
large crowd, led by his fellow gentleman Charles Wolverston, had gathered
at midnight outside his house, singing abusive songs 'in maner of a harvest
Songe the foot of wch Song was theis filthie wordes following ... Come kisse
our arse holes'. When Hall's wife told them to desist, the assembly 'did then
and there drawe forthe there prvytyes at her ... maydes' and Wolverston
declared that 'By Gods Wounds I have shitt in thy husbandes porridge
pot ev[er]y day this Fortnight & swore that by Gods wounds that he and
all his company would shite in his ponde ... before they would goe away'.
According to the complaint, 'the said ryotous & rowtous psons dyd accordingly p[re]sently p[er]forme the same'. In answer, Wolverston explained how
the crowd had in fact gathered to offer acclaim to the local gentry, there
being

> a Neybourly usadge ... emongest quiett and well disposed people a harmlesse
> custome ... yearley about the latter ende of harveste for the harvest folke to
> assemble themselves togther to synge ... harvest songes at or neere the dwellynge
> houses of the gentlemen or Cheife men of every p[ar]ishe and doe use in recom-
> pence of their love to bestowe harvest cheare uppon sutch syngers when they
> singe aswell as when they worke.[8]

The opposing accounts of the events in Culpho on 8 August 1604 highlight conflicting contemporary modes of social analysis: was this a world of
conflict, or an organic hierarchy of 'quiett and well disposed people', their
pastoral communities bonded by mutual 'love' and 'harmlesse custome'?

---

[8] The National Archives [TNA], STAC8/176/14. For harvest celebrations, see
T. Tusser, *Five Hundred Points of Good Husbandry* (Oxford, 1984 edn), 121–4; *Wiltshire:
Topographical Collections of John Aubrey, FRS, AD 1659–70*, ed. J. E. Jackson (Devizes,
1862), 198. For their survival see W. B. Gerish, 'An East Anglian Harvest Custom,
Known Locally as "Hallering Largees"', *Folklore* 5 (1894), 167–9; J. Glyde, *A Dyshe of
Norfolke Dumplings* (1898), 102–3; James Hooper, 'Horkeys, or Harvest Frolics', in *Bygone
Norfolk*, ed. William Andrews (1898), 196–209. For their adaptation in American slave
plantations, see Roger D. Abrahams, *Singing The Master: The Emergence of African-
American Culture in the Slave South* (New York, 1992). For the adaptation of broader forms
of English paternalism, see Anthony S. Parent Jr, *Foul Means: The Formation of a Slave
Society in Virginia, 1660–1740* (Chapel Hill, 2003), 197–235. American slaveholders'
pretensions extended to comparing themselves to European feudal lords. See Eugene
D. Genovese, 'The Southern Slaveholders' View of the Middle Ages', in *Medievalism
in American Culture*, ed. Bernard Rosenthal and Paul E. Szarmach (Binghamton, 1989),
31–52.

How 'real' was deference and paternalism? In contrast to some of the literature on the subject, which has presented popular deference as a 'mask' which 'on occasion ... was ripped away' to reveal 'thinly-veiled hatreds', this chapter treats paternalism and deference as genuine impulses.[9] I seek to raise fundamental questions about the nature of domination and cultural hegemony. In particular, such questions have preoccupied those working within the historical materialist tradition. Vulgar-Marxist understandings of the subject used to see subordinates as held in the grip of a false consciousness which blinded them to the reality of their exploitation.[10] This chapter seeks to demonstrate that something like Antonio Gramsci's concept of cultural hegemony more fully captures the complex interplay of domination, subordination and resistance. Still sometimes misunderstood as describing a one-sided relationship in which the dominant group imposes its intellectual will and ideological force upon the governed, Gramsci saw power as contested and social relations as dynamic.[11] Certainly, hegemony assumes that ruling groups try to impose their own world-view upon subordinates. But it also assumes that this process is never complete; that within many hegemonic orders, considerable space is left for subordinates to develop their own senses of the world; and that such spaces are won by subordinates in the process of a constant, never-ending struggle with their rulers.[12] As Roberta Pearson puts it, hegemony is best

conceived of as a fluid and unstable site of contestation between the dominant social formations in the ruling power bloc and those marginalized social formations seeking concessions from the dominant, and whom the dominant constantly strives to incorporate. A hegemonic order is not monolithic or totalizing; the dominant tolerate alternative world views and, even more important, the domi-

[9] Paul Griffiths, Adam Fox and Steve Hindle, 'Introduction', in *The Experience of Authority in Early Modern England*, ed. Paul Griffiths, Adam Fox and Steve Hindle (Basingstoke, 1996), 1–9, p. 6.

[10] Vladimir Il'ich Lenin, *What Is To Be Done?* (London, 1988).

[11] For such misunderstandings, see James C. Scott, *Weapons of the Weak: Everyday Forms of Peasant Resistance* (New Haven, 1985), 315; Mark Goldie, 'The Unacknowledged Republic: Officeholding in Early Modern England', in *The Politics of the Excluded, c. 1500–1850*, ed. Tim Harris (Basingstoke, 2001), 153–94, p. 155. For Scott on false consciousness, see his *The Moral Economy of the Peasant: Rebellion and Subsistence in Southeast Asia* (New Haven, 1976), 159–60, 225–40. For the original formulation of hegemony, see Antonio Gramsci, *Selections from the Prison Notebooks* (1971), 12, 181–2, 242–4; idem, *Selections from Cultural Writings* (1985), 191. For a perceptive introduction, see T. J. Jackson Lears, 'The Concept of Cultural Hegemony: Problems and Possibilities', *AHR* 90:3 (1985), 567–93.

[12] Raymond Williams, *Problems in Materialism and Culture* (1980), 31–49; Richard Maddox, 'Bombs, Bikinis and the Popes of Rock 'n' Roll: Reflections on Resistance, the Play of Subordinations, and Liberalism in Andalusia and Academia, 1983–1995', in *Culture, Power, Place: Explorations in Critical Anthropology*, ed. Akhil Gupta and James Ferguson (Durham NC, 1997), 275–90, p. 286.

nated have a potential for resistance that might produce change, perhaps even a different hegemonic order.[13]

In the early modern context, obvious examples of partial spaces within which subordinates had the potential able to develop their own senses of the world include some of those areas identified by Wrightson as constituting the 'politics of the parish': most importantly, neighbourliness, community and custom.[14] Paternalism maintained a set of dominant interests; and yet it gave subordinates room for manoeuvre, handing to them a tool which, if used carefully, could win important concessions. Sometimes, this dialectical dance was cynically self-aware; alternatively, one or both sides might place genuine faith in the exchange. Just as hegemony is not reducible to the notion of a dominant ideology, then, neither is elite paternalism always instrumental nor plebeian deference evidence of false consciousness. Rather, for some, deference was more than half-believed, so ingrained in their souls as to define for much of the time their social outlook.[15] For others, paternalism and deference defined the lived environment. Carving out a place within which life could be sustained in this profoundly unequal social order was, for many poorer people, an achievement in itself.

Deference was neither universal nor total: there would always be those individuals who would not know their place. In 1588, the husbandman William Gallant criticised the esquire Edward Barnes for overstocking the commons of Soham (Cambridgeshire). Gallant accused Barnes of having broken the 'anncyent customes ... by lawes and orders', adding defiantly that although 'he veryly beleveth that there be div[er]s of the Towne of Soh[a]m that are affrayed to offend the said [Barnes] ... he this deponent doth not feare the threatenings or displeasure of [Barnes]'.[16] Many villages and towns had their own William Gallants. In some regions, whole communities developed reputations for a bolshie assertiveness. In recent years, the histories of some of those groups have been explored: they included the lead miners of the Derbyshire Peak Country; the people of the fenlands; the weavers of the Stour Valley and the Vale of Berkeley; the free miners and smallholders of the West Country forests; and many London artisans.[17]

---

[13] Roberta Pearson, 'Custer Loses Again: the Contestation over Commodified Public Memory', in *Cultural Memory and the Construction of Identity*, ed. Dan Ben-Amos and Liliane Weissberg (Detroit, 1999), 176–201, p. 180.

[14] Keith Wrightson, 'The Politics of the Parish in Early Modern England', *The Experience of Authority*, ed. Griffiths, Fox and Hindle, 10–46.

[15] Keith Snell, 'Deferential Bitterness: The Social Outlook of the Rural Proletariat in Eighteenth- and Nineteenth-Century England and Wales', in *Social Orders and Social Classes in Europe since 1500: Studies in Social Stratification*, ed. M. L. Bush (1992), 158–84.

[16] TNA, DL4/30/17.

[17] Andy Wood, *The Politics of Social Conflict: the Peak Country, 1520–1770* (Cambridge, 1999); Buchanan Sharp, *In Contempt of all Authority: Rural Artisans and Riot in the West of England 1586–1660* (Berkeley, 1980); John Walter, *Understanding Popular Violence in the*

In such communities, as deferential values were marginalised, paternalism came to mean less and less. Paternalism was 'dominant' in the sense that it represented the publically stated social values of the dominant class. But it was never 'dominant' in the sense of winning complete acceptance. In attempting to capture the complexities of early modern social relations we need to keep this in mind: for all that challenges to the status quo were often localised and limited, so deference and paternalism were partial, contested and contingent.

Yet paternalism and deference remained powerful impulses in a great many social environments. With his eye for a telling flash of detail, in a vivid passage in *English Society*, Wrightson takes his readers into a seventeenth-century alehouse to spy on the apprentice Roger Lowe, who 'bought drinks for his equals, but never for his superiors. They bought drinks for him and he, in turn, as a promising lad, listened deferentially to their opinions and advice.'[18] The moment is well chosen. It points to the everyday nature of deference and paternalism: these were forces that defined age, gender, class and household relations, and which were lodged in everyday exchanges, unspoken rules, body language and etiquette. Paternalism was widespread; providers included landlords, wealthier neighbours, employers, masters and mistresses, magistrates and vestrymen. The fruits of deference might include favour, advice, land, food, fuel, housing, perquisites, charity, poor relief, credit, office, advancement or employment. Flattery helped. When the widow Agnes Wingfield wondered in 1604 whether she should marry again, she sought the advice of her landlord 'for she thought it good to speake wth him before marriage to crave his good will that she might be welcome to his land'.[19] Much of everyday paternalism lies beyond the written record. But sometimes we catch fleeting glimpses: occasional handouts to paupers recorded in a gentleman's notebook; the Christmas gift of clothing and fuel scribbled in estate accounts; provision of medical care to a poor woman, noted in a clergyman's letter; a gentleman writing to a 'Brother' magistrate, interceding on behalf of an accused witch; a steward's suggestion that his lord sell some calves 'to poore men at good prices'; a landowner allowing 'pore men' to place their horses on his pastures; a minister in a dearth year

English Revolution: The Colchester Plunderers (Cambridge, 1999); Clive Holmes, 'Drainers and Fenmen: The Problem of Popular Political Consciousness in the Seventeenth Century', in *Order and Disorder in Early Modern England*, ed. Anthony Fletcher and John Stevenson (Cambridge, 1985), 166–95; David Rollison, *The Local Origins of Modern Society: Gloucestershire 1500–1800* (1992); Keith Lindley, *Fenland Riots and the English Revolution* (1982); Norah Carlin, 'Liberty and Fraternities in the English Revolution: The Politics of the London Artisans' Protests, 1635–1659', *International Review of Social History* 39 (1994), 223–54.

[18] Wrightson, *ES*, 63. For the rupture of one alehouse code, see Susana Narotkzy and Gavin A. Smith, *Immediate Struggles: People, Power and Place in Rural Spain* (Berkeley, 2006), 186.

[19] Lichfield Joint Record Office, B/C/5/1604: Matrimony, Wirksworth.

opening his glebe lands to the use of 'my power neyghbours of this p[ar]ysh', each to have an acre 'the powrest having the first choise wtout paying any rent therfor'.[20] All of these small kindnesses mattered; they blunted the sharp edge of class relations, softening the experience of authority. Taken in aggregate, they comprised a distinct element within the early modern mode of social relations, holding together what was otherwise a harshly unequal social order.

Paternalism worked most effectively when operative within face-to-face social contexts. In 1596, a Petworth (Sussex) shearman noted that because the poor people who had settled in his village 'had the greater favour of the Tenntts', they had been allowed to erect cottages on the common. Moreover, if the Petworth tenants felt that a poor cottager sought only to keep a few animals upon the common, 'he maye doe yt and never be denyed yt of the other Tenntts yf they see he be a poore man and that he ys not able other-wise to provide yt but this at the gentleness of the other Tenntts'.[21] Even in the hard years of the 1590s, then, there could still be room for 'gentleness'. Looking back on his life from the 1650s, Bishop Godfrey Goodman recalled his happy days as a parish minister in pre-revolutionary Essex. He thanked God that in the parishes he had served there had been (in his remembrance) no beggars, alehouses, legal cases, quarrels, felonies, violent deaths or illicit fornication. Moreover, 'in the weeke dayes noe laboring man ever wanted a dayes worke' and 'on the Sunday noe poore man dined at his owne howse but was ever invited'.[22] Modern-day social historians would probably have found Goodman's parish a bit dull: apparently, there was no riot, serious crime, witchcraft, slander, no discriminatory systems of poor relief, or, it would seem, any of the other indicators of conflict which social historians have grown used to charting.

Having suggested that paternalist ethics underwrote a wide range of relationships – master and servant, employer and worker, rich and poor, overseer and pauper – for the rest of this chapter I concentrate on the rela-tionship between the gentry and that varied body of non-gentle men and women whom the Levellers knew as the 'lower and middle sort of people'.[23]

---

[20] S. Robertson, 'The Expense-Book of James Master, esq., AD 1646 to 1676', *Archaeologia Cantiana* 15 (1883), 161, 165, 174, 184, 185, 194; J. V. Beckett, *The Aristocracy in England, 1660–1914* (Oxford, 1986), 354–5; Pettit, *Royal Forests*, 175 n. 2; Lord Leconfield, *Sutton and Duncton Manors* (Oxford, 1956), 64; Sheffield Archives, BFM/2/88; *The Oxinden Letters, 1607–1642: Being the Correspondence of Henry Oxinden of Barham and his Circle*, ed. D. Gardiner (1933), 220–3; Essex Record Office, D/P 135/1/1, fol. 100v. For other instances, see Alan Everitt, 'Farm Labourers', in *Rural Society: Landowners, Peasants and Labourers, 1500–1750*, ed. Christopher Clay (Cambridge, 1990), 161–230, pp. 204–5; TNA, E134/1Jasl/Trin7.

[21] West Sussex Record Office [WSRO], PHA 5449, fols 64r, 65r.

[22] Wren Library, Trinity College Cambridge, MS C.6.3, unpaginated endpaper.

[23] Wrightson's work on the language of social description remains unsurpassed: 'Estates, Degrees and Sorts: Changing Perceptions of Society in Tudor and Stuart England', in

Paternalism assumes deference.[24] That deference may be forced; or it may be genuinely felt.[25] In many cases, the reality is likely to fall somewhere between these polarities, producing a partial, conditional deference which none the less damages subalterns' collective agency.[26] Patrick Joyce puts this well: 'Deference is to be construed as a continuum of feeling in which the affective and the coerced are never strangers, and the inwards and the outward never distinct ... Deference [has] a real inwardness.'[27]

Tudor and Stuart gentry were highly sensitive to body language.[28] This was clear in the embodied rituals that often underwrote public encounters between gentry and their subordinates.[29] Rituals of subordination were intended to demonstrate the structural imbalance of power: bodily and/ or verbal subservience was to be met with a show of authority – be that gracious kindness or patriarchal sternness. Deliberate disruption of such etiquette was one response, transgressing ritual forms in order symbolically to break dominant norms.[30] Alternatively, repentant plebeians, apologising for taking fuel from a lord's wood or for breaking his fences, were expected to kneel and perhaps also to weep before the lord would grant pardon.[31] It was not unusual for the authors of written petitions to deploy an image of themselves beseeching their superiors 'upon our bended kneese to take according to your wonted maner and Christian practise our condition in to your compassion'.[32] Admission as the tenant of a lord could be equally

Language, History and Class, ed. Penelope Corfield (Oxford, 1991), 30–52; *idem*, 'Sorts of People in Tudor and Stuart England', in *The Middling Sort of People: Culture, Society and Politics in England, 1550–1800*, ed. Jonathan Barry and Christopher Brooks (Basingstoke, 1994), 28–51.

[24] Daniel Miller, 'The Limits of Dominance', in *Domination and Resistance*, ed. D. Miller, M. Rowlands and C. Tilley (1989), 63–79, p. 64.

[25] The classic statement of the former view is James C. Scott, *Domination and the Arts of Resistance: Hidden Transcripts* (New Haven, 1990).

[26] Andy Wood, 'Subordination, Solidarity and the Limits of Popular Agency in a Yorkshire Valley, c.1596–1615', *P&P* 193 (2006), 41–72; *idem*, 'Fear, Hatred and the Hidden Injuries of Class in Early Modern England', *JSH* 39:1 (2006), 803–26.

[27] Joyce, *Work, Society and Politics*, 95. For a different tone, see Eugene D. Genovese, *Roll, Jordan, Roll: The World the Slaves Made* (New York, 1974), 5–6.

[28] Anna Bryson, 'The Rhetoric of Status: Gesture, Demeanour and the Image of the Gentleman in Sixteenth- and Seventeenth-Century England', in *Renaissance Bodies: the Human Figure in English Culture, c.1540–1660*, ed. Lucy Gent and Nigel Llewellyn (1990), 136–53; John Walter, 'Gesturing at Authority: Deciphering the Gestural Code of Early Modern England', in *The Politics of Gesture: Historical Perspectives*, ed. Michael Braddick, *P&P* Supplement 4 (2009), 96–127.

[29] Edward Muir, *Ritual in Early Modern Europe* (Cambridge, 1997), 3–6.

[30] Victor Turner, *Dramas, Fields and Metaphors: Symbolic Action in Human Society* (Ithaca, 1974), 37–42.

[31] For examples, see TNA, DL4/109/8; TNA, STAC8/227/3.8.

[32] TNA, C115/52/3655.

ritualistic. In 1523, John Fitzherbert described the ceremony of homage, explaining how the tenant

> shalbe ungirde and his heed uncovered and the lorde shall syt & the tenaunt shall knele before hym on bothe his knees and shall holde his handes stretched out togyder bytwene the lordes hands and shall saye thus. I become your man from this day forwarde of lyfe and of membre and of worldely honour. And to you shall be faythfull and lowly and shall beare faythe to you for the landes and teneme[n]tes the which I holde of you ... and the lorde so sytting shall kysse his tenau[n]t the which is a sygne of perfy[c]te love[33]

Such exchanges mattered. Historians have attempted to distinguish 'real' feelings of plebeian anger from the outward show of subordination.[34] In so doing, however, one of the key points about the social organisation of public emotion has been missed: rituals of humiliation, however much their participants may have kept inner thoughts to themselves, helped to define an order in which plebeian subordination was routine. Critically, this was materially embodied: authority and deference were written into gesture, speech and silence.

Formal gift exchange is often a characteristic of paternalism: thus, gentlemen and gentlewomen cherished the 'kynde pore mans harty rewarde' of gratitude for their charity.[35] Gervase Holles recalled how his Tudor ancestor Sir William Gervase 'would often say that the whole country was his garden: for [as a reward for his renowned hospitality] if there was anything in it rare or delicate he was sure to have it presented to him'.[36] A good reputation within one's 'country' was essential to the gentry; without it, they were worth much less.[37] The earl of Northumberland's exploitation of his tenants certainly increased his revenue. But it was achieved at the cost of his social standing. As Lord Henry Howard observed in 1602, the earl was

[33] J. Fitzherbert, *Here Begynneth a Ryght Frutefull Mater: and Hath to Name the Boke of Surveyinge and Improvme[n]tes* (1523), fol. 31v.
[34] This deserved fuller attention than it received in Andy Wood, '"Poore Men Woll Speke One Daye": Plebeian Languages of Deference and Defiance in England, c.1520–1640', in *Politics of the Excluded*, ed. Harris, 67–98.
[35] Felicity Heal, 'Food Gifts, the Household and the Politics of Exchange in Early Modern England', *P&P* 199 (2008), 41–70, p. 46. On the social logic of gift exchange, see Marcel Fafchamps, 'Solidarity Networks in Preindustrial Societies: Rational Peasants with a Moral Economy', *Economic Development and Cultural Change* 41:1 (1992), 147–74, p. 161.
[36] *Memorials of the Holles family, 1493–1656 by Gervase Holles*, ed. A. C. Wood, Camden Society 3rd ser. 55 (1937), 46. For a dispute over gifts to the poor, see TNA, REQ2/129/45.
[37] For the sensitivity of gentry to suggestions that they lacked charity or were harsh landlords, see Cheshire Record Office, EDC5 (1604) 66, Aldford; Sheffield Archives, BFM/2/88; TNA, STAC8/107/5.

'followed by none ... no, not by the gentlemen or peasants of his country in respect of his vexation and sport'.[38] The need for the gentry to maintain their local status gave their subordinates room for manoeuvre. When the widow Margaret Dickens of Froyston (Nottinghamshire) petitioned Sir Charles Cavendish for a reduction in her rents, she concluded her petition as follows: 'youre peticoner as dutie doth bynd [shall] daylie pray to the almightie for the preservation of yor estate & health and all happiness longe to continue'.[39] Such expressions are formulaic: therein lies their significance – they express everyday social expectations. In this case, both sides gained something: Sir Charles got the widow's prayers to a God known to favour the entreaties of the poor; Margaret Dickens got a lower rent.

Hierarchical ideas naturalised social inequality. Writing in the 1630s, the gentleman John Smyth regretted the end of serfdom in Aklington (Gloucestershire):

> if any thinke this kind of dominion [that is, serfdom] not to bee lawfull, yet surely it is naturall: And certainly wee finde not such a latitude of difference in any creature, as in the nature of man; wherin the wisest excel the most foolish of men by farre greater degree then the most foolish of men doth surpasse the wisest of beasts ... a man is animal politicum, apt even by nature to comaund or to obey every one in his proper degree.[40]

Smyth here recycled the central organising assumptions of early modern social authoritarianism: that some were born to command and others to obey; that it had always been so; and that it would always be so. These represented propositions about both past and present. Thus, the individual who defers to superiors does so 'because he takes [elite] superiority for granted, as part of the natural order of things'; this behaviour is generated by 'the continuing effect of tradition' and is seen as characteristic of 'traditional society'. A deferential society, therefore, is 'consensual in its political and social relations but hierarchical in its distribution of power and authority' and the authority of its rulers is taken to be 'natural'.[41]

In the prescriptive literature of the time, Tudor and Stuart society was typically conceptualised as a corporate body, comprising a sequence of clearly

---

[38] *Advice to his Son by Henry Percy, Ninth Earl of Northumberland* (1609), ed. G. B. Harrison (1930), 24. For the local context, see Andy Wood, '"Some Banglyng about the Customes": Riot, Resistance and Popular Memory in a Sussex village, 1549–1640' (forthcoming).

[39] Nottinghamshire Archives, DD/4P/52/231. See also Nottingham University Library, Mi6/177/144.

[40] John Maclean, ed., *The Berkeley Manuscripts*, 3 vols (Gloucester, 1885), III, 43.

[41] Pocock, 'Classical Theory of Deference', 516; Richard R. Beeman, 'Deference, Republicanism and the Emergence of Popular Politics in Eighteenth-Century America', *William and Mary Quarterly* 3rd ser. 49 (1992), 401–30, p. 403.

delineated social blocs, the welfare of each of which was dependent upon all the others. Paternalism comprised the fulcrum of this social structure, built upon the notion that, in a harsh and unpredictable world, rich and poor needed one another. Clientage networks stretched through the whole social fabric, from the monarch dispensing noble titles to the parish overseer extending relief. Thus, it was well remembered by the Jacobean inhabitants of Bradborne (Kent) how, in 1574, 'Certayne Rich men' had tried to break the customary arrangements governing common rights. They had been faced down by the lord, Sir Thomas Scott, who had 'caused the court rolls of the said mannor to be produced and read … wherein the said Custome and usage and bylawe was written and … upon his command herein the … greedy minded Ten[a]nts did desiste from theire … oppression'.[42] When the time came, gentlemen and women expected to be able to call upon the reciprocal loyalty of those for whom they had done such favours.[43]

Edward Thompson has argued that paternalism 'was as much theatre and gesture as effective responsibility … far from a warm, household, face-to-face relationship we can observe a studied technique of rule'.[44] This is at best a two-dimensional assessment. There is little doubt that gentry *could* be as cynical in their exercise of paternalism as could their social inferiors in their apparent displays of deference. But just as plebeian deference could be genuinely felt and just as the deferential impulse interacted with other (perhaps more antagonistic) thoughts, so gentry paternalism represented a more powerful and complex phenomenon than Thompson suggests. Paternalism could represent a significant check, for instance, upon the desires of lords to maximise their profits. In 1636, the Cheshire gentleman Sir Richard Grosvenor advised his son that he should 'Let your fines bee moderate & accept of such scirvises as may bee performed [by tenants] without just cawse of repineing, lest otherwise the poore tenant cry (with the oppressed Isaralites) unto God for ease & hee take theire cawse in hand.'[45] In 1604, Sir William Wentworth wrote a similar letter. He too felt that the pursuit of economic interest could conflict with Christian duties, advising his son to be '[j]ust and get nothing with a bad conscience. Avoide usury and selling anie thing to pore men to a long daie for a great pryce. Ne[v]er take a cruell advantage upon a mortgage, bonds &c of pore men.'[46] Wealth and power were felt by many gentry to come with certain conditions. Lord Burley warned his heir that he should 'Take no suit against a poor man, without

[42] TNA, C2/JasI/G5/70.

[43] For the activation of clientage networks, see TNA, REQ2/223/40; TNA, STAC3/3/46; TNA, STAC4/10/6.

[44] E. P. Thompson, *Customs in Common* (1991), 64.

[45] *The Papers of Sir Richard Grosvenor, 1st Bart. (1585–1645)*, ed. Richard Cust, Lancashire and Cheshire Record Society 84 (Stroud, 1996), 34.

[46] J. P. Cooper, ed., *Wentworth Papers, 1597–1628*, Camden Society 4th ser. 12 (1973), 21.

receiving much wrong: for besides that thou makest him thy competitor, it is a base conquest to triumph where there is small resistance.'[47]

We should not romanticise paternalism. Landlords might ameliorate the condition of those poorer or less powerful than themselves; but their ability to do so rested upon their position in a profoundly unequal social hierarchy. In presenting themselves as father-figures, gentry paternalists took upon themselves not only the duty to care, protect and guide, but also the authority to correct and punish. Challenges from below were to be stamped upon, even if later the magistrate responded positively to their demands.[48] This was explicit in the concept of magistracy – the paternalist responsibilities of the justice of the peace included the expectation that he would maintain the social order with necessary force.[49] Sir William Wentworth's hypersensitivity to rank was in part generated by some dark assumptions about human nature: he advised his son that if he found himself in the company of his inferiors to combine condescension with intimidation: 'he that wilbe honoured and feared in his cuntrie must beare countenance and authority: for people are servile, nott generous and do reverence men for feare, not for lo[v]e of their vertues'. Wentworth would have been unsurprised by the stress placed in recent anthropologies of power and resistance upon the superficiality of plebeian deference. He warned his heir against placing too much trust in his tenants, 'For notwithstanding all their fawning and flatterye, they seldom lo[v]e their landslorde in their hartes.'[50]

Seeming fixed and certain, in truth paternalism was shot through with anxieties; most notably there was a neurotic fear of levelling – and so, a tendency to see any sign of popular dissent as a fundamental challenge to the status quo. The dependence upon face-to-face relationships could make governors nervous: were displays of deference really to be trusted? Did tenants doff their caps solely from an expectation of reward? The ninth earl of Northumberland thought so. In 1609 he warned his son that in return for 'proffered service', the tenant 'intends to make you pay for their courtesy, for leases in reversion at under rates must declare your bountiful nature'.[51] When the gentleman handed out customary doles to the poor (the most

---

[47] *Annals of the Reformation*, ed. Strype, IV, 340. For a very similar formulation, see John Rylands Library, English MS 202, fol. 77r.

[48] John Walter and Keith Wrightson, 'Dearth and the Social Order in Early Modern England', *P&P* 71 (1976), 22–42.

[49] For the coercive underpinnings of magisterial paternalism, see Douglas Hay, 'Patronage, Paternalism and Welfare: Masters, Workers and Magistrates in Eighteenth-Century England', *International Labor and Working-Class History* 53 (1998), 27–48. See also comments in A. Russell, 'Local Elites and the Working-Class Response in the North-West, 1870–1895: Paternalism and Deference Reconsidered', *Northern History* 23 (1987), 154–5.

[50] Cooper, ed., *Wentworth Papers*, 12, 18.

[51] *Advice*, ed. Harrison, 53.

vivid example is the Tichborne Dole)[52] or he mounted feast days, were the common people laughing behind his back? The evidence of one much-quoted Gloucestershire proverb suggested so: 'A great housekeeper is sure of nothinge for his good cheare, save a great Turd at his gate.'[53] How, if we are to take paternalism and deference seriously, are we to account for such evidence?

One way of shifting the historiography of early modern social relations beyond the trading of examples of deference against counter-examples of social conflict might be by considering the broader cultural context within which social relations were operative. One important component of early modern culture was a respect for the past. Memory mattered in early modern England, perhaps to no class more than to the gentry: see, for instance, the emergence of antiquarianism, an intellectual pursuit tailored precisely to the desire of gentlemen and women to establish their ancient pedigrees.[54] Early modern gentry located themselves in a continuum that linked past, present and future, anxious not only to secure their reputation while they lived, but to see that their worth was communicated down the generations. As Lawrence Humfrey put it in 1563, 'All we good me[n] favour nobility, both, for it is profitable for the whole state, that they endevour to earne the state of their auncestours: and also, for the aged memorye of theyr weld-eserving sires of the commen wealth, (though dead) ought muche to avayle with us.'[55] The past also mattered to the common people of early modern England, albeit for different reasons: as the basis for systems of customary law, as the medium through which folkloric traditions were communicated, as a means of transmitting memories of earlier resistance, as a way of making sense of the world.

In what remains of this chapter, I explore the ways in which memories of past lordship informed social relations. I argue that we find in these memories a usable past which was deployed strategically not only to describe past events, but also to inform understandings of the present.[56] In this respect, memories of lordship went through a process of simplification and conden-sation which is often fundamental to collective remembering. As we shall see, those subordinates invoking memories of good lordship conjured up the

[52] John Walter is currently working on a major study of the Tichborne dole; for now, see Steve Hindle, *On the Parish? The Micro-Politics of Poor Relief in Rural England, c.1550–1750* (Oxford, 2004), 164–6.

[53] Maclean, ed., *Berkeley Manuscripts*, III, 27.

[54] Jan Broadway, *'No Historie So Meete': Gentry Culture and the Development of Local History in Elizabethan and Early Stuart England* (Manchester, 2006); Richard Cust, 'Catholicism, Antiquarianism and Gentry Honour: the Writings of Sir Thomas Shirley', *Midland History* 23 (1998), 40–70.

[55] L. Humfrey, *The Nobles or of the Nobilitye* (London, 1563), fols 50r–v. For an idealised account of the charity and hospitality of past gentry, see L. Jewitt, 'An Unpublished Elegy by Leonard Wheatcroft', *The Reliquary* 6 (1865–6), 45–8.

[56] Henry Steele Commager, *The Search For a Usable Past* (New York, 1967).

paternalist ideal, but in locating it in the past, they drew a sharp contrast with the present.

Good lords and kind monarchs were often lodged within local memory. The gift of common land to Newnton (Wiltshire) by King Athelstan, supported by Athelstan's consort and her knight, Sir Walter, was commemorated every year by the inhabitants, who (John Aubrey noted in 1687) would process from house to house, praying not only for 'the good posterity of our soveraigne Lord King Hen. VIII and his Royall Issue', for King Charles II and for the nobility, but also for 'King Athelstan & Dame Maud his good Queen [who gave] this ground to our forefathers & to us, and to all them that shall come after us, and to all them that shall come after us in Fee for ever'. They also prayed for the soul of 'Sr Walter the good black knight, that moved his heart to our forefathers' and for Abbot Loringe, who built the Earl House where they met.[57] Mendip miners held that their free mining rights had been granted by a nobleman called Lord Chocke; in 1675 they cited his laws against 'ill disposed persons' who were 'endeavouring to break the old ancient custom of Mendipp'.[58] The tenants of seventeenth-century Epworth (Lincolnshire) believed that they owed their common land to their fourteenth-century lord, John de Mowbray. A charter granted by de Mowbray was locked in a chest in the parish church, set 'under a window, wherein was the portraicture of Mowbray set in ancient glass, holding in his hand a writing which was commonly reputed to be an emblem of the deed'.[59]

All of this defined the popular sense of what a good lord should be. A good lord should respect and defend local custom: in 1570, Norfolk witnesses recalled how their mid-century lord Sir John Cornwallis had refused to refer to a false custumal drawn up by his corrupt predecessor, and had instead protected the villagers' common rights.[60] A good lord should be generous: the Somerset widow Anne Satie remembered in 1619 how 'ladie Hopkins that now is gave this dep[onen]t three young oaks to build her howse'.[61] Some folkloric traditions suggested that good lordship had its rewards: 287 years after the event, there endured a local tale that, following defeat at the Battle of Stoke in 1487, the lord of the manor of Ulverston (Westmorland) had escaped to his estate 'where he lived a good while incognito among his Tenants there, who were so kind unto him as to maintaine & conceal him; & he dying there, they buryed him, whose grave is yet knowne & there to

[57] BL, Lansdowne MS 231, fol. 187v; see also *Wiltshire*, ed. Jackson, 272–3.

[58] J. W. Gough, ed., *Mendip Mining Orders, 1683–1749*, Somerset Record Society 49, supplement (Taunton, 1973), 6–7. For Lord Chocke's customs see Wiltshire and Swindon Archives, 161/133.

[59] Holmes, 'Drainers and Fenmen', 192.

[60] TNA, DL4/12/6.

[61] TNA, E134/17Jas1/Hil9.

be seen'.[62] Given early modern people's regard for their 'posterity', it was essential that good lords had their reward beyond the grave. Writing in the Interregnum, Gervase Holles noted the popular reputation of his Elizabethan ancestor, Sir William Gervase: 'He was of so noble a nature and so good a disposition that even to theis dayes (among the country people) he is mentioned by the name of "good Sir William" and "the good lord of Houghton".'[63]

The gentry's regard for the reputation of their house made them sensitive to suggestions that their actions might harm their 'posterity'. The commons knew this and exploited it. Thus in 1650, the tenants of Litton (Derbyshire) wrote to the earl of Rutland asking for his intercession against an enclosing landlord. They linked their 'posteritie' to that of the House of Haddon, warning that

> as we cannot be insensible of that imm[in]ent danger which threatens us & our posteritie, soe are wee very sensible of the mouths which will be opened against & that vaile of disgrace which would be drawen over that Ancient and Ho[noura]ble house of Hadden if this should be written of her & recorded to future generations that she deserted her tenants & sold them over into the hands of a merciless man who endeavours at least the temporall destruction of them & consequently of the whole country.[64]

When the inhabitants of Ely petitioned the bishop against the drainage of their fens, they struck a similar tone, recalling how

> The memorable B[ishops] Abbotts & Priors of former ages (R[ight] Hon[or]able & very good L[ords]) seated in Ely & other places wthin the Isle & confines of the same besid[e]s their church government have been very carefull patrons & industrious travel[e]rs for the generall good of the common wealth of those p[art]s to their eternall prayse.[65]

The inhabitants of Jacobean Framsden (Suffolk) were also able to draw upon local history, showing to Star Chamber in 1618 that whereas their current lord was trying to undermine their copyhold tenures, upon sight of documentation proving the tenants' rights, his father had retreated from that policy, saying that the tenants were 'his good neighboures and his loving Tennants [and that he] did not meane to be worse to them then his Ancestors'.[66] It was a common claim that good lordship existed only in the past. In Chewton (Somerset), the 'ancient people' remembered in 1676 that in

62 Cumbria Record Office, Carlisle, DLONS/L12/2/18.
63 *Memorials*, ed. Wood, 45.
64 Sheffield Archives, Bagshawe Collection 2094.
65 Cambridge University Library, EDR/A/8/1, p. 94.
66 TNA, STAC8/284/24.

earlier years they used to give certain dues to the lord out of favour to him, 'the lord beinge then kind to his tennts'.[67] In 1686, Peak Country miners contrasted the restriction of their free mining rights by the lord of Newton Grange with the easier attitude of his grandfather, who not only allowed them to dig where they pleased but used 'frequently [to] bid the workemen that were mining in the said grounds god speed'.[68] Such generosity could cut both ways. In a similar case in 1623, miners from Wirksworth (Derbyshire) explained that in former times they had not pressed their claim to dig for lead in Steeple Grange because the owner 'was a very good housekeep[er] & generaly beloved of all the miners ... the myners did forebeare to worke in the Steeple farme rather for love than any other causes'.[69]

These memories were mobilised to a very deliberate purpose: to underpin open social criticism. Nostalgia, a powerful force in popular memory, here provided a kind of agency enabling subordinates, through praising the decencies of long-dead governors, to undercut gentle authority in the present.[70] The capacity of common people to deploy nostalgia in this way is clearest in depositions taken in 1596 during the dispute between the ninth earl of Northumberland and his Petworth tenants. Witnesses conjured up images of a lost world of paternalism and social harmony. Richard Lindars, a 72-year-old husbandman, remembered how the copyholders had once been 'gently handled ... in paeing of theire fynes'. The customs for sub-letting land were arranged to favour the tenant, 'especially if he were a poore man'. Lindars recalled how, upon the death of a 'poore man' whose estate did not include an animal that could be claimed as a heriot, the lord would decline to take anything. The basis of this harmony lay in the regulations for the governance of the manor: courts met regularly and enjoyed considerable powers; manorial officers were 'substaunciall wise men'; finally, the manorial customs 'did sett much quietness and ease betweene ... the lorde and the Tennants'.[71] William Bullaker provided further detail, describing the state of Petworth in the 1550s, when the manor was held by the Crown. At that time the manor had been surveyed, and the tenants had asked the surveyor to see that the fines be fixed. The surveyor

> tould theym that they needed not to make any suche request sayinge they were the kings Tennts and were favorablye used and payed noe fynes but suche as were reasonable and easye For ... yor fine ys smale ynoughe ... and yor custome ys for auncyent [time] that you neede not to feare anye newe pr[e]sedents for payinge

[67] TNA, E134/27ChasII/Mich9.
[68] TNA, DL4/124/1686/7.
[69] TNA, DL4/72/31.
[70] On nostalgia as agency, see the brilliant discussion in Ben Jones, 'The Uses of Nostalgia: Autobiography, Community Publishing and Working-Class Neighbourhoods in Post-War England', *Cultural and Social History* 7 (2010), 355–74.
[71] WSRO, PHA 7362, fols 203r, 209r, 266r–7r.

greater fynes And therefore ... praye for yor prince; and as you are nowe so there ys noe doubte but you shall bee well used hereafter.[72]

Harmony, it was recalled, defined all aspects of social relations in mid-sixteenth-century Petworth: the prosperous copyholders in turn supported their poorer neighbours. The sources of their prosperity were their customs and their good lord. This formed a stark contrast, said Lindars, to the state of the village in 1596:

> he well knoweth that a greate many of the same tennanuts of late tyme and at this day whose p[re]decessors having no greater charge than those now Tenna-nuts have are greatly decayed and ympoverished and lyve very barely and poorely upon theire copyholds over theire said p[re]decessors did & have muche a doe (although they be not evyll husbands) ... wherea[s] theire predecssors were wealthy men & able to doe for theire frends of neede had beene But the nowe Tennaunts cannot doe so.[73]

The same sense of changed times was articulated in 1581 by the copyholders of Combe (Suffolk) in a petition to their lord, Sir Nathaniel Bacon. 'Here-tofore', they explained, when the lord took timber from copyhold land, the tenants 'have usuallye of custome had the toppes therein', but this right was now denied by Bacon's steward, 'which heretofore have never been'. The copyholders noted that

> not knowinge whether yt be to your worship knowne or not, aswell what o[u]r custome hath been heretofore as also nowe the denyall to yor pore tenants theirof made ... we trusting your worshippe will be so favourable unto us, as to let us nowe have such customes, as by the former lords of the same manor have been usuallye accustomed[74]

Perhaps the most cutting deployment of memories of past lordship was to be found in the libel from Norwich in 1596 which denounced the county gentry. The anonymous author, punning upon the surname of one of the leading gentlemen of Norfolk, observed bitterly that 'Sir William Paston, who might have been called Passion for his former pity ... now is Paston because he is become as hard as a stone.'[75]

Witnesses in a Chancery case of 1630 concerning the manor of Lylley (Hertfordshire) contrasted their current lord, Thomas Docwra, who had enclosed their common, raised dues and restricted fuel rights, with his father and grandfather. The aged yeoman Edward Spencer, recalling his days as a

---

[72] WSRO, PHA 7362, fols 147r–8r.
[73] WSRO, PHA 7362, fols 204r–5r.
[74] Cambridge University Library, Hengrave Hall MS 90, unlisted petition 23 May 1581.
[75] HMC, *Salisbury*, XIII, 168–9.

servant in the household of the lord's grandfather (also named Thomas), described a conversation he had overheard between the grandfather and the current lord's father, Edward Docwra:

> he heard … Mr Edward Docwra saye to his father Mr Thomas Docwra, the grand-father, that he marveiled that he would not comon with his sheepe upon Lilley hooe seinge that he … had land lyeing in their Comon fields of Lilley And the same Mr Thomas Docwra then answered to the said Edward Docwra … shall I that have peacablye lived thus longe wth my neighbors begin nowe to wrangle wth them and trouble them, thou art a very foole Ned I will not meddle wth it And was verye angrye wth him for it

Francis Taverner, a local gentleman who supported the tenants, also had positive memories of Thomas Docwra senior, who had employed Taverner as his steward. Taverner remembered the grandfather for his 'wisedome & integritye', adding that

> he lived in all the tyme of this deponts knowledge who were neer twentye yeares of age at his said Grandfathers death wthout anye suite in lawe or anie differ-ence wth the tennts of his said mannor of Lylley being verye much beloved & respected bothe by his Tennts & neighbors[76]

The memories of past social harmony that circulated in Petworth and Lylley might be understood as mythic in that they occluded historical realities, distilling a complicated past into a simple essence, producing 'a world which is without contradictions'.[77] Far from being the neutral bearer of past knowl-edge into the present, it has here been argued that collective memory was an active and dynamic force: what is remembered and how it is remembered is contingent, unstable and potentially political.

It may be objected that the memories with which this chapter has dealt are generic, adopting the same form in one historical period as in another, such that subordinates employ positive memories of past superiors in order to criticise the behaviour of their successors. Way beyond our period, nostalgia was employed in this manner. Writing in 1848, the Lancashire radical Samuel Bamford had this to say of his grandfather's days:

> Gentlemen then lived as they ought to live; as real gentlemen will ever be found living; in kindliness with their tenants; in open-handed charity towards the poor; and in hospitality to all friendly comers. There were no grinding bailiffs and land-stewards in those days, to stand betwixt the gentleman and his labourer, or his tenant; to screw up rents, to screw down livings, and to invent and transact all little meannesses for so much per annum … The gentleman transacted his

---

[76] TNA, C21/S15/1.
[77] Roland Barthes, *Mythologies* (1957; Eng. trans., 1972), 142–3.

own business; he met his farmer, or his labourer, face to face. When he did that which was wrong, he was told of it in unmistakeable language; or, at any rate, he stood a good chance of being so told. When he did that which was right – which was noble-hearted – he got blessings, no doubt, and made friends who stood by him whilst living, and spoke well of him when dead; and that is a kind of speaking of which one does not hear over-much now-a-days.[78]

Reading Bamford's words in the light of what has gone before in this chapter, we might ask in what respect the memories of the copyholders of Lylley and Petworth differed from those conjured up by Samuel Bamford two centuries later. It would seem that very little had changed. Or had it?

The urge to essentialise social memory – to see in it merely a set of generic qualities that transcend time and space – risks turning social history into a kind of ahistorical mush, confirming conservative assessments of the field as defined by a 'charming quality of timelessness'.[79] The historian of memory needs to attend not only to the content of what is remembered, but also to the context within which remembering occurs. It has been argued in this chapter that social memory has historically specific qualities that are not easily transferable from one age to another. In this respect, there is a very important distinction to be drawn between popular memories of lordship in the sixteenth and seventeenth centuries and those of the early nineteenth century. When early modern working people recalled memories of pater-nalism in order to indict the actions of their current superiors, they held up their rulers' actions to the ethical standards to which those rulers claimed to adhere, and to which it was hoped they would return. Dominant discourses, in other words, were deployed in order to criticise local representatives of the dominant class. In contrast, in the early nineteenth century, memories of past paternalism were invoked in order to compare a vanished social world with the harsh values of its *permanent* replacement. It is for this reason that the voices of the nineteenth-century working-class are so often inflected by a sense of longing for a lost world. Parliamentary enclosure, the workhouse and the factory system not only produced new forms of exploitation but also generated a profound sense of historical rupture. It does no good for the twenty-first-century historian to protest that historical realities were more complicated than this; the sense that a long-established social contract had been permanently breached ran like a red thread through early working-class culture.

The new experiences of the nineteenth century were felt and under-stood within historically produced cultures: senses of the past were, for many working people, central to the process of class formation. In this respect, early nineteenth-century working-class culture inherited from its

78 *The Autobiography of Samuel Bamford*, ed. W. H. Chaloner, 2 vols (1967), I, 19–20.
79 G. R. Elton, *Return to Essentials: Some Reflections on the Present State of Historical Study* (Cambridge, 1991), 117.

early modern predecessors the sense that, in forcing new forms of exploitation upon them, their rulers were breaking old, inherited patterns of paternalism, custom and reciprocity. What differed was the nineteenth-century sense that this breach was *permanent* and *far from local*. In this context, especially for rural workers, the experience of parliamentary enclosure was central. Even for those who had not been born to see the hedges planted, the gates erected and the ditches dug, the social memory of enclosure conditioned a sense of lost rights that was vital to early working-class political culture. For nineteenth-century workers, the loss of common rights meant more than a simply material process of deprivation. It meant the loss of a distinct physical space that, in many villages, had provided the basis for a sense of community. In the destruction of the commons, the opponents of enclosure argued, something more than common rights was lost: a kind of social contract between ruler and ruled was *permanently* broken. This sense of *final* rupture was one of the things that made the working-class culture of the early nineteenth century qualitatively different from that of early modern working people; and it, too, was embedded in memory and encoded in a specific sense of landscape.[80] Let us finish where we started. John Clare provides us with the starkest sense of how this sense of political dispossession, ecological destruction and material immiseration came to be written upon the land. This was the world he had lost:

> There once were days, the woodman knows it well
> When shades e'en echoed with the singing thrush;
> There once were hours, the ploughman's tale can tell,
> When morning's beauty wore its earliest blush
> How woodlarks caroll'd from each stumpy bush;
> Lubin himself has mark'd them soar and sing:
> The thorns are gone, the woodlark's song is hush,
> Spring more resembles winter now than spring,
> The shades are banish'd all – the birds have took to wing
>
> There once were lanes in nature's freedom dropt,
> There once were paths that every valley wound –
> Inclosure came, and every path was stopt;
> Each tyrant fix'd his sign where paths were found,
> To hint a trespass now who cross'd the ground:
> Justice is made to speak as they command;
> The high road now must be each stinted bound
> – Inclosure, thou'rt a curse upon the land,
> And tasteless was the wretch who thy existence plann'd[81]

---

[80] For a fuller statement of this argument, see the closing chapter of Andy Wood, *The Memory of the People: Custom and Popular Senses of the Past in Early Modern England* (Cambridge, forthcoming).

[81] *John Clare: Selected Poems*, ed. W. Tribble and A. Tribble (1965), 50–1.

11

Work, Reward and Labour Discipline in Late Seventeenth-Century England

STEVE HINDLE

In June 1692, Sir Richard Newdigate of Arbury near Nuneaton (Warwickshire) condemned the indolence of one of the agricultural labourers who was employed on his estate. William Suffolk, he noted, 'lyes abed and will not work'.[1] Complaints of this kind were entirely characteristic of an economic context in which, for the first time in well over a century, the fortunes of employers, and especially of landlords, were being undermined by falling rents, stagnant prices and increasing wages.[2] Because labour was in relatively short supply in late seventeenth-century England, it was believed that 'the very fabric of society could be threatened, not just by rising wages and costs, but by a swelling independence among the working masses, which commonly manifested itself in a refusal to engage wholeheartedly in unremitting toil'. There was, accordingly, a growing consensus, emerging among the propertied elite in the century after 1650, about the 'utility of poverty'.[3] Employers, magistrates and political economists alike agreed both in print and in the administration of social policy that 'the higher the wages labourers and artisans received, the less they worked, and that, while low wages bred industry and diligence, high wages bred laziness, disorderliness and debauchery'.[4] This, then, was a particularly troubling time in the long history of labour relations and it presented particular challenges to

---

[1] Warwick County Record Office [WCRO], CR136/V17, p. 227 (1692).
[2] Margaret Gay Davies, 'Country Gentry and Falling Rents in the 1660s and 1670s', *Midland History* 4 (1977), 86–96. Christopher Clay, 'Landlords and Estate Management', in *The Agrarian History of England and Wales*, V: *1640–1750*, II: *Agrarian Change*, ed. Joan Thirsk (Cambridge, 1985), 230–2; D. R. Hainsworth, *Stewards, Lords and People: The Estate Steward and His World in Later Stuart England* (Cambridge, 1992), 54–5; John Broad, *Transforming English Rural Society: The Verneys and the Claydons, 1600–1820* (Cambridge, 2004), 141–2.
[3] John Hatcher, 'Labour, Leisure and Economic Thought before the Nineteenth Century', *P&P* 160 (1998), 64.
[4] *Ibid.*, 69.

employers who sought not only to recruit, retain and discipline the labour force but also to incentivise productivity among their employees.

As Keith Wrightson has argued, employers like Sir Richard Newdigate were attempting to discipline their workforce in the context of a highly distinctive labour market – one which was highly localised; differentiated by skill, by gender and by age; and shaped by the seasonal and irregular pattern of the demand for work.[5] These structural characteristics ensured that 'full-time' employment as modern observers would recognise it was almost unknown: late seventeenth-century labour forces generally consisted only of a very small core of partially employed workers surrounded by a much larger penumbra of even more casual labour. The employment found by most labouring people in the century after the Restoration was often 'so precarious and uncertain that they could not give it a name'.[6]

The identification of these characteristics nonetheless raises almost as many issues as it resolves. Historians might identify the structural factors – the seasonality of demand, for example, or the gendered and life-cyclical points of entry and exit – which governed access to labour markets. They might reconstruct the strategies through which employers attempted to control a workforce reputedly more interested in leisure than in labour. They might even speculate about the ways in which labourers may have carved out a certain social and psychological space of their own.[7] But they are confronted at every turn by the limitations of the evidence for the relationship between work, remuneration and standards of living among the labour force. The sheer irregularity of work makes it nearly impossible for historians to convert wage rates into annual earnings.[8] Even if it *were* possible, moreover, to calculate the cumulative contribution of wages to the household incomes of a labouring population working in an economy of diversified resources (and some historians have tried[9]), annual earnings mean little in the absence of evidence of household expenditure – on rent, on food, on clothing, perhaps even on those consumer goods which might constitute their material wealth – with the result that the *value* of work to those who actually undertook it in late seventeenth- and early eighteenth-century England remains obscure.[10]

It is in this tantalising context that this paper attempts to reconstruct the experience of work among the agricultural labour force employed on a late seventeenth-century gentry estate, that of Sir Richard Newdigate,

5 Wrightson, *EN*, 308–20.
6 *Ibid.*, 313.
7 *Ibid.*, 322.
8 *Ibid.*, 312–13.
9 Sara Horrell and Jane Humphries, 'Old Questions, New Data, and Alternative Perspectives: Families' Living Standards in the Industrial Revolution', *Journal of Economic History* 52 (1992), 849 80.
10 Wrightson & Levine, *Terling*, 36–42.

second baronet of Arbury Hall in the parish of Chilvers Coton, near Nuneaton (Warwickshire).[11] The unique combination of evidence generated by
Newdigate's impulse to measure his landed, mineral and human resources
at Arbury permits more detailed delineation of Wrightson's intuitive sketch
of 'lives of labour'. By correlating the remarkable 1684 'census-type listing'
(by name, by age, by occupation, by relationship to household head) of the
inhabitants of the parish of Chilvers Coton not only with the rentals generated as part of Newdigate's 'great survey' of his estate in 1681–84, but also
with a wages book which records the tasks performed by, and the daily- and/
or piece-rates paid to, labourers and craftsmen at Arbury every day of the
year for the three years between 1688 and 1691, it is possible to analyse
the size, structure and participation rate of the agricultural workforce; the
range of jobs undertaken and the skills thought requisite to perform them;
and the relationship between work, remuneration and other types of reward.
It also invites speculation about the contribution of estate earnings to the
household economies of a significant proportion of Newdigate tenants.[12]
The paper accordingly speaks to wider issues that have been of perennial
interest to students of seventeenth- and early eighteenth-century social and
economic change: the nature and extent of independence among labouring
populations[13]; the character and dynamics of 'paternalism'[14]; and perhaps
even the standard of living debate.[15] In its focus on an estate employer,
furthermore, it offers a remarkable opportunity to analyse relations with
the different constituencies – in particular with servants in husbandry;
with regularly employed agricultural labourers and craftsmen; and with the
seasonal workforce of women and children – with whom the landed classes
had to deal; and to reconstruct the terms on which those dealings were

[11] This paper is part of a wider project to reconstruct the social topography of this
particular rural community on the basis of this source. See Steve Hindle, 'Fiscal
Seigneurialism in Late-Seventeenth-Century Warwickshire: Sir Richard Newdigate
and the "Great Survey" of Chilvers Coton', in *William Dugdale, Historian, 1605–86:
His Life, His Writings and His County*, ed. Christopher Dyer and Catherine Richardson
(Woodbridge, 2009), 164–86; *idem*, 'Below Stairs at Arbury Hall: Sir Richard Newdigate
and His Household Staff, *c*.1670–1710', *Historical Research* 85 [no.227] (2012), 71–88.
[12] The Newdigate family archive is WCRO, CR136. The most significant sources for
this study are CR136/V12, pp. 64–73 (occupational 'census-type' listing, 1684); V109,
V101, V12 (the three volumes of the survey of the manor of Griff and Coton, 1681–84);
and CR 1841/6 (estate wages book, 1688–91).
[13] Alexandra Shepard, 'Poverty, Labour and the Language of Social Description in Early
Modern England', *P&P* 201 (2008), 51–95; Peter King, 'Social Inequality, Identity and
the Labouring Poor in Eighteenth-Century England', in *Identity and Agency in England,
1500–1800*, ed. Henry French and Jonathan Barry (Basingstoke, 2004), 60–86.
[14] E. P. Thompson, 'The Patricians and the Plebs', in *idem, Customs in Common* (1991),
16–96; Peter King, 'Edward Thompson's Contribution to Eighteenth-Century Studies:
The Patrician–Plebeian Model Re-Examined', *SH* 21 (1996), 215–28.
[15] See, most recently, Gregory Clark, 'Farm Wages and Living Standards in the Industrial
Revolution: England, 1670–1869', *EcHR* 2nd ser. 54 (2001), 477–505.

transacted.[16] Fundamentally, however, it seeks to reconstruct in microcosm (and arguably in unprecedented detail) the lived experience of rural labour in late seventeenth-century England.

The composition and character of the Arbury workforce

At the heart of the agricultural workforce at Arbury in the 1680s were the ten servants in husbandry who were most regularly employed about the estate. In 1689, these comprised a shepherd, a coachman, a wainman, a postilion, two husbandmen and four husbandry boys.[17] The detailed record of the work that they performed in the autumn of that year indicates, however, that the tasks required of them were far more varied than their formal job descriptions suggest. In the six days he worked during the third week of October 1689, for instance, the coachman Thomas Wright not only 'looked to the horses' but was also responsible for ferrying slates, muck, earth, lime and stubble around various parts of the estate. That same week, the postilion Robert Sergeant was three days absent in Oxford on estate business but spent another two days with Wright carrying slates and earth. The wainman Edward Bryan, meanwhile, transported deer, horses and cattle to Coventry; carried wood to the great stable; and still had time to perform three days' work winnowing maslin, threshing wheat and harvesting pease. One of the two husbandmen, Richard Edwards, spent five days fetching stone from the Red Quarry at Griff Hollows and a sixth ploughing. One of the husbandry boys, William Wells, spent one day with Edwards at the quarry, another with Bryan at Coventry Fair, a third delivering tiles and fetching wood and three further days threshing oats in the Middle Barn. Another of the boys, Thomas Daniel, spent three days tending the flock with the shepherd William Clark, a fourth harvesting pease, a fifth turning a winnowing frame and a sixth shovelling muck by the hay ricks.[18]

Such examples could be multiplied, the servants in husbandry being delegated to fetch stone, to cart wood and to plough fields as need required. There were no contractual limits on the number of hours or days these men and boys might be expected to work or on the tasks they might be

---

[16] The only comparable studies are those of Elizabethan Stiffkey (Norfolk): A. Hassell Smith, 'Labourers in Late Sixteenth-Century England: A Case Study from North Norfolk', *C&C* 4 (1989), 11–52, 367–94.

[17] WCRO, CR1841/6. The following discussion of servants in husbandry takes no account either of the household staff (including the dairy maids) who worked within Arbury Hall itself or of the four or five staff who worked in Sir Richard's gardens. Cf. Ann Kussmaul, *Servants in Husbandry in Early Modern England* (Cambridge, 1981); Hassell Smith, 'Labourers', 14–18.

[18] WCRO, CR1841/6, unfol. (19–25 October 1689). cf. Kussmaul, *Servants in Husbandry*, 34–5.

required to perform. With the exception of the coachman Thomas Wright and the postilion Robert Sergeant (each of whom will have occasionally been working on Newdigate business elsewhere), all of them were employed somewhere round the estate during at least fifty weeks in the agricultural year. The estate cash books do not record weekly payments made to them, for they were retained on yearly contracts remunerated at board wages.[19] Newdigate's own household account books, however, reveal that the husbandman George Pearce earned £5 10s a year, the wainman Edward Bryan £5, the coachman Thomas Wright £4, the shepherd William Clark £4 and the postilion Robert Sergeant £2.[20] Several of these rates in fact exceed the statutory annual *maxima* (£3 15s for a husbandman, for instance, or £3 for a shepherd) confirmed by the Warwickshire justices in 1684.[21] Where he did offer wages in addition to board, therefore, Newdigate was forced by labour shortage into paying above the statutory rate, at least for his adult farm servants. For the youngest of them, however, board was all that was to be had: although the slightly older husbandry boy William Wells received an annual wage of £2 10s (broadly in line with the Warwickshire magistrates' assessment of the remuneration appropriate for 'an inferior servant man'), three other boys received no wages at all and were rewarded only in clothing, their livery consisting of 'mild fustian' stockings, leather britches, boots, coat, apron and hat.[22]

Staff turnover among the servants in husbandry was relatively high.[23] Apart from the wainman Edward Bryan, the shepherd William Clark and the postilion Robert Sergeant, none of the men or boys employed in 1689–90 had been in Newdigate's service in 1684.[24] One of the farm servants in fact left during the course of that year, George Pierce departing at Michaelmas 1689 after a year's service. Whether Newdigate dismissed his farm servants so regularly as a matter of deliberate policy is unclear.[25] The experience of Richard Edwards, George Pierce's successor as head husbandman at Arbury, is nonetheless suggestive. Edwards had been recruited at Michaelmas 1689 and from 5 October the wages book suggests that he was tasked to work six days a week every week on the Arbury estate. Like many of Newdigate's employees, Edwards moved on after a relatively short period of service, although he apparently completed the statutory year required by his

[19] *Ibid.*, 35–42.
[20] WCRO, CR136/V84, p. 546 (Lady Day 1689).
[21] *Warwick County Records*, ed. S. C. Ratcliff, H. C. Johnson and N. J. Williams, 9 vols (Warwick, 1935–64), VIII, 92–3.
[22] WCRO, CR136/V90, pp. 118–23, 66, 220, 711.
[23] It was higher still among his domestic staff. See Hindle, 'Below Stairs'.
[24] WCRO, CR136/V12, pp. 64–73 [no. 175].
[25] On fifty-one-week hirings designed to prevent settlement, see K. D. M. Snell, *Annals of the Labouring Poor: Social Change and Agrarian England, 1660–1900* (Cambridge, 1985), 73–7.

contract. By the autumn of 1691, he had left Chilvers Coton and he and his wife and child were described by the Warwickshire justices as 'poor people' thought likely to become chargeable to the parishioners of Ansley, some four miles to the west. The JPs ordered Edwards and his family removed back to Chilvers Coton, presumably on the basis that his successful completion of a year's service with Newdigate conferred rights of settlement there upon him. There is, however, no evidence that Edwards was ever resident, employed or relieved in Coton after 1691, and it may well be that the parish officers successfully moved him on, by fair means or foul.[26] From this perspective, the very high turnover of staff at Arbury may even have been a deliberate strategy on Newdigate's part, designed to ensure that his farm servants did not achieve settlement. This suggestion is lent further credibility by the fact that, unlike Newdigate's household staff, agricultural wage labourers or craftsmen, very few of those who worked as servants in husbandry at Arbury were apparently recruited from the village of Chilvers Coton. Of those resident servants employed in 1684, only 'Robin' Sergeant was a local boy, the seventeen-year-old son of a labourer who rented a house and tiny garden in the Heath End.[27] The rest were almost certainly recruited either through word-of-mouth recommendations from local employers or at the great statute hiring sessions, the most significant of which was held every Michaelmas only nine miles away at Polesworth, where by the 1680s farm servants were doubtless playing increasingly assertive roles in the 'market drama' of wage-bargaining.[28]

The resident farm servants were nonetheless only the core of a very extensive work force of day-labourers who were employed under various terms and conditions around the estate. Analysis of the estate wages book between Lady Day 1689 and Lady Day 1690 in fact suggests that no fewer than 110 separate individuals were tasked to perform work around the Arbury estate during that year.[29] Although by no means all of them were recruited from Chilvers Coton, this number represents about one-in-six of the population of the entire parish. In fact, of the 176 households listed in the Chilvers Coton 'census' in 1684, the heads of twenty-seven (15.5 per cent) were employed by Newdigate on the Arbury estate in 1689–90. In fifteen of these cases, moreover, either the wife or the daughter (or both) of the household

[26] Warwick County Records, IX, 41.

[27] WCRO, CR136/V101, pp. 23–24, 25–26; V109, pp. 66–7, 78–9; V12, pp. 64–73 [no. 74].

[28] For the enduring significance of the Polesworth hiring fair which regularly attracted several thousand servants, see William Marshall, *The Rural Economy of the Midland Counties*, 2 vols (1796), II, 17–18; Kussmaul, *Servants in Husbandry*, 60, 161. Cf. Michael Roberts, '"Waiting Upon Chance": English Hiring Fairs and their Meanings From the Fourteenth to the Twentieth Century', *Journal of Historical Sociology* 1:2 (1988), p. 137.

[29] WCRO, CR1841/6, unfol. (23 March 1689–22 March 1690).

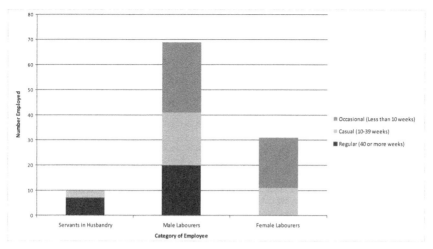

Figure 11.1. The structure of the Arbury Hall estate workforce, 1689–90.

head was also casually employed; and a further five women and girls were also working in Newdigate's meadows even though their husbands or fathers were not themselves employed at Arbury. All in all, therefore, thirty-two (18 per cent) of the households in Chilvers Coton drew all or part of their income from agricultural employment on the Arbury estate, and given the brief interval between the taking of the census in 1684 and the survival of the earliest wage books in 1689 this proportion is probably a significant underestimate of the gravitational pull exerted by the Newdigates in the local market for labour. It is apparent, moreover, that Newdigate recruited his employees not merely from the residents of the village but specifically from among his own tenants: almost one-third of the seventy-seven house-holders who rented property from him in 1689–90 found employment on the Arbury estate that year, the majority of them naturally being drawn from the ranks of the cottagers rather than those of the small farmers.[30]

As Figure 11.1 suggests, the workforce might usefully be disaggregated into three categories: those *regularly* employed (defined here as those who were employed in forty or more weeks during the year); those more *casually* employed (who were employed in between ten and forty weeks); and those only *occasionally* employed (who worked in less than ten weeks during the year). As might be expected, the twenty-seven 'regular' employees were exclusively male, mostly labourers and craftsmen, though seven of them were (as we have seen) resident servants in husbandry. The thirty-five 'casual' employees included not only another three of Newdigate's house-

30 WCRO, CR136/V84, pp. 530–1.

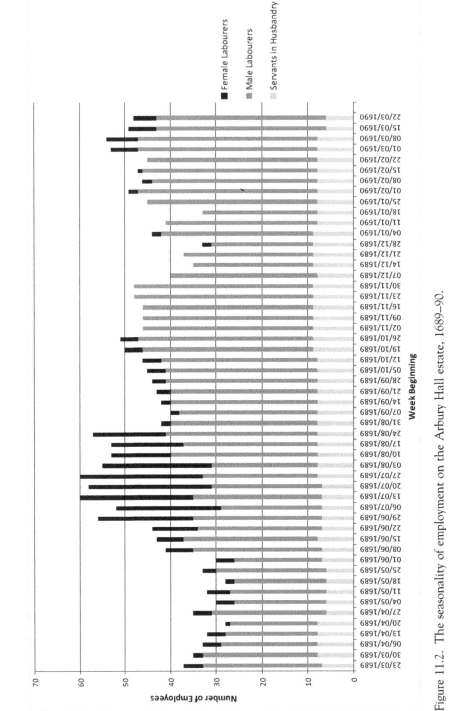

Figure 11.2. The seasonality of employment on the Arbury Hall estate, 1689–90.

hold servants whose duties were evidently split between the household itself and the estate, but also a significant penumbra of twenty-one male labourers and craftsmen and eleven women. The forty-eight 'occasional' workers comprised twenty-eight male labourers, several of them boys, and twenty women and girls, most of them, as we shall see, recruited seasonally. Newdigate himself evidently had a clear vision of the optimal size of his labour force. His own notes suggest that, in addition to his farm servants, he regarded sixteen male and four female labourers as adequate for the estate's needs, and accordingly decided at Lady Day 1689 that he could dispense with at least six men. He was, however, concerned to identify alternative roles for those laid off, suggesting that three of them be sent to fell wood at Weddington in Nuneaton and that another three could be employed either by the highway supervisors in mending the roads in the hamlet of Griff or in fencing around the park.[31] Nonetheless, the tendency for the workforce to grow as the bailiffs recruited more men and women on an *ad hoc* basis entailed further economies. In November 1689, Newdigate noted that he was regularly employing as many as thirty-seven workmen, five of whom he thought could 'go quite off', and a sixth could be put to better use making nails for him. The workforce could be brought down to the more economical number of twenty-six, he thought, if five other men were alternately laid-off and employed.[32] In this last proposal, he was anticipating the advice of those eighteenth-century estate stewards who argued that if supplementary labour was required, work should be shared out among as many as possible of those in need of employment.[33]

As these notes suggest, the wage-bill proved difficult to control, not least because the recruitment of casual and occasional labour swelled the workforce considerably. Indeed seasonal fluctuations were particularly marked: the average weekly number of workers tasked around the estate was approximately forty-four, characteristically consisting of seven or eight servants in husbandry, thirty male labourers and craftsmen, and five or six women. But this notional profile is a classic example of a meaningless mean, for as Figure 11.2 shows, there was a distinctly seasonal pattern of labour participation, with the number of employees ranging from a minimum of twenty-eight in the last two weeks of April to a maximum of sixty in the second half of July. This seasonal pattern is evident for male labourers, who were most regularly employed in harvesting and ploughing in the autumn: almost a quarter (24.2 per cent) of the man-days worked in 1689–90 fell in the nine weeks to the end of November 1689. It was even more obvious, however, in the case of the female labourers. There was a run of eight weeks

---

31 WCRO, CR1841/6, unfol. (25 March 1689).
32 WCRO, CR1841/6, unfol. (8 November 1689).
33 Clay, 'Landlords and Estate Management', 241.

in November and December, for instance, where no women were employed at all. By contrast, almost two-thirds (65.9 per cent) of all the days worked by women fell in the nine weeks commencing 29 June, the period associated with the hay harvest. The busiest week for females was 13–20 July, when twenty-eight women and girls were employed. Of these twenty-eight female employees, only four cannot be identified in the 1684 census. Of the remaining twenty-four, four were wives, and one a widow of Chilvers Coton householders. Nineteen of them, furthermore, ranging in age from eight-year-old Elizabeth Brown to thirty-three-year-old Catherine Atkins, were daughters of residents. The seasonal workforce was, therefore, overwhelmingly recruited from Newdigate tenantry.

Some indication of the extraordinary labour power required during the hay harvest is indicated by the distribution of tasks during the week beginning Saturday 20 July 1689. Between them, fifty-nine employees (including seven servants in husbandry) worked 281 person-days that week. To be sure, other tasks – ploughing, gathering tithe, hewing stone, fetching wood – were still being undertaken. Nonetheless, the activities associated with the hay harvest predominated. Twelve (28.6 per cent) of the forty-two days worked by resident farm servants were spent fetching, carrying or loading hay. Of the labourers, five men were tasked between them for nineteen days spent mowing specified meadows and a further four struck a bargain for payment to mow three others. A further seven labourers were tasked with helping at or 'topping-off' the ricks and between them spent seventeen days doing so. The actual haymaking – gathering the wet grass, turning it to ensure that it dried, loading it on to the wains and ricks – fell to twenty-eight women, boys and girls, who between them raked hay for 131 person-days. The fact that the ratio of haymakers to mowers was in excess of 3:1 suggests that, despite the increasing monopolisation of mowing by male labourers, very significant demand for female hay-rakers remained. Paying for the arduous, labour-intensive task of mowing nonetheless proved particularly expensive for Newdigate. It is instructive that the resident farm servants themselves were never asked to mow, possibly because they lacked the necessary skill, strength or experience to do so. Newdigate may even have been guilty of the false economy of deliberately recruiting servants in husbandry who could *not* mow on the basis that they could be hired for slightly lower wages, with the consequence that he had to strike bargains for mowing with day-labourers, who were therefore able to negotiate the terms on which they might be prepared to work in his meadows.[34]

---

[34] Michael Roberts, 'Sickles and Scythes: Women's Work and Men's Work at Harvest Time', *HWJ* 7 (1979), 3–28, pp. 9, 11, 13, 16–17, 22; *idem*, 'Sickles and Scythes Revisited: Harvest Work, Wages and Symbolic Meanings', in *Women, Work and Wages in England, c.1600–1850*, ed. Penny Lane, Neil Raven and Keith Snell (Woodbridge, 2004), 68–00, pp. 97–98. The classic contemporary description of the mechanics of the

Modes of payment: piece-rates and day-rates

So how was all this very significant collective effort – day after day spent sawing, digging, ploughing, carting, mowing and raking – actually rewarded? Although the farm servants were (as we have seen) paid fixed board wages, there was considerable flexibility about how the day-labourers were remunerated. Depending on the task they were expected to perform, they might be paid for specific jobs either at day-rates or at piece-work rates (that is, 'by [the] great', in the contemporary idiom). Although there was a general consensus that labourers were to be distrusted and disdained for their preference to subsist in idleness, opinion was divided over whether effort could best be incentivised through piece-rates or wage-rates. On the one hand, Thomas Tusser thought in 1573 that mowers and reapers rewarded at piece-rates would only 'deceive' their employers by 'lingring [the work] out'. Sir Edward Verney, by contrast, protested in 1635 about the 'knavery' of those labourers whose day-rates only encouraged them to 'fidle about' but who might be encouraged to work harder if they were by paid 'by the great'. By the 1660s, the Norfolk magistrate Robert Doughty feared that employers could not secure diligence whichever way they chose to pay: if labourers were paid day-rates, he thought, they would hardly 'do one dayes worke in twoe', but if they were employed at piece-rates 'then on the contrary they will as hastily slubber itt over'.[35] These conflicting perspectives complicate the analysis of the relationship between work and reward at Arbury: was the choice of the mode of payment a matter of Newdigate's own determination to incentivise effort, or does it reflect a process of negotiation in which the employees themselves exercised some agency? This question can be answered by a detailed analysis of who was paid, and how, for doing what on the estate between Lady Day 1689 and Lady Day 1690.

Of the 7,770.25 person-days worked by non-resident employees that year, almost one-quarter (22.8 per cent) were remunerated as piece-work, though the wages book never specifies the piece-rates for specific tasks, which were almost certainly customary. This pattern was, however, far from uniform across the labour force. The women, whether they were employed throughout the year or only casually during harvest, were always paid a daily wage. The overwhelming majority of them were paid 4d a day, though a small minority earned 3d, a differentiation which does not, curiously, seem

---

hay harvest is *The Farming and Memorandum Books of Henry Best of Elmswell 1642*, ed. D. M. Woodward (Oxford, 1984), 33–44.

[35] Thomas Tusser, *Five Hundreth Points of Good Husbandry* (1573), fol. 54v; F. P. Verney, ed., *Memoirs of the Verney Family During the Civil War*, 2 vols (1892), I, 128; Norfolk Record Office, Aylsham MS 304, unfol. ([undated memorandum on] '5 Eliz c. 4'). To 'slubber' up, or over, a task was to perform it in a hurried or careless manner: *OED* sv 'slubber' v.3a

to have depended on the age of the employee. Among the men, however, there was considerable variation between piece-rates and day-rates. As might be expected, the craftsmen, including the carpenter Thomas Nash (who was consistently paid a daily rate of 12d throughout the year) or the mason Andrew Hardy and his assistant Charles Hall (whose daily rates were 18d and 6d respectively in the summer and 14d and 5d in the winter), were invariably remunerated by the day. Some agricultural labourers were, however, similarly treated. Thomas Suffolk, for instance, worked almost 96 per cent of all the available person-days and was never rewarded at piece-rates. The five men for whom piece-work arrangements were most common, by contrast, were mowers, hedgers and ditchers, each of whom worked between 160 and 200 days a year, approximately two-thirds of them paid 'by the great'.

Complex calculations evidently lay behind the decision to reward effort in one way rather than another, for the same employee might be paid during the same week either at piece- or day-rates depending upon the specific task he was performing. A team of three men who were tasked together in the week beginning 19 October 1689, for instance, were each paid daily wages of 7d for the two days they spent removing wood and cutting windings in the New Park, but (unspecified) piece-rates for the four days they subsequently spent ditching in the New Park Wood. Some subtle distinctions may have been in play here. In July 1689, the sawyers Richard Nash and his son were paid piece-rates whenever they actually felled trees but daily wages whenever they clove wood, a decision which may either reflect a fine judgement about how ineffectively woodsmen could be supervised by the bailiff when they were cutting timber in the woodland as opposed to sawing wood once it had been collected; or the reluctance of sawyers to fell trees on any other terms than 'by the great'. Piece-rates certainly seem to have been retained for specific *tasks* rather than for specific *workers*. Only thirteen (11.5 per cent) of the man-days worked by male labourers and craftsmen in the week beginning 20 July 1689 were remunerated as piece-work, all of them in mowing. Mowers were generally employed either at a specially contracted rate for scything the grass on a particular meadow or at piece-rates per acre of grass cut. A similar situation prevailed with hedging and ditching in the autumn. Fifty-one (24.2 per cent) of the man-days worked by male labourers and craftsmen in the week beginning 19 October were remunerated at piece-rates, forty-two of them in ditching, six in felling trees and three in trenching. Virtually all the other tasks, from craftsmanship such as masonry, carpentry and thatching, through more menial jobs, such as muck-spreading, fetching or cutting wood, digging, pounding hemp and sowing acorns, were paid by the day. What seems to have been decisive here was the peculiarly masculine property of *skill*: those labourers who had the skills (largely understood in terms of sheer physical strength) required to fell trees or to mow meadows could dictate the terms on which they were employed, while their jobbing colleagues had no such bargaining power.[36]

On the other hand, there is some evidence that wage rates were the product of some negotiation. The wages paid to three labourers on 27 September 1689, for instance, were noted as 'towards their bargain for stocking roots in the New Park Wood'; and the remuneration for five days' hedging in April of that year was similarly regarded as part-satisfaction of a 'bargain'.[37] Ad hoc arrangements were particularly common during the hay harvest when the number of man-hours required to mow the extensive hay meadows was unpredictable and the irregular sums paid probably reflect some give and take. The four men who contracted to mow the Ox Meadow, the Barn Meadow and the Homestead in July 1689 agreed to do so for £1 10s between them, though the fact that the agreement itemises neither the number of acres to be cut nor the time to be taken over the task suggests that these grounds were so deeply inscribed in the mental maps of the workforce that they required no specification. How hard a bargain these men had driven cannot be known, though it is clear that at least one Arbury employee did succeed in arguing up his rate. Newdigate noted in June 1692 that the mason Charles Hall was to be paid a daily rate of 10d even though this was '1d more than my bargain' with Hall's former master Andrew Hardy.[38] Perhaps Hall really had held his hat in his hand but still found the courage to remind Newdigate to his face that his neighbours were prepared to pay more for his craftsmanship.[39]

Newdigate's position in these negotiations over wages was significantly weakened when his own long-standing and spiralling problems with debt were compounded by a chronic shortage of specie. John Locke regarded this situation as increasingly desperate for employers even *before* the recoinage crisis of 1696, arguing as early as 1690 that money was no longer 'running in the several channels of commerce'. The consequence, he argued, was that 'the farmer, not having money to pay the labourer, supplies him with corn'.[40] Newdigate's experience vindicates Locke's analysis, for by the mid 1690s the Arbury labourers and craftsmen were being 'paid' in tickets which they were ultimately able to redeem only for corn. The earliest evidence of this system dates from July 1695, when twenty tickets, each of 5s value,

---

[36] John Rule, 'The Property in Skill in the Period of Manufacture', in *The Historical Meaning of Work*, ed. Patrick Joyce (Cambridge, 1987), 99–118; Joyce Burnette, *Gender, Work and Wages in Industrial Revolution Britain* (Cambridge, 2008), 154–7.

[37] WCRO, CR1841/6, unfol. (5 April 1689, 27 Sept. 1689).

[38] WCRO, CR 136/V17, p. 227 (22 June 1692).

[39] Cf. Wrightson, *EN*, 326.

[40] John Locke, *Some Considerations of the consequences of the Lowering of Interest, and Raising the Value of Money* [2nd edn, 1696], repr. in Patrick H. Kelly, ed., *Locke on Money* (Oxford, 1991), 237. Craig Muldrew, '"Hard Food For Midas": Cash and its Social Value in Early Modern England', *P&P* 170 (2001), 78–120, p. 107.

were issued to four employees, but tickets of various denominations ranging from 2s 6d to £2 proliferated thereafter. On 25 October 1695, Newdigate's clerk Obidiah Key explained that he had signed sixteen tickets each valued at 2s 6d which he delivered to workmen ('i.e. towards paying this weeks work book'). He explained that he was to pay the money due upon them whenever they were brought to him, and subsequently recorded the specific dates on which he had burnt the tickets redeemed by particular workmen. By that winter, the entire estate economy had apparently been transformed from payment in cash to payment by ticket. On 15 November 1695, Key issued ninety-five more tickets to the cumulative value of almost £10 to twenty-five employees (including both craftsmen and labourers), many of their names being familiar from the wages book of the late 1680s.[41] After the recoinage of 1696, however, it was no longer possible for Key to redeem the tickets in cash, and by that winter Newdigate was effectively paying his employees in corn, which had itself become a very expensive commodity given the difficult harvest conditions of that year. In November 1696, twenty-one employees apparently 'purchased' corn from Newdigate at 3s 8d per strike in this way, sixteen of them initially 'paying' 3s 6d and remaining indebted for 2d, a transaction which in itself implies that small amounts could not be paid in cash and had to be held over as small debts.[42] What at first looks like a late flowering of the 'social economy of dearth', motivated by traditional gentlemanly ideals of hospitality, was in fact an early experiment in the truck system which did not become common elsewhere until the mid eighteenth century, an expedient forced upon Newdigate by the high price of labour and the shortage of coin.[43]

[41] WCRO, CR136/V168, reverse pagination [unfol.]: 'An account of tickets signed by Ob: Key'.
[42] WCRO, CR136/V17, p. 316 (Nov.–Dec. 1696). On high corn prices in the mid 1690s, see Andrew B. Appleby, 'Grain Prices and Subsistence Crises in England and France, 1590–1740', *Journal of Economic History* 39 (1979), 865–87; Peter Bowden, 'Appendix III: Statistics', in *Agrarian History*, V, ed. Thirsk, II, 829–30 (table 1).
[43] John Walter, 'The Social Economy of Dearth in Early Modern England', reprinted in John Walter, *Crowds and Popular Politics in Early Modern England* (Manchester, 2006), 124–80; cf. John Rule *The Experience of Labour in Eighteenth-Century Industry* (1981), 138; John Rule, *The Labouring Classes in Early Industrial England, 1750–1850* (1986), 64–5, 110; Craig Muldrew and Stephen King, 'Cash, Wages and the Economy of Makeshifts in England, 1650–1800', in *Experiencing Wages: Social and Cultural Aspects of Wage Forms in Europe Since 1500*, ed. Peter Scholliers and Leonard Schwarz (New York, 2003), 155–80, pp. 165–6; Beverley Lemire, *The Business of Everyday Life: Gender, Practice and Social Politics in England, c.1600–1900* (Manchester, 2005), 89–90, 96–7, 102.

Time discipline and labour discipline

Whether payments were made by the piece or by the day, in cash or on credit, there is some scattered evidence that Newdigate attempt to enforce both time and labour discipline on his workforce. A penny-and-a-half each (almost 25 per cent of their daily wage) was, for instance, deducted from the wages of sawyers Bartholomew and Francis Sergeant 'for giving over work on Saturday 2 November 1689 at 3 o clock'; and 2d each (an abatement of almost a third) was stopped from the wages of Henry and Edward Smith and of Thomas Clark for coming late to their hedging and ditching work on 13 December 1689. One Tuesday in late January 1690, John Ashby was threshing oats in the Middle Barn but went home 'sick' and was paid only for three-quarters of a day.[44] When labourers performed piece-work, moreover, Newdigate usually insisted that his estate bailiffs monitor their performance closely: thus he ensured, for instance, that Job Morton and Samuel Joyce, who worked four days trenching in Griff Hill Meadow 'by great' in November 1689, 'had their work measured'.[45]

Policing the punctuality, diligence and integrity of his craftsman and labourers was relatively easy. Wages could be abated at the end of the week, and claims about the volume of work completed could be verified on the spot. With his servants in husbandry, however, Newdigate had rather less room for manoeuvre: after all, these men and boys enjoyed some degree of security, being employed on yearly contracts at board wages. This did not prevent him from attempting to set the parameters of acceptable performance and behaviour by a disciplinary system of sanctions and rewards.[46] Newdigate's account books are replete with examples of farm servants being fined for infractions of this code, with those coachmen or wainmen whose roles took them furthest afield around (and often beyond) the Arbury estate apparently most often falling foul of his insistence on competence and punctuality. The coachman Thomas Wright, for instance, had his wages docked in 1692 to the value of windows broken through his negligence.[47] The wainman Robert Cholmly seems to have been a serial offender. In May 1696, he was in trouble for leaving ajar a gate at Griff Hill Farm, and in 1697 he was fined four times to the cumulative total of 12s (about 12 per cent of his annual wage). He forfeited 5s on 18 May for causing three teams another day's work by bringing home plaster that should have been sent to Astley; a further 1s on 21 May for mistakenly sending a cart to Coton; another 1s on 31 May for failing to appear promptly with a supply of marl; and finally 5s in early September for neglecting his business (riding 'out to the alehouse',

---

44 WCRO, CR1841/6, unfol. (8 Nov. 1689, 12 Dec. 1689, 27 Jan. 1690).
45 WCRO, CR1841/6 (13 Nov. 1689).
46 This system also applied to his household servants. Hindle, 'Below Stairs'.
47 WCRO, CR136/V17, p. 148 (May 1692).

for all Newdigate knew) so that oats were not brought home until midday.[48] Newdigate suspected that idleness and incompetence on this scale were often a consequence of drunkenness, and was particularly severe with those of his farm servants who over-indulged in alcohol. In 1695, accordingly, he fined his long-serving wainman Ned Bryan 10s for 'tempting James Morris and old Richard Nash to the alehouse and making Nash drunk'.[49] In the last resort, of course, Newdigate might dismiss these delinquents altogether. Thus Abraham Hans lost his job in 1696 when, having been instructed to purchase thirty-two strike of beans and provided with eleven horses and two husbandry boys for the purpose, he returned home from market with empty wagons.[50]

Despite Sir Richard's best efforts to secure punctuality and efficiency, there is nonetheless some evidence of absenteeism among the estate work-force. In the week 20–26 July 1689, the fifty-nine staff on the payroll should notionally have worked 354 person-days, but over one-fifth of these days were lost to absence, the majority of them on Saturday 20 July when only thirteen (or 27 per cent) of the employees turned in for work. The high level of absenteeism on this particular day may possibly have been due to the agricultural demands of the harvest on the employees' own strips, small-holdings and cottage gardens, but is more plausibly explained by the leisure opportunities afforded by the ancient fair at Polesworth associated with the feast of St Margaret. Newdigate's bailiffs would have been far happier with the situation in the third week of October, when only 7.5 per cent of the notional maximum number of working days were lost through absence, and these were spread almost equally throughout the week, the majority of them accounted for by children or youths who had presumably been called away to other duties at home. There is, therefore, little evidence of the leisure preferences associated with 'St Monday' among the agricultural workers on the Arbury Hall estate, no one day of the week standing out more than any other in the profile of absenteeism. If many of the workforce really had spent St Margaret's day revelling at Polesworth, the overwhelming majority of them nonetheless reported for work the following Monday.[51] Even though the late seventeenth-century market was not overburdened with surplus agricultural labour, therefore, Newdigate's employees did not take advantage of their relatively strong position, and patterns of Monday absence were not prominent at Arbury. These labourers were probably too poorly paid in absolute terms to take time off, and even if they were relatively well-off in other respects, the landlord's close supervision of village life meant that

[48] WCRO, CR136/V90, p. 1051 (7 May 1696); V17, pp. 441 (26 May 1697), 587 (16 Sept. 1697). For the docking of the wages of farm servants elsewhere, see Kussmaul, *Servants in Husbandry*, pp. 47–8.
[49] WCRO, CR136/V17, pp. 302–3 (21 Jan. 1695).
[50] WCRO, CR136/ V17, p. 405 (1696).
[51] Cf. Thompson, *Customs in Common*, 373–4; Malcolmson, *Popular Recreations*, 94–5.

rental and working opportunities could easily be restricted if they showed less than willing.

Agricultural wages, household economies and standards of living

The bulk of those regularly employed by Newdigate's bailiffs were agricultural labourers, who performed a remarkably wide range of tasks: a preliminary list based on close analysis of the wage books for late July and late October 1689 would include digging, ditching, haymaking, hedging, levelling, mowing, muck-spreading, ploughing, pounding hemp, sowing, threshing, trenching and woodcutting, to say nothing of the more generic tasks of assisting the various craftsmen or fetching or loading various raw materials such as clay, coal, muck, stone or timber, or building materials such as tiles or wood. Except when they were performing those tasks characteristically remunerated at piece-rates, Newdigate's labourers were generally paid daily rates of 10d during the harvest and 7d at other times. These rates also exceeded the statutory *maxima* reaffirmed by the Warwickshire justices in 1684, although they fell well short both of the wage rates in agriculture calculated by Peter Bowden, who suggested that average daily earnings across the year had risen to just over 11d by the first decade of the eighteenth century; and of the daily earnings of labourers in Terling (Essex) who were earning a shilling a day in the period 1680–1700.[52] Even during the harvest, therefore, Newdigate was probably paying something like 20 per cent less than the market rate. What these rates meant in terms of annual earnings is more problematic. Wrightson and Levine estimated that a labourer who found work for 220 days a year (that is, four days in most weeks and five days in some) in late seventeenth-century Essex would have earned a total of about £11, a sum which fell substantially short of the £13 14s probably required annually to support a family of five, though an equally industrious tailor (earning £12) or carpenter (£16 10s) would have fared slightly better.[53] In fact, only thirteen of Newdigate's employees (nine of them labourers) exceeded the Wrightson and Levine threshold of 220 days' labour. For the small minority who were able to get work five days a week in most weeks, therefore, it seems that relentless long hours remunerated at customary rather than at market rates were evidently the characteristic way of making a living at Arbury. Thomas Suffolk, for instance, was paid 6d per day for assisting the shepherd and making hay in July and 4d per day for fetching tiles, stubble and pease in October. Despite the fact that he worked 305 man-days (96 per cent of the notional maximum) for the Newdigates in 1689–90, he cumula-

---

[52] Peter J. Bowden, 'Agricultural Prices, Wages, Farm Profits and Rents', *Agrarian History*, V, ed. Thirsk, II, 5 (table 13.3); Wrightson & Levine, *Terling*, 41.
[53] Wrightson & Levine, *Terling*, 40–1; Wrightson, *EN*, 317–18.

tively earned only £3 12s 10d. Abraham Checkly, by contrast, worked 294 days (almost 93 per cent of the maximum) and earned only £6 1s 10d, a sum which in and of itself did not go far towards meeting the expenditure of a household which contained not only his wife but two teenage children.[54] As will become clear, however, the discussion of these earnings in isolation from other factors is highly misleading. Suffolk was unmarried and give-or-take £3–£4 was an invaluable supplement to the household income of his mother and father; and Checkly not only paid nominal rent but could also draw on the earning power of his wife.

Since there is no extant probate material for any of these labouring men (and almost all of them probably had goods of too little worth to justify the taking of a post-mortem inventory), one can only speculate how they made shift to support their families.[55] William Cox, who worked on the Arbury Estate for 275 days at the daily rate of 10d in the summer and 7d at other times and therefore earned just short of £9 from Newdigate in 1689–90 was able to supplement this income through the legitimate exercise of common rights associated with his cottage and two-and-a-half-acre homestall in the Paradise End. As a cottier, Cox could claim the right to keep two cows and a calf, a horse and foal and five sheep on the commons. If he exercised the right himself, Cox might annually earn somewhere between £14 and £20 from the dairy produce of his cattle.[56] Although at least two other regular Newdigate employees, the labourer and nailmaker Thomas Knight jr and the carpenter Joseph Smith, had plausible claims to common rights, it may well be that many others pastured their animals illegally.[57]

More decisive than the availability of common rights, however, was the value of subsidised rent. A significant proportion of Arbury employees were tenants of Newdigate and many of them were cottiers paying nominal rents of below 20s a year.[58] Thomas Knight jr, for instance, worked for Newdigate for 252 days at either 10d or 7d per day earning almost £8 in the calendar

---

[54] This calculation (and all those that follow) assumes that 'harvest' wages were paid only in eight of the fifty-two weeks of the working year. These earnings would have been higher still if Newdigate had chosen to distinguish not only between harvest wages and winter wages, but also between non-harvest 'summer' wages and winter wages, though he does not seem to have done so. Cf. Clark, 'Farm Wages', 478, 481.

[55] Margaret Spufford, 'The Limitations of the Probate Inventory', in *English Rural Society, 1500–1800: Essays in Honour of Joan Thirsk*, ed. John Chartres and David Hey (Cambridge, 1990), 139–74; Tom Arkell, 'Interpreting Probate Inventories', in *When Death Do Us Part: Understanding and Interpreting the Probate Records of Early Modern England*, ed. Tom Arkell, Nesta Evans and Nigel Goose (Oxford, 2000), 72–102.

[56] WCRO, CR136/V109, pp. 73–7. For estimates of the value of these common rights, see Leigh Shaw-Taylor, 'Labourers, Cows, Common Rights and Parliamentary Enclosure: The Evidence of Contemporary Comment, c.1760–1810', *P&P* 171 (2001), 95–126.

[57] WCRO, CR136/V109, p. 73.

[58] Cf. M. E. Turner, J. V. Beckett and B. Afton, *Agricultural Rent in England, 1690–1914* (Cambridge, 1997), 79–80.

year and yet was paying an annual rent of only 1s. William Mortimer was slightly less industrious, working for 160 days (the majority of them at piece-rates) on the estate, but only having to find annual rent of 2s.[59] Indeed, only two employees on the Arbury Hall estate – the labourer John Atkins and the mason Andrew Hardy – were paying Newdigate annual rents of over £2. In villages like Chilvers Coton, where landlords exerted very considerable control over the demand for labour, labourers' wages could be set at relatively low customary rates precisely because employees might be housed at the landlord's convenience in tied cottages for which they paid only peppercorn rents.

Tenure of Newdigate-subsidised property therefore conferred the opportunity to generate, through the effort of several family members, very substantial contributions to the household income of a labouring family. This is best illustrated through the case of Abraham and Alice Checkly, both of whom worked regularly on the Arbury estate in 1689–90. Abraham was forty-one in that year and (as we have seen) he worked 294 days – levelling, digging, cutting and loading wood, helping at the hay ricks and fetching slates – being paid 10d a day in harvest and 7d in the winter. His wife Alice worked 104 days on the estate, mainly in haymaking, for which she was paid a daily rate of 4d. At a time when they were leasing a house and garden in the Heath End from Newdigate for an annual rent of only 6s 10d, the couple were therefore between them earning almost £11 from employment by their landlord. In light of these preferential arrangements, it is little wonder that in November 1687 Abraham Checkly had opened negotiations with Newdigate about renting 'a piece of ground about £3 or £4 a year'.[60] In many respects, therefore, Chilvers Coton functioned as an estate village within which Newdigate's labour and rental policies were inextricably intertwined.[61] When their peppercorn rents and preferential leases are taken into account, regularly employed labourers might, it seems, make a tolerable living from working at Arbury.

The most obvious beneficiaries of Newdigate's demand for work, however, were the skilled craftsmen, who naturally fared rather better in terms of wages, and for whom the evidence of the rewards of labour is rather more robust. Probate material survives for two of the craftsmen most frequently employed on the Newdigate estate. The carpenter Thomas Nash was aged fifty-four in 1689 and he was paid 12d for each of the 231 days he worked – mending gates and horse-rails, repairing wheelbarrows and coaches, building shelves and making furniture – on the Arbury Estate. His annual aggregate earnings from Newdigate's bailiff alone therefore amounted to well over £16

---

[59] Although Wrightson and Levine allowed as much as £1 a year for rent, they conceded that the Terling housing stock *might* have included 'tied cottages with negligible rents' of the kind which predominated in Chilvers Coton. Wrightson & Levine, *Terling*, 40.

[60] WCRO, CR136/V84, p. 450.

[61] See the essay by H. R. French in this volume.

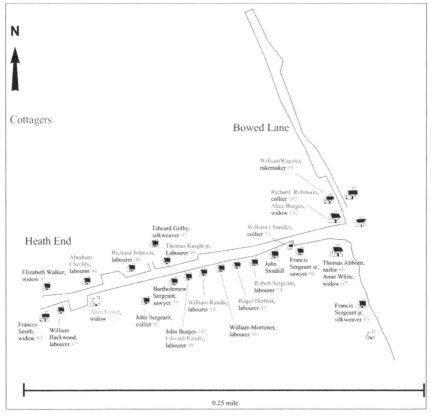

N

Cottagers

Bowed Lane

William Wagstcf,
rakemaker 69

Richard Robinson,
collier 103
Alice Burges,
widow 102

Edward Golby,
silkweaver 97

William Chandler,
collier 73

Heath End

Thomas Knight jr,
Labourer 98

Abraham
Checkly,
labourer 96

Richard Johnson,
labourer 96

Elizabeth Walker,
widow 95

John
Stonhill

Francis
Sergeant sr,
sawyer 90

Thomas Abbotts,
nailor 68

Anne White,
widow 67

Robert Sergeant,
labourer 74

Bartholemew
Sergeant,
sawyer 75

William Randle,
labourer 88

Roger Herbert,
labourer 85

Alice Foster,
widow

Francis
Sergeant jr,
silkweaver 83

Frances
Smith,
widow 93

William
Hackwood,
labourer 87

John Sergeant,
collier 91

John Burges 102
Edward Randle,
labourer 89

William Mortimer,
labourer 86

0.25 mile

Map 11.1. The households of the Heath End, Coton Town, 1684.

and he had a further three months' earning power to deploy elsewhere if he chose to use it.[62] Perhaps he worked for other employers, but he almost certainly worked his own land, described in 1684 as 'a middling farm' (probably in excess of thirty-four acres) which he leased from Newdigate at an annual rent of 30s. When he died in 1701 at the age of sixty-seven, his inventory, with a total valuation of over £136, listed consumer goods to the value of almost £19; livestock, including seven horses and four cows, worth almost £32; and agricultural produce worth £40. All this suggests a material wealth of over £111, which places him securely in the upper quartile of the entire Chilvers Coton probate sample for the period 1600–1750.[63] The

[62] Nash's earnings were therefore analogous to those carpenters in late seventeenth-century Terling who (just as he did) found work four days in most weeks and five days in some. Wrightson, *EN*, 317.

[63] Lichfield Record Office [LRO], inv. Thomas Nash, carpenter (25. Sept. 1701). For the categories of 'consumer goods' and 'material wealth' deployed here, see Tom Arkell, 'Introduction: Part I', in *idem*, ed., *Warwickshire Hearth Tax Returns*, 94–7.

mason Andrew Hardy did almost as well out of his employment at Arbury, although given that his daily rate was not consistent over the year, his aggregate earnings are more difficult to calculate. Nonetheless, he worked 160 days on the estate, earning either 18d or 14d per day, and therefore had an annual Arbury income of £9s 15s. When he died in 1702 aged fifty-nine, he left an inventory valued at £313, itemising over £13 worth of consumer goods; almost £33 worth of livestock (including two horses, twelve cattle and fifteen sheep); and £14 worth of agricultural produce. His household was clearly very active in dairying, since he owned forty cheeses cumulatively worth some 36s. Shortly before his death, he had in 1699 been able to expand his holding from the small farm in the Arbury Demesne he had rented from Newdigate in 1684 to property with an annual rental value of over £8.[64] Although he was owed the enormous sum of £247 on bonds and desperate debts, his material wealth of almost £65 compares very favourably with other craftsmen, and puts him in the top third of the sample.[65] These characteristics sit very comfortably with what has recently been discovered about the material culture of the middling sort of people who constituted the 'chief inhabitants' of rural communities in late seventeenth-century England.[66]

Of the living conditions of the labour force more generally, however, it is difficult to be so precise. Perhaps most instructive are the housing arrangements of a significant cluster of Newdigate employees who rented his cottages in the Heath End, effectively the sink estate of the village, extending for a quarter of a mile towards Arbury at the western fringes of the Chilvers Coton common field system (Map 11.1). The manorial jurors of 1684 had noted that the houses of the Heath End were 'mean tenements inhabitted by indifferent persons of which 3 or 4 are very poor' although they conceded that 'the land which belongs to them is, as most Gardens and Homsteads are, very good'. Twenty-two cottages and houses were huddled either side of the street, twelve of them occupied by tenants of Newdigate paying rents of less than 20s a year. Six of Newdigate's most regular employees in 1689–90 – the labourers Abraham Checkly, Thomas Knight, Robert Sergeant and William Mortimer and the sawyers Francis and Bartholomew Sergeant – lived here. Five of their six cottages had been exempted from payment of the hearth tax in 1670. The properties of Knight, Mortimer and Robert Sergeant were described as houses and little garden places for which they paid rents of only a shilling or two per year; and Checkly's as a house with a lean-to with a little garden for which he paid 2s 6d. Although neither of

64 LRO, inv. Andrew Hardy, yeoman (28 Mar. 1702).
65 Cf. Donald Woodward, *Men at Work: Labourers and Building Craftsmen in the Towns of Northern England, 1450–1750* (Cambridge, 1995), 241–2 on the high level of debts owed to building craftsmen such as masons.
66 H. R. French, *The Middle Sort of People in Provincial England, 1600–1750* (Oxford, 2007), 141–200, esp. p. 164 (Table 3.3).

the two Sergeants who felled trees for Newdigate were included in the list of cottiers, both were by 1689–90 paying nominal rents of 18s 4d and 19s 6d respectively. None of these properties had gardens exceeding a few hundred square yards, and conditions must have been impossibly cramped. Bartholomew Sergeant, for instance, lived in a one-hearth cottage with his wife and six children aged between nine and twenty-four; and William Mortimer shared his one-hearth cottage with a wife, two children aged twenty-three and eighteen, and a parish orphan aged ten. All these men enjoyed a relatively short walk of less than a mile to the Arbury estate, and one wonders how they felt each morning when they headed for work. For as they passed through the park gates into the 'polite landscape' of Arbury Hall, dominated by its Christopher Wren-designed stable block and its manicured gardens, to say nothing of its thirty-two chimneys, they were quite literally entering another world, one in which their perceptions of both time and space were likely twisted almost entirely out of shape.[67]

Conclusion

How, then, might we characterise the relationship between Sir Richard Newdigate and the men, women and children who worked on his estate; and what does that relationship tell us about the management of agricultural labour by a late seventeenth-century employer? To be sure, our understanding of the politics of agricultural employment on the Arbury demesne is skewed by the partial nature of these remarkable sources which by definition offer us only an elite view of the labour market. The voices of Newdigate's labourers are largely silenced by the very fact of their subordination. Despite the astonishing quality of the archival material, analysis of the implications of the Arbury wages and account books for rural social relationships necessarily remains speculative. On the one hand, Newdigate's significant degree of oversight of the living and working arrangements of his labour force suggests that he might have been able to exercise very extensive powers of control, perhaps even coercion, over his tenants and employees. His access to multiple sources of authority – as landlord, as employer, as poor-rate payer – gave him ample opportunity to manipulate the markets for housing, land and labour. On the other hand, however, there is abundant evidence that he had to bend over backwards to recruit labourers and to secure their diligence. When they worked for him, they rarely needed to work full time, and in the days not spent on the estate they might carve

---

[67] Tom Williamson, *Polite Landscapes: Gardens and Society in Eighteenth-Century England* (Stroud, 1995); Jonathan Finch, 'Pallas, Flora and Ceres: Landscape Priorities and Improvement on the Castle Howard Estate, 1699–1880', in *Estate Landscapes: Design, Improvement and Power in the Post-Medieval Landscape*, ed. Jonathan Finch and Kate Giles (Woodbridge, 2007), 19–37.

out an independent space of their own which might constrain Newdigate's freedom to manoeuvre.

Our account must also necessarily take account of personal factors. Newdigate evidently had a preference for micro-management. Although there was an estate bailiff (Henry Biddle, earning £9 a year by 1689) whose responsibility it was to record the performance of agricultural and building work at Arbury, Newdigate himself took a very close personal and discretionary interest in supervising the labour force.[68] This was evidently a habit of long-standing. On the morning of Saturday 7 October 1682, for instance, he recorded that he had risen at 6am and, pausing only for morning prayer, set his household and farm servants in motion: 'Sent Joseph White to Walsall to see for lime; [the coachman Richard] Drakeford to Arley to get a team to go with my 2 [teams]; [the brewer] Tom Tomson to Rugby with [the] lame [horse] Ophthene; [the butler] George [Nott] to Griffe about the highways; [the land agent Robert] Johnson to Coton to send Francis Kinder to Coventry for the [manorial court] paines; [the postilion] Jack Clark to fetch Coal; Thomas Musson to sow wheat; [the labourer] John Harris to plow for barly; [the wainman] Ned Brian to carry mud for barly; Robin Cox to carry brick etc for [the mason] Andrew [Hardy], with each a team; shewed Andrew [Hardy] where to build a root house; and employed the other workmen.'[69] Only then, after sending these men scurrying through and beyond the Arbury estate, did Newdigate stop to have breakfast.

There were equally, however, structural issues in play which complicated Newdigate's exercise of authority over his workforce. The sheer size of the estate and its concomitant demand for agricultural labour, compounded by the geographical origins of so many of those to whom he paid wages, meant that he had to be very careful about how his labourers were treated both during and after their employment. Getting the best performance out of the estate workforce was problematic. It seems likely that Newdigate and his bailiffs were forced to pay piece-rates rather than daily wages to incentivise the improved performance of certain agricultural tasks – especially mowing, hedging, ditching and tree-felling – required of his labourers. Where he did pay daily-rates, he was able to keep them at customary rather than market levels, but could only do so because so many of his labourers were his own tenants living in tied cottages at nominal rents. He did attempt to inculcate punctuality in the labour force, occasionally docking the wages of those day-labourers who started work late or left early and fining his farm servants heavily if they were incompetent, idle or drunk. In all these respects, Newdigate's workforce was subject to discipline both of their time and their productivity.

---

[68] In 1684 there had been two bailiffs resident at Arbury Hall: 31-year-old James Dowell and 22-year-old Samuel Moore. WCRO, CR136/V12, pp. 64–73 [no. 175].
[69] WCRO, CR136/B1306B (7 Oct. 1682).

These managerial aspects aside, the Newdigate archive discloses in unparalleled detail the lived experience of rural labour in late seventeenth-century England. Most labour markets in the early modern period were, of course, imperfect and the agricultural labour market at Arbury was more imperfect than most, for the presence of a very substantial landed employer generated significant distortions in the relationship between work and reward.[70] In an environment like Arbury, labour could not be an autonomous commodity which might be bought or sold for the highest price. Its worth was inextricably entwined with other factors of production, especially land and its associated rental value. In particular, the tied cottages in which so many of Newdigate's labourers were housed formed part of the raft of entitlements conferred when a labourer joined the Arbury workforce. In this sense, calculations of annual earnings among the agricultural workforce at Arbury (and elsewhere) are meaningless unless they take account of the negligible rents paid by so many of his employees.[71] This was doubtless a pattern reproduced across many estate villages by the early eighteenth century, but it is a valuable reminder to historians of living standards and industriousness that rental property was no less significant a commodity than labour time in the balance of resources between employer and employee.

The Arbury estate wages book is no less revealing of the considerable flexibility of the agricultural labour market in late seventeenth-century England. The casual contemporary identification of, and historical reference to, so many of Newdigate's employees as 'farm servants' or as 'labourers' conceals a very wide variety of tasks performed by, of skills inherent within, and of modes of payment negotiated among the workforce. Newdigate himself characterised the work done at Arbury as so much 'getting and threshing', a generic description which entirely fails to do justice to the range and complexity of the labour performed by men, women and children around the estate.[72] The farm servants, especially the husbandry boys, were jacks-of-all-trades, required (often in conjunction with day-labourers) to thresh, to plough, to fetch and to carry as needed. Singly and occasionally with assistants, the masons and carpenters exercised their craftsmanship with sufficient elegance to earn Newdigate's respect and the likelihood of regular work in the hall, the gardens and the park for years to come. In twos or threes, especially in the early summer and autumn, teams of skilled labourers hedged, ditched, felled and mowed on piece-rate terms which guaranteed them at least some control over the speed at which they worked;

[70] John Langton, 'Proletarianization in the Industrial Revolution: Regionalism and Kinship in the Labour Markets of the British Coal Industry from the Seventeenth to the Nineteenth Centuries', *Transactions of the Institute of British Geographers* 25 (2000), 31–49.
[71] Cf. Craig Muldrew, *Food, Energy and the Creation of Industriousness: Work and Material Culture in Agrarian England, 1550–1780* (Cambridge, 2011).
[72] WCRO, CR136/B2502H.

and they might even be able to name their price when it came to bargaining over the contract for the performance of a specific task. More commonly, the unskilled male labourers simply put in the hours throughout the year in digging, fetching and carrying, confident in the knowledge that so long as Newdigate was resident at Arbury there would always be demand for their brawn and stamina. And in July and August, the meadows of the estate were the site of a genuinely communal effort as a score or more of women and children raked hay for dozens of farm servants and labourers to load onto wains and ricks.

The late seventeenth-century agricultural labour market was undoubtedly, therefore, both segmented by skill, by gender and by age; and distorted by the highly seasonal nature of demand. The activities associated with the Arbury Hall hay harvest are, nonetheless, a powerful reminder that in the face-to-face world of local social and economic relations such distinctions might, on certain occasions at least, count for very little. At a time when labour was in relatively short supply, Newdigate and his bailiffs desperately needed all this collective effort. In negotiating with him over terms (and over the associated entitlements – including preferential rents, generous common rights and seasonal working opportunities for their wives and children), his employees might exercise significant agency over both when and at what rates they might work. And at the end of long hard week, they arguably enjoyed a standard of living which just might, from the perspectives either of their grandparents or their grandchildren, have seemed enviable.

12

Living in Poverty in Eighteenth-Century Terling

H. R. FRENCH

Samuel Payne was baptised in the mid-Essex village of Terling on 1 August 1736, the fifth child of Robert and Mary Payne. After marrying in 1757 or 1758, he and his wife Sarah went on to have twelve children between 1759 and 1778, including (remarkably) three sets of twins: Hannah and Mary, baptised in June 1768, Joseph and John, baptised in June 1770, and Rhoda and Amelia, baptised in August 1773. This exceptional fertility left the Paynes heavily dependent on relief from the parish throughout the period. Samuel received relief during bouts of 'sickness' in each winter between 1767 and 1771, in the summer of 1773, the spring of 1776, and the late summer of 1781. Similarly, Sarah was incapacitated by her repeated pregnancies, requiring assistance in 1766, 1768, from March to December 1770, 1772 and 1773, and the summers of 1776 and 1778, coinciding with the birth of her last two children. By the time Samuel died, aged fifty-two, in January 1789, only nine of these children survived, but they and their mother continued to depend on occasional relief payments until at least 1801. Indeed, Sarah's son Robert followed his father, and his paternal grandfather and namesake, in sometimes requiring poor relief to support his family, as he struggled to make ends meet in the very difficult years at the turn of the nineteenth century.

We know so much about the hard-pressed realities of their married life precisely because they were pushed repeatedly into the arms of the parish, and its overseers. Samuel and Sarah were recorded in at least 365 separate relief payments by Terling's overseers in the forty years between 1762 and 1801. The wider Payne dynasty (Samuel's father, his twelve children, and his son Robert's two sons) received 616 individual relief payments, plus weekly relief paid to Sarah in 1759 and 1760. In fact, the Paynes were the family with the highest dependence on poor relief in the parish, receiving occasional relief in *every* year between 1762 and 1801, averaging more than fifteen payments per year.

More generally, though, the Paynes were merely one of twenty families who received occasional payments in more than half of these forty years, and one family among the 360, comprising at least 809 named individuals, who received a total of 15,294 separate relief payments in the village between 1762 and 1801.[1] The decisions embedded in these discretionary relief payments are the focus of this chapter, because their dynamics illustrate both the ebb and flow of need and the shifting responses of parochial policy and provision, as well as (to some extent) the attitudes towards entitlement among the parochial elite. In focusing on them, we can also begin to decipher historical meaning out of the constant hubbub of hundreds of simultaneous reckonings of need versus entitlement.

I

In no small measure, the work of Keith Wrightson explains why two generations of historians have come to care about families like the Paynes, in places such as Terling. Indeed, Terling has become a totemic 'name' in the study of English social history, alongside other well-known (but little-visited) locations such as 'Wigston Magna', 'Colyton' or 'Myddle', precisely because it was the focus of the seminal study of social division and cultural separation between 1500 and 1700 published by Keith Wrightson and David Levine in 1979.[2] In fact, their study spawned a 'Terling thesis' within English historiography.

In line with earlier studies, Wrightson and Levine found that, as population pressure put agrarian resources under stress in the century after 1550, the process of social differentiation accelerated within the village producing a sharp increase in the numbers of the economically marginal, wage-earning segment and the more prosperous landholders and retailers.[3] They suggested that between 1524–25 and 1671 the proportion of the population in the bottom social category increased from 27.6 per cent to 50.8 per cent.[4] The

Research for this chapter was funded by a British Academy Small Grant SG091025. I am very grateful to Bethanie Afton for assistance in transcribing Terling parish overseers' rates and disbursements, 1745–1801, to Richard Smith, Director of The Cambridge Group for the Study of Population and Social Structure, for allowing me to consult family reconstitution records for Terling, 1550–1850, and, in particular, to Samantha Williams and John Broad for their detailed comments on this chapter.

[1]   In the database on which this research is based patrilineal family relationships have been recognised (by giving parents and children the same 'family' code), but each 'nuclear' unit of parents and children has been considered separately.

[2]   Wrightson & Levine, *Terling*.

[3]   Wrightson & Levine, *Terling*, 32–42; W. G. Hoskins, *The Midland Peasant: The Economic and Social History of a Leicestershire Village* (1957); D. G. Hey, *An English Rural Community: Myddle under the Tudors and Stuarts* (Leicester, 1974); Margaret Spufford, *Contrasting Communities. English Villagers in the Sixteenth and Seventeenth Centuries* (Cambridge, 1974).

[4]   Wrightson & Levine, *Terling*, 34–5. Miranda Chaytor, 'Household and Kinship: Ryton

most controversial element of the 'Terling thesis' was the suggestion that these growing economic and social distinctions resulted in a profound cultural separation between the more prosperous villagers and their poorer neighbours.[5] The purpose of this chapter is not to vindicate or disprove the broader 'Terling thesis', but rather to use its findings as the backdrop against which to view tears in the fabric of village life a century later. If historians of the sixteenth and seventeenth centuries have identified an ideological dimension to parochial disputes,[6] their counterparts investigating the eighteenth century have focused on the more immediately material, particularly struggles over the apportionment and disbursement of poor rates.[7] Detailed consideration of the intricacies in patterns of provision, perceptions of need, and questions of entitlement does allow several elements of the 'Terling thesis' to be projected forward into the eighteenth century.

Steve King has observed that historians of rural poverty and provision in the eighteenth and early nineteenth centuries seem to divide into optimists and pessimists, and has contrasted the more generous provision in the

in the late 16th and early 17th Centuries', *HWJ* 10 (1980), 25–60; Cicely Howell, *Land, Family and Inheritance in Transition: Kibworth Harcourt, 1280–1700* (Cambridge, 1983); Gwyneth Nair, *Highley: The Development of a Community, 1550–1850* (Oxford, 1988); Marjorie K. McIntosh, *A Community Transformed: The Manor and Liberty of Havering, 1500–1620* (Cambridge, 1991); John Goodacre, *The Transformation of a Peasant Economy: Townspeople and Villagers in the Lutterworth Area, 1500–1700* (1996); Pamela Sharpe, *Population and Society in an East Devon Parish Reproducing Colyton 1540–1840* (Exeter, 2002); Charles Cooper, *A Village in Sussex: The History of Kingston-near-Lewes* (2006).

5   Wrightson & Levine, *Terling*, 198–218. Additional contributions have come from Martin Ingram, *Church Courts, Sex and Marriage in England, 1570–1640* (Cambridge, 1987), 84–124; William Hunt, *The Puritan Moment. The Coming of Revolution in an English County* (Cambridge, MA, 1983), 159–82; Marjorie K. McIntosh, *Controlling Misbehavior in England, 1370–1600* (Cambridge, 1998), 186–209; Christopher Haigh, 'The Taming of the Reformation: Preachers, Pastors and Parishioners in Elizabethan and Early Stuart England', *History* 85 (2000), 572–88; *idem*, 'The Character of an Antipuritan', *Sixteenth-Century Journal* 35 (2004), 671–88; Eamon Duffy, *The Voices of Morebath: Reformation and Rebellion in an English Village* (New Haven, 2001).

6   Margaret Spufford, 'Puritanism and Social Control?', in *Order and Disorder in Early Modern England*, ed. Anthony Fletcher and John Stevenson (Cambridge, 1985), 41–57; Haigh, 'Antipuritan', 671–88; Eamon Duffy, 'The Godly and the Multitude in Stuart England', *The Seventeenth Century* 1 (1986), 31–49, p. 40; McIntosh, *Controlling Misbehavior*, 207–8.

7   Historians of the workings of the poor law have sometimes outlined a different pace of change. Cf. Steve Hindle, *On the Parish? The Micro-Politics of Poor Relief in Rural England, c.1550–1750* (Oxford, 2004), 363–4; Richard M. Smith, 'Some Issues Concerning Families and their Property in Rural England, 1250–1800', in *Land, Kinship and Life-cycle*, ed. Richard M. Smith (Cambridge, 1984), 1–86; Tim Wales, 'Poverty, Poor Relief and the Life Cycle: Some Evidence from Seventeenth-Century Norfolk', in *Land, Kinship and Life-cycle*, ed. Smith, 381–404; W. Newman-Brown, 'The Receipt of Poor Relief and Family Situation: Aldenham, Hertfordshire, 1630–90', in *Land, Kinship and Life-cycle*, ed. Smith, 405–22.

rural south with the parsimony practised in the industrialising north.[8] In lowland England, Keith Snell suggested in 1985 that the Elizabethan Poor Law embedded 'a face to face connection of administrators and the poor; while generous terms of relief and often humble officers facilitated agreement and mutual respect between the ranks and orders of parish society'.[9] More recently, Snell has noted that 'rising relief expenditure, dwindling access to commons and unenclosed land … rising population, often high unemployment, food shortages, near-famine prices, and the legal liability to maintain settled paupers' accentuated the role of the parish as 'a critical administrative, economic and apparently moral unit upon which the poor depended'.[10]

In Essex, such (qualified) optimism has been echoed by Thomas Sokoll's extremely detailed research. On the one hand, Sokoll is emphatic that 'there can be little doubt about the secular deterioration in the condition of the Essex agricultural labourer during the century after 1750'.[11] On the other, though, he argues that

> The evidence from both Ardleigh and Braintree has confirmed the notion of the Old Poor Law as a 'welfare-state in miniature' (Blaug) which offered relatively generous relief payments at critical points of the life-cycle.[12]

However, he admits that generosity had its limits, particularly in the very difficult years after 1795.[13]

By contrast, Pamela Sharpe has depicted parochial provision in eighteenth-century Essex in less positive terms, particularly in its treatment of women. The precipitous decline of the cloth trade in the county after 1720 removed a potentially valuable female by-employment, which had previously supplemented harvest work in rural parishes. Sharpe argues that this economic shift was compounded by new patterns of relief provision in the later eighteenth century, through which married women faced a 'double

---

[8]   This literature is reviewed comprehensively in Steven King, *Poverty and Welfare in England 1700–1850: A Regional Perspective* (Manchester, 2000), 49–65, 141–80, 181–226. See also Joan Kent and Steven King, 'Changing Patterns of Poor Relief in some English Rural Parishes circa 1650–1750', *Rural History* 14 (2003), 119–56.

[9]   K. D. M. Snell, *Annals of the Labouring Poor: Social Change and Agrarian England, 1660–1900* (Cambridge, 1984), 104.

[10] K. D. M. Snell, *Parish and Belonging: Community, Identity and Welfare in England and Wales 1700–1850* (Cambridge, 2006), 65. Nicola Whyte has demonstrated that many physical boundaries between parishes remained mutable: Nicola Whyte, *Inhabiting the Landscape. Place, Custom and Memory, 1500–1800* (Oxford, 2009), 90.

[11] Thomas Sokoll, *Household and Family among the Poor: The Case of Two Essex Communities in the Late Eighteenth and Early Nineteenth Centuries* (Bochum, 1993), 130.

[12] *Ibid.*, 291.

[13] *Ibid.*, 144.

deprivation'.[14] As Essex de-industrialised, and arable agriculture predominated, opportunities for regular and remunerative female employment in
the countryside remained infrequent.[15] Sharpe notes that by the turn of
the nineteenth century in Terling itself 'single or widowed women's wages
derived from agriculture were very small', with two-thirds of their income
being provided by poor relief.[16] Gleaning might supply flour worth 'from
an eighth to a tenth of total labouring family income', but Peter King has
shown that access to the fields was increasingly regulated by tenant farmers
in the county.[17] Joyce Burnette has also suggested that as labour competition in agriculture increased in the later eighteenth century as farmers
opted to support male rather than female employment, while R. C. Allen
has suggested this shift was most pronounced on larger farms.[18]

Similarly, Susannah Ottaway's detailed investigation of provision for the
elderly poor in eighteenth-century Terling has emphasised that price inflation put ever-greater pressure on parish pensions.[19] This echoes the work of
Richard Smith, who has suggested that these regular payments were eroded
significantly by inflation after 1760.[20] These trends were part of larger
changes which Steve King has suggested accelerated in southern England
after 1790, producing a marked 'change in the composition of the relief lists
from predominantly female and old to predominantly male and younger'.[21]

Samantha Williams's detailed examination of these trends in two Bedfordshire parishes, Campton and Shefford, shows that up to one-third of residents in these two communities were recipients of regular relief payments
at some point in their lives, with 46 per cent of rural Campton's population receiving relief during the crisis of 1801.[22] Williams argues that the
wartime crisis and its aftermath ensured that 'assistance from the poor law

[14] Pamela Sharpe, *Adapting to Capitalism: Working Women in the English Economy, 1700–
1850* (Basingstoke, 1995), 135.
[15] Sokoll, *Household and Family*, 264–6.
[16] *Ibid.*, 88.
[17] *Ibid.*, 82; Peter King, 'Gleaners, Farmers and the Failure of Legal Sanctions in England,
1750–1850', *P&P* 125 (1989), 116–50.
[18] Joyce Burnette, 'The Wages and Employment of Female Day-Labourers in English
Agriculture, 1740–1850', *EcHR* 2nd ser. 57 (2004), 664–90, p. 685; see also R. C. Allen,
Enclosure and the Yeoman: The Agricultural Development of the South Midlands, 1450–1850
(Oxford, 1992), 216–17, 247–52.
[19] Susannah R. Ottaway, 'Providing for the Elderly in Eighteenth-century England',
C&C 13 (1998), 391–418; *idem*, *The Decline of Life: Old Age in Eighteenth-Century
England* (Cambridge, 2004), 210, 222–8.
[20] Richard M. Smith, 'Ageing and Well-Being in Early Modern England: Pension Trends
and Gender Preferences Under the English Old Poor Law 1650–1800', in *Old Age from
Antiquity to Post-Modernity*, ed. Paul Johnson and Pat Thane (1998), 64–95.
[21] King, *Poverty and Welfare*, 143.
[22] Samantha Williams, 'Poor Relief, Labourers' Households and Living Standards in
Rural England c. 1770–1834: A Bedfordshire Case Study', *EcHR* 2nd ser. 58 (2005),
485–519.

was increasingly important in the economies of the poor in these communities, and in the rural south and east more generally', particularly within 'a narrowed economy of makeshifts', but that in general such provision was 'supplementary and limited in duration'.[23]

This chapter will assess these processes of development and the grounds for optimism or pessimism about the nature of rural poor provision by picking up the 'community narrative' in Terling in the second half of the eighteenth century. At this point, fifty years on from the close of *Poverty and Piety*, Wrightson and Levine suggest that the village had become 'a near classic example of the carefully regulated "closed parish"' under the control of a family of resident landlords, the Strutts.[24]

II

Although the Strutt family (later lords Rayleigh) only achieved complete control (and almost complete ownership) of Terling in the mid nineteenth century, John Strutt's purchase of the manor of Terling Place in 1760 was a decisive moment in the histories of the family and the village. The family were already substantial landowners in the parish, following the purchase of eight farms by Strutt's grandfather and uncle in the 1720s.[25] However, the purchase of Terling Place, and its five large leasehold farms, from Sir Matthew Featherstonehaugh added 843 acres to John Strutt's holdings in the village, at the cost of some £17,500. It also sealed Strutt's ambition to become the village 'squire', a status that he inscribed on the community by building an impressive Palladian residence, called Terling Place, between 1762 and 1771.[26] In 1776, Strutt added the Terling Hall estate, with three other leasehold farms and 271 acres, for a further £7,000. These purchases made him the largest single proprietor in the village.[27] Although this concentration was still relatively unusual in Essex, the Strutts fitted seamlessly into a county society populated by former cloth-manufacturers, London merchants, and tradesmen, East India 'nabobs' and more established landed families, such as the Mildmays, Honeywoods, Petres, and Abdys.[28]

[23] *Ibid.*, 516–17.
[24] Wrightson & Levine, *Terling*, 183–4.
[25] Sir William Gavin, *Ninety Years of Family Farming: The Story of Lord Rayleigh's and Strutt & Parker Farms* (1967), 2, 5.
[26] John Strutt moved to Terling in 1762, and Terling Place was completed by 1772, at a cost of £6,045 10s 5½d. Gavin, *Family Farming*, 7.
[27] In 1781 Strutt's lands (some 2,653 acres) comprised 82 per cent of the parish's area and 60 per cent of the parish's annual land tax valuation. *Ibid.*, 8; Essex Record Office [ERO], Q/RPL 1054–1075, Witham Hundred Land Tax Assessments, 1781–98.
[28] A. F. J. Brown, *Prosperity and Poverty: Rural Essex, 1700–1815* (Chelmsford, 1996), 76–107.

What kind of community was Terling at this time? The sale particulars for Terling Place described the village's situation in the following terms:

lying in the proper neighbourhood, five miles from Braintree and Bocking, three miles from Witham, and six from Chelmsford ... is in a very healthy country thirty four miles from London, and as above, from the three best Market Towns in Essex.[29]

The village was a nucleated settlement, encompassing 3,228 statute acres in the mid nineteenth century, with its centre arranged along the road south to Hatfield Peverel (where it joined the main London–Colchester highway). It was only half a day's ride from London, and its agriculture benefited from extensive local and metropolitan demand. This drove up land values and cereal prices.[30]

The period after 1760 was also an era when the processes of economic change within the county accelerated, as cloth manufacture declined to extinction and arable husbandry had to fill the void. Although Terling had never been a centre of cloth production,[31] spinning had provided a significant by-employment, supplementing the earnings of women and children within labouring households sometimes by more than 4s per week in the 1730s.[32] Industrial decline occurred in two phases. In the first, up to the beginning of the Seven Years War in 1756, the industry shrank back to its established centres (Colchester, Braintree, Bocking, and Coggeshall).[33] In the second phase, between 1763 and the late 1790s, the decline accelerated,[34] and earnings from spinning halved to approximately 2s per week in the 1790s, a level below the subsistence wage, although yarn production persisted after the final collapse of the Essex cloth industry.[35] Indeed, in November 1800, Terling vestry noted that, 'Such Poor Persons as belong to the Parish may be supplied with spinning by applying to Edward Garnett'.[36] Four months later, the parish paid Widow Thurgood 4s for teaching children how to spin.[37]

In rural parishes in central Essex, such as Terling, wheat cultivation

[29] ERO, D/DRa/E15, Terling Place Estate notebook, 1731–78, sale particulars of manor of Terling Place, 1760.
[30] Ottaway found that cereal prices in Terling were consistently above the national level: 'Providing for the Elderly', 409.
[31] Brown, *Prosperity and Poverty*, 16.
[32] Sharpe, *Adapting to Capitalism*, 34; Brown's 'tentative' estimates of household income suggest 5s per week for spinning by 'wife and daughter' between 1730–40 and 1760–70, declining to 4s per week 1785–90: A. F. J. Brown, *Essex at Work, 1700–1815* (Chelmsford, 1969), 134.
[33] Brown, *Essex at Work*, 1–28; Sharpe, *Adapting to Capitalism*, 19–38.
[34] Brown, *Essex at Work*, 22, Sharpe, *Adapting to Capitalism*, 27–30.
[35] Sharpe, *Adapting to Capitalism*, 34.
[36] ERO, D/P 299/8/3, Terling Vestry Minutes, 3 Nov. 1800.
[37] ERO, D/P 299/12/3, Terling Parish Overseers' Accounts, 1790–1801, 16 Mar. 1801.

Table 12.1. Social position in Terling, 1524*, 1671* and 1801

	1524		1671			1801		1801	All years
Category	Assessment	% Distrib.	Hearths	% Distrib.	Criteria		% Distrib.	% Distrib.	% Distrib.
I	£10–54 land or goods	11.8	6 to 20	8.2	Ratepayers >twice par. mean		7.7	7.7	7.7
II	>£2–£8 land or goods	36.8	3 to 5	23.8	Ratepayers		14.3	14.3	14.3
III	£2 goods	23.7	1	17.2	Not ratepayers, not on relief		47	47	29.8
IV	<£2 land or earnings	27.6	1 and excused	50.8	Receiving relief		31	31	48.2
Total		76 Persons		122 Families			168 Families		

Source: Wrightson & Levine, *Terling*, 34–5

dominated in the later eighteenth century, as population, demand, and grain prices all rose, albeit generally in advance of labourers' wages.[38] John Strutt of Terling Place was an agricultural 'improver' and correspondent of Arthur Young, interested in both increasing wheat and barley yields and the quality of his livestock, particularly sheep.[39] Between 1781 and 1816, Strutt also increased his income from Terling, from £1,887 to £3,909, achieving a 52 per cent increase in rent while expanding his estate in the village by a further 21 per cent.[40] A. F. J. Brown suggests that male wages in agriculture stagnated at around 7s per week in the centre of the county between 1760 and 1790, with decline in female earnings (resulting from falling piece-rates for spinning) and static wages for youths in husbandry. At the same time, he speculates that food costs had risen from one-third of weekly household incomes in the 1730s to just under half in the 1790s.[41] By 1796, during the wartime economic 'emergency', Sokoll found that 'there is no reason to assume that those above the poverty line were substantially better off' even though wages now averaged 8s 9½d per week.[42]

As a consequence, it is not surprising that Table 12.1 shows how social divisions had become entrenched in eighteenth-century Terling. The table categorises the 1801 census population in accordance with Wrightson and Levine's categories for the 1524 Lay Subsidy and the 1671 Hearth Tax. Categories I–III are broadly comparable; however, those who paid on land or earnings worth less than £2 in 1524 would probably have enjoyed access to more resources (allowing for inflation and rising consumption patterns) than their counterparts in category IV in 1801. Table 12.1 illustrates that the population of Terling in 1801 had increased significantly since the later seventeenth century. There were now 708 inhabitants living in the village, gathered together in 168 families. The wealthier section of the village, in categories I and II, comprised a smaller proportion of the total population (just over 20 per cent) than 130 years before. The number of wealthy property owners in the village was actually somewhat larger, but an increasing proportion no longer lived there. At first sight, it appears that the proportion of the village in the poorest social category had also declined, from 50.8 per cent to 31 per cent. However, it might be better to equate category IV in 1671 with some of categories III and IV in 1801. The census is, inevitably, a snap-shot. If we examine the 1801 census population through time, we discover that, in fact, twenty-nine families who did not receive relief in 1801 *had* done so in the recent past. This leaves category IV much closer to

---

[38] G. A. Ward, 'Essex Farming in 1801', *Essex Archaeology and History* 5 (1973), 185–201.

[39] Gavin, *Family Farming*, 11.

[40] *Ibid.*, 8–9.

[41] Brown, *Essex at Work*, 132–4.

[42] Sokoll, *Household and Family*, 119. By 1804 wages rates in Ardleigh increased 50 per cent to 13s 2½d per week, significantly above the county mean.

the 50 per cent level of 130 years before, with the proviso that, as a whole, members of this group were probably more dependent on parish relief than their peers in 1671. In these respects, the parish had continued filling up from the bottom of the social scale.[43] There were, perhaps, twenty additional poor families at the end of the eighteenth century compared to 1671, and their poverty was probably more intense.

III

While John Strutt was undoubtedly *primus inter pares* in Terling (as an MP, JP, and vestry member), the day-to-day running of the parish tended to remain in the hands of the largest tenant farmers.[44] A resident landlord could not execute all the offices of parish government himself, even if John Strutt maintained a close eye on the community and its administration.[45] By 1800, such surveillance was helped by the fact that nine out of the twelve largest ratepayers were his tenants, who between them had served as overseers thirty-eight times.[46]

The parish vestry provides a useful illustration of the concentration of power among the larger tenant farmers and of some of their social attitudes. For example, on 1 May 1775 the vestry observed that the village's two alehouses needed to be better regulated:

> These rules are meant to Restrain the Loose & Wicked who by Sotting at the Houses neglect & starve their Familys & whose Children are brought up in Idleness & Debauchery & are rendered unfit for service & not to deprive the industrious & Honest Labourer of proper Refreshment & enjoying the Accustomed Holydays of Christmas & Whitsuntide.[47]

The order was signed by seventeen parishioners, including the Rector, Charles Phillips, and John Strutt. Of these seventeen, sixteen had served as overseers of the poor, accounting for 36 per cent of all years served between 1745 and 1801. Only five had served in the more prestigious, but largely ceremonial, office of churchwarden, but they monopolised the office, accounting for 71 per cent of all the years served in this period. Similarly, this apparently random list of vestrymen eventually attended just over half (53 per cent) of all the vestry meetings between 1766 and 1801 (that is 1,698 out of 3,226 attendances). They also averaged rate payments that

---

[43] Wrightson & Levine, *Terling*, 36.
[44] Brown, *Prosperity and Poverty*, 88.
[45] He served as overseer five times between 1766 and 1794 and attended the vestry sixty-one times between 1753 and 1801.
[46] Brown, *Prosperity and Poverty*, 158–9.
[47] ERO, D/P 299/8/1, Terling Parish Vestry Book, 1 May 1775.

were 263 per cent of the yearly parish mean across their lives as ratepayers in Terling.[48] Of this group, at least five were tenants to Strutt's large farms.[49]

Although condemnation of misbehaviour among 'Labours and other Working Persons' was repeated within the vestry minutes each time the poor rates rose, it continued to reflect what Steve Hindle has termed 'the discretionary calculus of eligibility' that had become embedded within the Old Poor Law.[50] In fact, these comments were very similar in tone to the complaints of Terling's village officers in 1620 about drunken disorders 'whereby the name of god is highly dishonoured, idleness maintained and our parishe of itself poor enough impoverished and decayed'.[51] By the end of the eighteenth century, though, there were two differences. Firstly, the problem was now depicted primarily as one of household provision, rather than as a threat to individual, and collective, salvation. Secondly, the village elite depicted the matter as a one that followed, rather than spanned, a social divide. Drunkenness still threatened to impoverish the village, but mainly by affecting a distinct group of 'others', defined by their manual labour and (implicitly) their wage-earning status. Vestry orders continued to assume that the parish was a 'moral community', in which each group had a responsibility to the other, but the groups themselves were increasingly well-defined, and further apart.[52]

IV

By the latter half of the eighteenth century, the 'Elizabethan' poor law system had been in operation for almost 200 years. As Snell has suggested, it was embedded in people's lives, not merely as an administrative system, but also as a set of social and cultural practices. The generation that grappled with the Poor Law after 1750 had been born into it, as had their parents, grandparents, and great-grandparents.

---

[48] This approach requires the transcription of all rates in the series and the calculation of the indexed mean figure for each person in each year of the sample, involving 8,263 entries for Terling between Easter 1745 and Easter 1801. The eighty-eight parishioners who held office or attended the vestry between 1750 and 1801 paid rates that averaged 224 per cent of the parish mean for all ratepayers in this period.

[49] Isaac Ling (who held Great and Little Farsley farms, c.150 ac. between 1754 and 1791), John Speakman (who held one-third of Parsonage farm, c.100 ac, between 1764 and 1793), George Taylor (who held Maddox Farm, 1757–78), George Clarke (who held Sparrows Farm, 1759–81), and Philip Potter (who held Scarletts Farm between 1762 and 1801).

[50] Hindle, On the Parish?, 379–98.

[51] Wrightson & Levine, Terling, 136–7.

[52] See Keith Wrightson, 'The Decline of Neighbourliness Revisited', in Local Identities in Late Medieval and Early Modern England, ed. N. L. Jones and D. R. Woolf (Basingstoke, 2007), 19–49.

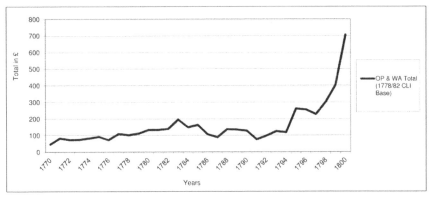

Figure 12.1. Terling, 1770–1800: occasional payments and weekly allowances.

Until the 1790s it appears that the system coped in Terling. As Figure 12.1 shows, although the real value of disbursements apparently doubled between the early 1770s and the mid 1780s, thereafter they fell back to their earlier levels until the mid 1790s, when absolute and relative levels of disbursements rocketed.[53] It is possible to correlate these peaks with the vestry's expressions of outrage and special initiatives. In 1785, when disbursements were three times the 1770 figure, even allowing for inflation, the vestry

> Resolv'd that such poor Persons who have been reliev'd within the last Twelve Months should give an Account to the Parishioners in what manner they employ themselves for their own and Family's support and what Money they weekly earn. Resolv'd that in order to obtain the above information it is necessary that some one principal Parishioner should visit a certain Number of Families and inquire into the same and also to observe their conduct and behaviour and that they be admonish'd to behave with regularity and in particular on Sundays.[54]

Figure 12.2 illustrates the annual value of weekly allowances and occasional payments, and the total annual nominal rateable value of properties in Terling, with these values deflated by cost of living index (CLI) data from Charles Feinstein.[55] It suggests that in the 1770s and 1780s the parish vestry was fairly successful in pegging relief levels and rateable values to the cost of

[53] Index figures for cost of living and average full-employment real earnings are taken from Charles H. Feinstein, 'Pessimism Perpetuated: Real Wages and the Standard of Living in Britain During and After the Industrial Revolution', *Journal of Economic History* 58 (1998), 625–58, pp. 652–3; the same trends in disbursements are found by Williams for Campton (Bedfordshire) and Sokoll for Ardleigh (Essex). Williams, 'Poor Relief', Figure 1, p. 492; Sokoll, *Household and Family*, Figure 5.2, p. 138.

[54] ERO, D/P 299/8/2, Terling Parish Vestry Book, 28 Nov. 1785.

[55] Feinstein, 'Pessimism Perpetuated', 652–3.

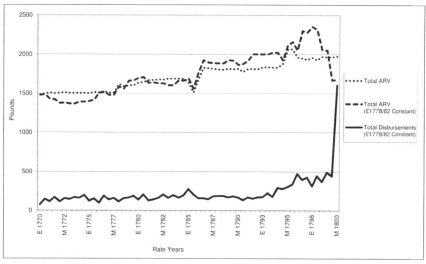

Figure 12.2. Terling, 1770–1800: annual rateable values (ARV) and disbursements.

living, perhaps helped by use of the parish workhouse to limit expenditure on those in long-term dependence, after spending increases following the economic down-turn of 1781–84. However, after Michaelmas 1793 the real value of expenditure began to rise, and the nominal value of the taxable base fell. In 1795, when relief levels were three-times the 1751 level, the vestry took special measures to limit wheat prices, sell more cheaply to the poor, and restrict gleaning rights to widows and poor families.[56]

In one respect, this crisis was partly of the ratepayers' own making. Although relief levels rose in real terms, the nominal valuations of properties on which the rates were based did not. Figure 12.2 shows how the annual property valuations on which rates were calculated were eroded by cost-of-living inflation, particularly in the late 1790s. Increasingly, these assessments of rateable value diverged from the rising real returns on the ratepayers' property, which must have been well in excess of the 52 per cent increase recorded in the Strutts' estate rents. However, the slowly rising annual rateable valuations represented the public 'story' about their estates, and highlighted the limits of their ability to bear substantial increases in expenditure. As the graph suggests, this story was undermined in the winter of 1800, when the ratepayers were forced to bear burdens apparently in far excess of the 'real' value of their rateable capacity.

Secondly, though, these parochial resolutions reflected an understanding that the Poor Law could act as a welfare mechanism both by fixing wage-rates and sharing out employment in ways that deviate distinctly from

[56] ERO, D/P 299/8/2, Terling Parish Vestry Book, 25 Mar. 1795, 6 July 1795, 21 July 1795.

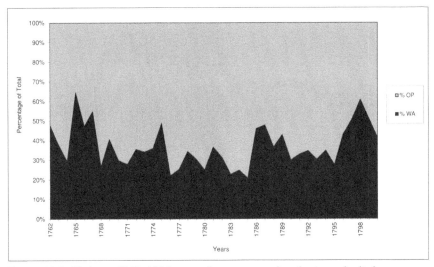

Figure 12.3. Terling, 1762–1800: annual percentage distribution of relief payments.

emerging notions of *laissez-faire*. The 1785 resolutions are faint echoes, but echoes nonetheless, of the interventionist policies of Essex vestries in the tough times of the 1620s.[57] These resolutions indicate that although social distinctions were increasingly entrenched, there was still a consensus among the parish rulers about the *function* of the Poor Law as an amalgam of social obligations and responsibilities. As Hindle and Snell have also pointed out, whatever their feelings, magisterial oversight ensured that vestries actually had little scope to cut off payments to the legally settled poor.[58]

At the end of the century, the wartime emergency of two consecutive harvest failures, heavy taxation and government borrowing, and rapid price inflation projected the existing Poor Law system into uncharted territory. Even allowing for the rapid price inflation between 1798 and 1801 (when prices rose by approximately 36 per cent), at constant 1778–82 prices the poor relief total in the village in 1800 was over 600 per cent of its 1770 level. In the winter of 1800, the parish was spending in one month what it had previously spent in six.[59] Eventually, in January 1801, the vestry instituted a system of direct doles of cheap substitute foods (flour, rice, and herrings), presumably to counter rising prices and limit the distribution of cash, which might find its way to the alehouse.[60] At the same time, inspection visits by

[57] F. G. Emmison, ed., *Early Essex Town Meetings: Braintree, 1619–1636, Finchingfield, 1626–1634* (Chichester, 1970), 86.
[58] Hindle, *On the Parish?*, 405–32; Snell, *Parish and Belonging*, 81–162.
[59] ERO, D/P 299/12/3, Terling Parish Overseers' Accounts, 1790–1801. Between Michaelmas and Easter 1797, the overseers disbursed £174 9s 1½d. Between 21 Dec. 1800 and 18 Jan. 1801, they disbursed £221 8s 5d.
[60] ERO, D/P 299/12/3, Terling Parish Overseers' Accounts, 1790–1801, 31 Jan. 1801;

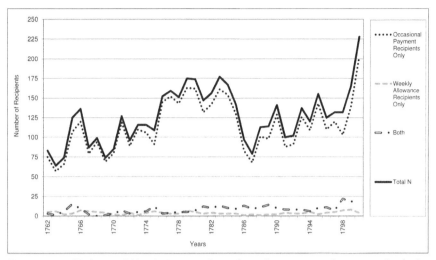

Figure 12.4. Terling, 1762–1800: annual number of recipients of occasional relief, weekly allowances and both occasional relief and weekly allowances.

individual vestry members to poor households were revived, according to a strict rota laid out in the vestry minutes.[61]

V

Figure 12.3 illustrates the balance of relief expenditure in Terling after 1762. Although there were regular fluctuations in the value of allowances and occasional payments, across the period weekly pensions accounted for just over one-third of the value of annual poor relief expenditure, while occasional payments comprised almost two-thirds. In fact, as Sokoll has suggested for eighteenth-century Ardleigh, the term 'occasional poor relief is something of a misnomer'.[62] In Steve King's south-eastern sample the balance shifted more towards occasional payments, so that 'by 1801 only around one-half of communal welfare resources were devoted to pensions'.[63] Historical attention has focused on weekly 'pensions' because they are easier to deal with than the jumble of irregular payments recorded from week to week in overseers' accounts. However, these occasional relief payments supply much greater detail about the operation of the poor law, and reached

'Return of the Poor Inhabitants of the Parish of Terling taken in the month of January 1801'.
[61] ERO, D/P 299/8/2, Terling Parish Vestry Book, 14 Nov. 1799.
[62] Sokoll, *Household and Family*, 147.
[63] King, *Poverty and Welfare*, 155–6.

Table 12.2. Terling, overseers' disbursements, 1762–1801: percentage distribution of the value of payments per category

Disbursement categories	Time Periods							
	1762–64	1765–69	1770–74	1775–79	1780–84	1785–89	1790–94	1795–1801
Settlement	9.64	3.56	3.67	1.02	1.74	1.28	1.59	4.76
Clothing	23.22	8.67	2.71	25.78	21.65	14.06	14.57	13.51
Shoes	2.01	1.42	0.17	13.71	10.1	6.37	6.92	4.24
Administrative Expenses	3.27	1.46	2.92	2.04	4.43	4.22	4.13	0.87
Sickness	8.11	32.17	24.94	21.58	9.43	6.17	10.26	4.33
Food & Drink	0.23	3	1.06	5.18	17.51	10.05	14.11	7.64
Care Costs	0.33	9.68	9.84	6.28	8.81	14.54	13.81	9.53
Baptisms, Marriages & Burials	8.56	9.42	9.64	3.97	6.64	4.37	5.09	3.44
Household Equipment	0.55	0.47	0.45	0.57	0.43	0.36	0.08	0.36
Fuel	0.55	1.87	1.69	0.94	2.1	2.68	0.57	1.22
General Allowances	30.64	24.93	38.84	16.99	16.48	35.81	28.45	50.09
Rent	12.88	3.34	3.93	1.96	0.68	0.08	0.41	0
Total %	100	100	100	100	100	100	100	100

a much larger population than can be observed from the weekly pension lists alone.

Figure 12.4 shows that the annual number of recipients of occasional relief always far outweighed the numbers of parish pensioners, even if the latter always received much more relief per capita. While the former rarely fell below 100 individuals per annum after 1770, the latter averaged eight per annum (half of whom also received occasional payments). By the 1790s approximately 120 individuals per annum were receiving some form of paro- chial assistance, compared to an average of ninety in the 1760s.

Table 12.2 is based on 15,294 individual payments made by the parish overseers to 809 relief recipients between 1762 and 1801, and shows the distribution of the value of expenditure between various payment categories in each five-year period. It suggests that the bulk of the overseers' disburse- ments were spent on direct individual relief provision (either non-specified money doles or 'allowances', or specific sums for clothing, shoes, heating, working tools or equipment, sickness, and care costs). Medical and care costs (primarily payments to other relief recipients for nursing) accounted for between 10 and 25 per cent of the total value (except between 1766 and 1774 when they exceeded 35 per cent). Administrative expenses and settlement cases rarely absorbed more than 5–6 per cent of the value of occasional payments.

As in most other communities, by the end of the eighteenth century the parish's poor relief system had generated a series of provisions that were comprehensive, responsive to individual need, and which retained the moral compass of the original legislation.[64] Ottaway has even suggested that weekly pensions in Terling were slightly more generous on a per capita basis than the national average.[65] However, Figure 12.5 implies that she and Smith are also correct in asserting that in general their value (which aver- aged less than 2s per week) was not increased in line with inflation until 1795.[66] Until then, on average 85 per cent of pensions in Terling amounted to no more than 2s per week, which is in line with Sokoll's findings for Ardleigh and Steve King's more general figures in the same period.[67] The system was really designed only to relieve immediate needs, and to supple-

---

[64] Barry Stapleton, 'Inherited Poverty and Life-Cycle Poverty: Odiham, Hampshire, 1650–1850', *SH* 18 (1993), 339–55; Samantha Williams, 'Malthus, Marriage and Poor Law Allowances Revisited: A Bedfordshire Case Study, 1770–1834', *Agricultural History Review* 52 (2004), 56–82; idem, 'Poor Relief', 506–15.

[65] Ottaway found that per capita spending in Terling between 1795 and 1800 was 12s *per annum*, whereas the national average in 1802–3 was 9.5s for the whole of England and Wales. Ottaway, *Decline of Life*, 222.

[66] Weekly pensions were increased in line with inflation in Campton (Bedfordshire) from the 1790s. Williams, 'Poor Relief', Figure 3, p. 494.

[67] Sokoll, *Household and Family*, 150. King gives an average pension of 1s 8d per week for his sample parishes in the 1770s, rising to 2s 4d per week by 1821: *Poverty and Welfare*, 152.

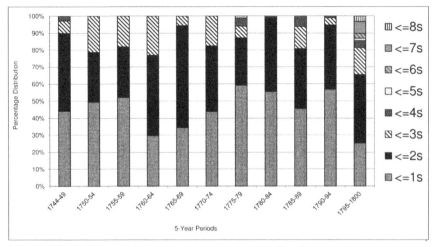

Figure 12.5. Terling, weekly allowances, 1744–1800: distribution of pension payments.

ment subsistence for most recipients rather than to secure it. Payments for clothing, shoes, and tools probably also had an 'enabling' aspect, that is, to provide equipment necessary for individuals to gain and maintain employment (and so reduce relief bills in the process).

Even so, this 'enabling' dimension of poor relief may have had another aspect. The database of payments allows month-by-month breakdowns of occasional payments. Across a year, the per capita size of these payments was small. However, the mean size of each payment per month was rather more substantial, averaging 8.4s per person. If we strip out specific allowances for food, shoes, clothing, fuel or rent, the mean figure for each individual (cash?) 'allowance' payment was 6.7s per person between 1762 and 1801. Given that each person received relatively few payments per year (on average only 2.6 payments per year through the period) these sums added up to relatively small amounts for each recipient in each year. However, if each payment is regarded as *replacement income* for the particular week or weeks in which it was granted, the pro rata levels of occasional payments were quite substantial. Although occasional payments generally amounted to an annualised figure of less than 1s per head, if they supplied missing weekly income at the rate of 6s or 8s in the one or two weeks of the year in which they were required, they may have been regarded as fairly 'generous' by the successful recipients. However, the Terling overseers' accounts do not tell us how many relief applications were rejected.

This represents a slightly different perspective on poor relief, and an acceptance that it was not a comprehensive social safety net but quite often simply sticking-plaster for the household economy in one or two weeks in the year. Viewed in this light, payments that amount to relatively trivial per annum levels of income support could function as fairly substantial stop-gap payments, in a system that was designed (and expected) to deal with infrequent 'emergencies' rather than persistent privation.

VI

What about the recipients? Although a full family reconstitution has not been attempted for this chapter, the categories of recipients of occasional relief in Figure 12.6 represent estimates of age and marital status based on Terling parish registers between 1730 and 1801, cross-referenced with data on individuals abstracted from the family reconstitution undertaken by the Cambridge Group.[68] Although there were considerable variations between 1762 and 1801, between one-third and a half of the value of all occasional payments were made to married adults under the age of sixty. In fact, when we break down the 'married' category by gender, married men as household heads tended to receive more payments than married women, receiving an average of 30 per cent of the value of all occasional payments across the time periods, compared to just over 17 per cent for married women. However, when payments to two-parent families were squeezed by disbursements to widows and widowers between 1780 and 1790, the amounts paid to married men and women were equal (at around 25 per cent of all payments), with the gap reopening after 1790.

A further 25 per cent of total expenditure was given to named children under the age of twenty (others were hidden in payments to adults), while between 10 and 20 per cent was spent on widows and widowers under sixty years old, with the remaining 5–15 per cent paid to those over sixty years old. Children were most often the named recipients of payments for clothing, footwear, and care-costs (when they were placed with other families, or when sums were paid for apprenticeships or boarding or wage costs). They also received sums for working equipment, because the parish maintained a consistent policy to the end of the period of buying spinning wheels for girls *and* boys. The parish also used a system of cross-payments, paying widows (in particular) who were already in receipt of poor relief for nursing and watching over sick neighbours. For example, between August 1762 and

---

[68] In MS Access, each occasional payment was coded according to the life-cycle/age/status category of the recipient *at the time of the payment*, as well as his or her gender, and the type of payment made. Coding each entry allowed assessment of changes in the status of each recipient through time. Individuals listed in the database were identified and differentiated by nominal and chronological linkage with ERO, D/P 299/1/4, Terling Baptism Register 1688–1802, Marriage Register 1688–1754, Burial Register 1688–1802 (accessed at seax.essexcc.gov.uk/Images.Net/?ID=966029&intThisRecordsOffSet=1&int OffSet=0); D/P 299/1/9, Marriage Register 1754–84; D/P 299/1/10, Marriage Register 1784–1812; and through the Cambridge Group Family Reconstitution Forms.

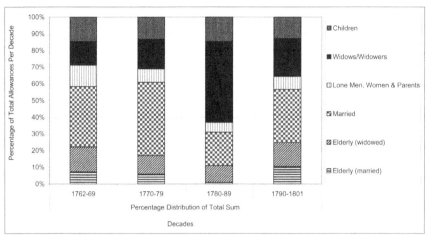

Figure 12.6. Terling, 1762–1801: percentage distribution of value of occasional payments and weekly allowances to recipient groups.

March 1798 Sarah Payne was paid for nursing, sitting with, and assisting with funeral preparations for sixteen of her neighbours.[69]

In line with Steve King's findings, the proportion of sums devoted to pensions for the over-sixties fell from over 50 per cent of the total value of weekly allowances before 1775 to under 25 per cent until the end of the century.[70] From this point, a much greater proportion (over 60 per cent of the annual value of pensions between 1785–89 and 1795–1801) was devoted to relieving younger widows and widowers, particularly those with dependent children. This shift reflected either the short-term fluctuations in the patterns of need or greater provision for the elderly in the workhouse.[71]

Table 12.3 is rather complicated, but breaks down the proportion of occasional payments according to the type of recipient, the type of payment,

[69] ERO, D/P 299/12/1c, Terling Overseers Accounts, 1762–77, payments to Sarah Payne for helping Hannah Tilbrook, 2 Aug. 1762; James Ward, 4 Nov. 1771; for Elizabeth Bass, 21 and 29 Sep. 1772 and 10 Jun. 1777; D/P 299/12/2, Overseers Accounts, 1777–90 for Mary Middleton, 5 Feb. 1784; washing for Richard Stacey's family, 4 May 1784; with Dame Cottis for Elizabeth Smith, 7 Feb. 1785; for a shroud for Sarah Wenden, 22 Apr. 1785; for Sarah Thurgood, 11 Mar. 1788; with Wid. Thurgood for Thomas Bass, 7 Sep. 1789; for Dorothy Dowsett, 12 Dec. 1788; for Hannah Stammers, 18 Oct. 1789; D/P 299/12/3, Overseers Accounts, 1790–1801, for nursing Sarah May, 14 Sep. 1795; Elizabeth Ward, 11 Mar. 1798.
[70] King, *Poverty and Welfare*, 168.
[71] In each year between 1775 and 1788, adult women (under sixty years old) comprised over 40 per cent of inmates listed in seven out of fourteen years, while female children comprised more than 40 per cent of inmates listed in six years. For two years after the revival of the workhouse in 1800 almost all its inmates appear to have been adult or elderly men.

Table 12.3. Terling, occasional payments, 1762–1801: recipient profile and payment types

Condition type	Payment category	1762–64	1765–69	1770–74	1775–79	1780–84	1785–89	1790–94	1795–1801
Children	Administrative Expenses	7.8	0	1.1	1	1.6	2	0.7	0.8
	Baptisms, Marriages & Burials	6	3.6	19.5	2.8	4.6	2.5	2.6	5.3
	Care Costs	1.5	11.5	47.8	9.6	27.4	28.7	26.6	39.7
	Clothing	30.4	28.5	6.8	45.1	39.9	13.1	14.3	13.6
	Food & Drink	0.2	0	0.3	0.6	0.4	0.3	3.6	0.8
	Fuel	0	0.1	0	0	0	0	0	0
	General Allowances	48.1	20.6	4.8	16.5	2.5	44.3	37.7	29.7
	Household Equipment	0	0	0	1.5	0.5	0.4	0.2	0
	Rent	0.2	0	0	0	0	0	0	0
	Settlement	0	3.2	0	0	0	0	0.2	3.8
	Shoes	5	3.8	0.9	21.4	18.6	4.9	7.3	4.1
	Sickness	0.8	28.5	18.7	1.7	4.5	3.7	6.8	2.1
Female (Married)	Administrative Expenses	0	0.2	0.4	0.1	12.8	0.7	21.3	1
	Baptisms, Marriages & Burials	15.5	12.2	11.1	4.8	6.5	13.6	5.4	5.6
	Care Costs	0	0.6	5.7	0.5	0	7.3	8	1
	Clothing	6.1	2.1	5.8	18.9	13.6	26.2	14.5	17.7
	Food & Drink	1.2	0.9	1.1	2.6	7.4	5.4	12.1	0.6
	Fuel	0	0	1.7	0.5	0	0	0	0.1
	General Allowances	28.3	20.2	25.2	3.1	36.1	20.8	1.3	61.9
	Household Equipment	0	0.2	0.3	0.4	0.2	0	0	0.4
	Rent	0	0.3	9.4	3.3	0	0	0	0
	Settlement	0	3.6	0.4	0	0.1	12.4	0	0.6
	Shoes	0	0	0	8.8	4.9	3.2	5	3.4
	Sickness	48.8	59.7	38.7	57	18.3	10.5	32.4	7.8
Male (Married)	Administrative Expenses	4	1.6	0.4	0.3	2.2	8.6	5.1	1.1
	Baptisms, Marriages & Burials	12.2	6.2	3.3	4.3	5.6	2.5	1.5	1.5
	Care Costs	0	7.9	13.3	2.1	0	8.3	6.6	1.7
	Clothing	7.1	2.5	2.7	19.7	14.5	11.9	11.3	8.3
	Food & Drink	0.4	5.5	1.3	16.2	35	33.2	30.3	12.4
	Fuel	1.7	5.7	2.3	2.3	5.9	4.3	0.5	2
	General Allowances	42.3	27.1	38.2	13.7	5.2	9.7	25.7	58.1
	Household Equipment	1.8	0.4	0.9	0	0.6	0.5	0.2	0.5
	Rent	15.9	9.9	2.6	0	0	0	1.6	0
	Settlement	0.8	7.2	8.3	0.9	3.5	4.1	1	5.9

	Shoes	2.5	2.1	0.3	16.4	12.8	10.6	7	3.8
	Sickness	11.4	24	26.3	24.1	14.7	6.4	9.3	4.6
Old Person (Married)	Administrative Expenses	0	28.4	0	0	0	0	0	0
	Baptisms, Marriages & Burials	0	0	0	11.2	20.1	0	0	0
	Care Costs	0	0	0	0	0	0	0.4	0
	Clothing	6.2	9.1	0	6.2	1.4	36.4	12	43.7
	Food & Drink	0	0	0	6.7	35.8	0	34.1	2.6
	Fuel	0	0	0	3.1	0.7	0	0	0
	General Allowances	6.6	10.8	23.6	11.5	1.5	25	36.9	41.9
	Rent	87.1	0	0	0	0	0	0	0
	Shoes	0	0	0	10.4	11	38.6	7.6	9.6
	Sickness	0	51.7	76.4	50.8	29.5	0	9	2.2
Old Person (Widowed)	Administrative Expenses	5.3	1.9	1.2	0	0.7	0.4	0	0.1
	Baptisms, Marriages & Burials	14.1	25	15.9	0	20.8	1.7	31.8	5.1
	Care Costs	0	13	0.5	0	0.1	0	0	0.4
	Clothing	18.4	2.1	0.5	21.9	31.7	16	29	33.3
	Food & Drink	0	0.5	0.4	4.1	3	2.2	11.3	2.3
	Fuel	0	0.6	0.9	0	0.9	7.6	1.2	2
	General Allowances	48	29.6	59	31.3	27.2	56.3	16.3	46.1
	Household Equipment	0	2.9	0	0	0.5	0	0	0.3
	Rent	14.2	0	3.5	9.5	0	0	0	0
	Settlement	0	0	0.2	4.4	0	0	0	0
	Shoes	0	1.2	0	8.7	10.9	10	4	8.9
	Sickness	0	23.1	17.8	20.1	4.2	5.7	6.4	1.6
Single	Administrative Expenses	0	0.9	8.2	21.1	15.1	15.7	2.7	0.7
	Baptisms, Marriages & Burials	10.4	27.4	28.6	3.5	18.4	3.7	17.8	5.5
	Care Costs	0	19.7	0	13	9.9	18.5	0	0.4
	Clothing	0	13.1	3.1	26.3	18.2	25.3	20.6	12.4
	Food & Drink	0	6.2	1	1.2	3.8	4.9	2.3	3.2
	Fuel	0	1.4	0	0.4	0.9	0.2	4.2	2.8
	General Allowances	2	11	39.4	7.3	12.2	12.3	20.2	53.6
	Household Equipment	0	0.5	0	0	0	0.8	0	0.2
	Rent	25.4	5.2	0.7	0.2	0	0	0	0
	Settlement	56.2	6.8	12.6	5.4	4.4	0	14.1	7.2
	Shoes	0	1.9	0	12.3	8.4	10.1	11.6	5.3
	Sickness	6	5.9	6.3	9.3	8.8	8.5	6.6	8.7

Widowed (<60)	Administrative Expenses	0.2	0.2	11.8	1.3	0.2	1	0	0.3
	Baptisms, Marriages & Burials	3.4	2.7	1.4	5.6	2.5	7.5	5.2	1.4
	Care Costs	0	0	5.2	3	10.2	5.5	16.2	9.9
	Clothing	70.2	10	0.5	11.8	14.4	13.3	13.2	14.3
	Food & Drink	0	3.7	1.9	5.2	28.3	11.1	4.4	8.9
	Fuel	0	1.3	3.4	1.2	2.9	6.3	0.3	0.2
	General Allowances	13.5	54.1	58.4	29.2	27.1	41.5	52.6	50.8
	Household Equipment	0	0.5	0.8	0.6	0.6	0.2	0	0.2
	Rent	10.8	8.9	5.5	3.4	3.3	0.3	0	0
	Settlement	0.6	0.6	0.9	1.4	1.1	0.3	1.3	9.4
	Shoes	0.2	1	0	4.7	2.8	3.2	6	3.3
	Sickness	1.1	17.1	10.1	32.8	6.7	9.9	0.9	1.4

and over time. Certain common patterns emerge. The provision of clothing accounted for at least 10–20 per cent of expenditure among each group of recipient, but the proportions were often substantially higher for children and the elderly, presumably because each group lacked the earning capacity to buy clothes.[72] Unsurprisingly, perhaps, the cost of sickness was significant for married women and the elderly, while the costs of care for (orphaned?) children were also important. Equally expectedly, unspecified 'general allowances' (usually undifferentiated payments of household running costs, such as food, drink, clothing, and fuel) dominated the payments made to male, female, and elderly householders, and became a larger component over time, either because of changes in recording practices or the jump in the cost of living at the end of the century. In addition, the costs of parochial registration of baptisms and burials accounted for 5–15 per cent of the occasional payments made to wives and the unmarried (usually single mothers), and even more for the widowed elderly, many of whom were buried at parish expense. The latter point tends to support the views of King and Ottaway that many parishioners came to depend on relief payments in old age.[73]

Most occasional payments were made on a case-by-case basis, but certain patterns can be observed. In general, unlike the Paynes, most of those who

[72] See John Styles, *The Dress of the People: Everyday Fashion in Eighteenth-Century England* (New Haven, 2007), 257–75; Peter D. Jones, 'Clothing the Poor in Early Nineteenth-Century England', *Textile History* 37 (2006), 17–37; Vivienne Richmond, '"Indiscriminate Liberality Subverts the Morals and Depraves the Habits of the Poor": A Contribution to the Debate on the Poor Law, Parish Clothing Relief and Clothing Societies in Early Nineteenth-Century England', *Textile History* 40 (2009), 51–69; Steven King, '"I Fear You Will Think Me Too Presumtuous in My Demands but Necessity Has No Law": Clothing in English Pauper Letters, 1800–1834', *International Review of Social History* 54 (2009), 207–36.
[73] *Ibid.*, 168–9; Ottaway, 'Providing for the Elderly', 402.

Table 12.4. Terling, 1745–1801: Weekly allowances and occasional payments

	Weekly allowances				Occasional payments		
Duration	Number	%	Campton Beds*	Mean N yrs elapsed	Number	%	Mean N yrs elapsed
<1 year	37	27	26	1	402	43.6	1
1–2 years	25	18.2	19	2.2	144	15.6	4.1
2–3 years	21	15.3	9	4.6	93	10.1	7.4
3–4 years	11	8	7	5.1	61	6.6	8
4–5 years	11	8	5	5.4	52	5.6	9.3
5–6 years	6	4.4	3	6	40	4.3	11.9
6–7 years	10	7.3	3	14.9	36	3.9	12.8
7–8 years	3	2.2	3	14.3	20	2.2	13.1
8–9 years	4	2.9	5	9	15	1.6	13.5
9–10 years	1	0.7	5	10	11	1.2	18.6
10–15 years	8	5.8	9	12.6	36	3.9	18.6
15–20 years	2	1.5	2	21.5	6	0.7	23.7
20+ years	0	0	5	0	7	0.8	28.4
	139				923		

Duration of pensions by types of recipient

					Occasional Payments	
Recipient Type	Number	Mean yrs received	Mean yrs elapsed	Campton Beds*	Number	Mean N months
Elderly (>60) married	7	5.9	6.4	6.3	16	15.8
Elderly (>60) widowed	24	4.5	5.2		54	15.7
Married Persons	33	2.9	3.6	2.9	303	10.1
Lone Men/Women/Parents	21	3.3	5.2		160	3.4
Widowed	41	4.4	6.2	4.3	99	13.7
Children	21	3.1	3.1		282	5.2

Source: S. Williams, 'Poor Relief, Labourers' Households and Living Standards in Rural England c.1770–1834: A Bedfordshire Case Study', *EcHR* 2nd ser. 58 (2005), Tables 3 and 4

received occasional relief payments in Terling in this period did so for a few weeks at a time, and in the main only in two or three years. Between 1762 and 1801 over two-thirds of those who received occasional payments from the parish did so over less than six months in total across this forty-year span. In fact, for 70 per cent of recipients less than three years elapsed between receipt of their first and last payments, although this may under-represent the dependence of those who only began receiving relief towards the end of the period. Even so, 18 per cent of recipients received occasional relief in more than twelve months through these forty years, while just over 5 per cent of recipients received relief in more than ten of these forty years. Only 16 per cent of recipients (127 out of 809) received weekly pensions in addition to occasional relief payments through this period. In almost all cases (80 per cent), these pensioners had already received occasional payments before being granted more sustained relief.

In general, then, 'occasional payments' were just that. By contrast, 'weekly allowances' were intended to be of longer duration. Table 12.4 shows that the patterns evident in Terling follow those outlined in Williams's study of the village of Campton (Bedfordshire).[74] There, 26 per cent of recipients received weekly pensions for between six months and one year. In Terling the figure was 27 per cent. From this point, however, relief patterns in the two settlements begin to diverge, with Terling's vestry apparently being less willing to tolerate long-term dependency than was the case in Campton, although Williams's study is based on a longer period of observation. In Campton, 66 per cent of recipients received weekly allowances for less than five years while in Terling 75 per cent of recipients did so. In Campton, 21 per cent of recipients received allowances for more than ten years while only 8 per cent of Terling's recipients did so. However, it is evident that in both communities widows and widowers received pensions for more than five years, on average, while married couples under the age of sixty received them for less than half that time, and single people (and parents) received them for three to four years. In these respects, the decisions about the forms of relief and the criterion of entitlement in Terling appear in line with those found elsewhere in southern England in this period, even if it is clear that Terling's overseers maintained a degree of vigilance against long-term dependence.

Although occasional payments were much more sporadic than weekly pensions, a relatively small number of dependent families and individuals also received a disproportionate number of payments throughout these forty years. If we define their 'dependency' arbitrarily as the receipt of an average of ten or more occasional payments in a single year, across the period we can see that there were thirty-six such families (out of 360 in receipt of relief) and fifty-one individual recipients (out of 809). Between them, they

---

[74] Williams, 'Poor Relief', Tables 3 and 4, p. 504.

Table 12.5. Terling, 1762–1801: age and gender profile of most dependent recipients of occasional payments*

		Percentage of number of payments made per recipient type							
		1762–64	1765–69	1770–74	1775–79	1780–84	1785–89	1790–94	1795–1801
Women	Children	0	8.9	0.1	0.6	0	0	0	0
	Single	0	0	0.3	5.5	16.3	8.9	3.9	0.5
	Married	45.5	53.2	39.8	11.7	9.3	2.4	0.2	3.8
	Widowed	0	9.7	11.3	49.1	52.5	54.9	12	14.7
	Over 60s	0	6.2	7.5	8.1	0	0	10.3	15.3
% Total		45.5	78	59.1	75	78	66.2	26.5	34.4
Men	Children	0	3.2	0	0	0	0.2	8.5	3.2
	Single	0	0	0	0	0	1.4	0	0
	Married	54.5	17.7	26.3	19.2	12.3	21.9	53.8	58.5
	Widower	0	1.2	0	0	0	2.7	1.1	4
	Over 60s	0	0	14.6	5.8	9.7	7.7	10.1	0
% Total		54.5	22	40.9	25	22	33.8	73.5	65.6

		Percentage of total value of payments per recipient type							
		1762–64	1765–69	1770–74	1775–79	1780–84	1785–89	1790–94	1795–1801
Women	Children	0	5.7	2.7	0.3	0	0	0	0
	Single	0	0	0.4	4	9.4	6.7	3.2	1.2
	Married	51	53.9	38.4	16	7.3	2.9	0.3	1.4
	Widowed	0	10.6	9.6	38.3	62.7	56.5	16.5	6.8
	Over 60s	0	5.5	6	12.5	0	0	7.1	7.2
% Total		51	75.7	57	71.2	79.3	66.1	27.1	16.6
Men	Children	0	4.2	0	0	0	0.2	5.9	2.5
	Single	0	0	0	0	0	0.7	0	0
	Married	49	19.2	30.6	21.9	15.3	24.6	56.6	75.6
	Widower	0	1	0	0	0	4.7	2.1	5.3
	Over 60s	0	0	12.4	6.9	5.3	3.7	8.4	0
% Total		49	24.3	43	28.8	20.7	33.9	72.9	83.4

* Most dependent recipients are those in receipt of an average of ten or more occasional payments in a single year.

accounted for 33 and 23 per cent respectively of the total value of occa-sional payments in the village. Not surprisingly, their dependence seems to have increased in difficult years, such as the mid 1780s and again after 1795 (although it was also high in the late 1760s and mid 1770s).

The relatively small size of this most dependent cluster means that its composition could alter quite rapidly. However, Table 12.5 illustrates some more concerted movements. Categories of expenditure also changed. Between 1780 and 1784, half the money paid to this group was spent on food and drink, clothing, and the costs of sickness. Between 1796 and 1801, two-thirds of payments went on unspecified 'general allowances' – that is, direct, but unspecified, cash payments. Elderly people of both sexes were relieved relatively consistently over time.

While widowed women had received a substantial proportion of all payments between 1775 and 1789, in the 1790s occasional relief was increasingly channelled to married men as household heads, instead of direct payments to married women. This shift from women to men is even more pronounced when we consider the value of payments. Before 1790 the most dependent women (initially married women, then widows) routinely received between half and two-thirds of the value of occasional payments. After 1790 the balance was reversed, with over two-thirds (and over three-quarters after 1795) of the value of these payments going to male house-holders. This does seem to confirm both changes in need, as the economic crisis after 1795 brought men as household heads into chronic depend-ence, and changing priorities among the parish overseers, who were swift in reducing the proportion of relief directed towards the most dependent married and widowed women.

The financial assistance provided to this particular group of dependent individuals was more consistent than that offered to other recipients, but not necessarily more generous per capita. Across the period the average annualised weekly income from occasional payments and weekly allowances combined did not exceed 2s for 62 per cent of the most dependent recipi-ents. However, as with other recipients of occasional payments, the *actual* sums provided were larger. In fact, between 1762 and 1801, they averaged 6.7s per person per month in occasional payments alone, but only within 2.8 months across 6.8 years. In this respect, despite receiving an average of at least ten occasional payments per year, the dependence on the parish of this 'most dependent' group was still quite limited, despite the relatively substantial size of each individual payment.

VII

Why did this group remain so dependent upon the parish? We can gain some insights from two snap-shots of family structure among the poor. One was 'A List of Labouring Persons in the Parish of Terling with their

Table 12.6. Terling, poor listings, 1775 and 1801: household structure

Household structure	1775	%	1801	%
Husband, Wife & Children	48	36.09	36	52.17
Widower & Children	7	5.26	2	2.90
Widow & Children	9	6.77	2	2.90
Married, No Children	20	15.04	7	10.14
Unmarried, No Children	46	34.59	22	31.88
Unmarried, Children	3	2.26	0	0.00
Total	133	100	69	100

Familys, May 5th 1775', while the other was information gathered by the parish alongside the 1801 census, as illustrated in Table 12.6.[75] As Sokoll has demonstrated, although such 'snap-shot' listings appear unproblematic, 'listings of inhabitants do not normally indicate which households are poor while pauper lists do not normally record households at all'.[76] In the 1775 census, households are reasonably well-defined, except in shared properties. The list comprised approximately ninety-three 'labouring families' resident in Terling, plus a further fifteen families with rights of settlement in the parish, but who lived elsewhere. There were a further twelve persons housed in the parish workhouse, nine of them children or adolescents. Of the 108 labouring families outside the workhouse, twenty-five (23 per cent) had more than five members, eighteen (17 per cent) were headed by widows, but only one widow headed a household of more than five members.

Comparing the composition of labouring households in 1775 with those listed as 'poor' in 1801 produces striking, but slightly misleading, results. Certainly, by 1801 many of those receiving relief did so because they were unable to provide for families that included five or more inhabitants. In 1775, 47 per cent of labouring households appear to have contained only one to two persons, while in 1801 only 22 per cent did so. Conversely, in 1801 51 per cent had more than five persons, while in 1775 only 28 per cent did so. Does this reflect population increase and the immiseration of those with larger families by 1801? It may do, but in fact, nineteen of the 'households' of one to three persons listed in 1775 were actually resident with other families, many of them not classified among the 'labourers'. In addition, the two lists were made for different administrative purposes. The 1775 list recorded all those whom the overseers thought *might* be at risk of poverty. The 1801 list identified the population in receipt of relief. In fact, eighty-two out of the ninety-three 'labouring' households (86 per

[75] Recorded in ERO, D/DRa/E15, Strutt Family Accounts.
[76] Sokoll, *Household and Family*, 75.

cent) in 1775 contained a member who received relief from the parish in the period. Of these, most (73 per cent) received occasional relief in the years before or after 1775, while fifty ended up spending time in the parish workhouse. Twenty-seven were from the most dependent occasional recipients, including Samuel and Sarah Payne and their seven children, who were living in a parish house in Mill Street (at the cost of 9s per week). This suggests that although occasional poor relief was scattered quite widely, reaching four-fifths of 'labouring' households in Terling, generally it was scattered very thinly, with only a small proportion of recipients receiving it with any regularity.

The group of twenty-seven 'most dependent' (occasional) recipients divided between those, like the Paynes, whose needs persisted for ten to twenty years, and those who suffered shorter-term emergencies over three to six years. The former outnumbered the latter two-to-one. Some were individuals, such as Ann Cass, John Gilder, or Thomas Hare Ogham (who had paid rates between 1745 and 1772), who were chronically sick and received support from the parish for a number of years before their deaths – twenty-eight years in the case of Ann Cass. Others were like the Paynes, or Margaret Edwards, and needed repeated support, particularly during the years of child-rearing. The latter included some, like John Royce and William Smith, who were only children themselves in 1775, but went on to have large families, leading to increasing dependence on the parish after 1795. Others, like Thomas Marshall, managed to avoid dependence on the parish until their old age (in Marshall's case until the age of eighty-three in 1798). Hannah Dowsett and Susannah Brewer gave birth to illegitimate children, suffered incapacitating illnesses over several years, and then died, while Benjamin Ward, Mary Davenish, and Henry Jeremiah Hollingsworth were plunged into poverty by acute bouts of illness over a couple of years, before recovering and leaving the lists of recipients.

Until the late 1790s, most of those in good health seem to have been able to meet their basic subsistence needs, most of the time. However, their relative dependence on parish assistance for items of clothing, footwear, and the unexpected burdens of caring for children or parents suggests that Paul Slack's 'shallow poverty' was endemic in this rural community, even before the price shocks at the end of the century.[77] Ottaway's research on parish pensions in Terling echoes these findings (primarily among the elderly). Pensions that had been providing a 'subsistence-level' stipend for the old or chronically sick in the 1770s were eroded by rapid inflation so that by the end of the century, poor pensioners 'could not have supported themselves even at the level of workhouse inmates unless they had other assistance'.[78]

[77] Paul Slack, *Poverty and Policy in Tudor and Stuart England* (1988), 73–5.
[78] Ottaway, 'Providing for the Elderly', 408.

Table 12.7. Terling, 1801 poor census: percentage distribution of health condition by age of recipients

Health	Age categories											
	0.5–2	3–4.9	5–9.9	10–14.9	15–19.9	20–29.9	30–39.9	40–49.9	50–59.9	60–69.9	70–79.9	80+
Good	92.86	94.44	93.75	92.59	100.00	91.67	97.06	73.33	100.00	45.45	20.00	0.00
Blind	0.00	0.00	0.00	0.00	0.00	0.00	0.00	0.00	0.00	0.00	0.00	25.00
Idiot	0.00	0.00	0.00	0.00	0.00	0.00	2.94	0.00	0.00	0.00	0.00	0.00
Ill	0.00	5.56	0.00	0.00	0.00	0.00	0.00	6.67	0.00	0.00	0.00	0.00
Indifferent	7.14	0.00	6.25	7.41	0.00	0.00	0.00	20.00	0.00	36.36	50.00	25.00
Infirm	0.00	0.00	0.00	0.00	0.00	0.00	0.00	0.00	0.00	9.09	20.00	50.00
Lame	0.00	0.00	0.00	0.00	0.00	8.33	0.00	0.00	0.00	9.09	10.00	0.00
Number	28	18	48	27	3	12	34	15	9	11	10	4
% Good	92.86	94.44	93.75	92.59	100.00	91.67	97.06	73.33	100.00	45.45	20.00	0.00
% Sick	7.14	5.56	6.25	7.41	0.00	8.33	0.00	26.67	0.00	54.55	80.00	75.00
% Disabled	0.00	0.00	0.00	0.00	0.00	0.00	2.94	0.00	0.00	0.00	0.00	25.00

In 1801, the parish correlated the state of health and earning-potential of 219 individuals in receipt of relief.[79] As Table 12.7 shows, the Terling poor were deemed by the parish authorities to be generally in good health.[80] Only over the age of sixty did infirmities, blindness, lameness, and 'indifferent' health come to dominate the descriptions. This profile affected both the estimations of earning potential and the patterns of relief payments. Among fifty-five male-headed recipient households in 1801, parish contributions only amounted to 100 per cent of income for nine men (16 per cent), eight of whom were aged over sixty years, plus William Cable, aged twenty-seven and described as 'lame'. These contributions averaged only 45 per cent of income in sixteen of the fifty-five male-headed households (29 per cent) who received them. Women and children's earnings in these households only comprised an average of 19 per cent of income, in the twenty-four of the male-headed households (44 per cent) which received them, much lower than in Williams's Bedfordshire study in 1795, but closer to her figure for 1834.[81] By contrast, allowances amounted to 100 per cent of the income of ten out of sixteen female-headed households (63 per cent) among the parish poor, and averaged 92 per cent of income in fifteen out of sixteen households (94 per cent) who received them. If the annual value of these weekly parish allowances is estimated (optimistically) over fifty-two weeks, the mean allowance for these wholly dependent households was only £8.1 for male-headed households and £7.7 for female-headed ones (although most contained only one person).

The mean income for the other forty-six male-headed households (from earnings and allowances) was £22.9 per annum, for a mean family size of 4.5.[82] Households with up to three members received the annualised equivalent of £4.4 in relief, out of a total projected income of £21.9. Those with four or five members received £5.2 out of a total income of £30.1, while those with six or more members received £5.5 out of a projected income of £26.1. These sums excluded the value of doles of rice, flour, and herrings through the winter of 1800–01, as well as housing costs, but they make it easier to understand why these marginal households were susceptible not merely to gross shocks caused by death or sickness, but also to less percep-

---

[79] ERO, D/P 299/12/3, Terling Parish Overseers Accounts, 1790–1801, 'Return of the Poor Inhabitants of the Parish of Terling Taken in the Month of January 1801'.

[80] Those over sixty years made up 11 per cent of relief recipients in 1801, but 32 per cent of all the elderly in the village. See Ottaway, 'Providing for the Elderly', 402.

[81] Williams, 'Poor Relief', 508. Obviously, these Terling families may have been in need in 1801 partly because women and children's earnings were deficient.

[82] Among ninety-six recipients of weekly doles of rice, herrings, and cash on 31 Jan. 1801 the mean weekly pension was only 2s 1d, representing an almost nominal cash sum on top of a basic subsistence diet. ERO, D/P 299/12/3, Terling Parish Overseers Accounts, 31 Jan. 1801.

tible forces, such as price inflation, or merely the burden of an extra pair of children's shoes.

Seventy-one households received food or money in 1801, comprising 42 per cent of all 168 households in the village and 35 per cent of its population.[83] If we set these households into the wider context of poor relief within the parish, we can see that they contained eighty-eight individuals (out of 251) who can be identified positively as recipients of occasional payments and weekly allowances in the years after 1762. This encompassed all but two of the seventy-one household heads in the group. Although thirteen recipients were drawn from the most dependent families (including Sarah Payne, now a 62-year-old widow), in many cases it is clear that apparently substantial histories of relief payments break down under closer scrutiny. While these eighty-eight individuals had received relief over an average of fourteen years before 1801, they received relief *in* only seven of these years. In fact, on average they received occasional payments in only twenty-two months, or in only 2.4 months per person. Once again, this meant that the *actual* amounts received on each occasion were reasonably substantial, averaging 7s per month, but only for a couple of months each in total. However, given that the estimated earnings of these poor households (from all sources) averaged only 7.9s per month in 1801, stop-gap income that was spread widely but thinly may have been able to preserve such meagre living standards, but only when the duration of dependence was very brief.

Indeed, fifty-six out of this group of eighty-eight relief recipients had only ever received occasional payments before 1801, while only thirty-two had received these and weekly allowances as well. Fourteen of the group were, or had been, residents of the workhouse. Half of these were now aged over sixty, and five were over seventy. Twenty-eight recipients among these households were described as ill, 'infirm', 'indifferent' or 'lame' in 1801, but the remainder were deemed to be in good health, like the bulk of those recorded in the pauper census.

By 1801, the pressure of costs had accumulated in the parish to the point where the vestry could only meet the basic subsistence needs of almost half the parish residents by direct purchasing of cheap 'substitute' foods, rice (instead of flour) and herrings (instead of meat), alongside sharply reduced monetary allowances and flour doles. Although many of these families received regular food doles in the spring of 1801, when divided by the numbers of recipients per family, on average they amounted to approximately 13 ounces of flour per person per week and 2½ ounces of rice. This marked the worst moment of the crisis, in which the parish's resources and the consent of its ratepayers were stretched to breaking point.

---

[83] This compares to 46 per cent in Campton in 1801 and 42 per cent in Ardleigh in 1796. Williams, 'Poor Relief', Table 1, p. 496; Sokoll, *Household and Family*, 150.

These changes did not go unremarked in Terling. In 1814, John Strutt received an anonymous threatening letter. In it, the writer stated

> I am ashamed of what you have been doing to the poor for you have been feeding them with scillerylee [celery?] and rice and I am shure you will be feed with powder and shot without great alterations ...
>
> Second act we will burn terling hall down just to make a beginning and then we will seek the avenge upon the farmer because they do not find we work ...[84]

However diligent Strutt and his fellow overseers were as administrators, accountants, and jugglers of expediency, need, and cost, the system they controlled and the society in which they lived were incapable of assuaging anger of this kind.

VIII

This study reveals two quite different perspectives on the 'generosity' of the Old Poor Law. On the one hand, it reveals a system more in line with the pessimism of King and Sharpe than the optimism of Snell and Sokoll. In total, per capita payments were small, and the bulk of relief payments were designed to be either stop-gaps or 'enabling' devices, to buy shoes, clothes, or household goods that would minimise immediate dependence. Pensions in Terling were not particularly generous by county standards nor distributed very widely, and until the rapid price-inflation after 1795 ratepayers exhibited a marked reluctance to make real increases in the value of the taxable base within the parish. However, by analysing the size of occasional payments month-on-month, this study has suggested that they were made at a *replacement level* that was much closer to the normal weekly income for 'poor' families. When families had to turn to the parish (and, crucially, when the parish agreed to respond), it seems that the overseers were prepared to fill the temporary gaps in income at realistic levels, but often only for a week or two at the most. This behaviour also raises deeper questions about whether or not annual per capita measures of relief are particularly meaningful, since they suggest that relief payments supplied immediate 'bridging' income rather than sustained wage 'subsidies'.

Such meanings undoubtedly depend on context, and it is difficult to judge the social 'temperature' of a rural community such as Terling from the laconic records left by vestry meetings or overseers' accounts. Like most of southern and central England in the eighteenth century, Terling reflected the inexorable economic 'logic' of mature agrarian capitalism, of large-scale rentier landlords living off the market-determined rents of sizeable tenant

---

[84] Quoted in Brown, *Prosperity and Poverty*, 187.

farmers, whose enterprises depended upon the labour of landless, wage-dependent agricultural workers, who were pushed increasingly by price inflation to the margins of subsistence. The increasingly bureaucratic responses of the parish authorities to the pressures of poverty also intimate the first stirrings of a Foucaultian 'governmentality' – in which those in need were assessed, graded, and assisted by reference to impersonal criteria of entitlement, rather than because of subjective, emotional, and neighbourly desires to help.[85] Undoubtedly, by the later eighteenth century, the governors of the parish regarded labouring families as a distinct group of 'working people', often because they had become *their* employees. As a consequence, by the crisis of 1800, it was increasingly easy to subject them to the disciplines of rational accounting, so as to correlate their earning capacity and relief needs with their health, age, family size, and food consumption requirements. However, tenant farmers probably did not attend the vestry several hundred times over a twenty- or thirty-year period merely out of a desire to act as bureaucratic functionaries, or to lord it over their poorer neighbours. In 1801, Terling remained a village of less than 1,000 inhabitants, in which the poor were known individuals, not merely names, and in which real human need was all too apparent. In this sense, social relations remained personal, discretionary, and 'emotional'.[86]

Our difficulty is that we have to characterise a system in which 'poor neighbours' were also 'labouring families', where people were *both* names and numbers, members of a parish community *and* representatives of an identifiable 'class'. Villagers in Terling 'belonged', but they did so within a hierarchy of economic advantage or disadvantage, and according to various criteria of social status. Tenant farmers acted on an obligation to help their disadvantaged neighbours, but did so by treating them as representatives of the 'labouring poor'. They scrambled to devise new expedients to stave off hunger, but assessed needs according to methods of dispassionate 'means-testing'. They versed their social perspectives in the conventional, paternalist, moral language of rights and obligations, yet they policed their own participation with a daily rota. To recognise this is to acknowledge not merely that historical settings can be 'complicated', or that interpretative decisions are difficult, but also that distinct, and different, social models can operate in the same place *simultaneously*, sometimes with contradictory effects. Terling's inhabitants attempted to make sense of a world that they did not fully understand, and which, at the turn of the nineteenth century, must have felt like it was spinning out of control. All the careful stratagems, rules, checks, and annual balances heaped up by a succession of overseers

[85] Michel Foucault, 'Governmentality', in *The Foucault Effect: Studies in Governmentality*, ed. Graham Burchell, Colin Gordon and Peter Miller (Hemel Hempstead, 1991), 87–104.
[86] David Eastwood, *Government and Community in the English Provinces, 1700–1870* (Basingstoke, 1997), 26–42.

and vestrymen in half-a-dozen thick vellum-covered ledgers looked like they could be undone by the inchoate rage of a single anonymous letter. In the end, though, the ledgers prevailed, rather than powder and shot. Yet, as the discretionary payments accumulated silently and steadily year-on-year within their pages, they provide a witness to the pinched realities of hundreds of lives like those of Samuel and Sarah Payne, and continue to ensure that 'a shudder of pain vibrates across the centuries'.[87]

---

[87] Wrightson and Levine, *Terling*, 185.

13

From Commonwealth to Public Opulence: The Redefinition of Wealth and Government in Early Modern Britain

CRAIG MULDREW

A common wealth is called a society or common doing of a multitude of free men collected together and united by common accord.
Although of all thinges or lyuing creatures a man doth shew him selfe most politique, yet can he not well live without the societie and fellowship ciuill.   Sir Thomas Smith (1583)[1]

That state is properly opulent in which opulence is easily come at, or in which a little labour, properly and judiciously employed, is capable of procuring any man a great abundance of all the necessaries and conveniencies of life…. National opulence is the opulence of the whole people, which nothing but the great reward of labour, and consequently the great facility of acquiring, can give occasion to.
                                    Adam Smith (c.1763)[2]

Although Adam Smith chose to title his great work on the economic organisation of society *An Inquiry into the Nature and Causes of the Wealth of Nations*, it is not about national power, but about the wealth of the people who happened to live in nations. The very first sentence in his introduction to the work describes how 'the annual labour of every nation' is the fund which 'supplies it with all the necessities and conveniences of life'.[3] The organisation of his book is evidence of what he considered to be most important. He began with the division of labour, and then moved on to the nature of money, exchange and capital formation, before finally dealing with

---

[1] Sir Thomas Smith, *De Republica Anglorum* (1583), ch. 10.
[2] Adam Smith, 'Early Draft of Part of the Wealth of Nations', in *Adam Smith, Lectures on Jurisprudence*, ed. R. L. Meek, D. D. Raphael and P. G. Stein (Oxford, 1978), 561, 567 [hereafter Smith, *LJ*].
[3] *Adam Smith, An Inquiry into The Nature and Causes of the Wealth of Nations*, ed. R. H. Campbell, A. S. Skinner and W. B. Todd (Oxford, 1976), 10 [hereafter Smith, *WN*].

systems of political economy and the revenue of a 'Commonwealth'. For Smith, labour, and the incentive to work at different occupations, was the foundation of his thinking about wealth. The division of labour arose out of the 'propensity to truck and barter' or to exchange goods as a means of fulfilling desires for a wider variety of goods than any single man or woman could produce by themselves. Smith built up his economic system on the basis of individual psychology, just as he had built his moral philosophy on benevolence and self-reflection in the *Theory of Moral Sentiments*. In an earlier draft of the *Wealth of Nations*, Smith had termed this multiplication of consumer goods through exchange and the division of labour 'public opulence', and for him the wealth of labouring producers was *the* necessary feature of an 'opulent' or 'wealthy' nation. By 'public opulence' he meant the wealth enjoyed by *all* employed members of society, and he used the term specifically to differentiate this sort of wealth from money.

The literature on Smith, it goes without saying, is vast; and much has been written about the division of labour as the basis of economic organisation. There is also much which interprets Smith ahistorically as the founder of the 'classical' theory of the market, which in turn laid the basis for theories of self-interested behaviour and market equilibrium modelling. Often in the popular imagination Smith is equated with absolute free markets and the absolute private right to accumulate wealth, as organisations like The Adam Smith Institute propagate such ideas. However, a more recent body of writing has placed Smith within his historical context, arguing that he was much more than a critic of economic regulation and an advocate of free markets.[4] It is also now widely accepted that Smith did not see men as the rational individual maximisers of much modern neo-classical economic theory. Near the beginning of the *Wealth of Nations* he stated:

> In civilized society [man] stands at all times in need of the co-operation and assistance of great multitudes, while his whole life is scarce sufficient to gain the friendship of a few persons. ... man has almost constant occasion for the help of his brethren.[5]

Here I wish to contribute to this contextualisation, arguing that Smith drew on a preceding genealogy of economic discourse which dealt above all with the importance of *labour* in British society. As Donald Winch has pointed

[4] Emma Rothschild, *Economic Sentiments: Adam Smith, Condorcet, and the Enlightenment* (Cambridge MA, 2001); Istvan Hont, *Jealousy of Trade: International Competition and the Nation-State in Historical Perspective* (Cambridge MA, 2005); E. G. Hundert, *The Enlightenment's Fable: Bernard Mandeville and the Discovery of Society* (Cambridge, 1994), ch. 5; Donald Winch, *Riches and Poverty: An Intellectual History of Political Economy in Britain, 1750–1834*, (Cambridge, 1996), chs 1–4; Jerry Z. Muller, *Adam Smith in His Time and Ours: Designing the Decent Society* (Princeton, 1993).
[5] Smith, *WN*, I, ii, 26–7.

out, Smith has been criticised for not sufficiently acknowledging his influences, but in stressing the fundamental role of labour as a foundation for society, he was building on a long tradition which can be traced back in England to the so-called 'commonwealth men' of the sixteenth century.[6] Even more than that, however, I wish to suggest that Smith was also an acute observer of *social* as well as economic change, which had actually occurred in British society over the previous century, and that he actively applied the concept of sympathy he developed in the *Theory of Moral Sentiments* when he wrote about the lives of ordinary workers. He was much more radical than almost all of his immediate predecessors in his concern for the material well-being of the ordinary working family, and this led him to stress not only the fundamental role of labour in creating wealth, but also the role of labourers as active savers of capital and as consumers of the goods they produced. He developed the idea that wealth came from the labour of a nation's workers, producing different things for exchange. He nonetheless rejected previous interpretations which saw labour productivity as beneficial because it was a means of making the state more powerful through its ability to raise taxes to build imperial might. On the contrary, he thought that war and colonial possessions were an impediment to economic growth and believed in the mutual advantage of international trade in specialised products of different regions.[7] He wanted to emphasise that 'wealth' was neither the luxury of elites nor the economic power politics of the state.

This essay will begin by tracing the changing conceptions of the relationship between society and wealth from the mid sixteenth century to 1776; and it will link these conceptual changes to actual processes of economic and social change. The idea of a 'commonwealth', as might be expected, has always contained a notion of economic well-being, but the interpretation of what this meant changed in a number of ways from the sixteenth to the eighteenth centuries, and by the time Smith came to write it was generally used to simply mean government, which is how Smith used it. In a short essay there is insufficient space to do justice to the profusion of relevant writings, and I will accordingly focus here on how labour came to be seen as crucial to national wealth, and specifically why Smith made both the productivity of labour and the well-being of labouring families the centre of his vision of 'public opulence'. Rather than looking at a broad range of pamphlet sources I will focus on how canonical texts actually reflected and interpreted the experience of social and economic change, and especially on how after 1650 increased labour output in agriculture supported a growing manufacturing and retail sector, a process contemporaries generally referred to as the growth of industriousness.

---

6   Winch, *Riches*, 35; Craig Muldrew, *The Economy of Obligation: The Culture of Credit and Social Relations in Early Modern England* (Basingstoke, 1998), 319, 123.
7   Hont, *Jealousy*, 72–5, 83.

The complex relationship between changing economic practice, social interpretation and lived experience has been a consistent theme in Keith Wrightson's work. His writing has always been sensitive to the problems of individuals, especially those without power, caught up in historical change. Individuals had to struggle to deal with both actual change and the fact that *understanding* of such change was developed by those with power, and such power, while it worked to support social order, was rarely uninterested.[8] In *Earthly Necessities*, for instance, he looked at how individuals came to 'live with the market' by the early eighteenth century, but also how society was redefined by elite commentators such as Gregory King away from reciprocal duties to the capacity to generate income.[9] This article aims to continue Wrightson's method of analysis into the late eighteenth century. It will attempt to show how Smith used his philosophy of moral sentiments to subvert previous economic ideas which he saw as self-interested justifications of the right to social and economic privileges. Smith was a sympathetic interpreter of *social* as well as economic change, who looked back at the feelings of labour rather than forward towards the abstraction of market equilibrium.

Wrightson demonstrated that the term commonwealth was a sixteenth-century keyword which meant 'both the common good, or common interest, and the social and political structures responsible for achieving that condition of public welfare'. It signified the idealisation of an organic society with a managed economy in which subordinates were looked after in exchange for deference. All this required the vital assistance of good government. The sheer number of statutes passed by Tudor parliaments concerning economic matters, and the development of quarter sessions as a means of enforcing these laws, testified to real administrative attempts to achieve this ideal. Wrightson used the example of Edmund Dudley's *The Tree of Commonwealth*, which depicted society as a great tree sustained by the roots of love of God, justice, trust, concord and peace and bearing the fruits of 'tranquilitie', 'good example', 'worldly prosperitie' and 'honour of god'. If all this was achieved, then commonwealth would be evident in a society distinguished by concord, material prosperity and full employment.[10]

However, by the beginning of the seventeenth century this reciprocal ideal was beginning to change as a result of the rapid growth of a competitive market economy, in which household profit was valorised because of the high risk of debt and economic failure. The number and scale of market

8 Keith Wrightson, 'Two Concepts of Order: Justices, Constables and Jurymen in Seventeenth-Century England', in *An Ungovernable People: The English and Their Law in the Seventeenth and Eighteenth Centuries*, ed. John Brewer and John Styles (1980), 21–46; Wrightson, *EN*, 332.
9 Wrightson, *EN*, 270–2.
10 *Ibid.*, 27–9.

transactions expanded rapidly in the years after 1550, leading to a great expansion of credit and increased litigation over unpaid debts. Society was redefined away from a corporatist notion of a Christian body politic to one based on natural law, on contract and on distributive, rather than commutative, justice. This conception of society reached its apotheosis in the natural law theory of Thomas Hobbes. Rather than the economy being guided through the management of a governor, wealth was created through individual production for the market and trust between competitors was increasingly based on contract law secured through a state legal system. The 'serial sociability' of the market came to predominate over the corporate economy, and success in this marketplace was also seen as providential.[11]

As a result, writing on economic matters shifted in the early seventeenth century from an emphasis on social good expressed as 'wealth' or 'weal' to the social utility of household wealth gained from application to business.[12] This was accompanied by the related development of the literature of 'reason of state' which grew out of the catastrophic and costly religious wars of the period.[13] With the influx of gold and silver from its New World mines, the Spanish empire was able to employ large well-equipped armies in its fight against the Dutch and other Protestant territories. This led governments to attempt to find new ways of taxing their subjects to pay for ever increasingly expensive warfare, and many writers offered advice on how gold and silver flowed in and out of a country.[14] In the 1620s, Thomas Mun claimed that foreign wars exhausted a kingdom's treasure because armies needed to be provisioned with foreign wares.[15] Such writings described the state as a mirror of an individual household competing in the market economy to become wealthier, and thus successful.

These writings linked the power of the state very closely to the amount of gold and silver coins or bullion within a realm or political territory. This was because war drew currency and bullion out of a country as troops fighting abroad needed to be paid in gold or silver coins if they were to be supplied from the local economy.[16] What came to be called mercantilist policy also stressed the need for the state to protect its own trading interests in order

---

[11] Muldrew, *Economy of Obligation*, 320–8.

[12] *Ibid.*, 140–1; Hont, *Jealousy*, 40–4.

[13] Richard Tuck, *Philosophy and Government, 1572–1651* (Cambridge, 1993), ch. 2.

[14] One of the first to write in this vein was Bernardo Davanzati in his *Discourse upon Coins* of 1588. Terence Hutchison, *Before Adam Smith: The Emergence of Political Economy 1662–1776* (1988), 17–20.

[15] Thomas Mun, *England's Treasure by Forraign Trade* (1664), reprinted in J. R. McCulloch, ed., *Early English Tracts on Commerce* (Cambridge, 1954), 21. Also see William Petyt, *Britannia Languens or a Discourse on Trade* (1690), reprinted in McCulloch, ed., *Early English Tracts*, 11; John Locke, *Some Considerations of Consequence of the Lowering of Interest, and the Raising the Value of Money*, reprinted in Patrick Hyde Kelly, ed., *Locke on Money* (Oxford, 1991), I, 232.

[16] Eli F. Hecksher, *Mercantilism* (1955), II, 13–49, 175–216.

to ensure that it could not be weakened militarily by enemies cutting off its access to world bullion flows. Adam Smith and many later economists interpreted this early seventeenth-century literature to have equated wealth with money, or what was termed 'treasure'. However, most of these early 'mercantilist' writers were well aware of the fact that wealth came from agricultural and industrial production.[17] Before the financial revolution, however, it was difficult to use such wealth to finance armies abroad, as war disrupted the international flow of merchants' bills of exchange. Thus, possessing more gold and silver than their potential enemies did indeed give states without access to stable national banks a greater degree of *power* in terms of the ability to pay for war.

Writers by the early seventeenth century stressed the importance to the commonwealth of merchants who traded overseas because it was through the growth of international trade that bullion entered the country.[18] This resulted in a redefinition of the term commonwealth. Now, instead of being based on a strong classical republican notion of moral guidance on the part of a governing elite, the commonwealth increasingly came to refer to the collective 'state' of all of the private wealth in the kingdom.[19] As Edward Misselden put it in 1623:

> Is not the publique involved in the private, and the private in the publique? What else makes a common-wealth, but the private-wealth ... of the members thereof in the excercise of Commerce amoungst themselves, and with forrine Nations?[20]

This type of definition was also linked to the origins of the word 'state', which derived from the term for a prince's 'estate', meaning his condition or the state of his wealth or holdings.[21]

In the second half of the seventeenth century, however, there was a shift in emphasis in many economic writings away from a primary concern with taxes and money to the importance of labour and the creation of wealth through industry. These ideas developed during the English Republic, most notably from the so-called Hartlib circle of radical puritan thinkers. Here ideas about how agrarian 'improvement' could benefit England were linked to projects for public education. For the first time, education for the poor in a skill was seen to be a way of improving the country's economy

[17] Lars Magnusson, *Mercantilism: The Shaping of an Economic Language* (1998), ch. 3.
[18] Rice Vaughan, *A Discourse of Coin and Coinage* (1675), reprinted in J. R. McCulloch, *Old and Scarce Tracts on Money* (1933), 60; Charles Davenant, *A Memoril Concerning the Coyn of England* (1695), 6–8.
[19] Thomas Elyot, *The Book Named the Governour* (1880 edn), 1–6.
[20] Misselden, *Circle of Commerce*, p. 17.
[21] Petty, *Political Arithmatick*, in *The Economic Writings of Sir William Petty*, ed. Charles Hull (Cambridge, 1899), I, 35–6.

by increasing the production of food and industrial products.[22] As is well known, the architects of Puritan republican government chose to call the regime a commonwealth in part to emphasise the common safety of its members, but in doing so they also drew on the way the term commonwealth had been used to describe participation in the self-governing institutions of corporate town and parish government.[23] In this way, they preserved not only the emphasis on the positive role of government but also the link between trade and economic well-being.

Under the Commonwealth and Cromwellian Protectorate, the institutions of parliamentary taxation were reformed and an excise tax was also successfully introduced for the first time. This allowed successful wars to be conducted against Scotland and Ireland and Spain. The first Dutch war also showed that the English navy could successfully challenge Dutch hegemony and it resulted in the passage of the Navigation Acts limiting colonial trade to English shipping. These successes meant that, while free trade in the Atlantic and with most of Europe was defended, government direction was now seen as a beneficial helpmeet of overseas trade.[24] Government had a role to play in encouraging overseas trade and colonisation through legalisation such as the Navigation Acts and the establishment of the Board of Trade, as well as in educating the poor and promoting schemes to increase wealth. However, because the term commonwealth was politically bound up with the English Republic, it not surprisingly fell out of favour during the Restoration, and words such as 'happiness' came to replace it.[25] In works written before 1650, commonwealth was the usual word employed to describe the English government or state. Misselden and Mun, as well as Malynes in his *Lex Mercatoria* and *Free Trade* and Lewis Roberts in *The Treasure of Traffike* (1641), all used it often. Thus Roberts explained that:

> Statists have noted, that the Arts and Sciences are very many, that are commodious and beneficiall to a Common-Wealth, and which consequently beget abundance, wealth, and plenty, not only to the Prince in his owne particular, but also to his people and Countrey in the generall.[26]

Later pamphlets such as Petyt's *Britannia Languens*, Dudley North's *Discourses on Trade* or *England's Great Happiness* did not use the term commonwealth.

---

[22] Paul Slack, *From Reformation to Improvement: Public Welfare in Early Modern England* (Oxford, 1998), 79.

[23] Phil Withington, *The Politics of Commonwealth: Citizens and Freemen in Early Modern England* (Cambridge, 2005), 76–84.

[24] The East India trade, of course, remained a controversial monopoly of the East India Company.

[25] Phil Withington, *Society in Early Modern England: The Vernacular Origins of Some Powerful Ideas* (Cambridge, 2010), 160–8.

[26] Lewes Roberts, *The Treasure of Traffike, or a Discourse of Forraigne Trade* (1641), reprinted in McCulloch, ed., *Early English Tracts*, 3.

These writers preferred the term nation. Of course, earlier writers had occasionally talked about the advantages of trade to 'England' or to 'the nation', but in *Britannia Languens* the term nation was used as many as 419 times, much more than previously.

In the period after the Restoration, the comparative advantage of England over other trading nations, most notably Holland and then France, became the central concern of writers. Much has been written about their supposedly 'mercantilist' nature, but all were concerned with what Istvan Hont, using David Hume's famous term, has called the' jealousy of trade'. Writers continued to be aware that warfare between nations, whatever the cause, was a type of national competition of military strength, and that since traders also competed for markets, those of certain nations did so more successfully than others.[27] Writers in England promoted the expansion of home manufacturing for export to increase earnings, and argued that exports were the proper concern of government because their production would employ more of the poor.

Although too little is still known about the 1650s, there is solid empirical evidence from customs records that overseas trade continued to expand from the Restoration until the outbreak of the American Revolution.[28] Naval power was used to both protect and expand the rapidly growing global trade in commodities such as tobacco, sugar and East Asian goods. With the growth of the French economy under Colbert, and the emergence of a strong Catholic state under a mature Louis XIV, a well-resourced navy was seen as essential.[29] The success of this symbiosis of naval power and increased trade has been well documented by John Brewer and Patrick O'Brien. A higher standard of living meant that Britain could afford the highest level of taxation of any of the major European powers. This in turn was used to secure a tremendous expansion of state credit primarily through borrowing from the Bank of England.[30] With a stable national debt, long-term credit could be used to finance expensive wars with paper financial instruments, which foreign merchants could rely on to retain their value after a war. Britain was therefore no longer vulnerable to the instability and danger of short-term credit.

What is less commonly discussed is the central role played in these debates by home manufacture and the need to employ more labour. Good

[27] Hont, *Jealousy*, Introduction, *passim*.
[28] C. D. Chandaman, *The English Public Revenue 1660–1688* (Oxford, 1975); Ralph Davis, 'English Foreign Trade, 1660–1700', in *The Growth of English Overseas Trade in the Seventeenth and Eighteenth Centuries*, ed. E. M. Carus-Wilson and W. E. Minchinton (1969), 78–98.
[29] Ronald Findlay and Kevin O'Rourke, *Power and Plenty: Trade, War, and the World Economy in the Second Millennium* (Princeton, 2007), 247–62.
[30] John Brewer, *The Sinews of Power* (1989); P. K. O'Brien, 'The Rise of a Fiscal State in England, 1485–1815', *Historical Research* 66 (1993), 129–76.

policy would result in material prosperity represented by the variety of goods supplied both through trade with other nations *and* through the industry of labourers and artificers at home. In the first part of the seventeenth century a growing population had meant that the supply of labour was greater than demand. Lack of rural employment led to increased labour mobility as the young took to the road in search of work, and the poor laws were established.[31] However, after the mid seventeenth century this situation was reversed and demand for labour outstripped supply. There were a number of reasons for this, including the emigration of a considerable number of young men to the New World and much slower population growth after 1650. At the same time, however, the rising food prices of the early seventeenth century had motivated farmers to engage in 'improving' their farms to profit by selling more food. This had the effect of increasing the demand for agricultural labourer to increase crop production, and by 1700 England was producing enough grain to export a surplus to the Continent in most years. The increased availability of food energy produced by agriculture also led to an increased number of people being able to work in non-primary sectors of the economy such as shopkeeping or cloth production. E. A. Wrigley has estimated that the proportion of the population engaged in primary agricultural production fell from 76 per cent in 1520 to only 36 per cent by 1801.[32] In absolute terms, this meant that the population engaged in agriculture in 1800 was about 3,140,000 compared to 2,870,000 in 1600, even though the amount of land under cultivation had increased considerably and crop yields were much higher. This certainly suggests that agricultural labour had become more productive per head over this period.

The authors who advocated 'improvement' also promoted the 'industriousness' of labour as necessary for that improvement. Their key terms became improvement, national interest, wealth, happiness and industriousness.[33] More employment would eventually lead to more production and more wealth for all. The increase in the consumption of middling sorts and elites in this period has attracted the attention of many recent historians, and Paul Slack and Jan de Vries have shown how this increase was reflected in the writings of Nicolas Barbon and Bernard Mandeville.[34] However, a

[31] Wrightson, *EN*, 115–31, 145–9, 194–20.
[32] E. A. Wrigley, 'Urban Growth and Agricultural Change: England and the Continent in the Early Modern Period', in *idem, People, Cities and Wealth* (Oxford, 1987), p. 170.
[33] Paul Slack, 'The Politics of Consumption and England's Happiness in the Later Seventeenth Century', *English Historical Review* 122 (2007), 609–31.
[34] Neil McKendrick, John Brewer and J. H., Plumb, *The Birth of a Consumer Society* (1983); *Consumption and the World of Goods*, ed. Roy Porter and John Brewer (1993); Lorna Weatherill, *Consumer Behaviour and Material Culture in Britain, 1660–1760* (London, 1988); Mark Overton, Jane Whittle, Darron Dean and Andrew Hann, *Production and Consumption in English Households, 1600–1750* (2004); Jan de Vries, *The Industrious Revolution: Consumer Behaviour and the Household Economy, 1650 to the Present* (Cambridge, 2008), 58–67.

study of labourers' inventories shows that in the 100 years after 1650 the median value of their total stock of household goods rose 77 per cent. Many more poor labourers became what contemporaries termed 'honest' or 'painful' labourers, meaning that they were earning enough not only to get by but to improve their standard of living after the previous century of hardship before 1650.[35] It was Adam Smith more than any other writer who correctly interpreted this development as *the* transformative change of the post-Restoration economy.

The key term to describe this prosperity, as Paul Slack has demonstrated, was 'happiness'. However, the word used in this sense did not refer to an individual psychological feeling of well-being (as it would come to do in the eighteenth-century philosophy of sentiments), but rather to providential good fortune.[36] The word happiness derives from the old English word 'hap' which means fortune, and a happy country was one upon which protestant providential fortune had shined. This usage was similarly employed by individuals accounting for business profit in their personal account books.[37] The most notable use of the term was, however, in John Houghton's argument in favour of free trade and consumption of foreign luxuries, *England's Great Happiness*. Houghton became famous for publishing his *Collection for the Improvement of Agriculture and Trade*, in which he claimed to have been 'stirred up' by Hartlib and others in the Royal Society. He was one of the first authors to argue for the benefits of luxury consumption as a spur to home improvement and industry, leading in turn to an increased demand for English industrial goods abroad. Such an increase in trade would also lead to an increase in customs revenue, therefore benefiting state power as well. Houghton was followed by others such as Nicolas Barbon, who argued that consumption could stimulate infinite economic growth through men's desire for material goods to 'promote the ease, pleasure and pomp of life'.[38]

Barbon's writings developed the idea that individual happiness might come from material possessions rather than from good government. This was a major turning point in how 'wealth' was to be conceived, and it was a development upon which Smith was to build. Previous theorists of the 'Commonwealth' had certainly noted the importance of commodities, but they had stressed that they should be consumed in proportion to one's place in society. Expenditure on luxury was always seen as a potential cause of over-indebtedness among the middling sort and of the loss of the self-control required for the exercise of authority by elites.[39] For Barbon, luxury

---

[35] Craig Muldrew, *Food, Energy and the Creation of Industriousness: Work and Material Culture in Agrarian England, 1550–1780* (Cambridge, 2011), 163–207, 298–309.
[36] Slack, 'Politics of Consumption', 629–31.
[37] Muldrew, *Economy of Obligation*, 144–6.
[38] Slack, 'Politics of Consumption', 613–16, 619.
[39] Muldrew, *Economy of Obligation*, 157–66.

consumption was now seen as potentially beneficial precisely because it created what we now understand as the 'economic function of demand'. Such demand, he argued, would lead to the creation of new inventions and industries, which would in turn provide employment. This, combined with labour discipline to encourage industriousness, would solve the perennial problem of poverty for governments.[40] The importation of luxury goods remained problematic for other authors, however, because they continued to emphasise the value to state power of a favourable balance of trade which would draw currency into the country and away from potential future military opponents. For William Petyt, this meant suppressing home spending on foreign luxuries, which drained money from the country, and expanding exports.[41] In addition, there were those who worried about the effeminating effect of luxury consumption on a classical masculine idea of virtue and military preparedness.[42] From this point on, however, authors could focus on the interrelated importance of both consumption and employment.

The most famous of the authors who subsequently developed this theme was Bernard Mandeville, whose *Fable of the Bees* constructed an entire sociology of consumption based on the egotistical satisfaction of private desires driven by passions.[43] Government, in his argument, was now based neither on virtuous authority, nor on an original contract to administer a body of laws. Rather, the authority and respect embodied in governmental offices channelled individual competition for power into beneficial administration, in which virtue was merely a display.[44] But, Mandeville was more interested in the unbridled consumption of luxury, which he thought was far more conducive to the promotion of prosperity than government. In the view of moralists, such consumption was 'private vice', but in Mandeville's view it led to public benefits:

> I shew that those very Vices of every particular Person by skilful Management, were made subservient to the Grandeur and worldly Happiness of the whole.
> [...]
> Frugality is like Honesty, a mean starving Virtue, that is only fit for small Societies of good peaceable Men, who are contented to be poor so they may be easy … and therefore very useless in a trading Country, where there are vast Numbers that one way or other must be all set to Work.[45]

---

[40] Hale, *A Discourse Touching Provision for the Poor* (1683), 5, 8, 15, 24.

[41] Petyt, *Britannia Laungens*, ch. 12.

[42] Istvan Hont, 'The Early Enlightenment Debate on Commerce and Luxury', in *The Cambridge History of Eighteenth-Century Political Thought*, ed. Mark Goldie and Robert Wokler (Cambridge, 2006), 379–418.

[43] De Vries, *Industrious Revolution*, 58–64.

[44] Hundert, *Enlightenment's Fable*, 62–75.

[45] Bernard Mandeville, *The Fable of the Bees*, ed. F. B. Kaye (Oxford, 1924), pt I, 104–6.

Although Mandeville emphasised industriousness and the beneficial employ-ment of labour, he was one of many early eighteenth-century commentators who thought that the poor should not earn more than they needed to keep their families in necessities, or they would not work hard enough to produce consumer goods either for the wealthy to consume or for the country to export.[46]

Mandeville very rarely used the term 'Commonwealth', preferring instead to discuss a flourishing 'society'. The word society was used, for instance, over 120 times in the first volume of *The Fable of the Bees*. In comparison, it had been used only twice in the *Treasure of Traffik*, and only three times in *Britannia Languens*. Mandeville used the terms state and nation very commonly, but he abandoned the idea of the importance of government for commerce, preferring to stress how the desire for material goods would lead to wealth and power:

> It is from this Policy, [promoting luxury] and not the trifling Regulations of Lavishness and Frugality ... that the Greatness and Felicity of Nations must be expected; for let the Value of Gold and Silver either rise or fall, the Enjoyment of all Societies will ever depend upon the Fruits of the Earth, and the Labour of the People; both which joined together are a more certain, a more inexhaustible, and a more real Treasure, than the Gold of *Brazil*, or the Silver of *Potosi*.[47]

We must be careful, however, not to single out consumption as the main theme of late seventeenth-century economic writing. Indeed, the majority of post-Restoration economic publications were about the problems of finance and taxation. This question of the relationship of the circulation of currency to economic growth remained important in the eighteenth century, when it preoccupied writers such as Turgot, Sir James Steuart and especially Adam Smith. In the eighteenth century, however, the question of how finance could be related to the creation of wealth through labour and exchange became paramount.[48] Britain's economic and imperial success led to writings on the subject of national wealth becoming increasingly inter-national, with many French, Italian and German tracts providing advice on how best to conceive or manage successful national economies, which might also involve colonial trade.

This aspect of the enlightenment project has come to be generally termed 'political economy'.[49] It was a term chosen by Sir James Steuart to

[46] *Ibid.*, 192–4, 197; 119–20, 128, 170–3. Cf. John Hatcher, 'Labour, Leisure and Economic Thought Before the Nineteenth Century', *P&P* 160 (1998), 64–115, pp. 69–71.

[47] Mandeville, *Fable of the Bees*, 6, 112–13, 197–8. Like Houghton he also saw the advantage of consuming foreign goods so as to encourage foreigners to consume more English-produced goods.

[48] I intend to investigate this in a companion piece.

[49] Rothschild, *Economic Sentiments*, 2–4, 57–60.

describe the relationship between wealth and society in his classic work *An Inquiry Into the Principles of Political Economy Being an Essay on The Science of Domestic Policy in Free Nations. In Which are Particularly Considered Population, Agriculture, Trade, Industry, Money, Coin, Interest, Circulation, Banks, Exchange, Public Credit, and Taxes*, published in 1767, but written over the previous two decades. The term political economy was still not common and was undoubtedly chosen by Steuart because of the emphasis he placed on the importance of the role of government (his term was 'a statesman') in directing economic policy. His work was written while he was in exile in France and Germany, and its overwhelming concern with the necessity of economic management shows the influence of writers like Montesquieu and the German cameralists.[50] Although his theory on how the economy functioned was based on the promotion of market production and economic liberty, Steuart still believed that the role of a governor was to promote the long-term competitive advantage of the national economy over others, so as to provide goods and employment for its own subjects:

> The principal object of this science is to secure a certain fund of subsistence for all the inhabitants, to obviate every circumstance which may render it precarious; to provide everything necessary for supplying the wants of the society. [51]

Smith, in contrast, did not discuss political economy until his introduction to Book IV of the *Wealth of Nations*, where he famously claimed

> Political oeconomy, considered as a branch of the science of a statesman or legislator, proposes two distinct objects; first, to provide a plentiful revenue or subsistence for the people, or more properly to enable them to provide such a revenue or subsistence for themselves; and secondly, to supply the state or commonwealth with a revenue sufficient for the publick services.[52]

Recent writers on Smith have focused on Books IV–V of the *Wealth of Nations* to refute the idea that for Smith market liberalism was a sufficient organising principle for society, and have pointed to the importance in his theory of those areas of economic activity where legislation and government were beneficial.[53] But these benefits were generally confined to public goods such as justice, the administration of infrastructure and most importantly the education of labourers.[54] It is nonetheless significant that it was

---

[50] Hutchison, *Before Adam Smith*, 335–7.

[51] Steuart, *An Inquiry into the Principles of Political Economy Being an Essay on The Science of Domestic Policy in Free Nations. In Which are Particularly Considered Population, Agriculture, Trade, Industry, Money, Coin, Interest, Circulation, Banks, Exchange, Public Credit, and Taxes* (1767), 2.

[52] Smith, *WN*, IV, 428.

[53] Hont, *Jealousy*, 99–111; Winch, *Riches*, 90–123.

[54] Smith *WN*, V.i, 723–31, 782.

only after he had described how people had provided 'such a revenue or subsistence for themselves' that he went on to discuss what role government should have in relation to this revenue. Famously, he opposed the localism of the corn laws in favour of the benefits of free trade in grain, except in cases of extreme necessity, arguing that higher market prices would lead to increased production and in turn to less shortage and eventually to lower prices.[55] He agreed with Steuart that there was a role for political economy (that is, government intervention), but he thought there was no advantage to be gained from intervening in free exchange as inevitably it would be to the advantage of those with power, or (in the case of the corn laws) to local rather than to universal good.[56]

Steuart's work also contains what seems to be the first use of the exact phrase 'public opulence' in England to describe the wealth of a country's people.[57] 'Opulence' is a French word which came into fairly common currency in the early eighteenth century, generally as a synonym for a society where a class of people could afford to live in luxury, which was usually contrasted with what was termed a 'primitive society', where wants were few. Pierre de Boisguilbert used the term 'opulence' often in his *Dissertation de la nature des richesses, de l'argent et des tributs* (1707), where he argued that wealth consisted of useful services and goods rather than of money, which was only a means of facilitating market exchange. Thus, he used opulence in a very similar way to Smith in order to contrast wealth-as-consumption with wealth-as-currency.[58] Boisguilbert also used the term public opulence, and was, like Smith, sympathetic to labourers and small traders.[59] Other authors, such as Montesquieu, Hume and Condillac, all used the term opulence fairly often.[60]

Smith, however, used opulence in a much more specific way to refer to the actual material wealth of labourers, and this is what distinguishes him from his predecessors. He used the phrase most regularly in his *Lectures on Jurisprudence* in the 1760s, and very often in an early draft of the *Wealth of Nations* entitled 'Of the nature and causes of public opulence'.[61] In the

[55] Smith, *WN*, IV.v, 524–43; Hont, *Jealousy*, 88–91.

[56] Smith, *WN*, II.v, 372, IV, 428.

[57] Steuart, *Inquiry*, II, 352, 357, 452

[58] Pierre de Boisguilbert, *Dissertation de la nature des richesses, de l'argent et des tributs* (1707), Texte numérisé et présenté par Paulette Taieb at www.taieb.net/auteurs/Boisguilbert/diss1.html, 1, 11.

[59] Hutchinson, *Before Adam Smith*, 107–11. Turgot used the term richesse, not opulence. Hont, *Jealousy*, 30–6.

[60] Hont, *Jealousy*, 74.

[61] The *Lectures on Jurisprudence* are of course two sets of formally copied lecture notes dated 1762–3 and 1766, the provenance of which has been carefully considered by the editors of the Glasgow edition. It is interesting that the taker of the first set of notes did not use the phrase 'public opulence', instead just writing 'opulence' or the 'nature of opulence'. However, since Smith himself used the term in his early draft it seems likely

published version of *Wealth of Nations* he was more analytical and less overtly rhetorical than in the lecture notes, and tended to prefer phrases like 'real wealth'. However, as the discussion below will show, his concern for the wealth of workers remained, even if his language became more prosaic. By 'public opulence' he meant the wealth enjoyed by *all* the employed members of society, and he used the term specifically to differentiate this sort of wealth from money:

> Observe the accommodation of the most common artificer or day-labourer in a civilized and thriving country, and you will perceive that the number of people of whose industry a part, though but a small part, has been employed in procuring him this accommodation, exceeds all computation. The woollen coat, for example, which covers the day-labourer, as coarse and rough as it may appear, is the produce of the joint labour of a great multitude of workmen. ... we shall be sensible that without the assistance and co-operation of many thousands, the very meanest person in a civilized country could not be provided.[62]

The wealth of a nation was its ability to provide a wide range of consumer goods for all its members, not just for the rich. In this sense, Smith ironically took a term usually associated with the luxury and wealth of a few and applied it to the public in general. In doing so, he was accurately interpreting a real change in eighteenth-century Britain to a higher wage economy in comparison to other parts of the world.[63] Increased food production reduced grain prices by about 20 per cent in the first half of the eighteenth century while agricultural wages rose and employment opportunities in high wage industries expanded. To Smith, therefore, it was actually public wealth, rather than that of the government, which mattered. By arguing that butchers, bakers and pin-makers contributed more significantly than overseas merchants to the creation of this wealth he gave productive workers an economically democratic role in the foundation of prosperity, thereby radically reinterpreting it:

> The uniform, constant, and uninterrupted effort of every man to better his condition, the principle from which publick and national, as well as private opulence is originally derived, is frequently powerful enough to maintain the natural progress of things toward improvement, in spite both of the extravagance of government, and of the greatest errors of administration.[64]

that this was the term he used in his lectures. In the *Wealth of Nations* he discussed the subject of opulence in terms of the historical development of the economic prosperity of different nations. Smith, *LJ*, Introduction, 561, and R. L. Meek and A. S. Skinner, 'The Development of Adam Smith's Ideas on the Division of Labour', *Economic Journal* 83 (1973), 1094–116.

[62] Smith, *WN*, I.i, 23.
[63] Muldrew, *Food, Energy and the Creation of Industriousness*, 257–9.
[64] Smith, *WN*, II.iii, 343.

The high price of labour is to be considered not meerly as a proof of the general opulence of society which can afford to pay well all those whom it employs; it is to be regarded as what constitutes the essence of public opulence, or as the very thing in which public opulence properly consists.[65]

This was a deliberate rhetorical strategy on Smith's part, designed to distance him from the concept of national wealth which stressed a favourable balance of trade with other countries to increase the amount of gold and silver coins in circulation. He also wanted to distance himself from those authors who chose to criticise labourers for their leisure preference.[66] He instead stressed that the opportunities opened up by the increase in manufactures in the eighteenth century had led workers to better their standard of living.

Smith was well aware of the inequalities of wealth brought about through competition as he had engaged with Rousseau's *Discourses on Inequality* in a review of 1755. It is clear that he agreed with Rousseau that private property led to great inequality, but Smith believed it was a necessary evil, because if it was not protected, the motivation to better one's own circumstances would be undermined.[67] Smith, however, explained that 'so much oppressive inequality' could be justified by 'the superior affluence and abundance commonly possessed even by this lowest and most despised member of civilized society'.[68] This was how he came to describe what he termed the slow progress of public opulence, which was an anthropological history of the effect of commerce on social organisation. Here he contrasted the *rude* state of mankind before the division of labour increased production, where only princes and aristocrats enjoyed opulent luxury, with commercial society, where opulence was public or universal.[69]

More pessimistically, however, he thought that government was usually used to enhance rather than lessen inequality. In the early draft for the *Wealth of Nations*, he was even more explicit about how the products produced by the labour of the poor are inordinately distributed to the wealthy who work less. This sounds surprisingly almost like Marx's theory of surplus value, but with a stoic acceptance of the class basis of society:

In a civilized society the poor provide both for themselves and for the enormous luxury of their superiors. The rent which goes to support the vanity of the slothful landlord is all earned by the industry of the peasant.

... with regard to the produce of the labour of a great society there is never any such thing as a fair and equal division. In a society of an hundred thousand

65 Smith, 'Early Draft', 567.
66 Hatcher; and cf. the essay by Steve Hindle in this volume.
67 Hont, *Jealousy*, 91–100.
68 Smith, 'Early Draft', 567.
69 Hont, *Jealousy*, 91–2; Winch, *Riches*, 60–3, 97–8.

families, there will perhaps be one hundred who don't labour at all, and who yet, either by violence or by the more orderly oppression of law, employ a greater part of the labour of the society. ... The division of what remains, too, after this enormous defalcation, is by no means made in proportion to the labour of each individual. On the contrary those who labour most get least.

... the poor labourer who has the soil and the seasons to struggle with, and who, while he affords the materials for supplying the luxury of all the other members of the common wealth, and bears, as it were, upon his shoulders the whole fabric of human society, seems himself to be pressed down below ground by the weight, and to be buried out of sight in the lowest foundations of the building.[70]

The division of labour, industry and consumer demand had been discussed a century or more before Smith published the *Wealth of Nations*, but none of the previous writers we have considered attempted to look at the process of labour with either such analytical thoroughness or with such sympathy. Smith's theory of how wealth was created through labour was not part of his advice for a legislator, but was an idealistic attempt to destroy the special interests found in government, monopolies and combinations of masters.[71] This was to be done by freeing the industrious labourer to earn what the market would give him in order to buy goods whose prices had not been inflated by monopolistic manipulation. He was very critical of the laws which allowed masters to enter into combinations to reduce wages but punished workmen for doing the same thing to maintain wages.[72] He had put such sentiments even more forcefully in his lectures:

Laws and government may be considered in this and indeed in every case as a combination of the rich to oppress the poor, and preserve to themselves the inequality of the goods which would otherwise be soon destroyed by the attacks of the poor, who if not hindered by the government would soon reduce the others to an equality with themselves by open violence.[73]

In a sense the *Wealth of Nations* was an answer to the question of how the poor could become wealthy enough to make violence unnecessary.

Finally it remains to consider whether Smith's sympathy with the aspirations of labourers is consistent with his theory of market motivation and profit. Modern neo-classical economists regard Smith as a libertarian, but in fact as Donald Winch has argued he took great pains to distance himself from mercantilist thinkers who stressed individualistic instrumental

---

[70] Smith, 'Early Draft', 563–4.
[71] Winch *Riches*, 47–9.
[72] Smith, *WN*, I.x, 158.
[73] Smith, *WN*, IV, 22–3, 208.

and utilitarian motivation.[74] Smith, as noted previously, made few specific references to previous authors, but one he did single out for criticism was Mandeville. Smith wished specifically to challenge Mandeville's more elitist conceptions of the benefits of luxury spending, but he also opposed on principle the sociology of self-love. Much of the *Theory of Moral Sentiments* was an attempt to undermine the assumptions of theorists like Mandeville, who derived their vision of an ideal society from self-interest, which Smith termed pernicious.[75] James Steuart also seems to have been influenced by Mandeville, since he stressed that individuals were motivated by the accumulation of private passions. Although Smith never mentioned Steuart's *Inquiry*, in a private letter he claimed that 'every false principle in it, will meet with a clear and distinct confrontation in mine'.[76] Steuart however, chose to use the phrase 'self-' or 'private-interest' rather than 'self-love':

> The best way to govern a society … is for the statesman … never to flatter himself that [a] people will be brought to act in general, and in matters which purely regard the public, from any other principle than private interest.[77]

Although these two terms – self-interest and self-love – have often been taken to be synonymous, their linguistic genealogy is quite different. Mandeville used the term self-love to imply the feeling of pleasure gained from individual competitive success in society. This concept had originally been formulated by the Cambridge Platonists in the mid seventeenth century as a way of reconciling the love of God both with Natural Law's emphasis on self-preservation and with new psychological theories of the mind such as that of Descartes. The Platonists had argued that a love of one's self was a reflection of the love of God as creator of the soul, and was an emotional feeling of desiring good.[78] For Steuart, self-, or private-, interest, on the other hand, implied a profit which was particular only to an individual or to a special interest group and which had no public aspect. In this sense self-interest was criticised often as being prejudicial to public interest:

> Private advantages are often impediments of publick profit; for in what any single person shall be a loser, there, endeavours will be made to hinder the publick gain, from whence proceeds the ill succes that commonly attends the endeavours for

74 Winch, *Riches*, 103.
75 Adam Smith, *The Theory of Moral Sentiments*, ed. D. D. Raphael and A. L. Macfie (Oxford, 1976) [hereafter Smith, *TMS*], 308.
76 Winch, *Riches*, 88.
77 Steuart, *Inquiry*, 163.
78 C. A. Patrides, ed., *The Cambridge Platonists* (London, 1969), 000–00; Hundert, *Enlightenment's Fable*, ch.1; Richard Cumberland, *A Treatise of the Laws of Nature*, ed. Jon Parkin (Indianapolis, 2005), 298.

publick good; ... Interest more than reason commonly sways most mens affections.[79]

Steuart went on to develop this theory of interest, which (like Mandeville) he based on consumer demand, but he was careful to distinguish luxury spending, which was desirable, from excess, which was detrimental to political economy.[80] Steuart's 'statesman' redirected Mandeville's exuberant and individualistic consumption of luxuries towards an economic vision which was mutually beneficial to all of society:

> to employ the inhabitants (supposing them to be free-men) in such a manner as naturally to create reciprocal relations and dependencies between them, so as to make their several interests lead them to supply one another with their reciprocal wants.[81]
> [...]
> Here then is a system set on foot, whereby the poor are made rich, and the rich are made happy, in the enjoyment of a perpetual variety of every thing, which can remove the inconveniences to which human nature is exposed. Thus both parties become interested to support it, and vie with one another in the ingenuity of contriving new wants.[82]

The concept of interest, when not attached to the prefix *self-*, was also used in the sense that it referred to the mutual advantage, benefit or profit of two or more parties, which is the usage Smith adopted. Henry Parker had claimed in 1648 that 'traffick' was something which 'every Subject of the Land has an interest in', and he quoted a proverb on the common advantage of interest, to the effect that 'every mans interest is nomans interest, & that every mans businesse is no man's busines'.[83] An 'interest rate' was also something quite different than usury, and referred to the interest the lender had in the success and profit of the borrower's business.[84] In this sense, interest had a link with the classical sense of 'utility', implied by profit and the exchange of goods.[85]

In contrast to Steuart, Smith stressed that exchange required the 'assistance' and 'co-operation' of many thousands of people, and argued that

---

[79] Samuel Fortney, *England's Interest*, 2.

[80] Steuart, *Inquiry*, 281, 306ff, 168.

[81] *Ibid.*, 1–2.

[82] *Ibid.*, 280.

[83] Henry Parker, *Of a Fee Trade: a Discourse Seriously Recommending to our Nation the Wonderful Benefits of Trade* (1648), 1, 7; Josiah Childe, *Discourse About Trade* (1690), reprinted in McCulloch, ed., *Early English Tracts*, preface, v; Petty, *Political Arithmatick*, preface.

[84] Eric Kerridge, *Trade and Banking in Early Modern England* (Manchester, 1988), 34–9.

[85] Slack, 'Politics of Consumption', 630; Hont, *Jealousy*, 40.

individual as well as social happiness would result from sympathetic benevolence as well as from self-command and from the desire to be well regarded by others:[86]

> When the happiness or misery of others depends in any respect upon our conduct, we dare not, as self-love might suggest to us, prefer the interest of one to that of many. The man within immediately calls to us, that we value ourselves too much and other people too little, and that, by doing so, we render ourselves the proper object of the contempt and indignation of our brethren.[87]

While he was willing to acknowledge that some benefit could come from the spending of the aristocracy, Smith thought that this was in no way as beneficial as popular consumption. When discussing the happiness which could be derived from material needs and wealth, Smith turned not to the self-interested satisfaction of desire, but to the mutual good which could be achieved through the utility of interest embodied in exchange, which had been discussed by previous authors.[88] This is the meaning of his famous passage about the butcher, brewer and baker in the *Wealth of Nations*:

> man has almost constant occasion for the help of his brethren, and it is in vain for him to expect it from their benevolence only. He will be more likely to prevail if he can interest their self-love in his favour, and shew them that it is for their own advantage to do for him what he requires of them. Whoever offers to another a bargain of any kind, proposes to do this. Give me that which I want, and you shall have this which you want, is the meaning of every such offer. …
> It is not from the benevolence of the butcher, the brewer, or the baker, that we expect our dinner, but from their regard to their own interest. We address ourselves, not to their humanity but to their self-love.[89]

In this way he could argue that self-love might have a beneficial effect by leading to market exchange. It was also crucial for Smith that this effect was unintended, because (as he argued in the *Theory of Moral Sentiments*) actions intentionally motivated by self-love would make one the object of 'resentment, abhorrence, and execration'. As he put it in the *Lectures on Jurisprudence*:

> We may observe that these principles of the human mind which are most beneficial to society are by no means marked by nature as the most honourable. Hunger,

---

[86] Smith, *TMS*, 166, 235–6.
[87] *Ibid.*, 138; cf. 64, 241, 245, 310.
[88] The propensity to trade was something previous writers had postulated: Muldrew, *Economy of Obligation*, 138–9.
[89] Smith, *WN*, 26–7. This idea also appeared almost verbatim in the *Lectures on Jurisprudence*: Smith, *LJ*, 340–3.

thirst, and the passion for sex are the great supports of the human species. Yet almost every expression of these excites contempt.[90]

Bargaining was the crucial step through which mankind co-operated in the market, as it provided a motivation for the division of labour through each individual's interest in obtaining a greater number of material goods:

> If we should enquire into the principle in the human mind on which this dispo-sition of trucking is founded, it is clearly the naturall inclination every one has to persuade. The offering of a shilling, which to us appears to have so plain and simple a meaning, is in reality offering an argument to persuade one to do so and so as it is for his interest.[91]

In all of Smith's descriptions of the socio-historical development of the division of labour, change occurred when labourers specialised their occupa-tion, motivated by the desire to obtain more sophisticated things through exchange for the more specialised goods they produced. Thus, the desire for a greater range of goods led to more efficient, cheaper production and to an expansion of the number of goods available, allowing the labourers them-selves to purchase them. It was this consumption, driven by prudent saving and expenditure, which led to a 'revolution of the greatest importance to the publick happiness'.[92] Smith was much more concerned to emphasise frugality over prodigality in order to promote popular saving, which he believed was as necessary as work if labouring families were to increase their standard of living:

> whatever a person saves from his revenue he adds to his capital ... so the capital of a society, which is the same with that of all the individuals who compose it, can be increased only in the same manner. Parsimony, and not industry, is the immediate cause of the increase of capital. ... whatever industry might acquire, if parsimony did not save and store up the capital, would never be the greater.[93]
> [...]
> ... in the greater part of men, taking the whole course of their life at an average, the principle of frugality seems not only to predominate, but to predominate very greatly.[94]

In this way, popular consumption was superior to the uninhibited gratifica-tion of self-love because it was based on a much more complex psychology

---

[90] Smith, *WN*, 449.
[91] Smith, 'Early Draft', 481. Also see Smith, *LJ*, 306.
[92] Smith, *WN*, III.v, 17; Winch, *Riches*, 69, 77.
[93] Smith, *WN*, II.iii, 337.
[94] Smith, *WN*, II.iii, 341–2; Winch, *Riches*, 77–80; de Vries, *Industrious Revolution*, 69–70.

which allowed for social improvement and progress. It also allowed capital to be created, and in making a connection between work, saving, capital formation, investment and consumption, Smith created a much more analytically coherent explanatory structure than his predecessors.

Smith's attack on what he termed the 'Mercantile System' was motivated in part by his thinking about the relationship between finance, production and demand, but also by his idealistic project of how public opulence could be increased and extended to benefit workers everywhere. He developed this line of reasoning to show how tariffs and restrictions on imports and exports were harmful to the production of opulence:

> The idea of publick opulence consisting in money has been productive of other bad effects. Upon this principle most pernicious regulations have been established.... The absurdity of these regulations will appear on the least reflection.
>
> All commerce that is carried on betwixt any two countries must necessarily be advantageous to both. The very intention of commerce is to exchange your own commodities for others which you think will be more convenient for you. When two men trade between themselves it is undoubtedly for the advantage of both.... The case is exactly the same betwixt any two nations.[95]

Here we can see how far Smith had modified the ideal commonwealth of the sixteenth century. The ideas of mutual interdependence and the natural propensity to bargain and exchange which had commanded such respect in the sixteenth century were endorsed by Smith. In the sixteenth century, however, mutuality had been achieved by emphasising the role of elite governance, through which the propertied exercised authority and the poor were cared for by market regulation and by being employed in service. Authority was stressed, and the independence of the poorer sort was feared as they were seen as 'the many headed monster'. In the seventeenth and early eighteenth centuries, theorists of the mercantile state downplayed mutuality, and instead stressed that the wealthy, especially traders and merchants, were valued for the taxable wealth they created. Prosperity created by these means might be used in a more instrumental fashion by government, or in Steuart's terms by 'the statesman', to create employment, but also to expand state power overseas. Mandeville went even further, dismissing both government and mutuality in favour of the benefits of economic growth driven by consumer self-gratification.

Smith, however, reintroduced a role for mutuality through the exercise of benevolence and stressed the social utility of interest in market exchange. However, he was much more sympathetic to the self-determination of the poor than the sixteenth-century commonwealth writers. For him government, when involved in the marketplace, was an institution whereby self-

---

[95] Smith, *WN*, IV.v, 511–12.

interest could easily distort mutuality to the advantage of the wealthy. Smith, unfortunately, said little about redistribution of wealth to those without work. But when discussing the English poor laws he did claim that, with the Elizabethan Poor Laws 'the necessity of providing for their own poor was *indispensably* imposed upon every parish' [my italics] to compensate for the loss of monastic charity. Thus Smith actually stressed the necessity of government intervention when he did not need to. He also objected to the way the freedom of the poor was 'cruelly oppressed' by the Laws of Settlement.[96] He thought that the hard work and frugality of labour would, when considered in an enlightened way, convince rulers that it was in their interest to let the pin-makers and glaziers get on with what they were doing, and that this production of material wealth would be the greatest benefit to the common labourer. It has been stressed often before but it is important to note that from the perspective of 1776 Smith was interpreting a vibrant economy of small producers. It was also an economy in which standards of living had risen. When describing the increase in production since the Restoration, he claimed capital had been accumulated 'by the private frugality and good conduct of individuals, by their universal, continual, and uninterrupted effort to better their own condition'.[97] In this reading of Smith, he was not just participating in the Enlightenment republic of letters, but was someone working with evidence of actual social change. E. A. Wrigley has noted that Smith thought there were natural limits to economic growth based on labour, organisation and machinery, and that he failed to see how the use of inorganic power would change the world out of all recognition.[98] He also failed to see that future economic power lay with large corporations of which he was so critical, and was equally blind to the possibility that state power might be needed to regulate the self-interest of corporate dominance.[99] This is because he was not an advocate of free markets for freedom's sake, but for the benefit of those labourers and small producers he felt were disadvantaged by the society of his time. In this sense he must have sought, and also, I feel, deserves, approbation.

[96] *Ibid.*, I.x, 152–7. Cf. Naomi Tadmor's essay in this volume.
[97] Smith *WN*, II.ii, 344–5.
[98] E. A. Wrigley, 'The Quest for the Industrial Revolution', in *idem, Poverty, Progress and Population* (Cambridge, 2004), 25–7.
[99] Smith, *WN*, I.x, 138–52.

Appendix

Bibliography of the Published Writings of Keith Wrightson from 1974 to 2011

COMPILED BY LINDSAY O'NEILL

Books and articles

2011

Ralph Tailor's Summer: A Scrivener, His City and the Plague (New Haven, 2011)

2007

'The "Decline of Neighbourliness" Revisited', in *Local Identities in Late Medieval and Early Modern England*, ed. Norman L. Jones and Daniel Woolf (Basingstoke, 2007), 19–49

'Elements of Identity: The Re-making of the North East, 1500–1760', in *Northumbria: History and Identity 547–2000*, ed. Robert Colls (Chichester, 2007), 126–50

2006

'Mutualities and Obligations: Changing Social Relationships in Early Modern England', *Proceedings of the British Academy* 139 (2006), 157–94

2002

'Class', in *The British Atlantic World, 1500–1800*, ed. David Armitage and Michael J. Braddick (Basingstoke, 2002), 133–53

2000

Earthly Necessities: Economic Lives in Early Modern Britain (New Haven, 2000)

1998

'The Family in Early Modern England: Continuity and Change', in *Hanoverian Britain and Empire: Essays in Memory of Philip Lawson*, ed. Stephen Taylor, Richard Connors and Clyve Jones (Woodbridge, 1998), 1–22

1996

'The Politics of the Parish in Early Modern England', in *The Experience of Authority in Early Modern England*, ed. Paul Griffiths, Adam Fox and Steve Hindle (Basingstoke, 1996), 10–46

APPENDIX

1994

'"Sorts of People" in Tudor and Stuart England', in *The Middling Sort of People: Culture, Society and Politics in England, 1550–1800*, ed. Jonathan Barry and Christopher Brooks (Basingstoke, 1994), 28–51

1993

'The Enclosure of English Social History', in *Rethinking Social History: English Society 1570–1920 and its Interpretation*, ed. Adrian Wilson (Manchester, 1993), 59–77 [a modified and expanded version of the article in *Rural History* 1:1 (April 1990), 73–82]

1991

'Estates, Degrees, and Sorts: Changing Perspectives of Society in Tudor and Stuart England', in *Language, History and Class*, ed. Penelope J. Corfield (Oxford, 1991), 30–52 [an expanded version of the article in *History Today* 37:1 (1987), 17–22]
Co-authored with David Levine, *The Making of an Industrial Society: Whickham 1560–1765* (Oxford, 1991)

1990

'The Enclosure of English Social History', *Rural History* 1:1 (April 1990), 73–82

1989

Co-authored with David Levine, 'Death in Whickam', in *Famine, Disease and the Social Order in Early Modern Society*, ed. John Walter and Roger Schofield (Cambridge, 1989), 129–65
'Kindred Adjoining Kingdoms: An English Perspective on the Social and Economic History of Early Modern Scotland', in *Scottish Society 1500–1800*, ed. R. A. Houston and I. D. Whyte (Cambridge, 1989), 245–60

1987

'Estates, Degrees, and Sorts: Changing Perspectives of Society in Tudor and Stuart England', *History Today* 37:1 (1987), 17–22

1986

'The Social Order of Early Modern England: Three Approaches', in *The World We Have Gained: Histories of Population and Social Structure*, ed. Lloyd Bonfield, Richard M. Smith and Keith Wrightson (Oxford, 1986), 177–202

1984

'Kinship in an English Village: Terling, Essex 1500–1700', in *Land, Kinship and Life-cycle*, ed. Richard M. Smith (Cambridge, 1984), 313–32

1982

English Society 1580–1680 (1982) [reprinted as a new edition in 2003]
'Infanticide in European History', *Criminal Justice History* 3 (1982), 1–20

1981

'Alehouses, Order and Reformation in Rural England, 1590–1660', in *Popular*

Culture and Class Conflict 1590–1914: Explorations in the History of Labour and Leisure, ed. Eileen Yeo and Stephen Yeo (Brighton, 1981), 1–27
'Household and Kinship in Sixteenth-Century England', *History Workshop Journal* 12:1 (autumn 1981), 151–8

1980
'The Nadir of English Illegitimacy in the Seventeenth-Century', in *Bastardy and its Comparative History*, ed. Peter Laslett, Karla Oosterveen and Richard M. Smith (Cambridge, 1980), 176–91
Co-authored with David Levine, 'The Social Context of Illegitimacy in Early Modern England', in *Bastardy and its Comparative History*, ed. Peter Laslett, Karla Oosterveen and Richard M. Smith (Cambridge, 1980), 158–75
'Two Concepts of Order: Justices, Constables and Jurymen in Seventeenth-Century England', in *An Ungovernable People: The English and their Law in the Seventeenth and Eighteenth Centuries*, ed. John Brewer and John Styles (1980), 21–46

1979
Co-authored with David Levine, *Poverty and Piety in an English Village: Terling, 1525–1700* (1979) [revised edition, Oxford, 1995]

1978
'Medieval Villagers in Perspective', *Peasant Studies* 7:4 (Fall 1978), 203–17

1977
'Aspects of Social Differentiation in Rural England, c. 1580–1660', *Journal of Peasant Studies* 5:1 (1977), 33–47

1976
Co-authored with John Walter, 'Dearth and the Social Order in Early Modern England', *Past & Present* 71:1 (May 1976), 22–42

1975
'Infanticide in Earlier Seventeenth-Century England', *Local Population Studies* 15 (1975), 10–22

Book reviews

2010
The Ends of Life: Roads to Fulfilment in Early Modern England by Keith Thomas, *English Historical Review* 125 (February 2010), 176–8

2009
Hunting and the Politics of Violence before the English Civil War by Daniel C. Beaver, *Journal of Interdisciplinary History* 40:1 (summer 2009), 89–90

2008
North-East England, 1569–1625: Governance, Culture and Identity by Diana Newton, *Journal of Interdisciplinary History* 38:4 (Spring 2008), 590–1

2007

The Social World of Early Modern Westminster: Abbey, Court and Community, 1525–1640 by J.F. Merritt, *English Historical Review* 122:495 (2007), 180–2

2002

Courtship and Constraint: Rethinking the Making of Marriage in Tudor England by Diana O'Hara, *Journal of Social History* 35:4 (summer 2002), 1010–12

Guilds and the Parish Community in Late Medieval East Anglia, c. 1470–1550 by Ken Farnhill, *Catholic Historical Review* 88:4 (October 2002), 769–70

2001

British Society, 1680–1880: Dynamism, Containment and Change by Richard Price, *Journal of Interdisciplinary History* 31:4 (spring 2001), 629–30

The Development of Agrarian Capitalism: Land and Labour in Norfolk, 1440–1580 by Jane Whittle, *Albion* 33:4 (winter 2001), 629–30

'Passions and Politeness' a review of *Civil Histories: Essays Presented to Sir Keith Thomas* edited by Peter Burke, Brian Harrison and Paul Slack, *The Times Literary Supplement* 5115 (13 April 2001), 34

'When the Lights Went Out' a review of *The Voices of Morebath: Reformation and Rebellion in an English Village* by Eamon Duffy, *The Times Literary Supplement* 5143 (26 October 2001), 12

1998

Ale, Beer, and Brewsters in England: Woman's Work in a Changing World, 1300–1600 by Judith M. Bennett, *American Historical Review* 103:3 (June 1998), 868

1997

The Shaping of a Community: The Rise and Reformation of the English Parish, c. 1400–1560 by Beat A. Kümin, *English Historical Review* 112:449 (November 1997), 1260–1

1996

The History of the British Coal Industry, I: Before 1700: Towards the Age of Coal by John Hatcher, *English Historical Review* 111:442 (June 1996), 709

Lordship and Community: The Lestrange Family and the Village of Hunstanton Norfolk, in the first half of the Sixteenth Century by Cord Oestmann, *English Historical Review* 111:443 (September 1996), 970–1

Societies, Cultures and Kinship, 1580–1850: Cultural Provinces and Local History by Charles Phythian-Adams, *English Historical Review* 111:440 (February 1996), 199–200

The Transformation of a Peasant Economy: Townspeople and Villagers in the Lutterworth Area 1500–1700 by John Goodacre, *Social History* 21:3 (October 1996), 383–4

1995

A Community Transformed: The Manor and Liberty of Havering, 1500–1620 by Marjorie Keniston McIntosh, *English Historical Review* 110:435 (February 1995), 173–4

APPENDIX

1994

Before the Luddites: Custom, Community and Machinery in the English Woollen Industry, 1776–1809 by Alan Randall, *History of European Ideas* 18:2 (March 1994), 298–9

'Round the Maypole' a review of *The Culture of the English People: Iron Age to the Industrial Revolution* by N.J.G. Pounds and *The Rise and Fall of Merry England: The Ritual Year, 1400–1700* by Ronald Hutton, *The Times Literary Supplement* 4796 (14 October 1994), 6

1993

'Untuned Strings?' a review of *The Pursuit of Stability: Social Relations in Elizabethan London* by Ian Archer and *Fire from Heaven: Life in an English Town in the Seventeenth Century* by David Underdown, *History Today* 43:1 (January 1993), 56–7

1992

A Rural Society after the Black Death: Essex, 1350–1525 by L. R. Poos, *Catholic Historical Review* 78:4 (October 1992), 647–8

1991

'Keeping Open House' a review of *Hospitality in Early Modern England* by Felicity Heal, *Times Literary Supplement* 4580 (11 January 1991), 20

1988

Women and Work in Pre-Industrial England edited by Lindsey Charles and Lorna Duffin, *The English Historical Review* 103:407 (April 1988), 489–90

1987

'Dogberry No More' a review of *The English Village Constable 1588–1642: A Social and Administrative Study* by Joan R. Kent, *The Times Literary Supplement* 4372 (16 January 1987), 67

Pettyfoggers and Vipers of the Commonwealth: The 'Lower Branch' of the Legal Profession in Early Modern England by C.W. Brooks, *Durham University Journal* new series 48:2 (June 1987), 381–2

1986

'The Bacillus and its Legacy' a review of *The Impact of Plague in Tudor and Stuart England* by Paul Slack, *The Times Literary Supplement* 4319 (10 January 1986), 43

Popular Culture in Seventeenth-Century England edited by Barry Reay, *Journal of Peasant Studies* 14:1 (October 1986), 135–7

The Transformation of English Provincial Towns 1600–1800 edited by Peter Clark, *Urban History Yearbook* 13 (1986), 177–8

1985

Forgotten Children: Parent–Child Relations from 1500 to 1900 by Linda A. Pollock, *British Journal of Developmental Psychology* 3:2 (June 1985), 199–200

'On the Road' a review of *The Great Reclothing of Rural England: Petty Chapmen and their Wares in the Seventeenth Century* by Margaret Spufford, *The Times Literary Supplement* 4266 (4 January 1985), 20

345

APPENDIX

'A Story without Characters' a review of *Economic Expansion and Social Change* by C. G. A. Clay, *The Times Literary Supplement* 4218 (19 April 1985), **444**

1984

Coram's Children: The London Foundling Hospital in the Eighteenth Century by Ruth K. McClure, *English Historical Review* 99:391 (April 1984), 437

The English Alehouse: A Social History, 1200–1830 by Peter Clark, *Albion* 16:2 (summer 1984), 167–9

Fenland Riots and the English Revolution by Keith Lindley, *Journal of Peasant Studies* 11:3 (April 1984), 126–8

Reading and Writing: Literacy in France from Calvin to Jules Ferry by François Furet and Jacques Ozouf, *Journal of Ecclesiastical History* 35:4 (October 1984), 675–6

The World of the Muggletonians by Christopher Hill, Barry Reay and William Lambert, *Economic History Review* new series 37:1 (February 1984), 134–5

1983

Marriage and Society: Studies in the Social History of Marriage edited by R. B. Outhwaite, *Social History* 8:3 (October 1983), 422–5

1982

Literacy and the Social Order: Reading and Writing in Tudor and Stuart England by David Cressy, *English Historical Review* 97:382 (January 1982), 136–7

The Population History of England 1541–1871: A Reconstruction by E. A. Wrigley and R. S. Schofield and *Population and Metropolis: The Demography of London 1580–1650* by Roger Finlay, *English Historical Review* 97:385 (October 1982), 850–3

'Portrait of an age' a review of *English Society in the 18th Century* by Roy Porter, *New Society* 60:1020 (June 1982), 400

Records of an English Village: Earls Colne 1400–1750 edited by Alan MacFarlane et al., *Social History* 7:2 (May 1982), 241

1981

In Contempt of All Authority: Rural Artisans and Riot in the West of England, 1586–1660 by Buchanan Sharp, *American Historical Review* 86:1 (February 1981), 127–8

1980

Family and Society edited by R. Forester and O. Ranum, *Urban History Yearbook* 7 (1980), 113–14

Wanton Wenches and Wayward Wives: Peasants and Illicit Sex in Early Seventeenth Century England by G. R. Quaife, *Social History* 5:3 (October 1980), 491–2

1979

Famine in Tudor and Stuart England by Andrew Appleby and *Crisis and Development: An Ecological Case Study of the Forest of Arden, 1570–1674* by Victor Skipp, *Social History* 4:3 (October 1979), 524–6

Reconstructing Historical Communities edited by Alan MacFarlane in collaboration with Sarah Harrison and Charles Jardine, *Social History* 4:1 (January 1979), 133–5

1978

Family and Inheritance: Rural Society in Western Europe, 1200–1800 edited by Jack Goody, Joan Thirsk and E. P. Thompson and *Family Life and Illicit Love in Earlier Generations: Essays in Historical Sociology* by Peter Laslett, *Social History* 3:3 (October 1978), 382–5

1977

Death, Disease and Famine in Pre-Industrial England by Leslie Clarkson, *Social History* 2:6 (October 1977), 840

The English People and the English Revolution by Brian Manning, *Journal of Peasant Studies* 4:4 (July 1977), 398–9

1975

Essex Quarter Sessions Order Book, 1652–1661 edited by D. H. Allen, *Historical Journal* 18:4 (December 1975), 893–4

'Villages, Villagers and Village Studies' a review of *Contrasting Communities: English Villagers in the Sixteenth and Seventeenth Centuries* by Margaret Spufford and *An English Rural Community: Myddle under the Tudors and Stuarts* by David G. Hey, *Historical Journal* 18:3 (September 1975), 632–9

1974

Law and Order in Historical Perspective: The Case of Elizabethan Essex by Joel Samaha, *Historical Journal* 17:3 (September 1974), 656–8

Index

Page numbers in *italic* refer to figures.

Tabula Gratulatoria

Susan D. Amussen

Joyce Appleby

Ian W. Archer

Tom Arkell

Jonathan Barry

Judith Bennett

Helen Berry

Jeremy Boulton

Michael Braddick

T. H. Breen

Christopher Brooks

Bernard Capp

Emily Cockayne

Robert Colls

Rich Connors

Brian Cowan

John Craig

David Cressy

Mark Dawson

David Dean

Simon Devereaux

Harry T. Dickinson

Heather Falvey

Margaret Ferguson

Chris Fitter

Adam Fox

Elizabeth Foyster

Henry French

Ari Friedlander

Malcolm Gaskill

Mark Goldie

Paul Griffiths

Mark Hailwood

Tim Harris

Cynthia Herrup

Steve Hindle

Jennifer S. Holt

Ralph Houlbrooke

R. W. Hoyle

Eleanor Hubbard

Martin Ingram

Norm Jones

David Scott Kastan

Lucy Kaufman

Krista J. Kesselring

Mary Laven

Matthew Lockwood

Peter C. Mancall

Christopher Marsh

Peter Marshall

Michael Mascuch

Andrea McKenzie

John Morrill

Craig Muldrew

Lindsay O'Neill

Geoffrey Parker

Margaret Pelling

Wilfrid Prest

Claude Rawson

David Rollison

Hamish Scott

Jim Sharpe

Pam Sharpe

Alexandra Shepard

Paul Slack

Greg T. Smith

Richard Smith

Peter & Margaret Spufford

Tim Stretton
Naomi Tadmor
Hillary Taylor
Stephen Taylor
Courtney Thomas
Keith Thomas
Robert Tittler
Barbara J. Todd
Richard Tuck

Brodie Waddell
Alexandra Walsham
John Walter
Paul Warde
Samantha Williams
Phil Withington
Andy Wood
Tony Wrigley

STUDIES IN EARLY MODERN CULTURAL,
POLITICAL AND SOCIAL HISTORY

Printed and bound by CPI Group (UK) Ltd, Croydon, CR0 4YY

09/06/2025

14685719-0005